Dagmar Brunow
Remediating Transcultural Memory

Media and Cultural Memory/
Medien und kulturelle Erinnerung

Edited by
Astrid Erll · Ansgar Nünning

Editorial Board
Aleida Assmann · Mieke Bal · Vita Fortunati · Richard Grusin · Udo Hebel
Andrew Hoskins · Wulf Kansteiner · Alison Landsberg · Claus Leggewie
Jeffrey Olick · Susannah Radstone · Ann Rigney · Michael Rothberg
Werner Sollors · Frederik Tygstrup · Harald Welzer

Volume 23

Dagmar Brunow

Remediating Transcultural Memory

Documentary Filmmaking as Archival Intervention

DE GRUYTER

ISBN 978-3-11-076458-1
e-ISBN (PDF) 978-3-11-043637-2
e-ISBN (EPUB) 978-3-11-043452-1
ISSN 1613-8961

Library of Congress Cataloging-in-Publication Data
A CIP catalog record for this book has been applied for at the Library of Congress.

Bibliographic information published by the Deutsche Nationalbibliothek
The Deutsche Nationalbibliothek lists this publication in the Deutsche Nationalbibliografie;
detailed bibliographic data are available on the Internet at http://dnb.dnb.de.

© 2021 Walter de Gruyter GmbH, Berlin/Boston
This volume is text- and page-identical with the hardback published in 2015.
Cover illustration: Victor Potasyev/iStock/Thinkstock
Typesetting: Konrad Triltsch, Print und digitale Medien GmbH, Ochsenfurt
Printing and binding: CPI books GmbH, Leck
♾ Printed on acid-free paper
Printed in Germany

www.degruyter.com

Acknowledgements

During the writing process I have felt privileged to be part of a wonderful network of colleagues, friends and family who have supported me in so many ways.

First of all, I owe tremendous thanks to my supervisor Johann N. Schmidt for his patience, generosity and intellectual rigour; to my second supervisor Astrid Erll for her enthusiasm for this project as well as the inspiration and vast knowledge she willingly shares; to Joan Bleicher for providing prompt advice whenever I needed it.

For their valuable feedback and for their inspiring scholarship my gratitude goes to Vanessa Agard-Jones, Ulrike Bergermann, Tim Bergfelder, Stella Bruzzi, Erica Carter, Simon Dickel, Jan Distelmeyer, Gayatri Gopinath, Liz Greene, Judith Keilbach, Annette Kuhn, Michael Rothberg and Alexandra Schneider. Thanks too to my film theory reading group in Hamburg: Malte Hagener, David Kleingers, Skadi Loist, Katja Schumann and Senta Siewert.

A number of invitations helped me to develop and test out some of my arguments. I feel grateful to Gunlög Fur, Ulla Manns and Tytti Soila for inviting me to talk about my work at the seminar of postcolonial studies at Linneaeus University, at the Gender Studies research seminar at Södertörn, and at the Film Studies research seminar at Stockholm University respectively. Thanks to Christine Achinger for inviting me to Warwick and to Heidrun Führer for inviting me to her seminar on intermediality studies at Lund University. A big thank you also goes to Ylva Habel for being a discussant at an early stage of writing and for co-chairing a panel with me at the CAAR conference in Bremen. I would also like to take this opportunity to thank John Sundholm and Lars Gustaf Andersson for their invitation to contribute to a special issue of *Studies in European Cinema* and to their panel at the MAGIS Spring School in Gorizia.

A special thanks goes to the filmmakers, artists, curators and archivists who generously gave of their time during conversations or interviews. Their work and experiences have been fundamental for shaping my ideas: John Akomfrah (Smoking Dogs Films), Kodwo Eshun, at the *mpz:* Ulrike Gay and Olaf Berg; at *bildwechsel:* the one and only Durbahn; and at *die thede:* Christian Bau, Maria Hemmleb, Barbara Metzlaff and Alexandra Gramatke. Thanks too to the late Harun Farocki, to Hito Steyerl, Thomas Tode, Sandhya Suri and Ulrike Schaz. The chapter on the Hamburg video collectives is dedicated to the memory of Jens Huckeriede (1949–2013), member of the collective *die thede*, whose films and art projects explore the dialectics of forgetting and remembrance, especially in relation to the cultural memory of the Holocaust, and which deserve a book on their own.

During the creation of this study my colleagues at Linneaeus University have been the most wonderful colleagues anybody could wish for: Anna Sofia Rossholm, Ingrid Stigsdotter, Tommy Gustafsson, Anna Arnman and Anders Åberg. For their collegiality and hospitality I would like to thank Anna Bachmann, Sofia Bull, Laura Horak, Anu Koivunen, Jakob Nilsson, Ingrid Ryberg, Nadi Tofighian, Patrick Vonderau, Malin Wahlberg, Eirik Frisvold Hansen, Åsa Bergström, Anders Marklund, Sanjin Pejkovic, Michael Tapper, Ann-Kristin Wallengren and Jonnie Eriksson. My fabulous colleagues at Södertörn University have been a constant source of inspiration: Jenny Sundén, Helena Hill, Ulla Manns, Ulrika Dahl, Katarina Mattson and Ann Werner. An extra "tack" goes to my inspiring teachers Karin Carsten Montén, Else Kjaer and Jahn Thon at Hamburg University. A big cheers goes to Dorota Ostrowska and Christine Achinger for tea time at the British Library. I am also highly grateful to Tytti Soila and to Steph Klinkenborg for encouraging me at an early stage of my work.

The MYMEM research network *(National Myths and Collective Memory in a Transnational Age)* and the COST-Action *ISTME (In Search of a Transcultural Memory in Europe)* have generously supported my participation at network meetings in Stavanger (2012), Paris (2013), Krakow (2013) and Budapest (2014). I feel grateful to be part of these transnational networks which are characterised by intellectual curiosity, openness and excellent scholarship. For this I would like to thank Barbara Törnqvist-Plewa, Bill Schwarz, Susannah Radstone, John Sundholm and Alexandre Dessingué.

The Arts and Humanities Department at Halmstad University and its research cluster "Kontext & Kulturgränser" have partly funded this research, enabling me to take time off teaching and travelling to conferences, among them Screen, NECS, IAMHIST and CAAR. I feel especially grateful to KG Hammarlund for his support.

The staff at the Stuart Hall Library in London, at the British Library, at the BFI and at Kungliga Biblioteket in Stockholm have been immensely helpful. A big thanks to Jenny Helstad at Halmstad University Library, who managed to get hold of basically every title or article I wished for.

For valuable feedback and comments I would like to thank Robin Curtis, Skadi Loist, Sonja Majumder, Karen Schulz, Thorsten Stobbe and especially Beeke Ropers, who edited and proof-read the bulk of the manuscript. I am also grateful to Sonja Uhlendorf who was generous enough to help me with the layout. My family and friends have reminded me both of the upcoming deadline and of life outside academia: Arne and Susanna Christensen, Manfred and Angelika Kutsch, Ursula Wallin, Traute Peschel, the late Werner Peschel, Mehmet Kocaaga, Ulrike Jensen, Gabriela Pichler, Tinna Hiller Andreasson & family, Britt-Marie and Gillis Hiller, Emelie Karlsmo & family, Anna Viola Hallberg, Kerstin

Janssen, Christian Schneider, Andreas Stuhlmann, Rolf Uhlendorf, Ann Sofi Lindberg and Mats Myrstener. I would also like to thank FSK radio station for offering me an outlet for thoughts and ideas, above all Ole Frahm and Torsten Michaelsen for never ceasing to inspire me, as well as my co-workers at my Hamburg office collective for being around. My London friends Beeke Ropers and Giorgio Frare cannot be thanked enough: their hospitality during my stays in London and their support on all levels have been beyond measure.

The biggest thanks goes to my parents Hella and Günter Brunow for always believing in me. This work has been written in fond memory of Tine Plesch and Martin Büsser, whose inspiration reaches beyond death. This book is dedicated – as always – to my sisters Hülya and Meyrem, and to the younger generation: Zuhal, Fatma, Narin, Berivan, Şevin, Ramia, Harun, Şilan, Rubar, Zülal & Elif Nisa: you are the hope!

Contents

1. **Introduction** —— 1
1.1 Mediated memories: the transcultural turn and its epistemological challenges —— 2
1.2 Memory communities and the audiovisual archive: whose memory is it? —— 6
1.3 Aims – Methods – Structure —— 14

2. **Theory** —— 21
2.1 Conceptualising transcultural and transnational memory —— 21
2.1.1 The notion of transculturality —— 21
2.1.2 Transculturality and its discontents —— 24
2.1.3 Transnational memory: using the insights of transnational film studies —— 27
2.1.4 Conclusion —— 32
2.2 The Archive —— 34
2.2.1 The archive in memory studies —— 34
2.2.2 Archive theory: power, knowledge and materiality —— 37
2.2.3 Archival interventions: remediation and curatorship —— 38
2.2.4 Conclusion: the archive as agent —— 40
2.3 Remediation —— 41
2.3.1 Remediation within media studies —— 41
2.3.2 Remediation within memory studies —— 45
2.3.3 Remediation and intermediality —— 46
2.3.4 Remediation and its discursive frameworks —— 49

3. **Mediatized memories in a global age: the transcultural turn?** —— 52
3.1 Remembering Turkish-German labor migration (Fatih Akin's *We Forgot to Go Back/Wir haben vergessen zurückzukehren*) —— 53
3.1.1 Mediating the cultural memory of migration —— 57
3.1.2 Migrant memories and national frameworks —— 60
3.1.3 Countering essentialism: aesthetic strategies —— 62
3.1.3.1 Transnational urban spaces —— 66
3.1.3.2 Transnational sonic spaces —— 68
3.1.4 Migrant memories: transnational approaches —— 69

3.2	Transcultural memories: post-punk Manchester in times of urban regeneration —— 71
3.2.1	The memory boom around 1980s post-punk Manchester and its gender dimensions —— 77
3.2.2	Feminist filmmaking practice as intervention (Carol Morley's *The Alcohol Years*) —— 83
3.2.3	Translating cultural memory: gentrification and subcultural nostalgia —— 90
3.2.4	Conclusion: multidirectional memories and the notion of transculturality —— 98

4. Reworking the archive —— 100

4.1	Archival interventions: excavating the cultural memory of video art and activism —— 105
4.1.1	The cultural legacy of video collectives: film historiography as memory work —— 109
4.1.2	The practice of the video collectives: production, distribution and exhibition —— 112
4.1.3	Archival practice in times of digitization —— 118
4.1.4	Conclusion: video collectives, archival politics and digitization —— 124
4.2	Filmmaking as archival intervention – reworking cultural memory in the essay film (*Handsworth Songs*) —— 126
4.2.1	Recoding news footage: television, whiteness and national memory —— 131
4.2.2	Sonic interventions – remixing cultural memory —— 140
4.2.3	The archive as inventory: traces and links —— 142
4.2.4	Conclusion: essay filmmaking, auteurism and canon formation —— 146

5. Remediation: reappropriations in digital media and in the essay film —— 149

5.1	Remediating the cultural memory of migration: reappropriating the audiovisual archive of the Windrush —— 151
5.1.1	Media specificity and the construction of the nation: The Pathé newsreel of the arrival of the Windrush (1948) and its Eurocentrism —— 152
5.1.2	Premediation and the discursive context of remediation —— 155
5.1.3	Digital archives of migration: reappropriating and reworking mediated memories on YouTube —— 158
5.1.4	Remediation and its discursive frameworks —— 165

5.2		Remediation and intermediality: media specificity and the discursive context (*Looking for Langston*) —— **166**
5.2.1		Contemporising the past: intermediality and transtemporal dialogue —— **175**
5.2.2		The discursive frameworks of media specificity: reworking photography —— **182**
5.2.3		Discursive frameworks: the context of the 1980s —— **190**
5.2.4		Remediating cultural memory: from 'memory matter' to mnemonic discourses —— **192**
6.		**Conclusion – Mediated cultural memory in a digital age —— 194**
6.1		Transculturality —— **195**
6.2		The archive —— **197**
6.3		Remediation —— **198**
6.4		Outlook —— **200**

Bibliography —— 203

Index of Names —— 239

Index of Titles —— 247

Index of Terms —— 251

1. Introduction

A piece of black and white archival footage shows a white British journalist approaching the Caribbean calypso singer Lord Kitchener, asking him to perform a song in front of the TV cameras facing him. The scene takes place as Kitchener is about to disembark from the SS Empire Windrush docking at Tilbury on 21 June 1948. Kitchener duly performs an a cappella version of his famous calypso "London is the place for me". Initially a piece of analogue film gauge, screened as part of a Pathé newsreel in British cinemas, this piece of archival footage has been remediated in a variety of contexts, from historical exhibitions to YouTube.[1] The footage has been used in British documentaries on Caribbean migration to Britain and in the legendary essay film *Handsworth Songs* by the Black Audio Film Collective (dir. John Akomfrah, 1986). Today the scene showing Lord Kitchener freestyling his calypso has become a central part of the cultural memory of post-war migration to Britain. As such it opens up to various ways of theorising around the relation of documentary film images and cultural memory.

Archival footage such as the above example raises questions on the mediation of memory, its media specificity and the way memory travels, how it is adapted, translated and appropriated. It invites us to reflect on the role of documentary film images for the construction of memory, on their alleged status as visible evidence and on the ontology of the image. Archival footage allows us to rethink notions of mediality, of the politics of representation, of the colonial and Eurocentric gaze and other power relations prevalent in image making, of historiography and canon formation. These introductory paragraphs reveal a pathway to examine the relation of cultural memory and filmic images and to give an overview over the issues addressed in this study.

This study situates itself at the intersection of memory studies and film and media studies. It regards itself as an intervention into ongoing theorisations about the mediation of cultural memory and its dynamics. As memory studies are currently entering into their third phase, defined by discourses about mediated memories and their transnational and global reach, this study sees itself as a contribution to the burgeoning (or rather currently emerging) field of media memory studies.[2] The impact of global media, geopolitical changes, retro cul-

---

[1] For a more detailed discussion, see chapter 5.1 *Remediating the cultural memory of migration: reappropriating the audiovisual archive of the Windrush*.
[2] This third wave of memory studies was suggested by Erll 2010. For a detailed account of the history of cultural memory studies, see Erll 2011a. The term "media memory studies" is currently emerging within cultural memory studies. If we regard all cultural memory as mediated, the

ture, fan fiction or street art demands new theorizations in a field which otherwise would have no problem to "keep generations of scholars busy, charting the mnemonic practices of all ages and places", as Astrid Erll has claimed (Erll 2011b, 4). Instead of turning into a mere additive project, memory studies needs to rethink and reconceptualise some of its theories and methodologies. Given the insight that cultural memory is always mediated, it is surprising to see how small the impact from film and media studies has been until now.

1.1 Mediated memories: the transcultural turn and its epistemological challenges

Mediated memories come in various forms and shapes: as fiction films, novels, newspapers, Facebook posts, Instagram images, digital material on a USB stick, newsreels, amateur home movies on 8 mm film, or archival footage discovered in a television archive and remediated in a documentary or essay film. Digital media, social media networks or satellite television are some of the factors why we can currently observe a transnational turn within memory studies. Within the last decade, cultural memory studies has increasingly shifted its focus towards the dynamics of memory and its global remediation (see Erll and Rigney 2009; Rothberg 2009; Garde-Hansen et al. 2009; Erll 2011b; Hoskins 2011; Rigney 2012). Both the dominant national perspective and the notion of collective memory have been challenged in favour of highlighting the dynamics of cultural memory, theorised in terms of "prosthetic memory" (Landsberg 2004), "multidirectional memories" (Rothberg 2009) or "travelling memory" (Erll 2011b). This ongoing shift towards perceiving memory as a process, as not fixed or stable, is the result of a heightened awareness regarding the impact of media on the construction of cultural memory.

Since the late 1980s, Pierre Nora's theorization of sites of memory, the *lieux de mémoire*, has set the tone for research within cultural memory studies (see Nora 1984–1992). Nora regards the nation-state as the privileged site for the enunciation of collective memory. However, Nora's focus on the nation-state has been called into question by Daniel Levy and Natan Sznaider (2002, 90) who criticise Nora for "his implicit normative claim and the fixation on the nation-state as the sole possible (and imaginable) source for the articulation of col-

---

term is to be understood neither in opposition to cultural memory studies, nor as its supplement. It is merely a heuristic device to highlight the importance of media for the construction of cultural memory.

lective memories".[3] In the meantime Nora's focus on the national paradigm has been contested by four kinds of studies. First, by research publications drawing on the notion of the *lieux de mémoire*, but whose perspective reaches beyond the nation-state, for example by setting out to study a common European heritage, as in the three-volume edition on European sites of memory (see Den Boer, et al. 2011–2012). Second, by studies which conceptualise memory beyond the national framework, as cosmopolitan (Levy and Sznaider 2002), European (Leggewie and Lang 2011), regional (Erll 2010) or global (Levy and Sznaider 2001). Third, by tendencies within memory studies focussing on the dynamics of memory, its multidirectionality, and its 'travelling' aspect (Rigney 2008a, 2008b; Erll and Rigney 2009; Rothberg 2009; Erll 2011b). This would also include studies on digital memories (Van Dijck 2007; Garde-Hansen, et al. 2009; Reading 2009, 2011a; Hoskins 2011; Garde-Hansen 2011). And, finally, the focus on the nation-state has been challenged by studies suggesting the transcultural turn within memory studies (Erll 2010, 2011b, 2011c).

The interest in mediated memories has been further triggered by Ann Rigney's emphasis on the dynamics of memory: "Although it has proven useful as a conceptual tool, the metaphor of 'memory site' can become misleading if it is interpreted to mean that collective remembrance becomes permanently tied down to particular figures, icons, or monuments," Rigney notes (2008a, 346). She suggests to take the performative aspect of remembrance into account. A site of memory should therefore not be conceptualised as something stable, but as a process of remembrance, acknowledging that *lieux de mémoires* are "constantly being reinvested with new meaning" (2008a, 346). Rigney thus suggests a "shift from 'sites' to 'dynamics' within memory studies [...], from a focus on cultural artefacts to an interest in the way those artefacts circulate and influence their environment" (Rigney 2008a, 346)[4]. Rigney's ideas helped pave the way for understanding processes of mediatization and remediation.

Memory is always mediated, as Astrid Erll and Ann Rigney claim: "Just as there is no cultural memory prior to mediation, there is no mediation without remediation: all representations of the past draw on available media technologies, on existent media products, on patterns of representation and medial aesthetics." (Erll and Rigney 2009, 4) Cultural memory is only accessible in its media

---

[3] Nora's focus on the nation-state has also been criticised by Confino (1997) and Tai (2001). Tai criticises Nora's concept from a post-colonial perspective for not taking the diversity of cultural memory into account.

[4] Despite the dominant role it has been playing within cultural memory studies, the concept of the *lieu de mémoire* has been described by Erll as "one of the most sorely undertheorized concepts of memory studies" (Erll 2011b, 27).

specific forms and genres, via TV news, as YouTube clips, feature films, novels or newspaper articles. James E. Young has pointed out "that none of us coming to the Holocaust afterwards can know these events outside the ways they are passed down to us" (Young 1988, vii). The role of media in the construction of memory thus needs to be reconsidered: from being regarded as an 'outlet' of memory, as an externalization, to acknowledging cultural memory as inextricably linked to its specific media forms. Accordingly, Marita Sturken describes media as "technologies of memory, not vessels of memory in which memory passively resides" (1997, 9). Also Aleida Assmann (2011) has pointed at the fact that cultural memory is defined by the kind of media available in a society at a given point in time. Paraphrasing Marshall McLuhan's famous dictum "the medium is the message", Astrid Erll suggests that "the medium is the memory" (Erll 2011a, 115). Therefore, a historical event can be said to have been created by newspaper articles, newsreels, photographs, diaries, historiographic works, poems, novels, plays, paintings, memorials, films, TV series, comics and blogs as well as Twitter and Facebook status updates (cf. Zelizer 2001; Edgerton and Rollins 2001; Neiger, et al. 2011).[5]

Despite the increased interest in the mediation of memory, the media specificity of memory has long been neglected within memory scholarship.[6] In Pierre Nora's collection *Les lieux de mémoire* no distinction is made between a monument, a song ("La Marseillaise") or a published novel, such as Marcel Proust's *A la recherche du temps perdu* (see Nora 1984–1992). Likewise, a German collection on the *lieux de mémoire* of the GDR does not distinguish between a rock band (Puhdys), a concept (anti-fascism), a shop (Intershop) and their specific mediations (see Sabrow 2009). Accordingly, Ursula von Keitz and Thomas Weber suggest that questions of memory culture and media specificity should be linked (Keitz and Weber 2013, 11). In their volume on the media transformations of the Holocaust, which examines comics, visual art, museum exhibitions or the role of the internet, their focus does not lie on historiography, but on the representation of history in specific contemporary moments (Keitz and Weber 2013, 12). This approach echoes Astrid Erll's statement that "memory studies directs its interest not toward the shape of the remembered pasts, but rather to the particular presents of the remembering" (Erll 2011a, 11). Since cultural memory is always mediated and cannot be accessed outside its mediatizations, audiovisual media need to be considered in their diverse forms, including documentaries,

---

[5] This does not mean to say that the historical event is a fiction or has not actually taken place. The point is that we can only access the event via the various media versions.
[6] Although attempts of acknowledging mediality can be traced back to Aby Warburg and Maurice Halbwachs (Erll 2011a).

essay films, videos or user-generated YouTube clips. These formats and genres are of equal importance for the transmission, translation and reworking of mediated memories of migration as are fiction films or written sources.

This study looks at documentary filmmaking and essay film. The films I examine are not "memory films" ("*Erinnerungsfilme*"), a notion conceptualised by Erll (2008b) referring to "memory-shaping" fiction films, such as *The Downfall* (*Der Untergang*, Hirschbiegel, 2004) or *Schindler's List* (Spielberg, 1993), which have a "potential for memory-making" (Erll 2008b, 395). These films play an important role for the construction of cultural memory in a specific historical context, as distributors of memory images. This potential is not inherent in the memory films as such, but unfolds in the process of reception. The basis for this remediation is prepared through a multiplicity of pluri-medial networks, such as reviews, DVD versions, marketing strategies, awards, political speeches or academic debates, "advertisements, comments, discussions, and controversies" which "constitute the collective contexts which channel a movie's reception and potentially turn it into a medium of collective memory" (Erll 2008b, 396). However, in most cases only widely distributed films can become memory films.

Cultural memory studies have so far dealt with fiction films or prime time television documentaries, focusing on the representation of historical events. I will argue that documentary films and essay films require special attention due to their alleged indexical relation to 'reality'. Moreover, they can themselves be regarded as epistemological tools of foregrounding the construction of reality through filmmaking. Rather than looking at the representation of history in the films, I regard them as theoretical tools in their own right. Drawing on Volker Pantenburg's (2006) notion of "film as theory", epitomised in the works by Harun Farocki and Jean-Luc Godard, I look at the ways essay films (Carol Morley's *The Alcohol Years* [2001], John Akomfrah's *Handsworth Songs* [1986] as well as Isaac Julien's *Looking for Langston* [1989]) function as a mode of theorization about media specificity, filmmaking, representation and memory.

The pictorial turn (Mitchell 1994) has led to a deeper understanding of images as historical sources in their own right. Documentary images are often considered a source of factual, positive knowledge. Therefore, conventional documentaries tend to use archival footage as a means of authentication, as visible evidence to show "how it really was" ("*wie es einst gewesen*") in the sense of Ranke. However, as John Tagg points out in *The Burden of Representation*: "Like the state, the camera is never neutral. The representations it produces are highly coded, and the power it wields is never its own" (Tagg 1988, 63–64). Such an understanding of a photographic image incorporating a "trace of a wordless power" (Tagg 1988, 64) has had repercussions on the work of museums or memorial sites: we can observe a tendency to relaunch exhibitions in a way that treats photographs or moving images not merely as illustrations of written information, but as historical sources in their own right. The notion of documentary images as visible evidence has also been challenged within documentary film theory (Minh-ha 1990; Steyerl 2008), via filmmaking (for instance in essay films by Chris Marker, Harun Farocki, Agnès Varda or John Akomfrah), as well as in theoretical writings on photography (e.g. Barthes 1982; Sontag 1977; Sekula 1986; Hall 1991). These theoretical interventions share the insight that image making cannot be conceptualised outside relations of power, such as the gaze of the camera and its potentially colonial, Eurocentric, patriarchal or heteronormative perspective. Moreover, we need to ask: who is entitled to take pictures of others and to distribute them? Who has the prerogative of interpretation over these images? Therefore, we have to regard documentary images not as exact copies of 'reality', but as representations and thus as constructs which are the result of entangled discourses, of iconographic traditions, narrative formula and specific media technologies and their dispositifs.

1.2 Memory communities and the audiovisual archive: whose memory is it?

New memory communities have been generated by global social media, such as YouTube, Facebook, Twitter, Instagram or Tumblr. While digital media has been celebrated for its democratic capacity (Garde-Hansen 2011), this study aims at complicating the notion of memory communities and transcultural memory. Although I agree with Landsberg (2004) that memory is prosthetic and can allow people to participate in experiences which are not their own, in this study I would like to highlight the multidirectional, travelling mode of memory, but without losing sight of the power relations. It would be problematic solely to celebrate user-generated content as a democratic victory, which enables a multifaceted representation, polyvocality and diversity. In fact, this is not actually the case, as most of the user-generated content reproduces hegemonic representations (for instance of race, gender and sexuality). Likewise "history from below" is not emancipatory per se, nor does the use of oral history or testimonial witnesses automatically imply a polyphony of voices, allowing different (and differing) experiences to be represented. The overall approach of this study oscillates between the understanding of documentary filmmaking as an intervention into the audiovisual archive, which implies the need to articulate a speaking position or a point of articulation, and the capacity of mediated memories to transgress these speaking positions. As the audiovisual archive I define the sum of images, sounds and narratives circulating in a specific society at a specific historical moment. The notion of the audiovisual archive also entails a diachronic dimension, including past representations, such as stereotypes, which continue to shape the way images are decoded. In this sense my conceptualisation of the audiovisual archive is reminiscent of Aby Warburg's notion of collective pictorial memory [Bildgedächtnis] (Warburg 1988–2009, Warburg 2000).

The term 'collective memory', which goes back to memory scholars' reception of Maurice Halbwachs,[7] is currently being abolished within memory studies. While the term emphasizes the meaning of cultural memory for the formation of identity and belonging, digital media has complicated previous conceptualisations of the term. The notion of 'collective memory' "rests upon the assumption that every social group develops a memory of its past; a memory that emphasizes its uniqueness and allows it to preserve its self-image and pass it on to future generations", Motti Neiger, Oren Meyers and Eva Zandberg note (2011, 4). The main problem with the concept, I would argue, lies in the understanding of the communities which share collective memory and, as a result, in the risk of homogenising these communities. Neiger, Meyers and Zandberg (2011, 16) also point to the fact that "[s]cholars who write about collective memory tend, in many cases, to view large-scale, dominant, widely popular media representations of the past as almost straightforward manifestations of the collective understanding of the past." The notion of collective memory has resulted in stabilising identities which have, more often than not, been conceptualised within the framework of the nation-state. As Levy and Sznaider (2002, 88) remark: "The conventional concept of 'collective memory' is firmly embedded within the 'Container of the Nation-State'. We argue that this container is in the process of being slowly cracked. It is commonly assumed that memory, community and geographical proximity belong together. We direct our attention to global processes that are characterised by the deterritorialization of politics and culture." According to Levy and Sznaider, the concept tends to perceive nation and territory in conjunction. As early as in the 1980s Black British Cultural Studies, most notably Stuart Hall (1988) and Paul Gilroy (2002), have pointed at the risk of sidelining the experiences of diaspora and migration in essentialising identity in terms of national belonging, territorial locatedness and ethnicity. Their ideas prove to be a hitherto rarely acknowledged intervention into essentialising conceptualisations within memory studies.

---

7 In his text *The Social Framework of Memory*, originally published in French in 1925 as *Les cadres sociaux de la mémoire* and now part of the Halbwachs edition *On Collective Memory*, Halbwachs (1992) does not employ the term 'collective memory'. The term first appears in the posthumously published *La mémoire collective* (1950), translated into English in 1980 (see Halbwachs 1980).

Migration and diaspora are part of everyday life, both in contemporary multicultural societies and throughout history. In most conceptualisation of the nation these factors have been overlooked. "Because of migrations that have been ongoing, in multiple directions, throughout the past century, there are practically no places left in the world which are not hybrid in terms of culture." (van Alphen 2002, 55) However, not all of these hybrid subjects can tell their stories on equal terms. For instance, the lack of access to filmmaking for Black Britons has had repercussions on their representation in the audiovisual archive. If we understand the archive as the foundation from which history is written, a diversification of cultural memory can only be granted if the archival context represents multiple narratives and images, instead of providing representation which would stabilise rather than re-negotiate hegemonic narratives. Filmmaking by minoritised persons can thus be regarded as an archival intervention. However, even when access to media representation by Black Britons was enabled, such as during the 1980s when municipal initiatives encouraged so-called 'ethnic filmmaking'[8], representation would not occur on equal terms: funding policies restricted the format (16 mm instead of 35 mm), and documentaries or filmic essays were produced instead of feature films, often with limited cinematic release. Black Britons are but one example for minoritised subject positions which challenge notions of collective memory. This study cannot represent all minoritised subject positions, but will discuss some of them exemplarily in the case studies.

In her essay "The Archive, the Activist, and the Audience" Fatima El-Tayeb points out the ambiguous role of the archive in a post-colonial context: "For [minorities], archives are sites of exclusion, a manifestation of the minority's irrelevance to their nation's history, rather than taken-for-granted containers of established history." (El-Tayeb 2005, 1) Taking as a point of departure Michel Foucault's (1982, 44) definition of the archive as a system of both control and of enunciation, our understanding of the archive can also be expanded from that of a building housing textual documents to that of the visual archive, housing images of the past that continue to exert an influence in the present. However, since archives have historically been dominated by a Eurocentric, colonialist perspective, immigrants have had few or no possibilities to represent themselves and to enter their stories into the archive of national historiography. Representation is not neutral and is pervaded by power relations. Racist imagery is not an exception of the rule, but the rule itself. As Richard Dyer (1997) has shown, the technological apparatus of analogue photography and filmmaking

---

8 See chapter 4.2 *Filmmaking as archival intervention – reworking cultural memory in the essay film.*

has been constructed in a way which prioritizes white skin tones. It constructs white skin as the norm.

Susannah Radstone has argued that memory is pervaded by discourses of power and is itself the result of networks of power and knowledge (see Radstone and Hodgkin 2003). Memory is therefore to be understood as a regime. Stories and images of the past, Helle Bjerg and Claudia Lenz 2008 state, "are elements in the negotiations and struggles about the distribution of material and symbolic resources within this society" (226). Cultural memory is always contested (see Hodgkin and Radstone 2003) and therefore subject to constant renegotiation. Drawing on Stuart Hall's reading of Michel Foucault (Hall 1997, 44), Bjerg and Lenz (2008) highlight the discursivity of cultural practice, while characterising discourse as something which "defines and produces the objects of our knowledge. It governs the way that a topic can be meaningfully talked about and reasoned with. It also influences how ideas are put into practice and used to regulate the conduct of others. Just as a discourse 'rules in' certain ways of talking about a topic, defining an acceptable and intelligible way to talk, write, or conduct oneself, so also, by definition, it 'rules out', limits and restricts other ways of talking, of conducting ourselves in relation to the topic or constructing knowledge about it." (Bjerg and Lenz 2008, 227) [9]

"Whose heritage is it?" is a question posed by Stuart Hall at a 1999 Arts Council conference in Manchester during his keynote address on heritage politics in Britain and the exclusions it produces. Hall criticises British heritage politics as targeting the white middle-classes, and suggests a more inclusive approach: "It follows that those who cannot see themselves reflected in its mirror cannot properly 'belong'." (Hall 1999, 14) Patricia Zimmermann has argued for a historical perspective "away from a single metanarrative [...] that is based on referentiality, realism, and facts that repress heterogeneity, toward a more particularised and multicultural construct of plural pasts" (Zimmermann 2008, 5)[10]. In more recent museum exhibitions we can see how notions of diversity are currently replacing the idea of a homogenous past. Museums in Britain have begun to include histories of ethnic minorities which were previously not represented. The Museum of London or the Slavery Museum in Liverpool try to acknowledge different experiences and pasts under the umbrella of contemporary multicultural Britain, acknowledging migrant and diasporic experiences and providing a discursive space for the articulation of cultural memory.

---

9 The use of the term 'discourse' throughout this study is based on Stuart Hall's Foucault reception, since this study does not attempt to provide an exegetic reading of Foucault's writings.
10 Patricia Zimmermann therefore applies Robert F. Berkhofer's concept of polyvocality to her study of the home movie.

In this respect, such endeavours could be classified as counter memories, challenging the hegemonic master narrative which constructs the "imagined community" (Anderson 1991) of the British nation as inherently white. However, the notion of counter practice is not unproblematic and its inherent binarism and risk of essentialism will be challenged throughout this study. Filmmaking can be a means for minoritised persons to gain agency.[11] Film has become a "fundamental tool with which we can rediscover and reconstruct our past", as Sarita Malik (1994, 13) put it. Disenfranchised groups use film as a way to counter their exclusion from hegemonic historiography. However, the question is on what grounds such archival interventions take place since counter practice implies the risk of self-essentialisation. If we want to address alternative memories which challenge official versions of the past, we have to accept the fact that a unified terminology and conceptualisation is lacking.

Memory in terms of a counter-practice has been classified as popular (Foucault 1975), counter (Lipsitz 1990) or vernacular (Bodnar 1992), for example. While the power dimension of memory and the modes of contesting hegemonic memory need to be addressed, their inherent binarism makes these concepts problematic. The risk is that these concepts become de-historicised and de-situated. Binary oppositions might stabilize what they actually criticize – on an epistemological level – when it comes to the perspective of the memory scholar (despite Derrida's insight of the slippery signifier and the power of the appendix to deconstruct), instead of perceiving memory as in flux and subject to change, thus granting agency to those who are not part of dominant structures. Moreover, popular/counter/vernacular/subcultural memories are not automatically counter-memories and not subversive per se.[12] Therefore the notion of counter-memory and its inherent binarism needs to be reconceptualised. The same goes for Foucault's notion of popular memory which is based on an idealised notion of the emancipatory qualities his concept entails. Non-official memory is not always more emancipatory than official memories, as the studies conducted by Harald Welzer and his research group have shown. Looking at the cultural memory of the Holocaust as transmitted through family memory (Welzer [2001] terms this 'social memory'), Welzer and his team were able to show that Germany's official memory about the Holocaust does more justice to the victims than the practices of amnesia or denial to be found within the majority of the German popu-

---

11 The notion of agency has been emphasised by John Sundholm in his current work on migrant filmmaking in Sweden and I am grateful to him for reminding me of the importance of this concept.
12 See chapter 3.2. *Transcultural memories: post-punk Manchester in times of urban regeneration.*

lation (see Welzer, et al. 2002). The dichotomy between official memory and unofficial memory, which is handed down within the family or in specific groups, is highly problematic, as hegemonic discourses influence and rework the communicative memory. In order to flesh out the flaws and limitations created by such a dichotomous theorization, this study critically examines the idea of alternative media practice. Both the video collectives discussed in chapter 4.1 and British film collectives of the 1980s have contextualised themselves either within the 'counter public sphere' or in opposition to it.

Drawing on Michel Foucault, Natalie Zemon Davis and Randolph Starn (1989, 2) define counter-memory as "the residual or resistant strains that withstand official versions of historical continuity". Marita Sturken (1997), however, criticises Foucault's concept of memory as naive and romantic when he conceptualises popular memory as unofficial memory with a capacity to subvert official historiography. While I agree with Sturken that Foucault's rather binary approach would need further theorization, I argue that, instead of providing an exact definition of the term counter-memory, it would be more important to include the specific context, as Zemon Davis and Starn (1989, 2) argue: "By whom, where, in which context, against what?". The specific social and historical context, or – to put it another way – the specific discursive formation at a given historical moment, should be considered in order to avoid an a-historical understanding of power relations as fixed and stable, as a binarism of "oppressed" and "suppressed", denying agency to those lacking power in a specific situation.

In film studies the notion of cinematic counter practice has been theorised by Peter Wollen (see Wollen 2002) in his 1972 outline of a binary classification which distinguishes modernist filmmaking from classical Hollywood narration. In 1973 Claire Johnston (see Johnston 1999) utilised the notion of 'counter' from a feminist perspective in order to outline the possibilities for a subversive filmmaking practice challenging and undermining the inherently patriarchal structure of classical Hollywood cinema. However, while these theoretical interventions were important for offering alternatives to oppressive structures, their use of binaries entails the risk of positioning Hollywood cinema as the norm – with the result that modernist/feminist/alternative filmmaking becomes its 'other'.

In the field of historiography, interventions have often aimed at adding previously hidden voices to the dominant version of history. In the case of feminist historiography the dominant 'history' was to be complemented with a 'herstory'. While the work of feminist historians has been important in excavating forgotten stories, the structures, presuppositions and modes of exclusion prevalent in hegemonic history remain untouched. One remains stuck in a hierarchical position in relation to hegemonic historiography (which still has the prerogative of definition) instead of questioning its epistemological prerequisites. Under the influence of gender studies, post-colonial theory and queer theory, though, the construction of masculinity, of heteronormativity, of whiteness and their positioning as a norm has been questioned.

Counter practice, therefore, runs the risk of, on the one hand, perpetuating the hierarchies of 'centre' versus 'periphery' and, on the other hand, homogenising and essentialising the most diverse groups of people (blacks/migrants/women/queers). The ambivalences within a community will not be addressed. From a feminist and/or queer perspective, criticism has been raised that counter practices, conceptualised this way, will eventually lead to new exclusions. Examples can be found in Pan-Africanism or the Black Power Movement. The risk is that feminist or queer positions are marginalised. Therefore, the question is: how are films able to criticise hegemonic historiography without at the same time having to refer to essentialism?

During the 1990s critical perspectives have increasingly challenged the concept of the nation and pointed at its constructedness (Anderson 1991; Hobsbawm and Ranger 1992; Bhabha 1990, 1994). In his seminal 1987 book *There Ain't No Black In the Union Jack*, Paul Gilroy (2002) targets the understanding of British national identity as inherently white. Gilroy was able to draw on the debates around Black Britishness during the 1980s.[13] Notions of Black British identity were not only explored within Black British Cultural Studies, but also within filmmaking (Black Audio Film Collective, Sankofa), photography (Rotimi Fani-Kayode) and art (Sonia Boyce, Keith Piper, Donald Rodney) as well as in exhibition practice.[14] These multiple forms of rethinking who belongs to the nation have not only contributed to redefining Britishness, but have also impacted the reconceptualisation of 'cultural heritage' (for a conceptualisation of cultural heritage within memory studies, see Erll 2011a).[15] "Identity politics [...] suggest that people belong to recognizable social groups, and that delegated representatives can speak on their behalf." (Shohat and Stam 1994, 343) This notion, however, is not unproblematic, as Ella Shohat and Robert Stam explain, because it always entails the risk of essentialism, which, in turn, has consequences for canonisation and the works' place in historiography. "How can scholarly, curatorial,

---

13 See Mercer 1988a, Cham, et al. 1988.
14 See Eshun and Sagar 2007, Bailey, et al. 2005.
15 The notion of heritage as part of cultural memory is characterised by Erll (2011a, 48) as one of several "concepts of memory research" which also include 'the invention of tradition' or the 'archive' among others. While heritage is part of cultural memory, it is often guided by official politics, by incentives by the state (see Erll 2011, 52–53) and, according to Stuart Hall (2002), by hegemonic whiteness.

artistic, and pedagogical work 'deal' with multiculturalism without defining it simplistically as a space where only Latinos would speak about Latinos, African-Americans about African-Americans and so forth, with every group a prisoner of its own reified difference?" (Shohat and Stam 1994, 343) In short, how can "ethnic insiderism" (Paul Gilroy 1993, 119) be avoided? This is one question. The other, more acute issue in the context of this work is how academic writing can avoid re-essentialising minorities when these have actually attempted to get out of the limiting frames of self-essentialising?

Not all forms of essentialism are automatically reactionary, as Diane Fuss (1989) has conceded in *Essentially Speaking: Feminism, Nature, and Difference*. She distinguishes between 'deploying' essentialism strategically and 'falling into' or 'lapsing into' essentialism, which is problematic. Such notions of 'strategic essentialism' (Spivak 2006) can also be found in Judith Butler's theorization of the "double movement". According to Butler, "learning the double movement" implies the necessity to "invoke the category and, hence, provisionally to institute an identity and at the same time to open the category as a site of permanent political contest" (Butler 1993, 222). These considerations have formed a point of departure for my work. The guiding question has been: how do the films negotiate the paradox of, on the one hand, employing a form of strategic essentialism, for example making films as the Black Audio Film Collective or films which deal with migrant historiography, while, on the other hand, trying to escape essentialism?

Anti-essentialism is also a way to leave the "burden of representation" (Mercer), to avoid making films for the community. Isaac Julien, former member of the London-based film collective Sankofa, points out how important it has been for Sankofa to "speak *from* experiences rather than *for* experiences" (Julien 1992b, 267 [italics in the original]). Instead of being a mouthpiece for a community, it was more important for Sankofa to engage in a "dialogic relationship to communities of interest" (Julien 1992b, 267). In his text Julien also expresses that he is sceptical about the term "black" if it is used as a term connoting union ("unitary blackness [...] is a fiction", Julien 1992b, 271) while it contributes to excluding Black Britons (for example LGBT persons). Julien (1992b, 274) suggests the following: "To create a more pluralistic interaction in terms of difference, both sexual and racial, one has to start with de-essentialising the notion of the black subject because it's very fixed at this moment, especially in the domain of the cinema."

Identity politics and the notion of self-representation for marginalised groups have become prevalent at a time when Barthes and Foucault propagated the death of the subject, alternatively the author. As cultural critics have famously observed, it seems symptomatic that white males propagate the death of the subject at a time when minorities struggle for recognition. As Elizabeth Fox-Genovese states: "Surely it is no coincidence [...] that the Western white male elite proclaimed the death of the subject at precisely the moment at which it might have had to share the status with the women and peoples of other races and classes who were beginning to challenge its supremacy." (quoted in Shohat and Stam 1994, 345) Consequently, in their seminal study *Unthinking Eurocentrism*, Ella Shohat and Robert Stam pose the relevant question: "How, then, should the struggle to become subjects of history be articulated in an era of the 'death of the subject'?" (Shohat and Stam 1994, 345–346).

1.3 Aims – Methods – Structure

Not only does memory "pervade every aspect of cinema", as Pam Cook (2005, 82) notes, a memory dimension can also be found in a variety of analogue and digital media practices, such as remediation (Bolter and Grusin 2000), convergence culture (Jenkins 2006) and remix culture (Lessig 2008, Groo 2012). Media memory studies therefore need to widen their scope from representations of the past towards questions of the archive, the collection and preservation of films, the use of archive footage in television programmes and/or in documentary filmmaking as well as processes of distribution and reception. Still, it is surprising that the politics of representation have so far been sidelined in media memory studies. In fact, the notion of representation seems to have been out of fashion, due to the increased interest in performativity. However, while I regard all cultural practice as performative, I argue that the power dimension entailed in the conceptualisation of representation will offer fruitful ways of analysing mediated cultural memory.[16] I will draw on the theorisation on representation within British Cultural Studies (Hall 1997), but also critical approaches to representation within film studies, such as Ella Shohat and Robert Stam's seminal work on Eurocentrism (Shohat and Stam 1994). While I am in favour of moving beyond the study of representation towards acknowledging the performative aspect within media cul-

---

[16] My understanding of the notion of performativity differs from its use in documentary theory. Both Bill Nichols and Stella Bruzzi deal with "performative documentaries", though their understanding of performativity is based much more on concepts of "performance" than on Judith Butler's notion. For Bill Nichols, performative films "stress subjective aspects of a classically objective discourse" (Nichols 1994, 54). For Bruzzi, a performative film is "one whose truth is enacted for and by the filmmakers' encounters with their subjects for the benefit of the camera" (Bruzzi 2002, 126). She distinguishes between "films that are performative in themselves and those that merely concern performative subject matter" (154).

ture and memory, I argue that critical theories of representation offer useful tools for the analysis of mediated memories, both in terms of a diachronic perspective on the colonialist, Eurocentric audiovisual archive and in terms of hands-on ways of analysing film images.

The discourses on digitisation as well as on the disappearance of the last generation of Holocaust survivors address a notion inextricably linked to remembrance: the notion of forgetting, which has been emphasized by Aleida Assmann (1999). A similar rhetoric of loss can also be found in discourses about the urgent need to preserve analogue film from decay. Only a fraction of the audiovisual heritage on analogue film stock has survived until now (see Fossati 2009), thus the question is how to preserve today's film heritage for future generations. Digitisation might be an option for preservation, but it is doubtful whether it actually can be a sustainable solution (see Holmberg 2011).

The filmic works I examine in this study are interventions against forgetting, against disremembering politically disenfranchised groups in hegemonic historiography and in popular visual culture. Images and narratives can change from being what Aleida Assmann terms 'storage memory' (which can be described as dead memory) to becoming 'functional memory' (which implies living memory) (see Assmann 2008).[17] Therefore they need to be remediated and have to be circulated again and again, for example via novels, TV series and documentaries, exhibitions or online platforms, such as YouTube, Flickr or Tumblr. The remediation of these images can enable them to become part of the 'functional memory' in a specific socio-historical context, instead of being relegated to an existence on a shelf in the archive. Aleida Assmann's distinction between storage memory and functional memory is echoed in the relation between archive and remediation. Remediation frees footage from forgetting by liberating it from the shelves. What is not continuously remediated, will soon be forgotten. As Erll states, "remediation tends to solidify cultural memory, creating and stabilising certain narratives and icons of the past" (Erll 2008, 393). However, while memory studies has hitherto focused on popular genres and mainstream cultural practice (Erll 2009; Rigney 2012), I would like to take a look at the remediation of archival newsreel footage and other archival images, since the archive is the foundation of how history is written. Or, as Stuart Hall has put it: "The past cannot speak, except through its 'archive'." (Hall 1991, 152) Arguing that the relation between

---

[17] Although I find Assmann's distinction highly useful I am sceptical about the term "storage memory", as memory needs to be constantly circulated and remediated. "Storage" is not memory. See chapter 2.2 *The Archive* for a discussion of Assmann's contributions to theorisations of the archive for memory studies.

documentary images and the dynamics of cultural memory needs to be theorised more fully, this study readdresses the concepts of the 'archive' and 'remediation'.

As most of the research centres on US-American filmmaking, I want to focus on European filmmaking while looking at film practice ranging from independent and experimental film-making to avant-garde practice. As a common denominator we could call the films in this study 'minor cinema' in the broad sense of David E. James, who has adopted the concept of 'minor cinema' as an umbrella term for "experimental, poetic, underground, ethnic, amateur, counter, noncommodity, working-class, critical [and] artists' film-making" (James 2005: 13).[18] The films I examine are documentaries in the widest sense of the term, ranging from first-person documentaries to essay films.[19] While this study perceives both filmmaking and archival practice as 'acts of remembrance', it also looks at filmmaking *as* archival practice. The films examined in this study can all be regarded as an intervention into the archive, as a way of reworking the visual archive of the nation for example, or the colonial archive, or the archive of Black gay memory. Film-makers make use of the archive, for instance by incorporating archive footage such as photographs, newsreels, found footage or home movies into their works. At the same time the films I examine can all be said to create a new (visual) archive of memory which foregrounds the politics of exclusion. What links the works I examine in my study has been described by Kobena Mercer (with regards to Black British artists) as "how their work interrupts commonsense essentialism in favour of a relational and dialogic view of the constructed character of any social identity" (Mercer 1994, 222).

As has become evident, my theoretical foundation has been (in)formed by the insights of post-structuralism, post-colonialism, feminist and queer theories as well as Cultural Studies. Yet, in analysing the aesthetic strategies of the films, my study tries to provide a way out of the impasse that Cultural Studies-inspired criticism has reached. Especially in Anglophone film studies the impact of Cultural Studies has brought about the risk of neglecting the films' aesthetic qualities. Looking for evidence of the power structures of race, gender and class in the specific (filmic) texts to be examined, seems to have become an end to its means. While Cultural Studies should be credited for having put these issues on the map, we should be aware that literary or cinematic texts are not only sociological case studies, but, while pervaded by various discourses, are the result of conscious (and of course sub-conscious) auteurist strategies.

---

18 The term 'minor cinema' is based on the notion of 'minor literature' put forward by Deleuze and Guattari (1986) and introduced into film studies by Tom Gunning (1989–1990).
19 On the notion of the essay film, see chapter 4.2 *Filmmaking as archival intervention: reworking cultural memory in the essay film*.

Alexandra Schneider and Vinzenz Hediger have pointed at the chances of departing from a position of marginality (Schneider and Hediger 2011, 153). As Derrida has shown, the margins can develop into a highly productive place (see Schneider and Hediger 2011, 153). Among others, Schneider and Hediger maintain, a marginal perspective allows us to better realize the mechanisms of control and exclusion at work in academic life and its production of knowledge. Moreover, the margins are never static, but constantly in flux, never fitting in. While Schneider and Hediger use, for instance, Hindi film or non-theatrical films such as industrial filmmaking as a point of departure for their discussion, I would like to depart from essay film or minor cinema. Likewise, Tim Bergfelder (2005, 320) suggests to make "liminality and marginality" fundamental characteristics of European cinema, proposing a transnational perspective on film studies which sets out to overcome the exclusions produced by a national framework. Although, for instance, film production in Central and Eastern European countries might be considered to be "liminal" and "marginal" from the perspective of national filmmaking, my ambition goes beyond analysing the works of hitherto neglected film-producing nations. Instead, my objective is to challenge questions of liminality and marginality in those cinematographies which have been playing an essential role in debates on national cinemas (see Higson 1989, 2000a, 2000b). Using examples from British and German films, my goal is to show how questions of canonisation and the archive can be complicated.

This study discusses three concepts: (trans)cultural memory, remediation and archive. Of course, the division made here is merely heuristic, as these concepts overlap and contribute to each other. The aim of this study is to offer theorizations around current concepts within memory studies from a film studies perspective. The research departs from documentary and essay films which rework the hegemonic (national) historiography and the colonial/Eurocentric/heteronormative visual archive. It looks at filmmaking as a theoretical tool to reflect on the modes of historiography and its exclusions. Each theoretical concept is discussed in two case studies.

The first section (*3. Mediatized memories in a global age: the transcultural turn?*) points at the risks inherent in the current transcultural turn within memory studies. My point of departure has been Astrid Erll's (2011) observation that the notion of 'culture' has been increasingly narrowed down and essentialised in cultural memory studies. She recommends the use of the term 'transculturality' based on Wolfgang Welsch (1999), and reintroduced into English Studies by Frank Schulze-Engler and Sissy Helff (2008). Despite its current boom, I will outline some of the risks accompanying an uncritical use of the concept, for instance when the notion of transculturality is merely employed in relation to ethnicity and national belonging. Drawing on the theorisation of transnational memory within film studies I will take a look at the possibilities the notion of 'transnationality' might offer for cultural memory studies. I argue that instead of conflating transnational and transcultural memory, it would be more fruitful to distinguish the two terms. At the same time I will argue for the need not to lose sight of the national perspective. The case of migrant memories shows the need for memory scholars not to 'other' migrant or diasporic persons in the research process by situating them outside a national framework. Chapter 3.1. *Remembering Turkish-German labour migration* examines the mediation of migrant memories within its industrial and discursive context. Looking at Fatih Akin's autobiographical documentary *We Forgot to Go Back* (2001) the chapter shows the limitations of self-representation. It analyses the aesthetic means used in the film, setting out to challenge essentialist notions of conflating identity, nation, ethnicity and territory. However, despite the films' anti-essentialist aesthetic strategies, its director and his work tends to be re-essentialized in the process of distribution and reception. Chapter 3.2. *Transcultural memories – post-punk Manchester in times of urban regeneration* examines the multidirectional memories and their power relations within contemporary retro culture and its current 'memory boom' of punk and post-punk subcultures. I argue that memory travels not only through space, but also through different cultural contexts within the same (g)local space: Manchester. The chapter examines how subcultural memory is translated and appropriated within neoliberal politics of urban regeneration. My hypothesis is that notions of vernacular, popular or counter memories need to be challenged both for their inherent binarism and for their conceptualisation as emancipatory or even subversive. I will use Carol Morley's feminist experimental film *The Alcohol Years* (2000) as a theoretical tool to point at the exclusions and gendered power relations at work in the construction of Manchester's post-punk memories. Other films, such as *24 Hour Party People* (Winterbottom, 2002) and *Control* (2007) will be briefly discussed, too.

The next section *(4. Reworking the archive)* re-introduces the notion of the archive into memory studies. I suggest to reconceptualise the notion of the 'archive' from the perspective of media memory studies while thinking together the archive's material and discursive aspects. Chapter 4.1 *Archival interventions: excavating the cultural memory of video art and activism* argues for the urgent need to preserve the currently decaying cultural memory of independent video workshops. The chapter, a first attempt to map the underresearched field of video collectives, examines the archival practice of Hamburg's video workshops. I will both emphasize the media specificity of video as a dispositif in its own right and highlight the role of the archive as an agent of memory. In this context the impact of curatorial decisions for granting access to the collections is examined. The chapter suggests to critically reflect on the modes of selecting films for preservation and online publication. The essay film as an epistemological tool for the investigation of the audiovisual archive is dealt with in chapter 4.2 *Filmmaking as archival intervention – reworking cultural memory in the essay film*. Drawing on the example of *Handsworth Songs*, the various functions of the film's self-reflexive aesthetics in relation to cultural memory, canonisation, the audiovisual archive and national belonging are examined.

The final section (*5. Remediation: reappropriations in digital media and in the essay film*) offers a new approach to remediation. Chapter 5.1 *Remediating the cultural memory of migration* examines the question: "What triggers remediation?" In the following chapter I examine in what ways archival newsreel footage of the now iconic arrival of the Windrush in Britain in 1948 has been reappropriated. I suggest that remediations of documentary images can be used to acknowledge the cultural memory of migration, and, more specifically, highlight the legacy of Black immigration and its impact on contemporary Britain. Analysing remediations of the footage available on YouTube, this chapter examines the media specificity of the cultural memory of migration and its different forms of mediation (mediatization). Moreover, it not only looks at the media specificity of these visual representations and their roles as performative acts, but also their specific discursive context. Arguing that the relation between documentary images and the dynamics of cultural memory needs to be theorised more fully, the case study readdresses the concept of 'remediation'. In order to understand the remediation of cultural memory and its inherent power structures, the case study highlights notions of media specificity, genre, the politics of representation at work, its discursive as well as its industrial contexts (production, distribution and exhibition). It also discusses the remediation of archival footage as a possible way to rework a colonial and Eurocentric perspective. Critical interrogations into the archive can create appropriations of cultural memory which might offer emancipatory potential instead of stabilising essentialist notions of belonging. This perspective could allow cultural memory studies to get away from essentialising concepts of cultural or transcultural memory as based on the notions of container cultures.

Studies on remediation have had the tendency to focus on the remediation of specific historical (mediatised) events (*The Indian mutiny*) or literary sujets (*the Odyssey*) or the impact of certain works (such as the novels of Sir Walter Scott) (see Erll 2009, 2011d, Rigney 2012). In contrast, the objective of this chapter is to look at remediation as a way to carve out discursive spaces which allow for a variety of subject positions. Using the example of *Looking for Langston* (1989), directed by Isaac Julien, by that time a member of the Sankofa Film and Video Collective, the potential functions of remediation are examined. Chapter 5.2 *Remediation and intermediality: media specificity and the discursive con-*

text suggests to look at intermediality studies to theorise the media specificity of remediation. While previous theorisations of intertextuality (Lachmann 1997) and intermediality (Dickhaut 2005) within cultural memory studies have focused on literature, media memory studies is in need of media specific theorisations for audiovisual media. The question of intermediality is relevant for cultural memory studies for various reasons. To name but a few: the use of archival footage in a film, remediating and translating archival footage within different formats, for instance from 8 mm to 16 mm; digitising analogue footage for online publication; the changing media of oral history interviews and witness testimonies, for instance at Holocaust memorial sites or exhibitions[20], re-editions and re-publications of documentary images (on video) in galleries, museum exhibitions, or online.

---

[20] To illustrate, at the concentration camp memorial site Bergen-Belsen video interviews with Holocaust survivors are circulating and/or stored in different formats, depending on their place in the exhibition or their role as archival source for research purposes (see Gring and Theilen 2007).

2. Theory

In this chapter I will outline the theoretical premises on which this study is based. The first section is dedicated to the question of culture in 'cultural memory', the transcultural turn and the notion of transnational memory. In the second part the notion of the archive is addressed. A brief overview over archival theory and archivology is given before introducing the concept of the 'audiovisual archive'. The role of filmmaking as archival intervention is discussed, especially in view of the essay film as an epistemological tool. In the third and final section the concept of remediation is presented and its limitations for memory studies will be outlined.

2.1 Conceptualising transcultural and transnational memory

Over the past few years cultural memory studies has undergone a 'transcultural turn', with an increasing number of studies dedicating themselves to what they term 'transcultural' or 'transnational memory', more often than not conflating both terms. However, as Erll (2011b) has pointed out, the notion of 'culture' has recently been increasingly understood in terms of homogenous 'container cultures' with clear-cut borders. In order to counter this trend toward essentialism, Erll recommends the use of the term 'transculturality' based on Wolfgang Welsch (1999), and recently introduced into English Studies by Frank Schulze-Engler and Sissy Helff (2008). I would like to point at some of the possible pitfalls of the use of the term 'transculturality' in memory studies. First, I will give an overview over the conceptualisations of transculturality suggested for memory studies, before highlighting some of the theoretical problems which arise. I will turn to the way transnationality has been theorized within film studies and then outline a possible mode how concepts of transnationality and transculturality could be employed in memory studies as a way to avoid essentialism.

2.1.1 The notion of transculturality

The notion of 'transculturality' has been conceptualised by Frank Schulze-Engler and Sissy Helff in their edited volume on transcultural English Studies (Schulze-Engler and Helff 2008). In the introduction Schulze-Engler (2008) outlines four areas of research in which the notion of transculturality has become increasingly prevalent: 1) "theories of culture and literature that have sought to account for the complexity of culture in a world increasingly characterized by globalization, transnationalization, and interdependence" (ix), 2) collective or individual lifestyles and spheres which are a result of "transnational connections and the blurring of cultural boundaries" (ix), 3) works of literature or film (or media in general) which "explore these realities, negotiate the fuzzy edges of 'ethnic' or 'national' cultures, and participate in the creation of transnational public spheres as well as transcultural imaginations and memories" (ix–x), and 4) the field of pedagogy and didactics, "where 'target cultures' refuse to sit still for pedagogical purposes" (x). Schulze-Engler and Helff draw on the conceptualisations of transculturality as put forward by Ortiz in the 1940s, and Wolfgang Welsch in the late 1990s.

When Cuban anthropologist Fernando Ortiz (Fernandez) introduced the concept of transculturality in his *Cuban Counterpoint: Tobacco and Sugar* (Ortiz 1995) in the 1940s, he used it as a means to conceptualise cultural exchange in order to transcend models of a one-way cultural imperialism. Despite the hierarchies of power existing between a country such as the US as opposed to Cuba, Ortiz emphasizes the mutual cultural exchange, thus empowering Cuban cultural practice and granting it a sense of agency.[21] However, as Schulze-Engler (2008) points out, despite its focus on cultural exchange, Ortiz' conceptualisation of transculturality has two limitations: first, it remains confined by the framework of the nation state, and second, it is tied to a concept of one culture being the dominating one and the other culture the dominated one. Instead, transculturality sets out to question both the paradigm of the nation as well as the dichotomy between periphery (which transcultural phenomena would be relegated to) and centre. Schulze-Engler therefore concludes that "the dynamics of contemporary 'transculture' can no longer be understood in terms of classical dichotomies such as colonizer vs. colonized or centres vs. peripheries" (Schulze-Engler 2008, xi). Instead, it is crucial to acknowledge that transculturality is not limited to diasporic or minoritarian cultural practice, but is a characteristic of all cultures.

Schulze-Engler's and Helff's theorization of 'transculturality' in the field of English Studies have inspired Astrid Erll to rethink the concept of 'transculturality' for its use within memory studies. For this purpose, Erll makes use of Wolf-

---

[21] The notion of mutual exchange is also prevalent in Mary Louise Pratt's concept of 'contact zones', which she develops to account for mutual influences in order to get away from notions of 'container cultures' and concepts of borders (Pratt 1992). Also Homi Bhabha, in his seminal *The Location of Culture*, reminds us of the importance to "locate the question of culture in the realm of the beyond" (Bhabha 1994:7). For the question of the locatedness of transculture, see also Stein (2008) in Schulze-Engler/Helff's volume.

gang Welsch's 1999 essay "Transculturality: The Puzzling Form of Cultures Today"[22], which marks the second wave of theorizations around transculturality Schulze-Engler and Helff draw on. Welsch puts forward the term 'transculturality' in order to find an adequate concept which acknowledges the impact of globalization, migration and transcultural exchange. He develops the concept in contrast to a national romantic understanding of culture as ethnically and socially homogenous (Herder), as a clearly demarked container separate from other (container) cultures (cf. Welsch 1999).

This notion of separate cultures, which forms the critical point of departure for Welsch's understanding of transculturality, was outlined by Johann Gottfried Herder in his *Another Philosophy of History for the Education of Mankind* (1774) and his *Outlines of a Philosophy of the History of Man* (1784–1791). Herder's philosophical writing had a strong influence on the German Romanticist conceptualisation of culture,[23] which, as Welsch has outlined, is characterized by three aspects: 1) social homogenization (culture as an expression of a people, without acknowledging inherent differences within his group, such as class or gender); 2) ethnic foundation (culture being the intrinsically unique expression of a specific people's mentality) and 3) intercultural delimitation (cultures separated from each other by clearly demarcated boundaries) (Welsch 1999, Welsch 2008, 5). Welsch considers the focus on ethnicity as a basis for cultural practice – as well as the notion of homogenous cultures and the idea of boundaries – highly problematic. As none of these criteria can incorporate the realities of contemporary multicultural societies, culture would have to be conceptualised in a different way: not in terms of 'container cultures', but as being inherently transcultural. "Today's cultures can obviously no longer be described as closed spheres or in terms of inner homogeneity and outer separation. Rather, they are characterized by a wide variety of mixing and permeations" (Welsch 2008, 6). Moreover, Welsch (1999) makes sure to distinguish transculturality from 'interculturality' and 'multiculturality', both of which are based on traditional understandings of container cultures, i.e. of cultures as spheres or islands. He sees the concept of 'interculturality' as based on the premise of different cultures which tend to collide and result in conflict. Welsch finds astonishing similarities to the concept of 'multiculturality' which also departs from a notion of homogenous cultures

---

22 The concept was initially presented by Welsch in 1991. For the edition history of his article and an overview over the different (language) versions, see Welsch 2008: 3, fn.1.
23 The Herderian concept is still visible in the German citizenship law which is largely based on a notion of *ius sanguinis*, see chapter 3.1.

with clearly demarked borders, only co-existing *within* the frameworks of a nation state.[24]

2.1.2 Transculturality and its discontents

In taking a closer look at the use of the concept of 'transculturality' in memory studies, I found that some aspects are still in need of further theoretical exploration: first, the notion of culture and its inherent risk of essentialism; second, the focus on nationality and ethnicity; and third, the temporal dimension of transculturality if we look at the concept from a diachronic perspective. Welsch's concept can prove fruitful in its understanding of multiculturalism as not only defined by ethnicity, but by class and (sub)cultural practice. Welsch's outline contains aspects of an intersectional perspective, encompassing categories such as gender, race and generation as well.[25] These ideas are not new, though. One of the major shortcomings of Welsch's approach is the national (German) perspective dominating the choice of his (white and predominantly male-authored) sources. Thus, while Welsch celebrates hybridity underlying the theoretical concept he promotes (as his), hybridity is lacking in his own academic practice. Anti-essentialist approaches to the nation-state have been provided by Homi Bhabha (1990), Benedict Anderson (1991), Hobsbawm and Ranger (1992), Arjun Appudarai (1995) or Nira Yuval-Davis (1997). Moreover, the insights of 1980s Black British Cultural Studies are completely ignored by Welsch. In their writings, Stuart Hall (see Hall 1996), Homi Bhabha and Paul Gilroy (see Gilroy 1987, 1993) have put forward ideas about identity as relational, as defined not by an essence, but by cultural practice, uncoupling ethnic identity from territory. Culture, as both Stuart Hall and Homi Bhabha (and many others) have argued, is

---

[24] The risk of these notions of cultural purity can lead to "regressive tendencies which by appealing to a particularistic cultural identity lead to ghettoisation or cultural fundamentalism." (Welsch 1999, 197)

[25] Welsch distinguishes between what he calls 'horizontal' and 'vertical' differences in society which have an impact on lifestyles and cultural practice. Vertical divisions would be "the culture of a working-quarter, a well-to do residential district, and that of the alternative scene", whereas horizontal differences would be "gender divisions, differences between male and female, or between straight and lesbian and gay" (Welsch 1999, 195). The examples chosen to illustrate vertical differences are not very convincing, since in times of neoliberal city planning and fast changes within the demographic structure of these areas these divisions are difficult to uphold. Instead, they constantly overlap, which is why I would not agree with Welsch's (1999, 195) conclusion that they "hardly exhibit any common denominator". (See also chapter 3.2 of this study on 1980s Manchester and the dynamics of remembrance in urban spaces).

inherently hybrid, it is never stable and fixed, but in constant flux. This understanding of culture is completely different from the concept of container cultures which both Welsch and Erll have criticized with good reason.

Erll's notion of transculturality, though influenced by Welsch, is more hybrid in its outset. For her, the "transcultural lens" is directed at modes of remembering across cultures, and she sees three particular advantages to the concept of transculturality: it allows us to see first "the many fuzzy edges of national cultures of remembrance, the many shared sites of memory that have emerged through travel, trade, colonialism and other forms of cultural exchange; secondly, the great internal heterogeneity of national culture, its different classes, generations, ethnicities, religious communities, and subcultures [...]" and third, formations which exceed national boundaries, such as world religions, music culture, consumer culture, football (Erll 2011a, 65).[26] However, what also remains unclear is the difference between 'transculturality' and 'hybridity'. It should be explored more closely whether the notion of 'hybridity' is about to be replaced because its terminology stems from post-colonial theory. Moreover, we should also examine what we actually do gain if we leave post-colonial theorising and its analysis of power structures behind. The question is if another approach might open up a perspective on artist practice without the risk of 'othering' the artist. The change from the term "post-colonial literature" to "literatures of the English language" can be regarded as a symptom for this tendency. Erll (2011b) in fact suggests to incorporate post-colonial theory into transcultural memory studies, especially concepts such as 'writing back', colonial nostalgia or the Middle Passage as a traumatic event, all of which provide a memory dimension.

While the notion of 'transculturality' might serve as a useful concept to overcome an understanding of culture in terms of 'container cultures', it contains the risk of contributing to re-essentialising the notion of 'culture'. To illustrate, the concept of 'transculturality' might be used in a way which would allow the term 'culture' to remain conceptualised as 'container cultures'. As a consequence, 'transculturality' would refer to phenomena associated with contemporary multi-cultural societies, such as migration, diaspora or ethnic minorities. Therefore, an uncritical use of the concept of 'transculturality' can contribute to re-essentialising the notion of 'culture' (in the Herderian sense). A 'minor cinema' perspective shows the need to reflect on the consequences the use of termi-

---

[26] However, it should be pointed out that while democracy, feminism, Buddhism, Catholicism or Islam exceed national boundaries, the national discourse, which finds its expression e.g. in laws or public debates, still has an important impact on the ways these phenomena are negotiated.

nology might have for the subsequent canonisation of migrant and diasporic artists, writers and filmmakers. Conceptualising Fassbinder, Goethe or Shakespeare in terms of 'cultural memory', whereas Akin, Zaimoglu and Kureishi are examined from the perspective of 'transcultural memory', implies an 'othering' of artists' practice which has repercussions for their status as artists. Therefore, the question remains: If the idea of transculturality is to get away from concepts of container culture, how then can a conceptualisation of 'transculturality' make sure that it does not walk into the trap of essentialism? Above all, an ethnicised understanding of the concept of 'culture', often conflating 'culture' with 'ethnicity', needs to be challenged. Studies on transculturality need to critically reflect on their use of ethnicising concepts of the 'transcultural'. For instance, if Welsch (1999) regards transculturality as a practice across countries and nations, he might actually conflate transculturality and transnationality. He names Naipaul or Rushdie as examples of writers whose cultural practice is informed by transcultural references, and who are "shaped not by a single homeland, but by differing reference countries, by Russian, German, South and North American or Japanese literature" (Welsch 1999, 198). However, not a single writer worldwide would be influenced by one single national literature alone. Such a limited understanding of transculturality reduces the concept to questions of national (and ethnic) belonging.[27] Moreover, the prevalent focus on contemporary culture within the use of 'transculturality' sidelines a diachronic perspective.[28]

For Welsch, transcultural phenomena are first and foremost a characteristic of today's multicultural societies. While he briefly acknowledges that 'cultural mixing' has occurred in previous eras[29], he sets out to conceptualise 'transcultur-

---

[27] Welsch also overlooks the impact of translation and adaptation processes at work in transnational reception. For a more profound account, using the example of cross-cultural film reception, see Bergfelder 2005, especially pp. 324–329.

[28] Erll 2011d and Rigney 2012 are notable exceptions.

[29] Welsch acknowledges that transculturality "is in no way completely new historically" (IV.1.), he modifies this statement when he claims that transcultural phenomena, which characterize the lifestyle and cultural practice of individuals today, "once may have applied to outstanding persons like Montaigne, Novalis, Whitman, Rimbaud or Nietzsche" (Welsch 1999, III.2.). In his 2008 article "On the Acquisition and Possession of Commonalities", a 'supplement' to his earlier theorisations of transculturality, Welsch lists a few "classical examples" of "[c]ultural mixing" or hybridisation, such as "Puccini and Chinese music; Gauguin and Tahiti; expressionism and African art; or Messiaen and India" (Welsch 2008, 7). Although Welsch contends: "When I introduced the term 'transculturality', I thought it was a new one" (Welsch 2008, 3), he does neither address the works by Stuart Hall or Paul Gilroy and other representatives of British Cultural Studies, which have dealt with the complexity of cultural practices, nor does he abstain from speaking of "cultures" in the plural form.

ality' as a predominantly contemporary phenomenon. In contrast, Astrid Erll (2011b) emphasizes the importance of a temporal perspective: Instead of focussing on the 'transcultural lens' as a perspective on contemporary literature, film or art alone, works from all periods ought to be regarded as inherently 'transcultural'. For instance, the writings of Homer and other canonical texts could be analysed from a transcultural perspective. In stressing the relevance of a diachronic perspective on transculturality, Erll states that "transcultural remembering has a long genealogy. [...] There is the Persian influence on the Old Testament; Egyptian fairy tales in Homer's Odyssey, Islam's substantial contributions to the European Renaissance; or the French origins of the Grimm brothers' German fairy tales" (Erll 2011a, 65). The notion of transculturality can thus contribute to a fruitful revision of canonical texts. At the same time it can help researchers to overcome the notion of the Romantic male genius in favour of emphasising the impact of migration and transnational reception. An example of such a paradigmatic shift towards employing the 'transcultural lens' in a diachronic perspective would be the 2012 exhibition "Migrations" at Tate Britain in London. Acknowledging the influences of travel and migratory movements, the exhibition set out to revise dominant art-historical paradigms, such as the notion of the artist-genius and the framework of the nation-state as the structuring principle for art exhibitions. Through this change of perspective, artists' practice which was previously marginalised within national art historiography became the centre of attention, for example the impact of Anglo-French relations or the multicultural art scene after World War II. While the British nation still formed the major point of reference, since the exhibition was based on the collections of Tate Britain, this project can be regarded as a fruitful way of undermining the dichotomy between 'centre' and 'periphery'. However, maybe the approach ought to be conceptualised as employing a 'transnational' rather than a 'transcultural' perspective. Since the terms 'transcultural' and 'transnational' are often used as synonyms, the advantages of distinguishing between these two concepts need to be reconsidered. In turning to transnational film studies I will now outline what insights the 'transnational' might offer.

2.1.3 Transnational memory: using the insights of transnational film studies

Conceptualising cultural memory as moving beyond and across national borders has at times resulted in conflating the terms 'transculturality' and 'transnationality'. I argue that using both terms almost as synonyms would forfeit the chance of also encompassing other categories than the nation. Actually, 'transculturality' is a broader concept than 'transnationality', transgressing at best not only the notion of the nation-state, but also class or subcultural belonging. In the following paragraphs I would like to use the theorizations of 'transnationality' within film studies as a point of departure for suggesting how memory studies could employ this concept as a fruitful perspective on the dynamics of remembrance.

In film studies the concept of 'transnationality' was developed in the late 1990s and early 2000s as a reaction to the dominant national perspective. If we depart from the main paradigms within film studies, which are structured along the lines of 'Hollywood cinema', 'European art cinema' and, more recently 'World cinema'[30], we find that Hollywood cinema has a tendency to be conceptualised either as universal or as an expression of national identity.[31] European art cinema has predominantly been conceptualised in terms of national cinema. In recent years, however, while the notion of national cinema has both been perpetuated and challenged within film studies (see Higson 1989, 2000a, 2000b), we can observe a tendency setting out to replace the paradigm of the nation.

Focussing on national film production overlooks the transnational exchange that has characterised filmmaking since the times of early cinema: co-productions between different nations were the rule rather than an exception and so was the exchange of actors and directors. Transnational film studies aims at acknowledging these mutual influences; it came about in the 1990s as a result of changing film production politics by the European Union and in the wake of multicultural filmmaking, of migrant and diasporic filmmaking entering the mainstream (such as Gurinder Chadha's *Bend It Like Beckham* or Fatih Akin's *Gegen die Wand (Head-on)*). Transnational film studies are also a result of the geopolitical changes in Central and Eastern Europe, such as Perestroika, the fall of the Berlin Wall and the Balkan wars. A transnational perspective on

---

[30] For a model which allows for more variations, see for example Stephen Crofts' "Concepts of National Cinema" (1998). In order to get away from the classic (and highly problematic) distinction between Hollywood cinema, European art cinema and Third cinema (African, Asian and Latin American cinema), Crofts outlines seven varieties of nation-state cinema (among them "Asian commercial successes", "Other entertainment cinemas", "Totalitarian cinemas" and "International co-productions", Crofts 1998, 390). However, these classifications contain a number of pitfalls in themselves and ought to be understood in a rather heuristic fashion as a way to challenge the dominant distinction. For a critique of Crofts, see Bergfelder 2005, 323–324. In the meantime conceptualisations of World cinema (Chaudhuri 2005; Durovicova and Newman 2010; Nagib, et al. 2012) and European cinema through a transnational perspective (Elsaesser 2005; Bergfelder 2005) have added new dimensions to the debate, denouncing the classical view of Hollywood cinema as the main point of reference for global film practice.

[31] For example within genre cinema. For conceptualisations of the Western from a national versus a transnational perspective, see Brunow 2013a.

film studies has not only left its marks on academic works on contemporary film, but also on studies of early cinema or 1930s and 1940s film production or on popular post-war cinemas. In short, it not only offers a new perspective on canonical works, but can also help to acknowledge those works which do not fit into the grid of 'national film' and which therefore have been marginalised and sidelined within film studies. As a result, mutual influences of national cinema cultures have been highlighted, as well as popular genre cinema of the 1960s or 1970s (see for example Distelmeyer 2006, Bergfelder 2005). Both Tim Bergfelder (2005) and Thomas Elsaesser (2005) have offered highly useful contributions to the theorization and historical study of European cinema from a transnational perspective.[32] Furthermore, in recent years, the trend has continued within film studies, especially with efforts to rethink national cinema (Hjort and Mckenzie 2000, Iordanova 2003), to introduce concepts of transnational cinema (Ezra and Rowden 2006) or to theorize World Cinema (Durovicova and Newman 2010, Nagib, et al. 2012). In the following paragraphs I will present Bergfelder's useful overview in more detail.

In his article "National, transnational or supranational cinema? Rethinking European film studies" Tim Bergfelder (2005) puts forward the notion of transnational filmmaking as a way to acknowledge the geopolitical changes in Europe during the 1990s, the impact of migration and the aftermath of Perestroika.[33] Bergfelder first outlines the problems implied by the concept of 'European art cinema'. While its focus on auteurs and the alleged 'universality' of their works undermines a national perspective and "promotes the wider project of an interconnected European culture", one of its inherent problems is that it "advertises this project through traditional Western – and frequently high bourgeois – values" (Bergfelder 2005, 317). On the one hand such a perspective on cinema risks to exclude popular filmmaking. On the other hand popular filmmaking, such as genre cinema or exploitation films, has increasingly come into focus of film scholarship, especially in the wake of cultural studies. However, while many of these studies set out to analyse "European popular cinema", their

---

[32] Thomas Elsaesser (2005) develops his concept of European cinema along the lines of distribution contexts, aesthetic practices and topics, such as festivals, the notion of 'double occupancy' and memory. Festivals as glocal events have become the major platform for European cinema and nowadays often a presupposition for a cinematic release. Second, the notion of 'double occupancy' is outlined as a theoretical concept to acknowledge the plural and multidirectional modes in which the filmmaker relates to the dominance of Hollywood cinema on the one hand and national filmmaking on the other. Third, memory, which for Elsaesser has a post-national (Elsaesser's term for transnational) quality, transgresses the national paradigm.

[33] Bergfelder's use of the term 'transnational' is inspired by Ulf Hannerz, who uses this term in preference to the term 'globalisation' (see Bergfelder 2005, 321).

framework is more often than not dominated by a national perspective. Thus, the concept of European cinema does not automatically mean that research on arthouse cinema or popular filmmaking is conducted from a transnational perspective, but is often used as an umbrella term for studies of national film cultures in Europe. As Bergfelder (2005, 315) has pointed out, "in most cases, research into European cinema still equals research into discrete national cinemas". Therefore, he promotes an understanding of European cinema as "more than just the sum total of separate and divergent national film styles" (329). In order to outline a transnational perspective on European cinema – instead of studying national cinema cultures in Europe – Bergfelder builds his argument along the lines of three phenomena which undermine the national paradigm: 1) migrant and diasporic filmmaking, 2) the industrial context of international co-productions, and 3) cross-cultural reception, which is highly influenced by the reception studies undertaken by Joseph Garncarcz (1994)[34].

One important challenge for the theorization of national cinema, especially within British cinema, but also in French and German film culture, has been the rise of migrant and diasporic filmmaking. Drawing on the seminal works of Sarita Malik (1996) and Deniz Göktürk (1998, 2001, 2002), Bergfelder challenges traditional film historiography in stating that migration is not a marginal phenomenon, but "fundamentally linked to the development of European cinema" (Bergfelder 2005, 320).[35] Within a national cinema framework, migrant and diasporic filmmaking is usually conceptualised as non-mainstream, as peripheral, as 'other', as Sarita Malik (1996) and Deniz Göktürk (1998, 2001, 2002) have shown.[36] Both Malik and Göktürk have criticised the way a perspective on national film cultures has so far not been able to cope with ethnic difference as a result of today's multicultural societies, resulting in marginalising and sidelining a great number of films. Yet, in times where migrant and diasporic filmmakers are 'bidding for the mainstream' (see Korte and Sternberg 2004), the dichot-

---

[34] Thanks to his research of cinema-going practice after WWII in West Germany, Garnkarcz was able to show that Germans did not at all favour those American productions screened in the allied zones. This result contributes to challenging traditional myths of Hollywood's economic power automatically guaranteeing (or leading to) cultural (or so-called "cultural-imperialist") dominance on international markets.

[35] Moreover, Bergfelder posits the question how "contemporary Europe's multicultural diversity within and across national boundaries can be represented through a framework which is so strongly rooted in Western aesthetic traditions and cultural norms. The fact that the overwhelming majority of European auteurs have been and still are white and male underlines this dilemma." (Bergfelder 2005a, 317)

[36] More recent studies are collected in Berghahn and Sternberg 2010.

omy between centre and periphery cannot be upheld.[37] In contrast to these tendencies, Bergfelder finds notions of liminality and marginality highly neglected in European film studies: "while the influence of exile and immigration have been readily acknowledged as essential to the multicultural composition of Hollywood, migration has not become an equally integral element in the discursive construction of national cinemas in Europe itself" (Bergfelder 2005, 320). As a consequence, research on European cinema remains to a high extent "couched in a rhetoric of cultural protectionism and fear of globalization" (Bergfelder 2005, 321), perpetuating the notion of stable and unchanging container cultures.

Another factor which challenges the national paradigm are international co-productions. In national film historiography they have been treated merely as "a cursory footnote, or as a tolerable exception to the more desirable norm of indigenous and self-reliant national film production" (Bergfelder 2005, 323). Yet, far from being an exception, transnational collaborations have played an important and defining role in European film production. A transnational perspective could also reposition these works in film historiography, where they have often been sidelined, either as being too banal (as popular thrillers or horror films) or too bland (as the so-called *Europuddings*). In addition, the fact that some of the works by auteurs, such as Bergman or Fellini, have been the result of international co-funding, is often neglected.[38] However, a national – or transnational – perspective should not only be theorized on the level of production, but also of reception.[39]

National audiences and their preferences are not static and fixed; the meaning of films is constantly renegotiated through strategies of cultural adaptation

---

37 *Bidding for the Mainstream* is the title of Korte and Sternberg's study on the shift in British filmmaking from the mid 1990s, when a number of British-Asian filmmakers managed to cross over to mainstream audiences, most notably Gurinder Chadha (see Korte and Sternberg 2004). However, this was not the case for Black filmmakers. While the late 1980s opened up possibilities for Black British filmmaking, especially due to the Workshop Act and the collaboration with Channel 4, the 1990s saw this trend reversed. According to Alexander (2000), the decline of Black British filmmaking throughout the 1990s was mostly due to economic reasons, such as cuts in film funding and the abolishing of ethnic arts funding in favour of the highly competed National Lottery money. For more recent developments, see also Sarita Malik's article in Berghahn and Sternberg 2010.
38 I would add that films by auteurs, such as Ingmar Bergman, which were made abroad, often do not gain the same status in their oeuvre as films made in their home country. In Bergman's case, films such as *Ormens Ägg* or *Ur Marionetternas Liv*, which he made during his exile in Germany, are often dismissed as marginal works or failures by critics and film historians alike.
39 The importance of getting away from merely looking at production in favour of reception contexts has also been pointed out by Higson 2000.

and translation. Drawing, above all, on the reception studies conducted by Joseph Garncarz (see, for instance, Garncarz 1994), Bergfelder highlights transnational modes of reception by looking at "the strategies and practices by which filmic texts 'travel' and become transformed according to the specific requirements of different cultural contexts and audiences" (Bergfelder 2005a, 326). For instance, censorship or different practices of subtitling and dubbing can vary enormously between different European countries and can have a decisive impact on the filmic representation, its content and narrative.[40] Bergfelder's approach to transnational film studies is especially useful since he does not limit himself to textual analysis or the focus on individual auteurs, but takes the industrial context of production, distribution and exhibition into account. His approach seems therefore highly fruitful for the aims of this study and will guide my understanding of the workings of mediatized cultural memory to be examined in the following six case studies, especially the ones in the first section.

2.1.4 Conclusion

The example of film studies' current paradigm shift towards a transnational perspective illustrates the importance of overcoming the methodological nationalism within memory studies.[41] Instead of adopting the essentialist understanding of culture as purist, authentic, homogenous and stable, conducting our research into cultural practice tied to a specific nation-state, the notion of *cultures* in plural needs to be questioned. Rather than assuming stable concepts, the focus should lie on transnational translations and adaptations, in short, on dynamics and practices, on formations and performative aspects. For memory studies this means that in the context of 'transcultural memory', three aspects need to be further highlighted and reflected upon: first, to avoid the risk of re-essentialising the notion of 'culture'; second, to get away from the focus on nationality and ethnicity; and third, to take the temporal dimension into account by employing a diachronic perspective instead of limiting the study of transcultural memory to contemporary practices.

---

40 Bergfelder (2005) compares Britain and Germany.
41 A perspective on transnational memory, grounded in film studies, has been suggested by John Sundholm (2011). Using the examples of Fatih Akin's film *Auf der anderen Seite* (2007) and Michael Haneke's *Caché* (2005), Sundholm analyses the translocal and the 'inclusive distinction' (Beck) in the films. Drawing on Ulrich Beck, Sundholm remarks that the transnational approach is "not anti-national, but non-national and ambivalent" due to migration, increased mobility and geopolitical changes.

Although this sub-chapter has argued for the use of a transnational perspective on film and minor cinema, media memory studies should not completely dismiss a national perspective. To illustrate, four reasons can be named: 1) immigration and citizenship laws are guided by national frameworks or national specifications of European legislation; 2) global media has a national dimension, for example the decentralised system of public service broadcasting in Germany or localised media formats adapted to national audiences; 3) legal constraints affect the use of global media (specific countries' censorship of Facebook or Twitter, national property rights legislation denying access to YouTube videos); 4) despite the impact of international co-productions, a national system of film funding has repercussions on the production, distribution and exhibition of film.

In order to avoid an othering of migrant or diasporic (or minoritarian) artists, one possible way out could be to employ the notion of 'transcultural memory' in fruitful revisions of already established canonical text, as Ann Rigney (2012) has successfully shown using the example of the novels of Sir Walter Scott. Analysing canonical works from the perspective of transculturality also helps to reduce the risk of essentialising migrant and diasporic cultural practice as 'transcultural', while white cultural practice is regarded as 'cultural' (e. g. "Fassbinder and cultural memory" or "Fatih Akin and transcultural memory"). Another way would be to stress other aspects of 'transculture' apart from ethnicity, for example gender, class or subcultural memory, as I will explore in the chapter on the dynamics of the (sub)cultural memory on 1980s post punk Manchester. A notion of transculturality which is not dominated by ethnicity is put forward by Astrid Erll (2011, 10) when she conceptualises transculturality as "part of everybody's individual everyday experience", as our "multiple memberships". These multiple memberships reflect the complexities of identity, such as, for example, that of an upper-class Afro-Swedish lesbian death metal fan or of a white working-class heterosexual Catholic country singer. They are modes of belonging which are not constantly of equal importance, but which do become important according to the specific context the individual is situated in. This understanding of multiple memberships or belongings has already been theorized within Black British Cultural Studies during the 1980s, especially in the writings of Stuart Hall and Paul Gilroy. And finally, the diachronic perspective which we find in transnational film studies could be adopted and developed within transcultural memory studies.

2.2 The Archive

This section looks at ways the notion of the archive has been theorized in memory studies and in film studies. The aim of this section is to take a critical look at the prevalent theorizations of the archive. My objective is to show the importance of the audiovisual archive and its discursive formations for the practice of minor cinema. As Jussi Parikka suggests, it is as important "to outline the centrality of the archive for media studies as has been done for philosophy and cultural theory" (Parikka 2012, 6). However, the following paragraphs will not be able to give a profound introduction into archive theory after the archival turn, nor will they be able to consider all those publications dedicated to film archives within film studies. Instead, this sub-chapter will outline some tendencies within the theorizations of the archive within film and media studies with the ambition to carve out concepts which might be useful for cultural memory studies, especially if we conceive memory as mediated, as transnational, and permeated by power relations.

2.2.1 The archive in memory studies

"Modern memory is, above all, archival. It relies entirely on the materiality of the trace, the immediacy of the recording and the visibility of the image." (Nora 1989, 13) Despite Pierre Nora's observation, the notion of the archive is conspicuously absent from memory studies. A notable exception is Aleida Assmann's discussion of the archive and the canon in her book *Erinnerungsräume* (Assmann 1999), translated into English as *Cultural memory and Western civilization* (Assmann 2011a) as well as her article "Canon and Archive" (Assmann 2008) which is based on a chapter of her 1999 book.[42] We need to keep in mind, though, that while Assmann briefly acknowledges audiovisual media, her focus is on printed archival stock. From the perspective of film and media studies, three of her concepts can provide useful points of departure for theorizations of the archive within media memory studies: a) the distinction between *functional memory* and *storage memory* which is helpful for the conceptualisation of re-mediation as well as for theorization of the archive, b) the dimension of active and passive forgetting, and c) the relation between archive and canon which enables us to rethink the mechanisms of canon formation.

---

42 Another chapter of the book was separately published as Assmann 2001.

Assmann's distinction between storage and functional memory is a useful starting point for a reconceptualisation of the archive.[43] Her distinction shows the importance of the uses of the archive, of keeping the archival stock in circulation. Functional memory, at times translated as 'working memory', is characterised by its relation to groups, and by its selectivity. It conveys values and norms, and is oriented towards the future (Assmann 1999, 134–136). Storage memory, in contrast, is the 'amorph mass' of the unused memories (Assmann 1999, 136), but it also contains the memories which have gone out of use and become obsolete. Assmann's concepts point at the fact that an archival artefact, although it once was considered important enough to be included into the archive, is not automatically part of cultural memory: it may well have been forgotten in the meantime. "When thinking about memory, we must start with forgetting", Assmann (2008, 97) reminds us, highlighting that, more than about remembrance, memory is about loss, forgetting and oblivion.

According to Assmann, the notion of forgetting is inextricably linked to remembrance. This insight is crucial for film studies since only 10–20% of the nitrate films from the silent film era have survived (see Fossati 2009). The majority of silent films cannot be remediated and therefore have no chance to become functional memory again, unless long-lost film reels are rediscovered. Assmann's conceptualisation, albeit unintendedly, emphasizes the role of the archivist in the process of selecting which films and which archival holdings will be preserved for future generations. The notion of remembrance implying forgetting is also a relevant insight in times of digitisation. Eivind Røssaak (2011b) has described the impossible challenge the National Library in Norway is currently facing in its attempt to preserve the nation's digital content, such as websites, or social media content. "In order to remember things, other things must be forgotten", Assmann (2008, 97) states, regarding forgetting as "part of social normality". Memories can be "hidden, displaced, overwritten, and possibly effaced" (Assmann 2008, 97). She distinguishes between two kinds of forgetting as a cultural practice: active forgetting, which implies "intentional acts such as trashing and destroying" (Assmann 2008, 97–98), for instance the cassation of archival documents, but also censorship. Within film studies the issue of censorship is a good example of illustrating the mechanisms of storage and functional memory, at any rate if a film is not completely forgotten in the archive, but is re-released at another historical moment. In contrast to the active mode of forgetting,

---

[43] Assmann's conceptualisation of storage versus functional memory was based on an attempt to overcome the opposition between memory and history claimed in the writings of Nietzsche, Halbwachs and Nora (Assmann 1999, 130–133).

the passive mode is defined by its non-intentionality. It includes acts such as "losing, hiding, dispersing, neglecting, abandoning, or leaving something behind" (Assmann 2008, 98). Usually the archival holdings are not deliberately destroyed, but "fall out of the frames of attention, valuation, and use." This goes for the majority of the film stock stored in film archives. The case study of the video collectives in Hamburg will show how the cultural memory of a generation is fading away due to passive forgetting, in conjunction with active forgetting. However, Assmann's conceptualisations do not cover the reality in todays' film and video archives according to which preservation, for instance in the form of digitisation, does not occur, simply due to a lack of funding.

In order to acknowledge the dimension of forgetting in cultural memory, Assmann (2008) introduces a (heuristic) division between the archive and the canon. The canon would stand for active remembering while the archive would refer to passive remembering. For Assmann (2008, 100), the "active dimension of cultural memory supports a collective identity and is defined by a notorious shortage of space. It is built on a small number of normative and formative texts, places, persons, artefacts, and myths which are meant to be actively circulated and communicated in ever-new presentations and performances". This memory is "continuously recycled and re-affirmed" (Assmann 2008, 100). These works are the result of "rigorous processes of selection" (Assmann 2008, 100) to secure a lasting space which would lead to canonization. I would argue that today functional memory is not only defined by canonization, but by much more short-term processes (e.g. YouTube videos or memes which might circulate for a short time, before they will be forgotten again). Other than such short-lived functional memory, "[a] canon is not a hit-list, it is instead independent of historical change and immune to the ups and downs of social taste" (Assmann 2008, 100). Assmann emphasizes the longevity and durability of the canon. Instead of changing from generation and generation, it "outlives the generations who have to encounter and reinterpret it anew according to their time" (Assmann 2008, 100). However, while the religious canon is rather fixed and stable, the literary canon has been challenged and renegotiated, especially in the wake of postcolonial theory. The canon is exhibited in museums, performed on theatre stages, taught at school and university.[44]

---

44 Assmann epitomizes the dynamics/struggle between canon and archive with the two different approaches used by the Harold Bloom versus Stephen Greenblatt for literary criticism.

2.2.2 Archive theory: power, knowledge and materiality

In her theorizations of the archive Assmann draws on the conceptualisation of the archive by Michel Foucault and Jacques Derrida. Acknowledging the archive as an instrument of power has influenced archive theory, archivology (see Ebeling and Günzel 2009) and media archaelogy alike (see Ernst 2004; Parikka 2012). Michel Foucault was the first to challenge the notion of the archive as a repository of knowledge in *The Archaeology of Knowledge* (1972) (originally published in French in 1969). In his understanding, the archive is not only a repository of material, but a discursive system, the "law of what can be said, the system that governs the appearance of statements as unique events" (Foucault 1972, 145). The archive is therefore not to be understood as an objective and neutral collection of artefacts. Foucault does not offer a comprehensive discussion of the term 'archive', but his idea of the archive as a construction, being the result of power relations, was reconsidered within post-structuralist and deconstructivist theorizing, notably by Jacques Derrida. In his "Archive Fever: A Freudian Impression" Derrida (1995, 4, note 1) famously remarks that "there is not political power without control of the archive, if not memory. Effective democratization can always be measured by this essential criterion: the participation in and access to the archive, its constitution, and its interpretation." Foucault's and Derrida's influential theorizations have initiated a paradigmatic turn from the storage of knowledge to its production which challenges the alleged neutrality and objectivity of the archive. The archive is not a space in which facts remain unchanged, but a process in which knowledge and facts are continuously recreated and transformed. As Aleida Assmann (2008, 102) states: "Archives always belonged to institutions of power: the church, the state, the police, the law, etc." Such an understanding of archives as top-down instruments, however, does not allow for any agency of those subjugated to these power structures. Digitization, but also grassroot archives challenge such an understanding of the archive as necessarily connected to hegemonic power structures (see Cvetkovich 2003; Van Dijck 2007). Left-wing archives or LGBT archives were founded as a counter-practice to official or commercial archives and set out to challenge dominant narratives. Digital archives with user-generated material, such as YouTube, contest the forgetting or marginalization of minorities' narratives provided by official archives.

In order to acknowledge the materiality of the archive, Aleida Assmann (2008, 102) rephrases Foucault's famous saying "the law that determines what can be said" into "The archive is the basis of what can be said in the future about the present when it will have become the past". Moreover, while Assmann, drawing on Foucault and Derrida, acknowledges the discursivity of the archive, media memory studies need to employ a media specific perspective on archival stock (such as nitrate film, video, super 8), taking the impact of power relations on the materiality of the archive into account. To add, in line with the ongoing shift in cultural studies "from products to processes" (Rigney and Erll 2009, 3), the archive can be regarded as a process rather than a product. Julia Noordegraaf (2011, 3) puts forward the understanding that "the meaning of archival records is located in their use, including their use at the various stages of the archival process itself". The use of the archive would be an important aspect to study. Markus Friedrich (2013), although he examines archives housing content from the Early Modern period, has suggested to focus on the uses of specific archives, rather than on abstract theorizations. For media memory studies this means that scholars would need to take a look at metadata, at the circulation of stock, for instance via loans, and at the way the previously conflicting interests of access and preservation are negotiated in the specific archive (see Holmberg 2011; Noordegraaf 2011).

2.2.3 Archival interventions: remediation and curatorship

Arguing to further think about the impact of remediation and curatorship, I will exemplify my ideas drawing on a specific example of archival practice. "We believe that an archive can only be significant if it refers to the practices of the present"[45] the Living Archive-website claims. "Living Archive – Archive Work as a Contemporary Artistic and Curational Practice" is a project established by the Arsenal – Institute for Film and Video Art in Berlin[46]. Starting in June 2011, the project invited 30 curators, filmmakers, researchers and visual artists to take a closer look at the Arsenal's collection of 8000 films and to use the archive as a springboard for their own projects. These projects can take the form of film programmes, exhibitions, performances or lectures, for example. As the website states: "Living Archive thus represents the attempt to undertake archival work that does not serve self-preservation only but is contemporary, creates something new and enables new approaches."[47] The project is an attempt to resurrect the archive stock and can therefore be regarded as an active intervention against the threat of forgetting. The Living Archive project has both enabled the digitiza-

---

45 http://www.arsenal-berlin.de/en/living-archive/about-living-archive.html (30 May 2012).
46 The Living Archive project is funded by the Federal Cultural Foundation and the Stiftung Deutsche Klassenlotterie Berlin. In addition, the Goethe-Institut has funded the grant program of the project Living Archive.
47 http://www.arsenal-berlin.de/en/living-archive/about-living-archive.html (30 May 2012).

tion of films from the archive, for example Laura Mulvey's and Peter Wollen's seminal film experiment *Riddles of the Sphinx* (1977), which, after being issued on DVD, has become avaible (apart from occasional screenings) for the first time in thirty years. Yet, the project has not only lead to films from the archives becoming accessible for the first time in years, it has also inspired other forms of remediation, such as concerts, books or exhibitions. Projects such as Living Archive, I argue, will have consequences for film historiography, since they provide film historians and film scholars with access to analogue film material, hitherto difficult to access, and – through programming and curatorial contexts – open up new ways of reconceptualising these works.

Also films themselves can remediate footage from storage memory to functional memory. Compilation films or collages of archival footage, such as *Handsworth Songs* or *Looking for Langston*, are examples of films turning into a deterritorialized image bank. Assmann's division between the canon and the archive needs to be revisited by media memory scholars. Are these notions to be understood as opposites or as two entities in a dialectical relation? Moreover, not every work of art or cultural practice which is met with "[e]mphatic reverence" (Assmann 2008, 101) is part of the canon (Steve Jobs, Samsung Galaxy, a new computer game, Playstation, Gangnam Style, an internet meme) – though, of course, it can become part of the canon in the future once the canon is re-negotiated. The notion of canon, characterised by "the privilege of repeated presentation and reception which ensures its aura and supports its canonical status" (Assmann 2008, 101) is also linked to the concept of remediation. As such it has repercussions on minor cinema practice, since remediation allows for agency as well. The user, when accessing the archive, might not always be able to re-circulate or remediate the archival stock, but curators and programmers can do so. Film festivals, cinémathèque programming or other forms of film curatorship are ways to turn storage memory into functional memory. Yet, also filmmakers, by incorporating archival footage into their work, can remediate archival stock. Its presentation in a new context as well as new modes of circulation will create new meanings, new ways of identification, in short: new uses of the archival images. Film studies scholars might want to examine in what way filmmakers, by remediating their works in different contexts, can inscribe themselves into a specific tradition of cultural practice or a creative network. John Akomfrah, for example, has recently started to created different versions of his work, one for the film festival circuit, possibly followed by a cinematic release, and another one for the arts context, often involving a multiple screen installation.[48] Here remediation

---

48 A shorter version of John Akomfrah's essay film *The Nine Muses* (2010) was exhibited unter

can be part of the self-inauguration of an artist. Moreover, the increased interest of experimental filmmakers in the art context (the shift from the black box to the white cube), is another example which shows how the archive, processes of canon formation and remediation engage with each other.

2.2.4 Conclusion: the archive as agent

Film studies have analysed the work of film archives mostly from the perspective of preservation, restoration and digitization (Fossati 2009; Flückiger 2012; Heller 2012; Bohn 2013). However, archives are not only storehouses of neutral material, but play a crucial role in the construction of 'historical sources', of documents through selection, classification and categorization, for instance through metadata. Thus, the archive itself is an agent in its own right. It entails a performative dimension in constructing documents and sources and, as a consequence, in creating the grounds from which history is written. The debate about the archive as an agent in its own right and the need to develop a self-reflexive perspective on the modes of selection and the impact of curatorial decisions will be a topic to be developed further, but valuable contributions have been made, such as the discussion on film curatorship and film archives in times of digitization between Paolo Cherchi Usai, David Francis, Alexander Horwath and Michael Loebenstein (Cherchi Usai, et al. 2008) as well as Heike Klippel's edited volume *The Art of Programming* (Klippel 2008). These works have directed the focus onto the impact of curatorial decisions on functional memory and therefore on the reworking of the audiovisual archive. Also Giovanna Fossati has increasingly included the role of the archivist as a curator as well as modes of exhibition into her work, both in *From Grain to Pixel* (Fossati 2009) and in later talks and conference presentations. Jan Holmberg, head of the Ingmar Bergman Archives, has also used the archival practice of the Ingmar Bergman Archives as a point of departure for theoretical considerations about the archive (see also Holmberg 2011). Also the evolving field of media archaeology, inspired by Foucault and Derrida, has contributed to an increased theorization of the archive as an agent of its own. Jussi Parikka (2012, 38) has suggested that we therefore need to look at specific, concrete archives, not only at abstract conceptualisations. In this study I will look at three specific archives, run by members of former independent video collectives,

---

the title *Mnemosyne. The Stuart Hall Project* (2013) toured the festival circuit and had a cinematic release. A version of the same footage was exhibited as a triple screen installation as *An Unfinished Conversation*.

to discuss some of the methodological possibilities the burgeoning fields of archive studies, archivology and media archaeology provide for memory studies.

2.3 Remediation

If we understand cultural memory as mediated and, as such, as constantly 'remediated', the concept of 'remediation' needs to be theorised further within memory studies. While my ambition is to complicate the prevalent uses of 'remediation', at this stage I will first give an overview over the prevalent theorizations of remediation within media studies and their adaptation for cultural memory studies. I will then look at the relationship between remediation and intermediality before outlining some aspects of remediation which are in need of further theorization, especially in view of the dynamics of mediatised memories and their power structures.

2.3.1 Remediation within media studies

The most influential conceptualisation of remediation goes back to Jay Bolter and Richard Grusin's 1999 *Remediation. Understanding New Media*. Drawing on Marshall McLuhan's (1964, 23–24) statement that "the 'content' of any medium is always another medium", Bolter and Grusin (2000, 45) define remediation as "the representation of one medium in another". Moreover, remediation "is a defining characteristic of the new digital media" (Bolter and Grusin 2000, 45). Digital media remediates analogue media, but, as Bolter and Grusin refine their argument, analogue media can remediate digital media as well. Remediation also entails a diachronic perspective since its workings are not only characteristic "of contemporary media, but also of visual media at least since the Renaissance, with its intervention of linear-perspective painting – as evidenced by the recent interest among art historians in the role that optical devices (including the camera lucida, camera obscura, and photographic projection) played in the history of realistic painting" (Grusin 2004, 17–18).

Four kinds of remediation can be distinguished in Bolter and Grusin's approach: First, remediation can provide access to older media, for example digitised galleries of paintings or photographs on DVD, CD-ROM or online, or digital archives of literary texts. This also includes the download option on websites. Here new media is not set in opposition to old media, but "instead, the computer is offered as a new means of gaining access to these older materials, as if the content of the older media could simply be poured into the new one" (Bolter and Grusin 2000, 45). For Bolter and Grusin this is an example of the digital medium aspiring to reach immediacy, erasing itself, trying to allow the recipient the same experience as without the computer screen ("but this is never so", they acknowledge) (Bolter and Grusin 2000, 45). While transparency "remains the goal" (46), the computer screen intervenes and "makes its presence felt in some way" (46). Second, remediation can emphasise the difference between old and new media – for example, encyclopaedic works on CD-ROM, which complete the text-based book version with film clips and sounds. We could also add digitally restored film versions, launched at film festivals as "improved" versions compared to the analogue 35 mm footage. Such remediations leave the character of the older medium and the status of an image intact. Third, Bolter and Grusin provide the category of "aggressive" remediation which is similar to – if not identical with – the concept of self-reflexivity.[49] In this case the older medium is torn out of its context, implying that it is "presented in a space whose discontinuities, like those of collage and photomontage, are clearly visible" (Bolter and Grusin 2000, 47). The last example of remediation outlined by Bolter and Grusin is "trying to absorb the older medium entirely" (47), such as computer games remediating cinema or the World Wide Web remediating television.

Bolter and Grusin's attempt to categorise four modes of remediation can be regarded as a first mapping of the concept. However, several of its aspects are in need of revision and modification. To illustrate, Bolter and Grusin mention literary adaptations as a way to borrow content, though without appropriating or quoting the medium, for instance the novel a film version is based on. According to them such adaptations cannot be classified as cases of remediation since no hypermediacy is involved. Another example would be the case of 'repurposing', which can generally be defined as taking "a 'property' from one medium and [reusing] it in another" (Bolter and Grusin 2000, 45) – a practice characteristic for contemporary convergence culture. Examples would be a graphic novel or comic series made into a live-action film or a film made into a video game. Acts of repurposing create new contexts which in turn redefine the work, although the interplay between media is only noticeable for audience members or users who are familiar with both versions. Moreover, repurposing also "reveals the inseparability of the economic from the social and material", as Bolter and Grusin (2000, 68) note. Apparently these cases would not be instances of remediation for Bolter and Grusin. Their definition as to what practices can be classified as processes of remediation remains unclear. Moreover, Bolter and Grusin's ideas will also

---

[49] The notion of self-reflexivity will be examined in further detail in chapter 4.1 *Archival interventions: excavating the cultural memory of video art and activism.*

need to be further theorised from the perspective of minor cinema and documentary film images.

Documentary filmmaking is completely left out in Bolter and Grusin's conceptualisation of remediation. Their book contains a single chapter on film which focuses on two film styles: animation film (Disney) and Classical Hollywood (Hitchcock). The case of animation film provides an example of 'retrograde' remediation, where older media imitate and absorb newer media, as in the more recent Disney productions *Beauty and the Beast* (1991), *Aladdin* (1992) and *Toy Story* (1995). The second example, illustrated by Hitchcock's *Vertigo* (1959) and *Spellbound* (1945), is conceptualised as "the Hollywood style", by which Bolter and Grusin obviously mean to refer to the specific mode of Classical Hollywood filmmaking. Finally, they take a look at computer graphics in live-action film, drawing on the examples of *Terminator 2* (1991), *Jurassic Park* (1993) and *The Lost World* (1997) as well as the Lumière brothers' film *The Arrival of a Train at the La Ciotat Station* (1895) to which they apply Tom Gunning's influential concept of early cinema as a "cinema of attractions", in which moments of spectacle dominate over the narrative process. The guiding question throughout the chapter is the relationship of immediacy and transparency between which all these films oscillate.[50]

Bolter and Grusin speak of the "double logic" of remediation, which means that media oscillate between hypermediacy and immediacy, constructing the impression of immediacy or transparency via hypermediacy. In this sense Bolter and Grusin's theorizations refashion Peter Wollen's seminal distinction between Classical Hollywood narration and modernist filmmaking exemplified by European art cinema (see Wollen 2002). Instead of outlining the distinctions between these two divergent film styles, Bolter and Grusin deconstruct the binary opposition by claiming that hypermediacy paves the way for an impression of immediacy. "Immediacy depends on hypermediacy", Bolter and Grusin (2000, 6) maintain. They do not conceptualise these two phenomena as mutually exclusive, but as two poles between which both old and new media oscillate. However, Bolter and Grusin do not consider the discursive framework of remediation. Rather than looking at the relations of power, Bolter and Grusin are more concerned with the formal relations between media. Therefore, what needs to be ex-

---

[50] In fact Bolter and Grusin (2000) included a brief reference to newsreels since it used to be screened before the main feature. According to them the cinema of attractions, in which immediacy and hypermediacy are merged, never disappeared entirely during the period of Classical Hollywood Cinema, for example newsreels "often appealed to the audience's sense of wonder that something (an exotic location or a war scene) could have been captured on film at all" (Bolter and Grusin 2000, 156).

plored further is both the reasons of remediation and the impact of its changing contexts: When and why are which media remediated? How does remediation alter the way audiences make use of the images?

In an attempt to complicate the notion of remediation, Richard A. Grusin has developed the notion of 'premediation' in his 2004 article "Premediation", drawing on Kathryn Bigelow's *Strange Days* (1995) and Steven Spielberg's *Minority Report* (2002). For Grusin, 'premediation' refers to the remediation of "future media practices and technologies" (Grusin 2004, 18). While the existence of the past prior to mediation was missing in the conceptualisation of 'remediation', "[t]he logic of premediation, on the other hand, insists that the future is also already mediated, and that with the right technologies [...] the future can be remediated before it happens" (Grusin 2004, 19). Grusin turns to the example of September 11, 2001 which has become a template for all subsequent mediations of catastrophic events. While immediacy is created through hypermediacy, as in remediation, the case of 9/11 implies a conceptual shift. During the events of 9/11 remediation's double logic of hypermediacy and immediacy was played out, working "simultaneously to erase the televisual medium in our act of witnessing the horror and to multiply mediation through split screens, scrolling headlines, the importation of radio feeds, cellphones, videophones, and so forth" (Grusin 2004, 21). According to Grusin, premediation is the order of the day in the current media regime which sets out "to make sure that when the future comes it has already been remediated, to see the future not as it emerges immediately into the present but before it ever happens" (Grusin 2004, 21). Grusin also takes the media specificity of (p)remediation into account by acknowledging the differences between televisual and cinematic depictions of disasters and catastrophes – most notably in terms of formal characteristics, such as "visual framing and the deployment of semiotic markers of the real" (Grusin 2004, 25)[51], but also in terms of structural or psychological distinctions. To sum up, in contrast to remediation, premediation "represents not a desire for immediacy but rather a fear of immediacy, of the kind of extreme moment of immediacy or transparency that 9/11 produced, in which the burning and collapse of the Twin Towers were perceived as if free from their mediation by radio, TV, the Web, and so forth, even while these mediations were multiplying at an almost dizzying pace" (Grusin 2004, 26). Both remediation and premediation cannot be perceived as isolated concepts, but focus on different aspects: in the case of remediation on the media forms, in the case of premediation on future events.

---

51 Here Grusin (2004, 38, footnote 8) draws on the insights provided by Geoff King in an unpublished essay.

2.3.2 Remediation within memory studies

For memory studies the concepts of remediation and premediation prove highly useful in acknowledging the dynamics of cultural memory and its mediatisation. Both Erll and Rigney have adopted the concept of remediation for cultural memory studies in a number of articles (Erll 2008; Erll and Rigney 2009) outlining its functions, possibilities and methodological challenges. Astrid Erll defines the term 'remediation' as follows: "With the term 'remediation' I refer to the fact that memorable events are usually represented again and again, over decades and centuries, in different media: in newspaper articles, photography, diaries, historiography, novels, films, etc." (Erll 2008b, 392). Repeated remediation then contributes to stabilising cultural memory: "remediation tends to solidify cultural memory, creating and stabilising certain narratives and icons of the past" (Erll 2008, 393) and creates *lieux de mémoire:* "Repeated representation, over decades and centuries, in different media, is exactly what creates a powerful site of memory." (Erll 2011a, 141) Remediation also allows us to rethink the notion of the *lieux de mémoire,* which is constructed through a genealogy of remediations. Remediation stabilises a *lieu de mémoire* and renegotiates it (see Erll 2011d, 132–133). It exists as long as it is remediated. As Erll concludes: "What is not constantly represented in new, other and newly combined media has lost its function as a lieu de mémoire." (Erll 2011d, 133) Unlike Bolter and Grusin (2000), Erll and Rigney (2009, 2) also observe the dynamics of remediation and the need to examine "the factors which allow certain collective memories to become hegemonic or […] allow hitherto marginalised memories to gain prominence in the public arena". The reason why some icons and narratives are more dominant than others can be explained through the concept of 'premediation', which "draws attention to the fact that existent media which circulate in a given society provide schemata for future experience" (Erll 2008b, 392) as well as "its anticipation, representation and remembrance" (Erll 2011a, 142). The dynamics of memory imply a theoretical and methodological challenge for research related to memory and the media.

Erll points out that notions of immediacy and authenticity play a crucial role in the debate around film and memory. Transparency and immediacy are constructed in memory media by multiplying other memory media. Erll (2011d) gives a number of examples: a) Yad Vashem, which assembles an online archive of photographs, a database collection of testimonies, an online exhibition as well as virtual tours through the memorial site, all of which can be accessed globally; b) the prime-time television genre of 'docudrama' which attempts to open a 'window to the past' in its collage of testimonial witness interviews and dramatised re-enactments. Docudramas evoke the impression of an unmediated access to the past rather than to the experience of a memory medium; c) Hollywood blockbusters such as *Saving Private Ryan* (Spielberg 1998) or *Flags of our Fathers* (Eastwood 2006) which incorporate or re-enact press photographs or archival newsreel footage. Erll argues that this practice is used to employ the 'reality effect' of media forms such as newsreels or press photographs, which due to their indexical quality are usually understood as representing reality. These examples differ in terms of media technology, degrees of fictionalization and memory functions. What they have in common is this: "Only through remediation and thus the multiplication of media do memory media create the illusion of an unmediatised access to the past." (Erll 2011d, 130) Most of the memory media draw on the notion of immediacy, they claim to be a window to the past, they stage themselves as transparent media, creating the illusion of an 'unmediated memory' (see Erll 2011d, 129), although they are characterised by hypermediacy. As opposed to immediacy, hypermediacy foregrounds the processes of mediatisation. Examples would be Anselm Kiefer's paintings, Atom Egoyan's self-reflexive fiction film *Ararat* (2002), Christopher Nolan's film *Memento* (2000) or W.G. Sebald's novels which incorporate photography. For Erll, even the Holocaust memorial in Berlin and its combination of different memory media is an example of the workings of hypermediacy in memory culture.

Appropriating the concept of remediation (and premediation) for memory studies has helped to acknowledge both the diachronic aspect and the intermedial dynamics at play in the construction of cultural memory (see Erll 2011a, 141). Their functions range from making "the past intelligible; at the same time, they can endow media representations with the aura of authenticity; and finally they play a decisive role in stabilising certain mnemonic contents into powerful sites of memory" (Erll 2011a, 143).

2.3.3 Remediation and intermediality

The relation between remediation and intermediality has been addressed only briefly so far. For example, Bolter and Grusin do not mention intermediality and intertextuality at all.[52] For memory studies, Ann Rigney and Astrid Erll have put forward the concept of remediation as a means to acknowledge the dynamics of cultural memory, both from a diachronic perspective and in view of

---

52 However, they briefly mention *ekphrasis*, drawing on Mitchell (1994) who defines it as "the verbal representation of a visual representation" (Bolter and Grusin 2000, 151–152; also on p. 45), and they briefly mention literary adaptations (Bolter Grusin 2000, 44–45).

their intermedial relations, drawing on examples of the plurimedia remediations of the Indian mutiny and of Homer's *Odyssey* (see Rigney and Erll 2009; Erll 2011d; Rigney 2012).

This study sets out to explore in how far insights from the burgeoning field of intermediality studies might prove useful for the understanding of remediation. My hypothesis is that Bolter and Grusin's concept of remediation does not capture the complexities of remediation and that we therefore ought to take a closer look at current developments within intermediality studies. Their focus has traditionally been around literature as well as the relation between different arts, but recently more studies have dealt with film (see Pethö 2010a, 2010b). These will deserve our special attention.

From the perspective of intermediality studies, Bolter and Grusin's concept of remediation has been criticised as being too broad and generalising, levelling out crucial differences between media and various modes of remediation (see Rajewsky 2005, 61–64). Lars Ellestöm calls for a more precise distinction between different modes of 'representation' and 'remediation' in Bolter and Grusin (2000) and finds "the authors' notions of media and remediation [...] conspicuously vague" (Ellestöm 2010, 47). While Bolter and Grusin address the complexity of media relations, they do not offer theoretical or methodological tools for analysing these, he argues. I agree with Irina Rajewsky and Lars Ellestöm in that Bolter and Grusin's concept needs to be complicated. As Irina Rajewsky (2005, 44) suggests, intermediality studies, despite the lack of a unified theory, can account for new ways of thinking about "medial border-crossing and hybridization" while pointing to "a heightened awareness of the materiality and mediality" of cultural practices, not least when it comes to artistic practices. Intermediality studies also allow us to think about media specificity. As Agnes Pethö states in her article on ekphrasis in Godard's films: "the moving picture as a medium can remediate all other media forms used by human communication" (Pethö 2010b, 211). Due to its mixed mediality, cinema "consists of a very unstable set of interrelationships". Cinema is not an additive project, adding sound to images, for example, but is characterised by spaces in-between. Therefore, the "mediality of cinema can always be perceived as intermediality as its meanings are always generated by the media relations that weave its fabric of significations" (212). Cinema can thus "be defined as an impossible, heterotopic space where intermedial processes take place, and where figurations of medial differences are played out" and "in which all other forms of representations can be inscribed and all other media can be re-mediated" (Pethö 2010b, 212). Such an approach challenges essentialist notions of media specificity.

For Irina Rajewsky (2002, 203) film is inherently plurimedial. The question discussed in intermediality studies, then, is the following: If film is plurimedial (or all texts anyway), how do we account for intermedial references? Unlike in the case of intermedial references, in "the case of intramedial references the referencing itself remains within *one* medium and consequently does not involve any kind of medial difference" (Rajewsky 2010, 62). I would like to complicate this notion since it does not account for the materiality of film footage. For instance, remediating 8 mm or 16 mm footage in a feature film can foreground a medial difference. Therefore, I will take a quick detour to three different uses of archival footage in fiction film. The first example is the remediation of archival footage in Helma Sanders-Brahms' *Deutschland, bleiche Mutter* (1980), a film into which an archival newsreel clip is inserted, showing a little boy among ruins. Although the boy in the footage is intercut with the protagonists' gaze and thus sutured into the diegesis, the grainy quality of the footage and its colours disrupt classic narration. Thus, the intertextual reference in Sanders-Brahms' film turns into a Brechtian element of 'Verfremdung'. Through its 'aggressive remediation' (Bolter and Grusin 2000) the footage becomes an alien element ["Fremdkörper"] within the fiction film, thereby turning into a self-reflexive device, breaking the illusion, disrupting continuity and breaking into the diegesis.[53] In the second example, the use of archival footage in *Milk* (Van Sant 2008) has the function of creating authenticity and immediacy. Altering the filmic images by giving them the grainy quality of 16 mm or 8 mm or by turning them into black and white images, has become a conventional means to create the illusion of authenticity (see also Erll 2011d). The third film used to illustrate the media specificity of repurposing is *Saving Private Ryan* (Spielberg 1998), in which remediation occurs via digitally altered images and intermedial reference to analogue photography. The blurry quality of Robert Capa's iconic photographs taken during the 1944 Normandy invasion (D-Day) was simply due to an accident in the lab when a young assistant damaged the film. In order to create the impression of authenticity in Spielberg's film, the visual style of Capa's black and white photographs is remediated in the film's introductory sequence. In contrast, in *Deutschland, bleiche Mutter*, remediation occurs through montage, by inserting analogue newsreel footage into an analogue fiction film, creating an intertextual reference to film. In Sanders-Brahms' film the remediation of the newsreel footage is used as a means of defamiliarization (Sklovskij). As opposed to this, *Milk* plays out a tension between analogue and digital film footage by both remediating 16 mm footage and recreating the 'look' of analogue archival

---

[53] The examples show that hypermediacy does not automatically imply immediacy (cf. Bolter and Grusin 2000) and that the division between 'old' (analogue) versus 'new' (digital) media is not as clear-cut as we might assume.

footage through digitally altered images. Both *Saving Private Ryan* and *Milk* are characterised by a hypermediacy which creates intertextual reference to 'older' media and its materiality in order to heighten the impression of 'authenticity'. These examples show that the materiality of film footage is another reason to rethink the relation between film, intermediality and cultural memory within the concept of remediation.

2.3.4 Remediation and its discursive frameworks

In studies of remediation the power dimension has so far been neglected. I argue for an understanding of remediation which not only takes the media specificity of remediation into account, but also its power dimension. Remediation does not occur in a vacuum, but is triggered by specific discursive constellations, by mediated events. The questions to be examined are: What triggers remediation? What kind of events are remediated more than others – and in which media formats? We therefore need to take a closer look at both the media specificity and the discursive context of remediation.

My attempt at rethinking the notion of remediation has been inspired by Stuart Hall's article "Reconstruction Work. Images of Post-War Black Settlement" (Hall 1991). In this article Stuart Hall looks at the visual archive of Black diaspora in Britain after the Second World War. For Hall, photography is not a "unitary thing", but a set of multiple "practices, institutions and historical conjunctures in which the photographic text is produced, circulated and deployed" (Hall 1991, 152). When employing photographs from the Black settlement in Britain after WWII one should keep in mind that many of them have already been published before, for example, in magazines and press publications. Therefore, these images are "already inscribed or placed by that earlier positioning" and most of them "will already have been organised within certain systems of classification" (Hall 1991, 152). Each renewed publication might create a new context for these photographs and adds a new layer of meaning. For that reason it would be impossible to recreate the original meaning of these photographs, and to look for their 'true meaning' would be an illusionary endeavour. Instead, the images are "essentially multilayered in meaning" (Hall 1991, 152), they are always inscribed into a set of practices and into their industrial context of production, distribution and reception. Therefore they cannot transcend time without having their meaning altered in the process of translation and recontextualisation. Images can evoke contradictory meanings, they are characterised by intertextual relations to other photographs and, as I would add, to the audiovisual archive. Using the example of the now famous photographs showing the arrival of the so-called

Windrush generation during the late 1940s and 1950s[54], Hall explains how the individual viewer's knowledge, affect, empathy and understanding contribute to the way the photographs will be 'decoded' (Hall). What is "beyond the frame", as Hall (1991, 154) puts it, "registers inside the frame". Both in this text and others (see Hall 1997a), Stuart Hall has offered a useful framework for understanding the politics of representation in its industrial context.

As we have seen, every production of meaning is the result of its context. If we want to expand the notion of remediation we therefore need to reconsider the impact of production, distribution and exhibition. While the industrial context will be analysed to a greater extent in the upcoming case studies, I would like to point at the impact of programming (see Klippel 2008).[55] Programming practice has ramifications for the critical reception of a film, and consequently, it contributes to defining the status of the director, his (or her) role in film historiography, which, in turn, has repercussions on his/her canonisation. Programming also creates horizons of expectations – via the title and the programme slot chosen, it guides and structures the viewers' assumptions of what to expect. This goes for cinema, but also for television. For instance, the labelling of a film series or the time slots chosen for a film at a festival or in a television schedule provide an interpretative framework and may guide, though not determine, the reception of a film. To illustrate, Fatih Akin's *We Forgot to Go Back* (see chapter 3.1 *Remembering Turkish-German labour migration*) could be programmed under a variety of headers, such as "Culture clashes", "Between two worlds: diasporic filmmaking in Germany", "Ethnic minority filmmaking", "Migration Stories", "German Family Stories" or "Road Movies". The categorizations represent different modes of relating to the work of a filmmaker whose family has immigrated to Germany. "Culture clashes" or "Between two worlds" are defined by an essentialist understanding of culture as container culture with clearly demarcated borders. "Ethnic minority filmmaking" in turn, does not automatically imply an essentialist understanding of culture, but it entails the risk of an othering. The same goes for "Migration Stories". "German Family Stories" includes the film into a German cultural tradition, while the header "Road movies" has a more international or transnational approach, avoiding an 'othering' in which the filmmaker is reduced to his parents' national origin and assigned/ascribed ethnic identity. Here the film would be an example of a global or transnational film cul-

---

54 See chapter 5.1 *Remediating the cultural memory of migration: reappropriating the audiovisual archive of the Windrush.*
55 The focus of the edited volume by Klippel (2008) is on programming as an aesthetic practice rather than on its political implications.

ture, maybe including films by other international filmmakers. This example shows how programming can play a part in creating an auteur – or hinder it.

The same programme, broadcast via another TV station, can reach different audiences (Hasebrink 2005, 390). These considerations might lead us to rethink the definition of remediation. Does the concept of remediation include changing contexts of distribution and exhibition? Reissuing a silent film on DVD would undoubtedly be an example of remediation, but would the concept also apply to the repeated screening of the film on different television channels? Drawing on the insights by Klippel (2008) and Hasebrink (2005), it might as well be called remediation, as the changing contexts imply changing modes of reception and new ways of 'decoding' the meaning of the programme.

Apart from the question posed above, we also need to consider the role of distribution, of the curator and of the user. Moreover, I would like to examine whether the concept of remediation can be expanded towards including curatorial practice. Can we broaden the scope of 'remediation' to include archival and curatorial practice, such as festival programming and cinemathèque programming, and focus on the role of the curator as an agent for turning storage memory into functional memory? Another question would be how remediation can be conceptualised in relation to adaptation, appropriation, translation, reappropriation, remakes, parodies and pastiches. While a detailed investigation into each of these concepts' relation to remediation would go beyond the constraints of this study, I would at least point out the need to further examine these notions, before focusing on intermedial appropriations in chapter 5.2 *Remediation and intermediality: media specificity and the discursive context*. Finally, given that Bolter and Grusin's conceptualisation of remediation and film has exclusively centred on Hollywood filmmaking, the notion of remediation needs to be further developed from the perspective of 'minor cinema' and documentary filmmaking.

3. Mediatized memories in a global age: the transcultural turn?

If we agree with Astrid Erll's (2011a) understanding that remediation stabilizes cultural memory, we have to ask, following Stuart Hall (2002): whose heritage is it? Whose narratives and images are remediated and therefore have the chance to enter the audiovisual archive? Cultural memory is dynamic and transnational, but at the same time it emerges within specific national or (g)local frameworks, as this chapter will argue. It is embedded in different, at times overlapping, cultural practices. Michael Rothberg and Yasemin Yildiz (2011, 33) have noted that "a singular site of memory can accommodate a diversity of histories that resonate with each other instead of erasing each other". The idea of "memories erasing each other" has been challenged by Rothberg's (2009) concept of 'multidirectional' memories. Memories do not simply replace each other, but overlap and are entangled. However, we need to take a closer look at the power relations involved in this process. I argue that memories are indeed multidirectional, but they are still subject to power structures either permitting them some discursive space for being articulated, or not. While memory due to its multidirectionality cannot be claimed by one specific group alone, it can open up or close discursive spaces for articulating non-hegemonic subject positions. Since memory is always mediated, the role of the media in which memories are enunciated is crucial for the impact they might have: memory films, reaching broader audiences, can influence cultural memory more than productions with limited distribution. Memory films are both remediated more often, but they will also most likely be the ones to trigger new remediations (e. g. remakes, remixes, fan fiction) compared to works of minor cinema.[56]

This chapter has several aims: first, it suggests to reconceptualise the notion of 'culture' in 'cultural memory' and in 'transcultural memory'. Second, it argues for the need to make cultural memory more diverse and to acknowledge the het-

---

[56] It would indeed be worthwile conducting further research on this issue, especially highlighting the impact of amateur videos going viral. YouTube-videos such as "Charly bit my finger" have triggered innumerable remakes, remixes, parodies on YouTube. However, the impact of such remediations might not have a crucial impact of our understanding of the past, at least if they stop being remediated after some time. Another more interesting case in this context are the Hitler parodies which remediate the same scene from *Downfall* (Hirschbiegel 2004) by adding new subtitles to the film images and the original German dialogue which can be heard on the soundtrack. These parodies remediate the footage into new and changing contexts, ranging from Jane Austen to Harry Potter, the iPod or Barack Obama.

erogeneity of cultural practice and of memory. Third, it suggests to conceptualise transcultural memory not merely in terms of ethnicity and national identity, but rather in terms of cultural practice. This would avoid the othering of citizens whose memory is claimed to be 'transcultural' instead of 'cultural'. This chapter departs from two examples of autobiographical filmmaking: Fatih Akin's *We Forgot to Go Back* (Germany, 2001) and Carol Morley's *The Alcohol Years* (UK, 2000). The first example looks at migrant memory from a national and transnational perspective, whereas the second case deals with the translation of memory into various context: from subcultural memory into retro culture and into the culture-led regeneration of a city. The first case strengthens the importance of a national framework when analysing dynamic transnational memories. The second case suggests a new way to employ the notion of transculturality within memory studies in moving beyond the realms of ethnicity and national belonging. As Rothberg and Yildiz (2011) emphasize, migrants are the subject of both national and transnational memory. Therefore memory scholars should keep in mind not to 'other' migrants again by solely conceptualising migration in terms of transnational or transcultural memory.

3.1 Remembering Turkish-German labor migration (Fatih Akin's *We Forgot to Go Back/Wir haben vergessen zurückzukehren*)[57]

"I wanted to make a film about my family. I wanted to show, hey, these guys came over here, didn't even have a loo ... maybe that's why I'm making this film ... so that I can show my kids some day, hey, come on and have a look, these are your grandparents, that's where they come from, their German sounded

---

57 Earlier versions of this chapter on Fatih Akin were presented at the conference "Families and Memories" at the Holocaust Centre in Oslo in 2009 and at The Warwick Workshop for Interdisciplinary German Studies in 2010. I would like to thank Christine Achinger for the invitation to Warwick and both Erica Carter and Astrid Erll for their generous feedback. A German version was published in 2011 as Dagmar Brunow, "Film als kulturelles Gedächtnis der Arbeitsmigration: Fatih Akins 'Wir haben vergessen zurückzukehren'". In: *50 Jahre türkische Arbeitsmigration in Deutschland. ed.* Şeyda Ozil, Michael Hofmann, Yasemin Dayioglu-Yücel, 183–204, Göttingen: V&R Unipress (Türkisch-deutsche Studien, Jahrgang 2011). An earlier version of this chapter has been published as: "Mediated Memories of Migration and the National Visual Archive: Fatih Akin's 'Wir haben vergessen zurückzukehren'." In: Angelica Fenner, and Robin Curtis, eds. *The Autobiographical Turn in Germanophone Documentary and Experimental Film.* Rochester, NY: Camden House, 2014.

like this ... this was their attitude."[58] This is how critically acclaimed director Fatih Akin explains his intentions in his documentary *Wir haben vergessen zurückzukehren* (*We Forgot to Go Back,* Germany 2001, Megaherz), which was commissioned for German television. According to the voice-over, Akin, who was born in Hamburg in 1973, decided to make the film after his parents told him stories and anecdotes about their early years in Germany. Only then did he realize how little he knew about the experiences of his father who came to Hamburg from Turkey as a worker in 1965 and of his mother, a primary school teacher, who followed a few years later. Akin's lack of knowledge about the memories of labor migration is not surprising. Despite recent attempts to diversify cultural memory through publications, exhibitions and conferences, the cultural memory of labor migration to Germany is still sidelined and marginalized in historiography. Even in cultural memory studies the notion of labor migration is only rarely addressed. A symptomatic example would be the deliberate exclusion of labor migration and other migrant movements in François and Schulze's *Deutsche Erinnerungsräume* (2001), published in the same year as Akin's film premiered on television. The editors explain the omission by arguing that migration is not yet distinct within cultural memory.[59]

Neither history books nor school education have so far adequately acknowledged the presence of multicultural Germany and its history of labor migration or other migration movements. Instead artists and activists have made efforts to create such "deutsche Erinnerungsräume" (*lieux de mémoires*) in order to counter these absences in the archive and to open a discursive space for migrant experiences. Several activist projects have challenged the hegemonic discourse on West-German labour immigration and historiography. In April 2001, for example, the activist group Kanak Attak presented a *KanakHistoryRevue – Opel Pitbull Autoput* at the Berliner Volksbühne theatre in order to address the invisibility of immigrants in national historic discourse and to grant them agency by pointing at migrant resistance during the strike at Ford Motors in Cologne in 1973.[60] In

---

58 ["Ich wollte 'nen Film über meine Family machen. Ich wollte zeigen, ey, die Typen sind hier rübergegangen, hatten nicht mal ein Klo ... vielleicht mach ich deswegen diesen Film... dass ich meinen Kinder irgendwann mal zeigen kann, ey guckt mal, das sind eure Großeltern, da kommen die her, die haben soundso deutsch gesprochen ... so waren die drauf."] All German quotations are translated by the author, unless otherwise stated.
59 In order to counter the research gap, studies on the representation of labor migration in school book or history books have been published (see Alavi 2004; Jamin 2004). However, a fundamental, pivotal account of multicultural Germany and its history is still to come.
60 http://www.kanak-attak.de/ka/archiv/vb01/index.htm (1 October 2009). Despite being a marginal phenomenon in the German public sphere, *Kanak Attak* acts as a counterbalance to both official politics of control, policing and regulation and to the often paternalistic attitudes

their book on hip hop in Germany, titled *Fear of a Kanak Planet* (2002), Hannes Loh and Murat Güngör fold the history of the first immigration labour migrants into their account of current hip hop practice, while dedicating the book to Güngör's father and the first generation of labour migrants [Gastarbeiter] in Germany. In 2013 the CD sampler *Songs of Gastarbeiter*, compiled by Imran Ayata and Bülent Kullukcu, gained widespread attention for having created a sonic archive of migrant memories. This practice among second generation[61] migrants of carving out a discursive space for articulating the experiences of the first generation has finally arrived in the mainstream via literary fiction; for example, in Emine Sevgi Özdamar's novel *Die Brücke vom Goldenen Horn* (1998) and Feridun Zaimoğlu's epic tale *Leyla* (2006). Cinematic releases such as *Solino* (Fatih Akin, 2002) and *Almanya... Willkommen in Deutschland* (Yasemin and Nesrin Şamdereli, 2010) have contributed to the cultural memory of migration as well.[62]

Several documentary or essay film projects by second-generation migrants have also addressed their parents' immigrant history.[63] To name but a few, Yüksel Yavuz' *Mein Vater, der Gastarbeiter* (*My father, the guest worker*, 1994) focuses on Kurdish labour immigration from Turkey, while Ainoah Arteabaro's *Die vergessene Generation* (*The forgotten generation*, 2006) is based on interviews with the first generation of Spanish immigrants in Hamburg.[64] These films, however, em-

---

towards migrants found in left-wing politics. In anti-racist, left-wing contexts the image of the migrant is often defined by "assumed poverty, helplessness, and even a certain degree of stupidity". Heidenreich and Vukadinović 2008, 141. For a critical perspective on German immigration politics, see Serhat Karakayali, "Die freundliche Einwanderungsgesellschaft. Eine Analyse bundesdeutscher Einwanderungspolitik." *Diskus* January 2001. Online: http://www.kanak-attak.de/ka/text.html (28 April 2009). For an innovative theoretical perspective on migration see also TRANSIT MIGRATION Forschungsgruppe (2007).

61 Despite using the terms "second" or "third" generation migrants, I am highly critical of these concepts and agree with Robin Curtis (2006, 120) who problematises categories which cannot possibly account for the multiplicity of migrant experiences, but concedes, "Nonetheless a descriptive model such as this allows useful distinctions and comparisons to be made."

62 One should keep in mind, though, that while the literary examples I give have entered the mainstream, the activism of Kanak Attak is a marginal phenomenon, rarely observed in dominant media discourse which they in turn try to challenge and intervene in.

63 Curtis (2006) also mentions *Gülüzar*, a short film by Hatice Ayten (1994, video, 8 min.) as well as Seyhan Derin's, *Ben Annemin Kiziyim (Ich bin Tochter meiner Mutter) 1996* (16 mm, 89 min.)

64 Yüksel Yavuz had a similiar motivation for making his film *Mein Vater, der Gastarbeiter* as Akin for *We Forgot to Go Back*, although both films have highly different takes on territory and ethnic identity. When his brother's first child was born, Yavuz wanted to tell him the story of its grandfather's migration to Germany. (Yüksel Yavuz introducing his film at the series "Zweite Heimat" at the Metropolis-Kino, Hamburg, 2009).

ploy diverse aesthetic and formal strategies and should not solely be regarded as portraits of the migrant experience. Angela Melitopoulos' *Passing Drama* (1999), for example, a filmic essay about forgetting, articulates doubts about the capacity of the filmic image to convey reality, even as filmmaking does offer one way of challenging or reflecting upon gaps and absences in hegemonic national historiography. While these examples show the importance of considering the media specificity of cultural memory, for instance the genre and its formal aesthetics, we should also look at the power relations involved in the construction of mediated cultural memory. "A discourse and the subject positions it generates are power-related since they regulate articulation", as Bjerg and Lenz (2008, 226) observe. Who is authorized to tell their own stories and who has the prerogative of definition over their versions of the past?

Processes of remembering are framed by regulating mechanisms which impact on the ways the past is spoken about. While several oral history projects on migration have been launched in recent years,[65] Fatima El-Tayeb points out: "The only incarnation in which non-majoritarian ethnic subjects entered the 'history from below' was that of the *Gastarbeiter*, who appeared within the context of workers' histories." (2) Moreover, "the *Gastarbeiter* was still assigned the role of the mute, oppressed object that needed the enlightened German to tell/translate his story." As a result, "what was collected [...] inevitably reflects the bias of dominant society." (2) Thus, as a memory practice oral history projects are the result of contemporary needs and reflect the power relations in a society at a specific sociohistorical moment. These needs can be analysed by taking the funding structures of these projects into account – as well as their mode of publication, distribution and exhibition. However, this study is not a discourse analysis, but I would like to point out the importance of acknowleding the discursive framework which shapes the construction of cultural memory. As oral history projects, so is art practice always discursively framed by the institutional circumstances under which it is produced, disseminated and received.[66] Thus, not only *what* is collected, but also *how* it is framed, should be examined.

---

[65] For example at the *Forschungsstelle für Zeitgeschichte* in Hamburg. See also Eder 2003 and http://www.migration-audio-archive.de (24 September 2009), a German web-based project, initiated by Sefa Inci Suvak and Justus Herrmann in 2004.

[66] For an in-depth methodological and theoretical reflection on the use of oral history, see Jureit 1999.

3.1.1 Mediating the cultural memory of migration

Akin's autobiographical film *We Forgot to Go Back* offers insights into the way the concept of cultural memory challenges the alleged binary of private recollections and collective memory. The film takes the audience along on the reverse journey from Hamburg-Altona via Istanbul to the little fishing village of Filyos on the Black Sea. Along the way Akin meets his family and friends in Hamburg, but also his relatives in Turkey, some of whom returned to their country of origin after many years in Germany. Akin interviews them about their experiences abroad and upon returning to Turkey. While Akin simply could have made a home movie to bring the family memories alive for his future children, his autobiographical documentary creates "prosthetic" memories (Landsberg 2004), allowing wider audiences to share experiences which are not their own. Whereas in home movies the family is at once the production unit, its subject, and its audience, autobiographical documentary filmmaking complicates this constellation because personal recollections also create new meanings upon entering the public sphere as circulating text.[67] Annette Kuhn (2002, 5) has examined how personal and public spheres fold into each other, coalesce and interconnect: "if the memories are one individual's, their associations extend far beyond the personal. They spread into an extended network of meanings that bring together the personal with the familial, the cultural, the economic, the social, and the historical." Kuhn's concept of 'memory work' can offer a useful starting point for the study of autobiographical works since it allows "to explore connections between 'public' historical events, structures of feeling, family dramas, relations of class, national identity and gender, and 'personal' memory" (Kuhn 2002, 5). As Helle Bjerg and Claudia Lenz (2008, 224) point out, family memories are not handed down "as fixed stories passed on to the next generation, but as an active and mutual construction of these memories through speech (and/or silence)". In the case of *We Forgot to Go Back* the memories of friends and family members were constructed in the presence of a camera. Certainly the interviewees were aware of the fact that Fatih Akin was not about to create a home movie, but a documentary film to be shown on public television. The media specific memories created in the process of filming are the result of a specific interview situation in the presence of a film team and of Akin performing different roles: as son, nephew, cousin, friend – and director. Thus, in line with oral history scholars such as Ulrike Jureit I would like to argue that witness interviews cannot be seen as a mode of 'authentic' self-representation.

---

[67] See Schneider 2004. For the role of amateur home movies in this context see Brunow 2012.

The cultural memory of migration has mostly been transferred orally from generation to generation, as Hannes Loh and Murat Güngör have observed: "Via oral history, stories are handed down and preserved that do not continue their life on paper, but rather, in the memories of individuals."[68] Due to the lack of visual imagery in the historiography of migration to Germany, the filmed documentation of private family stories and their release within the public sphere can be said to contribute new images to Germany's national visual archive. Thereby it can counter the exclusion of migrant and diasporic experiences from cultural memory. Akin's autobiographical family movie, this article argues, constitutes a form of memory work which represents "the lives of those whose ways of knowing and ways of seeing the world are rarely acknowledged, let alone celebrated, in the expressions of a hegemonic culture", as Annette Kuhn (2002, 9) states. According to Aleida Assmann (2006) artworks such as films or novels are automatically part of cultural memory. However, they do not belong to specific groups, but travel across generations, communities and nations (Erll 2011a).

Despite the fact that cultural memory is not fixed and stable, but dynamic and multidirectional, though, it does not mean that its content is arbitrary or contingent (Rothberg 2009). While completely agreeing with Ernst von Alphen (2002, 55) according to whom migration has ensured that "there are practically no places left in the world which are not hybrid in terms of culture", I would claim that not all of these hybrid subjects can tell their stories on equal terms. Thomas Elsaesser (2002, 64) suggests that filmmaking can function as a counter strategy: "By marking what is personal about the past, by bearing witness, and giving testimony, such films add a new dimension to memory, connecting the speaking subject to both temporality and mortality, creating 'pockets of meaning', in the sense one can speak, in a guerrilla war, of 'pockets of resistance'." While *We Forgot to Go Back* challenges national German historiography, to reduce its significance to that of a mere counter-narrative would perpetuate the binarism between hegemony and resistance and an essentialist notion of subjectivity upon which counter politics are so often predicated. The notion of counter-memory is based on the idea that 'lost' and 'hidden' memories are simply out there and merely need to be excavated and recovered. Therefore the concept of 'memory work' as "a method and a practice of unearthing and making public untold stories" (Kuhn 2002, 9) needs to be refined. Ann Rigney (2005,

---

[68] ["Das Wissen über das 'Herkommen nach Deutschland' wird von Generation zu Generation weitererzählt. In einem Prozess der Oral History werden Geschichten, die nicht auf Papier, sondern in den Gedächtnissen der Einzelnen weiterleben, durch Erzählung tradiert und bewahrt. So wird das Geschehene vor dem Vergessen gerettet."] (Loh and Güngör 2002, 56)

212) points at the dangers of this conception which entails the risk of a self-essentialisation: "This recovery project is itself linked in complex ways to contemporary identity politics and to the desire of particular groups to profile their common identity by claiming distinct roots in a particular historical experience". One of the epistemological problems Fatih Akin's film project faces is the desire to represent his family's experiences while trying not to engage in self-essentialism. Self-essentialising can serve as a strategic means to counter asymmetrical power relations, but also tends to level internal power conflicts that may exist along the lines of gender and class. While counter practices often assume a unified essentialist stance that speaks for an entire migrant or diasporic population, I would suggest that Akin's film uses anti-essentialist aesthetic strategies that defy notions of homogeneity and authenticity. As Robin Curtis (2006, 121) has pointed out, *We Forgot to Go Back* "critically addresses the myth of a unified Turkish identity capable of being transposed from one geographical location to another, and passed from one generation to the next". This chapter argues that Akin's film employs various strategies to counter this myth. One way of challenging concepts of purity, authenticity and essentialism that seem to accompany ethnic absolutism is to put forth the situatedness of knowledge. Another one is that Akin's film decouples identity from territory in the way he uses music to map space. While essentialising and stabilising notions of 'home', 'identity' or 'culture' have become increasingly problematic, artists' practice can help us to find more adequate understandings of these concepts.

Kuhn's idea of 'memory work' enables us to conceptualise autobiographical documentary filmmaking both as an act of remembrance and as an act of empowerment granting agency to the filmmaker. The process of filming also becomes an act of self-inauguration as a director. As Laura Rascaroli (2009, 2) claims when it comes to subjective and personal filmmaking: "To speak 'I' is, after all, firstly a political act of self-awareness and self-affirmation." While Akin's film project can be regarded as a way of self-inauguration, the film avoids any self-essentialisation in terms of ethnicity or national identity. However, in spite of employing aesthetic strategies which defy essentialist notions of culture, identity and ethnicity, Akin's work faces the risk of being re-essentialised throughout the film's industrial context: in the process of production, distribution via programming as well as through the film's critical reception.

Anti-essentialist concepts of culture and identity have been theorised in Black British Cultural Studies, especially in the writings of Stuart Hall and Paul Gilroy (see Hall 1999; Gilroy 1993). Gilroy's concept of "The Black Atlantic" undermines the idea that identity is determined by geographical territory: there is no locationally bound essence, but rather, a sense of in-betweenness. In the German context, however, this sense often bears the negative connotation of belonging neither to the home country nor to the new country. The oft-invoked trope of dwelling "zwischen den Stühlen" or of "falling between the cracks" shows that it is important to specify the socio-historical context of an autobiographical work. As Maurice Halbwachs (1992) reminds us, memory cannot be conceived outside of its socio-political context. Like other contemporary witnesses, artists, too, are shaped by contemporary discourses specific to their socio-historical context. Although migration is an international phenomenon, the situation for migrants varies from country to country according to specificities of legislation, attitudes, and media debates. Before taking a closer look at the aesthetic strategies employed in Akin's film, it is therefore important to outline the specificities of the German case.

3.1.2 Migrant memories and national frameworks

Although cultural memory is dynamic and transnational, hegemonic national discourses provide "an extremely enduring and effective interpretative framework" (Bjerg and Lenz 2008, 224) for its construction. Despite the fact that migration has extensively shaped German society since the Second World War, the hegemonic discourse frames national identity as inherently white and homogenous. Multiculturalism, instead of being appreciated, is regarded as a problem. To illustrate, until 2000 it was next to impossible for non-ethnic Germans to gain citizenship.[69] In 2005 a new Immigration Act was passed acknowledging Germany as an "immigration country". Previously, immigrants were mostly regarded as guest workers (*Gastarbeiter*) who one day would return to their home country. The title of the film *We Forgot to Go Back* alludes to this understanding of labour immigrants as temporary guest workers in Germany.[70] Akin explains in the voice-over: "We grew up with this. Throughout my whole upbringing my parents told me that some day we would return. It was always there in the background. Well, some day, we'll return. We won't be here forever."[71]

---

[69] The data in this passage is derived from http://www.bundesregierung.de/nn_646700/Content/DE/StatischeSeiten/Breg/IB/Einbuergerung/gp-a1-voraussetzungen.html (16 October 2009) and the Multicultural German Project at Berkeley University: http://mgp.berkeley.edu/?page_id=10 (19 October 2009). See also Deniz Göktürk, et al. 2007.

[70] See www.integrationsbeauftragte.de (16 October 2009); Curtis (2006); Heidenreich and Vukadinović (2008).

[71] ["Wir sind damit groß geworden. Meine Eltern haben mich damit erzogen, dass wir irgendwann zurückgehen. Das war immer latent da. So, irgendwann gehen wir zurück. Wir sind nicht für immer hier."]

When it became obvious that many *Gastarbeiter* in Germany were not returning to their countries of origin, the primary political goal became that of achieving their assimilation into German society, rather than working towards a truly multicultural society. In contrast to countries such as Canada or the USA, whose history was built upon immigration, notions of assimilation have dominated the German discourse on migration.[72]

It was only following the Second World War that immigrants were actively recruited to rebuild the country, thereby contributing to West Germany's and other western industrial nations' rapid economic growth. Yet, the German government soon expressed the need for regulation. In 1961 an agreement on labour recruitment was signed between Germany and Turkey, on the heels of the first bilateral contract on labour migration with Italy in 1955. German recruitment policies prevented foreigners from becoming German citizens and, as such, from becoming a part of the nation. In 1983 the Law of Return (Rückkehr-Gesetz) was passed, offering a financial incentive for immigrants to "return home." Family members were not eligible for work permits and newborns did not automatically count as German citizens. The reason is the long tradition of the German concept of *ius sanguinis* (Latin for the "right of blood"), according to which citizenship is only granted if one's ancestor is a citizen of the state. In contrast, the *ius soli* (Latin for the "right of soil", also known as birthright citizenship) practised in France would automatically convey citizenship to a child born in the French territory. Before the new citizenship law was passed in 2000, only *ius sanguinis* was valid in Germany, but the concept prevailed and, moreover, dual citizenship was not allowed (see Heidenreich & Vukadinović 2008, 137; Brubaker 1992).

After reunification, debates around national identity revived following a surge of attacks on visible minorities. During these years new groups of immigrants were arriving from the Soviet Union, so-called Russian-Germans (Russlanddeutsche), who were automatically granted the same rights as Germans according to the principle of *ius sanguinis*. Unlike them, second and third-generation Turkish immigrants still could not vote despite having lived in Germany their whole lives, worked there and paid taxes. Accordingly, Rogers Brubaker comes to the conclusion that "the ethnocultural, differentialist understanding of nationhood in Germany is embodied and expressed in a definition of citizenship that is remarkably open to ethnic German immigrants from Eastern Europe and the Soviet Union, but remarkably closed to non-German immigrants" (Brubaker 1992, 3). Further discussion was triggered when the government announced

---

[72] As Heidenreich and Vukadinović (2008, 139) conclude: "integration has been the guiding principle in implementing racist subordination in Germany."

plans to issue green cards to qualified migrants, e. g. IT experts from India. After heated xenophobic criticism, the government abolished this plan. Public debates about the viability of dual citizenship fuelled perceptions of migrants as a potential problem and as troublemakers. This discussion gained further momentum in 2000 from the results of the international PISA study, a comparative evaluation of the quality of 15-year-olds' scholastic performance; Germany's low ranking was explained by using non-achieving migrant children as scapegoats. By 2005, one in four immigrants in Germany was of Turkish descent; nonetheless, prevailing public discourse continued to revolve around the notion of an incompatibility of "cultures." Statistics published in 2009, for example, indicated that Turkish immigrants were least willing to assimilate, a claim that only exacerbated post-9/11 anti-Muslim sentiment.

The fact that immigrants have had an impact on West German society after World War II has not sunk in. Concepts of assimilation have dominated the discussion of immigration, while multiculturalism has been declared a failure almost before any attempts to realize it in Germany were implemented. In one scene in *We Forgot to Go Back* Fatih Akin's uncle warns him:

> When you have children and they go to school there will always be other children who call them foreigners. They will always experience some kind of discrimination. That is the disadvantage of staying. They'll look at your German passport and say 'Fatih Akin' – you'll say, 'I'm a German.' And they'll say, 'Fatih Akin? You're not German; you're Turkish.'[73]

In another sequence, Fatih Akin's female cousin, who spent her childhood and youth in Germany and now lives in Istanbul, points to the absurdity and injustice of the fact that visa regulations prevent her parents from visiting Germany, despite having lived there for half their lives. Hegemonic discourses, such as the notions of assimilation and integration, might thus impact on the self-fashioning of individuals. Against this background the next section will examine the possibilities and limitations of self-representation within autobiographical cultural practice.

3.1.3 Countering essentialism: aesthetic strategies

We Forgot to Go Back is Fatih Akin's first documentary work and, to date, the only one of his films without DVD distribution. It was originally produced for

---

[73] I use the translation by Robin Curtis (2006, 123), though with a slightly different punctuation. For an in-depth analysis of everyday racism in Germany, see Terkessidis 2004.

the television series "Denk ich an Deutschland, Filmemacher über das eigene Land" [When I think of Germany. Filmmakers on their own country, 1997–2004], a co-production of Bayrischer Rundfunk and Westdeutscher Rundfunk, which aired in 2001.[74] In October 2002, the film aired again as part of a series of programmes called "'Jung, deutsch und türkisch'. Die zweite und dritte Einwanderergeneration" ("'Young, German and Turkish.' The second and third generation of immigrants") on 3SAT.[75] Apart from these TV broadcasts, the film also screened at various film festivals, among them Hofer Filmtage and Münchner Dokumentarfilmfestival, and was later included in the Goethe Institute's international programming. At the time, Akin was only starting his career: After his debut film *Short Sharp Shock* (*Kurz und Schmerzlos*, 1998), which was followed by *In July* (*Im Juli*, 2000), it took until 2004 for Akin's international breakthrough with *Head On (Gegen die Wand)* to gain him classification as an 'auteur'. The fact that *We Forgot to Go Back* was then screened as part of a "Fatih Akin night" on German television is a symptom of Akin's changed status from migrant filmmaker to German filmmaker and 'auteur.'[76] However, *We Forgot to Go Back* is still mostly programmed in the context of events on migration and 'integration'.

We Forgot to Go Back can be categorized as a German representative of what Michael Renov (2004, xxii) has called the "autobiographical outbreak of the 1980s and 1990s" in documentary filmmaking. As Renov (2008, 41) suggests, autobiographical filmmaking, "even when constructed of indexical parts, remains an agnostic in the house of certainty." In using documentary filmmaking not as 'visible evidence', but as a way of carving out a discursive space for the articulation of situated knowledge interacting with hegemonic discourses, autobiographical filmmaking can undermine essentialist notions of identity. Moreover, the narrative structure of Akin's film de-essentialises identity as something not given and stable, but rather, as created in an interrelational process. During

---

74 The series, which was commissioned by the production company Megaherz in München, included several German filmmakers. Its title alludes to a well-known line from the poem "Nachtgedanken" (1844) by Heinrich Heine: "Denk ich an Deutschland in der Nacht / Bin ich um den Schlaf gebracht", which freely translates as "When I think of Germany at night, I cannot sleep of mere fright" (my translation).
75 Akin's film is included in a series of migrant cinema productions as well as several documentaries, most of them with an ethnographic perspective on the young migrants. For an account of the hegemonic media representation of migrants see Geißler and Pöttker 2005.
76 At Bayrischer Rundfunk on 26 October 2008. The shift occurred after Akin won the "Golden Bear" at the Berlin Film Festival in 2004, after which he was claimed as a German director by German media and as a Turkish director by Turkish media. Since his film *The Edge of Heaven* (2007), starring Fassbinder star Hanna Schygulla, he has often been compared to Fassbinder, thus enhancing his status as an 'auteur' with a unique style.

the film Akin is the main focalizer, often directly addressing the camera to give explanations to the audience and to situate himself. While this is a common approach in American documentaries, it is fairly uncommon in German autobiographical filmmaking, with the notable exception of directors such as Michael Brynntrup or Jan Peters. In speaking the voice-over himself, Akin contributes to the film's subjective stance by guiding the audience through the film, thus pointing at the situatedness of knowledge. For Stuart Hall this is a sign of anti-essentialism, being "a recognition that we all speak from a particular place, out of a particular history, out of a particular experience, a particular culture, without being contained by that position as 'ethnic artists' or filmmakers" (Hall 1996a, 169–170).[77] Laura U. Marks, however, characterises the dominance of dialogues, voice-overs and oral histories as a structural element typical for diasporic filmmaking: "Words suture the work together in the absence of a stable, informative image or a linear story-line." (Marks 2000, xv). Yet, it is worth noting that the narrative mode of Akin's film displays similarities to Carsten Knoop's low-budget production "Der Vorführ-Effekt" (Germany, 2001), in which the filmmaker Knoop himself cycles through Hamburg. Both talk directly into the camera while we witness their encounters with several interviewees (in Knoop's case these are film projectionists). Both films share the narrative mode of having the director travel through the city, of establishing him as someone "at home" there. Thus, I would argue, this mode of presentation does not necessarily need to be conceptualised by taking a post-colonial perspective. The film's narrative mode makes Akin a traveller and a mediator between his family and the audience.[78] At first glance, the similarities to Martin Scorsese's *Italianamerican* (1974) are striking.[79] Like Akin, Scorsese interviews his parents, but unlike

---

[77] At the same time we should keep in mind that the director/auteur of a film is not identical with its subject. The filmic representation, as Christina Scherer has pointed out, "splits the I of the narrator into a personal and a narrative identity, transforming and 'fictionalising' him/her." (Scherer 2001, 30, *my translation*).

[78] In a way, this can be seen as a reversal or an echo of the traditional structure in ethnographic documentary (for example in Flaherty's "Nanook of the North", 1922), where the white filmmaker becomes a mediator between the white audience and the ethnic deviant "other." Akin works in a similar way in his documentary *Crossing the Bridge* (2005), in which Alexander Hacke, member of the Berlin avant-garde band "Einstürzende Neubauten" functions as the traveller on his quest for "the sound of Istanbul" and thus as a mediator between western audiences and musical forms the reception of which has hitherto been fairly limited in the west. This form is also used in Wim Wenders' *Buena Vista Social Club*, a clear source of inspiration for Akin's film, with Ry Cooder as the mediator. See also Siewert 2008.

[79] When he made *We Forgot to Go Back*, Akin had not seen Scorsese's film, only heard about it (personal communication with the author, Dec 2009).

him, Akin defies the ethnographic gaze inherent in Scorsese's film, which shows the mother cooking traditional food, employs Italian folk music, and hails stereotypical images about Italian-Americans.[80] At one point, Akin's mother Hadiye returns a possible ethnographic gaze when she recalls her arrival to Germany facing the reality of having to live in a flat without running water: "I would never have believed this ... In Turkey everybody has a toilet and a small bathroom, but in Germany ... a flat without a shower and a toilet, you'd never believe this."[81] Akin's mother hereby also counters prevalent stereotypical media images and the victimisation of Turkish women in German cinema which Deniz Göktürk has examined (see Göktürk 2002, 251).

Although Akin's aesthetic approach highlights the audible und visual presence of the filmmaker in a manner reminiscent of Michael Moore's film practice, Akin does not operate on the basis of preconceived notions of what his interviewees might share. He also refrains from commenting on the witness's testimonies in order to present a polyphony of voices. While the use of testimonial witnesses in conventional documentaries often serves to stabilise an already given argument[82], this is not the case in Akin's film. Instead, he uses the film camera as a means of examining different, at times even conflicting opinions, as when his parents contradict each other on camera. In abstaining from deleting these elements from the interview footage, Akin's film allows space for different experiences and attitudes. The film, using the example of Akin's parents, also shows how gendered experiences of migration can be. Internal power relations are played out, rather than covered up to force a coherent presentation.[83]

Unlike the conventional use of witness testimonies in German documentaries, in which witnesses are filmed in front of a neutral, often black background, Akin's film presents the interviewees in their specific surrounding at a certain

---

80 On the use of stereotypical images in Scorsese's film, see Lane 2002.
81 ["Ich hab nie geglaubt ... In Türkei haben alle Toilette und kleines Badezimmer, aber in Deutschland ... eine Wohnung ohne Dusche und ohne WC, man kann nie glauben."]
82 See Keilbach 2008 as well as Brunow 2009.
83 In this context it is interesting to look at the way Akin's film differs from Martin Scorsese's documentary *Italianamerican* (1974), in which Scorsese similarly interviews his parents about their migrant experiences. Scorsese presents an image of his parents which is much more compatible with the hegemonic US discourse on Italian ethnicity, esp. with images of Italian-Americans in Hollywood productions. In contrast, Akin does not try to reproduce existing stereotypes. While Scorsese's mother is shown preparing traditional food in her kitchen, Akin shows his parents working side by side in the kitchen, thus countering prevalent stereotypes about Turkish patriarchs – which are perpetuated in 1970s and 1980s German cinema dealing with migrants.

moment in time.[84] In some cases Akin surprises them with his camera, thus giving a more spontaneous impression of them being "caught in the act." In one scene, for example, his aunt complains of not having been warned about the film team showing up, so that she could have cleaned the front steps. It is also interesting to note that Akin, as the film's protagonist, is almost always on the move, visually stressing "routes" instead of "roots."[85]

3.1.3.1 Transnational urban spaces

The filmmaker Fatih Akin, by repeatedly showing his rootedness in Altona and, for example, filming himself with his transnational crowd of friends in Adam Bousdoukos' Greek restaurant "Sotiris," constantly performs his identity as a non-essential one.[86] It is a transnational identity, neither German nor Turkish, but "Altonian" and "Hamburgian." Throughout the film, Akin repeatedly points out that he feels "Altonian" or "Hamburgian" rather than German or Turkish and calls Adam a "Hamburg-Altonese." As Akin explains in voice-over: "I come from Hamburg-Altona, that's my home, I was born here, here you'd find people from I don't know, man, fifty-five different nations [...] you'd find Greeks, Turks, Yugoslavians."[87] Altona and the "Sotiris" restaurant function as chronotopes in the Bakhtinian sense and as heretopia according to Foucault. This same transnational space of Altona and Adam's "Sotiris" restaurant also reappears in a production for the TV channel *arte*, "Durch die Nacht mit..." (Through the night with...), starring Akin's close friend, the actor Moritz Bleibtreu, who played lead roles in *In July* (2000), *Solino* (2002) and *Soul Kitchen* (2009). I argue that the districts of Altona in Hamburg as well as Beyoğlu in Istanbul serve as transnational, cosmopolitan spaces in Akin's filmic imagination. These areas are inhabited by people from various different regional and national backgrounds,

---

84 Although this is of course the case for the traditional use of testimonial witnesses, TV documentaries, like the ones by Guido Knopp, instrumentalize this practice, which originally stems from interviews with survivors of the Shoa, by presenting the testimonies as final, fixed knowledge that is timeless and therefore true. Knopp even has an archive of interviews which he can cut into various different films – where they are totally decontextualised and can be used wherever they might fit in.
85 For the concept of "Routes" for diasporic studies, see Clifford 1997.
86 After the shooting of *Soul Kitchen* (2009) in which he plays the lead role, Bousdoukos sold the restaurant.
87 ["Ich komm aus Hamburg-Altona, das ist mein Zuhause, hier bin ich geboren, hier leben Leute aus was-weiß-ich, Alter, fünfundfünzig verschiedenen Nationen [...] hier sind Griechen, Türken, Jugos."]

thus transgressing national boundaries.[88] Akin's feature film *Soul Kitchen* (2009), which was launched as a *Heimatfilm* by the production company Corazòn International, exemplifies this in the way it reappropriates the genre. Still, we should keep in mind that the notion of *Heimat* is a typically German concept and basically untranslatable – the word "homeland," for example, does not do justice to the almost metaphysical quality this term embodies. *Heimat* not only references the place of birth and childhood, but is also associated with endless longing for a lost and irretrievable place. While the notion of home in the *Heimatfilm* was a rural concept, the term is now reappropriated for a multicultural urban inner city area, threatened by gentrification. The press kit for *Soul Kitchen* announces the film as a "cheeky, dirty" *Heimatfilm* and conceptualises *Heimat* as a "place which has to be protected in an increasingly unpredictable world."[89] Like Akin's other films, *We Forgot to Go Back* shows, I would argue, an identity of affiliation, not of origin.

Both Paul Gilroy and Stuart Hall have regularly pointed out the impossibility for diasporic subjects to return "home." The home one leaves will never be the same when returning, as both people and places change. At the beach of Filyos Akin explains the changes the village has undergone during the past decades. The family members who have returned to Turkey all mention the difficulties of adapting to the new situation. Akin's uncle states that it takes as long to readjust to Turkey as the time you have been away. Still, the family members have all chosen different paths of dealing with it, from writing poetry about Hamburg, to deciding not to travel back and forth all the time to dreaming about taking the ship back to Germany. To be able to return to an unchanged past, the lost home, is a myth. The film shows – to both the television audience and the other family members – how the Akins negotiate this insight. As Annette Kuhn (2002, 10) points out: "memory work can create new understandings of both past and present, while refusing a nostalgia that embalms the past in a perfect, irretrievable, moment." Far from the tropes of alienation and displacement persistent in postcolonial film studies, Akin exhibits his sense of belonging to the district of Altona.[90] The film's focus on mobility further enhances the view of identity as constantly changing and in flux.

---

88 Akin frequently returns to these places in his work. While Altona features in *Short Sharp Shock*, *In July* and *Head On*, Akin discovered Istanbul during the shooting of *In July* (2000) whereupon he returned to the Turkish capital for *Head On* (2004), *Crossing the Bridge* (2005) and *The Edge of Heaven* (2007).
89 http://www.pathefilms.ch/libraries.files/soul-kitchen_PH_DCH.pdf (12 November 2009).
90 In *Soul Kitchen* (2009) Altona as a heterotopia is replaced by Wilhelmsburg, which is on the verge of gentrification.

3.1.3.2 Transnational sonic spaces

While it is true that music travels across borders, I would claim that music on a soundtrack can also contribute to establishing essentialist notions of identity. For instance, if conventional radio or TV productions play Turkish arabesque folk music when talking about second or third generation Turkish migrants in Germany, the music clearly connects them to the homeland of their parents or grandparents, thus – maybe unintentionally – implying that these people do not really belong to Germany. Fatih Akin defies this conventional practice by abstaining from linking his parents to a certain country via the soundtrack. Neither does he employ specifically traditional Turkish nor music associated with a German context, but rather uses globally popular sounds like US soul and funk. The film opens with a photograph of Akin's family, vividly coloured and reminiscent of the cover of a soul LP. On the soundtrack we hear the soul classic "It's a Family Affair" performed by Sly and The Family Stone in the 1971 version. Right from the start, Akin does not tie his family to a specific geographical space. Instead of playing traditional Turkish folk music, the film employs soul music in order to transgress national boundaries. As opposed to Scorsese, who uses traditional Italian folk in *Italianamerican* (1974), Akin places himself in a Third space (Bhabha) and opens up a transnational sonic space.[91]

Anahid Kassabian has argued that a soundtrack consisting of pre-existing songs creates a new sonic space by broadening existing identifications. Songs actually control identification to a lesser extent than a score specifically composed for the film might: "it means that perceivers bring external associations with the songs into their engagements with the film." (3) Akin's way of compiling the soundtrack does not derive from ethnic identifications, but from what Kassabian terms "affiliating identifications" (3), which instead of narrowing the "psychic field" of the listener, open it up. Thus, identity it not so much about where someone is from, but about what he or she aspires to. Another example occurs later in the film, while we see Akin travelling to the village of his grandfather. On the soundtrack we hear a version of the funk classic "Going Back to my Roots" performed by Odyssey in 1981. Here, the notion of "roots" instead of "routes" is

---

91 Senta Siewert (2008) employs Elsaesser's concept of "double occupancy" for the sampling of sounds and "cultures" in Akin's *Head On*. However, in order to avoid the inherent risk of binarism in this concept, despite its usefulness, I prefer to depart from Kassabian. I am highly sceptical towards the notion of "cultural and ethnic borders" (Elsaesser) since they presuppose the existence of homogenic entities, but would agree that this notion of borders is created through various essentialising strategies. Akin's documentary *Crossing the Bridge* is a good example. The film shows that the notion of an authentic Turkish music as an expression of an authentic, pure and essentialist Turkish culture is a myth. Instead, it celebrates hybridity.

employed for the first time throughout a film in which the notion of "routes," of "travelling" and of "nomadic" experiences otherwise predominate. Yet, while the lyrics speak of "roots" and territory, the funky music, associated with 1970s (Black/US) funk and disco function to deterritorialise the images.[92] Music thus serves to challenge the essentialist concept of identity prevalent in the national discourses that try to "other" immigrants according to their allegedly different "ethnicities" or "cultures." The film disrupts notions of belonging and offers an alternative to metaphysics of nation, race and bordered territorial cultures encoded in human bodies.

3.1.4 Migrant memories: transnational approaches

The example of *We Forgot to Go Back* has shown how cultural memory is constructed via filmmaking and how autobiographical documentary filmmaking can function as a memory work to address the experiences of migration. Akin's film can thus be regarded as an act of remembrance challenging the hegemonic national discourse which sidelines or silences migration. At the same time the film refrains from taking an essentialist stance towards notions of identity, culture or ethnicity by employing various de-essentialising strategies: putting forth the situatedness of knowledge as well as the decoupling of belonging, identity and territory through the use of space and music. The stories shared by the Akin family complicate the dominant perspective on labor migration which is still marginalized in German historiography. Countering the risk of being forgotten within national historiography, Akin's film creates a discursive space in which different experiences of labor migration can be articulated. Therefore, the film can be read not only as a complement to the prevailing master narrative, but also as a suggestion to re-narrate the story of the nation. Akin's film presents an act of remembrance for contemporary multicultural societies while at the same time highlighting that experiences are not universal, but specific. If such a variety and diversity of experiences can be collected within just a single family, it becomes evident that the cultural memory of labor migration will need many more contributions in order to do justice to its multifacetedness.

This case study also argues that while the film deconstructs essentialist notions of stable, fixed identities being determined by territorial origin, its industrial context of production, distribution and reception risks to re-essentialise the film despite its aesthetic strategies. Thus, a mere textual analysis might

---

[92] I am using the concept of deterritorialisation according to Deleuze 1989.

not be sufficient to tease out the complexities of autobiographical documentary filmmaking. These insights also have epistemological consequences for the researcher, as the chapter has argued. Yet, while the national perspective within film studies currently tends to be left behind in favor of transnational approaches, the construction of cultural memory – despite its dynamics – is shaped by national frameworks. The impact of the nation-state and its power structures is still strong. For instance, discourses on migration are entangled with nationally specific legislation, they are embedded in a diachronic perspective, which has had an impact on the self-fashioning of a nation and its visual archive.

Despite its anti-essentialist strategies, the film faces the risk of being re-essentialised in the process of critical reception which is shaped by discourses on assimilation. While the critics are positive about *We Forgot to Go Back*, the focus is not on the film's aesthetics, but on the content. As often in documentary criticism the film is treated as a sociological case study, with one reviewer stating: "when Hamburg boy Fatih Akin follows the roots of his family back to Istanbul and the Black Sea, it saves you five German-Turkish cultural conferences."[93] Another critic claims: "The mighty ideological slogans of 'German Leitkultur' and multiculturalism prove completely devoid of meaning when we look at the everyday practices by which Germans and foreigners have managed to coexist for years."[94] Concepts of assimilation, integration, and ethnic absolutism frame these reviews.

If institutional contexts not only discursively frame migrant artistic expression, but also its critical reception, what then about academic scholarship and the conceptualisation of migrant and diasporic filmmaking in film studies? How can the risk to "other" migrant and diasporic filmmaking be avoided? Does research on Fatih Akin always have to revolve around questions of ethnic identity and belonging?[95] Gerd Gemünden has pointed out how Akin and his contemporaries like Angelina Maccarone are more influenced by US-cinema than Wim Wenders and his generation would ever have wanted to be. For Akin and Maccarone, the US offers an alternative to German culture, otherwise

---

[93] Die Welt 29 October 2001. ["... und wenn der Hamburger Jung Fatih Akin den Wurzeln seiner Familie zurück nach Istanbul und ans Schwarze Meer folgt, kann man sich fünf deutsch-türkische Kulturtagungen sparen."]

[94] Neue Zürcher Zeitung 1 December 2001. ["Die wuchtigen ideologischen Schlagworte von 'deutscher Leitkultur' und 'Multikulti' erweisen sich als völlig bedeutungslos angesichts dieser Lebenspraxis, in der Deutsche und Ausländer längst zusammengefunden haben."]

[95] Meanwhile I am well aware that this article cannot escape from this dilemma either. See for example Berghahn 2005; Burns 2006, 2009.

considered to be too limiting in its "insistence on homogeneity, purity, and authenticity" (Gemünden 2004, 181). I would like to suggest that the recent paradigmatic shift from national cinema to transnational cinema, and from national film cultures to European cinema, can contribute to rescuing films from the margins.[96] For example, Akin's *In July* (2004) and *Head On* (2004) could very well be conceptualised as road movies in both an American and European tradition, represented by filmmakers and their works such as Wim Wenders (*Alice in the Cities*, 1974; *Kings of the Road*, 1976), Rossellini (*Viaggio in Italia*, 1954), Hopper (*Easy Rider*, 1969) or Polat's *Tour Abroad* (1999).[97] Thus, perceiving Akin's work as transnational or European filmmaking can avoid the risk of homogenising works by the most diverse filmmakers and "othering" them in the process of critical reception. Interestingly, Fatih Akin's film *Soul Kitchen* (2009) was deliberately launched as a "Heimatfilm" at the time, indicating that a shift of perspective may have been underway. A transnational perspective drawing on the theorizations of Deleuze and Guattari inspires the collected volume "Kultur als Ereignis" compiled by Özkan Ezli in 2010 (Ezli 2010). Most of its contributions examine Akin's *Auf der anderen Seite* (2007) as an example of contemporary transcultural filmmaking within the context of global World Cinema. Thus, filmmaking oscillates between transnational and national frameworks and these tensions are played out in Fatih Akin's documentary road movie *We Forgot to Go Back*.

3.2 Transcultural memories: post-punk Manchester in times of urban regeneration

The notion of 'transcultural memory', as outlined above, entails the risk of perpetuating an essentialist understanding of 'culture', ethnicity and the nation-state. This chapter sets out to move beyond a conceptualisation of 'transculturality' which is limited to the realms of ethnicity and nationality. It argues that memory studies would profit from taking a broader perspective on 'transcultural memory' which acknowledges the complexities of cultural practices even within the same geographical framework, for instance a nation, a region or a city. Since regional memories have had a tendency to be overlooked due to the prevalent national perspective within memory studies, as Astrid Erll (2010) has observed, I would like to examine the formation of memory in the English Northwest, and, more specifically, in the Manchester city region. With this approach I attempt to

---

96 See for example Bergfelder 2005; Elsaesser 2005 and Gemünden 2004.
97 For a transnational perspective on European road movies see Mazierska and Rascaroli 2006.

broaden the scope of transcultural memory which, according to Erll (2010, 312) "often unfolds within regions that are located at the intersections of different nations", for instance in border zones such as the Baltics or the South China Sea Region. However, I would like to show how a transcultural perspective is not limited to border zones between different nations and will therefore choose a specific city space. According to Erll, the transcultural lens allows us to see "the many fuzzy edges of national cultures of remembrance, the many shared sites of memory that have emerged through [...] cultural exchange; second, the great internal heterogeneity of national culture, its different classes, generations, ethnicities, religious communities, and subcultures", which "will all generate different, but in many ways interacting frameworks of memory" (Erll 2010, 311–312). Music culture, apart from popular culture, religion or ideologies, among others, is one of the "formations beyond national culture" (Erll 2010, 312) which require a different analytical framework which exceeds the national perspective.

Instead of understanding 'transculturality' in terms of a geographical area alone, I will focus on the dynamics of memory and the way it travels and translates into different contexts. Although memory studies is currently turning from the sites of memory towards its dynamics, I deliberately choose the memory of a city because the memory of a place not only entails a geographical, but also a diachronic perspective, and travels via specific discursive frameworks. Thus, my point of departure is one of the research questions outlined by Erll for future studies of regional transcultural memories: "How does memory 'travel' within a given region?" (Erll 2010, 313) In her article "Travelling Memory" Astrid Erll has pointed out that "a transcultural perspective also implies questioning those other grids (territorial, social, temporal), which we tend to superimpose upon the complex realities of remembering in culture" (Erll 2011b, 8). In this sense, transculturality could be used as a tool to analyse a diversity of cultural practices and the multidirectionality of memory within the same national or regional framework. Two of the guiding questions are: How is memory translated into different cultural contexts within the same geographical space? What are the power relations at work?

In *Time Passages* George Lipsitz (1990) conceptualises popular memory as counter-memory, characterised by localized experiences rather than official histories. As opposed to historical narratives that begin with the totality and then locate specific actors in it, counter-memory operates the other way around, according to Lipsitz. It "starts with the particular and the specific and then builds outward toward a total story." (Lipsitz 1990, 213). The following chapter will complicate such an understanding of the connection between different frameworks. I argue that local memories are not necessarily distinct from official memories and are not to be understood as 'counter-memory' per se. The same goes for regional memory which is not automatically more emancipatory than national memory.

In this chapter I look at the ways the cultural memory of 1980s post-punk in Manchester has been reworked, adapted and reappropriated into a new context: that of urban regeneration. The recent 'memory boom' of films and other retro phenomena concerning 1980s post-punk Manchester has contributed to the shaping of glocal identities. My example will examine the construction of transcultural memory by looking at the way the memory around 1970s and 1980s subcultures has been employed within official urban and regional politics in Manchester during the last two decades. Starting with an overview of the various remediations of post-punk Manchester's (sub)cultural memory, this chapter sets out to analyse what kind of memory is constructed in the process of ongoing remediation. The case study of Carol Morley's experimental film *The Alcohol Years* serves as yet another example of minor cinema's capacity to foreground the power relations at work in the construction of cultural memory. Moreover, this chapter sets out to questions notions of subcultural, popular, vernacular or other concepts of alternative memories as counter-hegemonic.

Concepts of "travelling" or "multidirectional memory" have challenged the binary structure on which memory studies' notions of alternative memories are predicated. This might mean that the emancipatory potential ascribed to the concept of subculture (Hebdige 1996) might have to be reconsidered. In fact, the notion of subculture is used here in a merely heuristic fashion, rather than pointing at a discursive formation situated within a specific context.[98] My use of the term 'subculture' goes back to Dick Hebdige's seminal conceptualisation in his 1979 book *Subculture: the meaning of style*, developed in the context of Birmingham's CCCS, in which he defines subculture as "expressive forms and rituals of those subordinate groups – the teddy boys and mods and rockers, the skinheads and the punks – who are alternately dismissed, denounced and canonized; treated at different times as threats to public order and as harmless buffoons" (Hebdige, 1996, 2). Such varying and conflicting discourses evolving around subcultures are also part of the transcultural memory of post-punk Manchester. If we agree with Hebdige, that the "meaning of subculture is [...] always in dispute" (1996, 3), the same might be the case for the memory of these subcultures.

Such an understanding of (sub)cultural practice as counter-hegemonic is put forward by Dave Haslam when he describes Manchester's subculture, here epit-

---

[98] If we perceive 'culture' as including multiple cultural practices, as this study does, the notion of 'subculture' is obsolete. However, as a discursive construct it can be the object of research.

omized in 1990s "Madchester", as a "culture that embraces the geographical and political margins, a pop culture long ago divorced from the dominant culture" (Haslam 2000, 256). Yet, the question remains if subcultural memories ought to be conceptualised in terms of alternative, emancipatory counter-cultures alone. The relation between subculture, nostalgia and commodification is understood by Dylan Clarke (2003) as follows: "The classical subculture 'died' when it became the object of social inspection and nostalgia, and when it became so amenable to commodification." (Clarke 2003, 223) Since debates about the commodification of punk are almost as old as punk culture itself, I would like to turn Dylan Clarke's argument around by following Alison Landsberg (2004) who approaches the debate from a different angle: for her everything is already commodified, but some cultural practices, despite their commodification, would allow for a counter-hegemonic stand. However, as this study argues, the notion of counter practice has to be critically examined. Its critical stand might not be as far-reaching as it perhaps seems. My hypothesis is that subcultural memory is not as emancipatory as one might expect.

I argue that we need to examine the workings of multidirectional, transcultural memories drawing on specific cultural practices, such as Rothberg did when he analysed how Holocaust memory is appropriated in different texts within the discourse of decolonization. My example will look at the cultural memory around 1980s post-punk Manchester and the era of the emergence of Joy Division, the Fall, the Smiths, the Haçienda (Manchester's legendary nightclub and concert venue), and the Factory label. To a lesser degree I take the 'Madchester' years into account, a term referring to the era of rave culture at the Haçienda during the second half of the 1980s, with the advent of house, the drug culture around ecstasy and bands like The Happy Mondays, The Stone Roses or The Inspiral Carpets.[99]

This chapter also deals with the notion of space for cultural memory. Although both digital and analogue memories have increasingly been conceptualised as transnational, the locatedness of cultural memory remains an important question for memory scholars. I argue that remediation creates certain nodal points around which a number of narratives of the past are constructed. One of these mnemonic nodal points is the legendary Haçienda, a nightclub and concert venue situated on Whitworth Street, which operated between 1982 and 1997. After its final closure in 1997 the Haçienda was torn down in 2002.[100] Two years

---

[99] I will also leave out the songs themselves, whose self-reflexivity and intertextuality also includes an important memory dimension.
[100] The Haçienda was temporarily closed in 1991, following the death of a clubber due to Ecstasy poisoning.

earlier 'memorabilia' from the Haçienda were auctioned off. Michael Winterbottom's film *24 Hour Party People* contributed to the club's legendary status in 2002.[101] In August 2007 an exhibition celebrated 25 years of the Haçienda. The club, musealised at the Manchester Museum of Science and Industry, also figures in Peter Hook's memoir *The Haçienda. How Not to Run a Club* (Hook 2009), and was recreated at the Victoria and Albert Museum for an exhibition of iconic British design in 2012. Different acts of remembrance and plurimedia remediations have transformed The Haçienda to a *lieu de mémoire* in the sense of Pierre Nora. For Nora *lieux de mémoires* come into existence first when the original places disappear. However, in order to get away from the national perspective associated with Nora's concept Bakhtin's notion of the chronotope could prove fruitful. Drawing on Bakthin the term "mnemotope" has come into use to stress the memory dimension of the chronotope. My ambition is not to engage with the vast research on Bakhtin, but to use his concept in a heuristic fashion. For rethinking the relation of iconic images and urban space Bakhtin's concept of the chronotope proves highly useful. Bakhtin uses the concept to refer to the "intrinsic connectedness of temporal and spatial relationships that are artistically expressed in literature" (Bakhtin 1981:84). He conceptualises the chronotope as a spatial-temporal dimension which in turn contributes to merging past and present and which develops a certain sense of locality for a music culture with a transnational reception.[102] Merging 1980s post-punk culture and 1990s rave culture (Madchester) the mediated cultural memories of the Haçienda turn it into a chronotope, or mnemotope. However, not only remediations, but also intermedial and intertextual references contribute to creating a chronotope I would argue.[103] For example, the club's name "The Haçienda" is an intermedial reference to Ivan Chtcheglov and his 1953 text "Formulary for a New Urbanism", which inspired the lettrists and the situationists.[104] Different cultural practices are placed in a continuum encompassing time and space. In the case of naming

---

[101] Even though, ironically enough, the film scenes set at the Haçienda had to be recreated in a warehouse in Ancoats, at the other side of the city.
[102] On a similar note, Redfern 2005 argues that *24 Hour Party People* is not so much about the specific bands and actors, but about Manchester. It places a variety of subcultures in a spatial continuum. He states: "Thus different sub-genres of the 'punk'/'indie' scene in Manchester are to be distinguished by different drugs, clothes, and music influences, but are united in their spatial contiguity: in placing the Happy Mondays in the same spaces as Wilson, Hannett, and New Order this proximity of bands in a single place links them as being Manchester bands and affording them a cultural continuity that is otherwise not apparent." (Redfern 2005, 304)
[103] The relation between the concepts of remediation and intermediality will be explored in chapter 5.1. (on *Looking for Langston*).
[104] One of the lines in the text goes: "the Haçienda must be built".

the Haçienda cultural distinction might have been one reason for the decision. Perceiving oneself as culturally distinct from mainstream culture has been important for the self-fashioning of post-punk Manchester.

I argue that in the former industrial cities of the Northwest of England, especially in Liverpool and Manchester, the heritage of popular music has contributed to relaunching the cities as creative clusters.[105] However, I will neither offer a comprehensive account of city politics, nor conduct an ethnographic/anthropological, sociological study of the changes the city underwent. Instead, I will go beyond this and discuss to what extent subcultures actually are the basis for alternative archives. I will argue that they are not necessarily alternative, but can feed into neoliberal discourses. Along with other media, filmmaking creates a psychogeography of the city. Remediation constructs mnemonic spaces which are predominantly heteronormative and male-oriented – all the more surprising since Manchester has been a traditional stronghold for LGBT-culture for decades. Therefore, the formation of Manchester's cultural memory is a highly gendered process. In the construction of memory "men and women are given very different subject positions and very different possibilities of identification", as Bjerg and Lenz (2008, 228) have emphasized. Using Carol Morley's experimental film *The Alcohol Years* (2000) as an example, the chapter critically examines the highly gendered remediations of popular music heritage and the appropriation and reworking of subcultural memories into an official narrative. *The Alcohol Years* foregrounds the construction of cultural memory by revealing which discursive spaces are opened and which are closed in the processes of remembrance. The chapter outlines the exclusions produced by mediated memories, and it poses the question on whose versions cultural memory is based.[106]

This chapter is divided into three parts. First, it critically examines the construction of subcultural memory and its plurimedia constellations. It will take a critical look at the memory boom and analyse "whose heritage" (Hall 2000) is celebrated in the multiple remediations of post-punk Manchester. Second, it uses Carol Morley's experimental film *The Alcohol Years* as an example of a feminist filmmaking practice which might allow us to reflect on the construction of cultural memory, its homosociality, its gaps and absences. It adds an intersectionalist perspective on the notion of remediation, taking a look at the way hegemonic constructions of gender, sexuality and ethnicity pervade the construc-

---

[105] For the case of Liverpool see Cohen 2007, Roberts 2012b.
[106] The notion of discursive spaces, and how film can be a way of opening them up, will be further examined in the section on remediation – using the example of Isaac Julien's *Looking for Langston*.

tion of cultural memory.[107] Finally it readdresses the notion of transcultural memory in looking at the ways subcultural memory is translated into practices of city branding in the context of urban regeneration and gentrification. Rather than looking at the ways cultural practices such as writing or filmmaking construct the memory of an event, this chapter examines in a first step the discursive spaces opened or closed through these operations. In a second step it analyses how the memory of cultural practices (clubbing, playing in a band, belonging to a subculture) is remediated and translated into different cultural contexts (from the self-fashioning for a subculture to city branding).

3.2.1 The memory boom around 1980s post-punk Manchester and its gender dimensions

For the last two decades a veritable 'memory boom' (Jay Winter) can be observed around 1970s punk and 1980s post-punk in Britain.[108] The cultural memory of this era is remediated via documentaries, feature films, memoirs, re-releases of records, band reunions, exhibitions, websites, uploads on YouTube or memorabilia, such as commemorative stamps[109].

The ongoing memory boom about post-punk Manchester is not limited to the Manchester music scene, but is part of the ongoing memorialisation of punk and post-punk culture. The rise of retro-culture in the first decade of the new millennium finds its expression in the opening of rock and pop museums, in band reunions, 1980s revival gigs and the growing number of music documentaries (Reynolds 2011). In his book *Retromania* Simon Reynolds defines the term 'retro' in its strictest sense as "a self-conscious fetish for period stylisation (in music, clothes, design) expressed creatively through pastiche and citation" (Reynolds 2011, xii), though the meaning of the word has become fairly vague over time. Reynolds' use of the concept of 'retro' in this wider sense is derived from Raphael Samuel's chapter on "retrochic" in his seminal *Theatres of Memo-*

---

[107] On the notion of intersectionality, see Crenshaw 2003, Yuval-Davis 2006, Degele and Winker 2009.
[108] While the memory boom seems to have started by the end of the 1990s, tendencies for the memorialisation of post-punk Manchester were already initiated by Factory Record in the late 1970s. In 1979, on 13 September, Factory Records announced a film event at the now legendary Scala Cinema in London, near King's Cross station. The event, which catalogued FAC9, included 8 mm-footage of Joy Division. On the label's information sheet the screening was announced as an "hommage [sic!] to the already golden age." (http://blog.factoryrecords.org/1979/09...)
[109] In January 2010 the Royal Mail released a first-class postage stamp which reproduces Peter Saville's record cover for New Order's 1983 album, *Power, Corruption and Lies*.

ry, first published in 1994. Samuel finds "retrochic" within 1950s and 1960s alternative youth cultures, such as the Teddy Boys, in the appropriation of the iconic styles of Marlon Brando or James Dean by 1970s gay culture, but also in the rise of charity shops, in vintage food trends, vintage clothing, in furniture design, Merchant-Ivory films and in pop music. Samuel states: "In pop music, the re-release of many older albums on CD, the discovery of hitherto unused recordings and tapes such as those of Jimi Hendrix, and not least the progressive ageing of many hard rock and heavy metal followers, is producing a veritable explosion of nostalgia." (Samuel 2012, 104). While Samuel speaks of remediation "producing" nostalgia, I would claim that nostalgia might also be an incentive for remediation in order to target a niche within the highly differentiated consumer culture for 'retromania'.

The recent wave of pop historiography can be said to be one factor in creating a cultural memory about popular culture. Books such as *Please Kill Me* (McNeil and McCain, 1997), *England's Dreaming* (Savage 2005) or *Rip It Off and Start Again* (Reynolds 2005) do not only offer accounts of the eras of punk and post-punk, but serve as modes of self-assurance and self-positioning for their readers. Their impact is more than a mere positivist rendering of facts. Popular music belongs to the symbolic system of representation in which our identities are negotiated. Due to its impact on our formative teenage years, popular music plays a decisive role in the construction of generational memory and is therefore highly affected by nostalgia (see Boym 2001). For subcultural audiences a variety of independent music cultures, among them punk and post-punk, have become fundamental for their self-fashioning, for creating a sense of identity and for pronouncing their cultural distinction against commercialized mainstream culture. As Sarah Thornton has pointed out in her article "The Social Logic of Subcultural Capital"[110]: "Subcultural ideologies are a means by which youth imagine their own and other social groups, assert their distinctive character and affirm that they are not anonymous members of an undifferentiated mass" (Thornton 1997, 201). Members of subcultures create a sense of identity in defining themselves in contrast to the mainstream. This sense of identity also affects the construction of cultural memory because it has repercussions on the stories individuals want to tell about their past and the cultural distinction they want to achieve through their self-fashioning.

Subcultural memory contributes to situating individuals from various generations into a (sub)cultural context. Manchester's musical heritage, but also the

---

110 Although Thornton looks at club culture, esp. rave culture, her insights on the performativity of gender in these subcultures provides a fruitful perspective on other subcultures as well.

prosthetic memories generated via widely circulating feature films such as *Control* (Landsberg 2004), allow even later generations to inscribe themselves within the legacy of punk and post-punk. Mediated cultural memories contribute to our "Selbstverortung", an untranslatable German term, which Robin Curtis (2006) uses as a starting point for her study on autobiographical German filmmaking. Curtis explains it as "a localization specifically with regards to the self; it emphasizes the spatiality of our being, the relevance that our placement in space and time has for our 'situation', in every sense of the word" (Curtis 2006, 7). Films such as *24 Hour Party People* (Winterbottom, 2002) or *Control* have already entered the archive of Manchester's pop-cultural memory. These films have become "memory films" in the sense of Astrid Erll and Stephanie Wodianka (2008). 'Memory films' are playing an important role for the construction of cultural memory in a specific historical context through their dissemination of memory images.[111] As Peter Bradshaw (2007) exclaimed about Anton Corbijn's *Control* (2007): "the period music detail of this movie makes it a very powerful madeleine". Memory films such as *Control* or *24 Hour Party People* allow global, transnational audiences to engage in the cultural memory of post-punk Manchester which they more often than not have never been part of themselves, for either temporal or spatial reasons. These memory texts tie into a retro culture which is crucial for the self-fashioning of a generation which feels connected to punk or post-punk. Although not every film is a 'memory film' as conceptualised by Erll and Wodianka (2008), all of them are acts of remembrance in their own way. While they contribute to the "plurimedia constellation" of Manchester post-punk memory, they are also intertwined in a discursive framework, some of the dimensions of which will be outlined in this chapter.

Two of the earliest accounts of Manchester's post-punk memory have been Mick Middles' *From Joy Division to New Order* in 1996 (Middles 2002, re-issued as *Factory. The Story of the Record Label* in 2009) as well as Dave Haslam's 1999 *Manchester England* (Haslam 2000). Michael Winterbottom's film *24 Hour Party People* (2002) was accompanied by the book publication *24 Hour Party People: What the Sleeve Notes Never Tell You,* authored by Tony Wilson (Wilson 2002). Deborah Curtis' *Touching from a Distance (Curtis 2005),* a memoir of the author's life with Joy Division singer Ian Curtis, was adapted into Anton Corbijn's *Control* (2007). Joy Division and Ian Curtis were also commemorated in *Joy Division. Piece by Piece* by Paul Morley (2008), in *Torn Apart. The Life of Ian Curtis* by

---

[111] In contrast, Carol Morley's *The Alcohol Years* has so far only played a minor role for the creation of post-punk culture's audiovisual archive. This can be regarded as a result of the film's limited circulation which in turn is due to the programming practice of cinemas or festivals and to the lack of academic research on Morley.

Mick Middles (2009), in Kevin Cummins' *Joy Division* (Cummins 2012) as well as in Peter Hook's *Unknown Pleasures: Inside Joy Division* (Hook 2013). Other publications include James Nice's *Shadowplayers: The Rise and Fall of Factory Records (Nice 2010)*, Peter Hook's *The Haçienda. How Not to Run a Club* (Hook 2010), Lindsay Reade's memoir of her life with Tony Wilson: *Mr Manchester and the Factory Girl (Reade* 2010) as well as Kevin Cummins' *Manchester* (Cummins 2010). John Robb's *The North Will Rise Again: Manchester Music City (Robb 2010)* is a collection of oral history accounts in the tradition of his earlier volume *Punk Rock (Robb 2006)* which in turn is modelled after *Please Kill Me* on 1970s punk culture in New York (McNeil and McCain, 1997). Grant Gee's documentary film *Joy Division* (2007), which even had a cinematic release, adds to a long list of television documentaries on post-punk Manchester, but also to countless remediations of live performances and television appearances now uploaded on YouTube.

This brief overview shows how the memory boom around post-punk Manchester has increasingly been focussing on nodal points such as Joy Division (the band), Factory Records (the label) and The Haçienda (the club), most notably in films such as *24 Hour Party People* by Michael Winterbottom and Anton Corbijn's *Control*.[112] These nodal points are perpetuated by the ongoing remediation stabilising the cultural memory. At the same time through remediation discursive spaces for different subject positions are opened or closed within cultural memory. This process in turns has repercussions on canon formation: it highlights some bands (especially Joy Division), while side-lining others (for instance The Fall or The Durutti Column). In most of the 'memory works' around 1980s Manchester the dominant narrative is defined by a homosocial (Sedgwick) and patriarchal perspective, which is white and heteronormative and in which feminist, queer or Black voices are excluded. To illustrate my point I will briefly discuss Winterbottom's *24 Hour Party People*.

24 Hour Party People is a highly self-reflexive film, with Brechtian moments of breaking the fourth wall, with cameo appearances (by Mark E. Smith, the singer of The Fall, or Howard Devoto), thus all the time blurring the boundaries between fiction and reality.[113] Another self-reflexive element is the casting of Steve

---

[112] Both the *Haçienda* (FAC 51) and *24 Hour Party People* (FAC 451) were issued with Factory Records' catalogue numbers.

[113] At first glance *Control* and *24 Hour Party People* seem to epitomize Bolter and Grusin's (2000) distinction of immediacy versus hypermediacy. In contrast to *Control*, which has been praised for its authentic look (see Davenport 2007), Winterbottom's film plays with notions of authenticity. For a more detailed discussion of *24 Hour Party People* see Brabazon 2005, Redfern 2005, Barton 2012, for a study of *Control* see Fauteux 2009.

Coogan, whose character Alan Partridge from the televised comedy series had gained nationwide prominence. In mocking the traditional mode of rockumentaries, *24 Hour Party People* inscribes itself into the tradition of music mockumentaries such as *Spinal Tap* (Reiner, USA 1984), about a British heavy metal band, and *All You Need is Cash*, Eric Idle's television film about the band "The Rutles" (Idle and Weis, UK 1978), an ironic take on The Beatles. However, despite its self-reflexive take *24 Hour Party People* does not offer a norm-critical perspective which might have contributed to subverting hegemonic representations of masculinity, whiteness or heteronormativity. Its playfulness does not undermine conventional representations of gender or sexuality prevalent in pop historiography.

Reducing the story of the Factory label to "a highly masculine tale of great men", as Tara Brabazon (2005, 142) observes, the film writes women "into the familiar roles of wives, girlfriends, prostitutes, cloakroom girls and anonymous mobile bodies in a club" (Brabazon 2005, 142). The film therefore constructs a discursive space for male homosociality, which according to Eve Kosofsky Sedgwick (1985) is not only based on the exclusion of women, but also on the premise of heterosexuality. As a consequence, LGBT-memories have been completely erased from the cultural memory of the Haçienda in *24 Hour Party People* (see Brabazon 2005, 142). The importance of gay culture at the Haçienda, both the "Gay Traitor Bar" and the gay nights at the "Flesh" club which attracted busloads of visitors from all over the North of England, is not acknowledged in the film. Although these gay clubs provided the economically challenged Haçienda with a necessary financial contribution, gay culture is as absent as is the representation of homosexual or bisexual desire. Without exception, the romantic or sexual encounters depicted in the film are either related to the male protagonists' wives, female lovers or female sex workers. Through the omission of queer desire the film strengthens both Tony Wilson's and the other characters' "heterosexual credibility" (Brabazon 2005, 142).[114] My point here is not to criticize a lack of historical record or to make suggestions about the protagonists' sexual preferences, but the point is that a queer, norm-critical perspective allows us to show in what way cultural memory is constructed: in *24 Hour Party People* it is through a highly gendered, heteronormative, patriarchal perspective while LGBT-memories are excluded from the film's 'memory work'.

---

114 Moreover, Vini Reilly, the singer of The Durutti Column, was edited out of the film (Redfern 2005, 296). No matter what his sexual preferences might have been, Reilly's gender performance could permit a 'queer reading' since he performs a more effeminate version of masculinity which is highly different from the one of the other male characters in the film. His presence in the film would have challenged the representation of male homosociality in *24 Hour Party People*.

Outlining the memory boom around post-punk Manchester allows us therefore to critically examine the kind of cultural memory constructed and to analyse which stories are included – or excluded. What at first glance appears to be a myriad of accounts is less polyvocal than it looks, despite its style or genre. If we regard cultural memory following Marita Sturken (1997: 1) as a "field of cultural negotiation through which different stories vie for a place in history", we can observe a tendency that the stories are actually not as different as it might seem. Diversity is lacking in the cultural memory of 1980s post-punk Manchester. As a tendency, the contribution of female artists is hidden in these works while women generally tend to be reduced to wives or groupies. The "role of women in the male, often macho, world of rock", as Jon Savage writes in his preface to Curtis (2007, xiii), is often side-lined, even in biographies such as Deborah Curtis' *Touching From a Distance* (Curtis 2007) or Lindsay Reade's *Mr Manchester and the Factory Girl: The Story of Tony and Lindsay Wilson* (Reade 2010). The trajectory of the narratives in both books – written from the perspective of a former wife of one of the main protagonists of the Manchester's music scene – is based on the career of the narrators' husband. Moreover, if we look at the choice of testimonial witnesses we find that in the majority of the accounts, independent of its genre within non-fiction books or documentary filmmaking, the testimonial witnesses are either male or are framed in a patriarchal setting. For Deborah Curtis and Lindsay Reade their discursive space of enunciation is limited to writing from the standpoint of being the wife of Ian Curtis or Tony Wilson respectively.

The mapping of Manchester as a pop city is therefore highly gendered. Its accounts are very much based on homosocial bonding and as a consequence on the exclusion of female artists, band members, DJs or clubbers from the cultural memory of the city. Hegemonic gender constructions are no less prevalent in the self-fashioning of independent culture. As Sarah Thornton has pointed out in her study on club culture, the distinction between mainstream and independent culture entails a gender dimension: "when the culture came to be positioned as *truly* 'mainstream' rather than just behind the times, it was feminized" (Thornton 1997, 205). While Thornton has looked at 1990s rave culture, Simon Reynolds and Joy Press (1995) have shown how punk culture – and post-punk – is based on the exclusion of femininity and the construction of a masculinity based on misogyny. We could therefore conclude that subcultural memory is not automatically emancipatory.

In the next section of this chapter I would like to introduce Carol Morley's film *The Alcohol Years* which allows us to reflect on questions such as 'whose memory is it?' The research process becomes a 'memory work' (A. Kuhn) in itself by introducing an essay film which has so far gone unnoticed by film scholars. Morley's film, which has not been circulated as widely as *24 Hour Party People* and *Control*, is an act of remembrance which offers a different perspective on Manchester pop cultural memory. While Carol Morley's prize-winning British documentary *Dreams of a Life* (2011) was funded by Channel4 and the British Film Institute (BFI), thus increasing its chances of being widely distributed, *The Alcohol Years* was funded by the Arts Council and had only a limited distribution.[115]

Drawing on Julia Kristeva's notion of intertextuality, which is derived from her reading of Bakhtin, I would like to examine Morley's film informed by my knowledge of Corbijn's and Winterbottom's work. Julia Kristeva understands intertextuality not only as a matter of influence, but of a text's dialogical relation to other, even later texts. In "Word, Dialogue and Novel" Julia Kristeva explains how "Bakhtin *situates the text within* history and society, which are then seen as texts read by the writer, and into which he inserts himself by rewriting them" (Kristeva 1980, 65). This perspective allows me to examine Morley's film as an intervention in the audiovisual archive of post-punk Manchester and its mediated memories. Carol Morley's experimental *The Alcohol Years* (2000) can be read as a filmic counter-project against the male dominated memory boom of the 1980s Manchester music scene. In this sub-chapter I am going to present a feminist reading of the film's aesthetic strategies and its reworking of the gendered archive of post-punk memory.

3.2.2 Feminist filmmaking practice as intervention (Carol Morley's *The Alcohol Years*)

The autobiographical *The Alcohol Years* is based on the director's teenage past during the early 1980s when she used to spend her nights at the Haçienda in Manchester. Carol Morley's state of notorious drunkenness, her sexual activities as well as the fact that she almost married Buzzcocks' singer Pete Shelley, but left him right before the wedding, contributed to turning her into a local myth. "Manchester was a real boys' town and I would freak people out because I'd fuck anybody, men or women. And of course I had this huge reputation", Morley states in an interview (Morrow 2000). The film came about, long after Carol Morley had moved to London, when an old friend from Manchester told her a story he had heard about her during her teenage years. The disparity between his rec-

---

[115] In 2000 *The Alcohol Years* was the winner of the City of Melbourne Award for Best Short Documentary at the Melbourne International Film Festival. A DVD edition of *The Alcohol Years* was published in 2005 including the shorts *Everyday Something* (2001), narrated by legendary BBC DJ John Peel, and *Stalin, My Neighbour* (2004).

ollections and her own, or rather, her own amnesia about this period in her life, triggered off the idea to make a film about the memories circulating about her. Morley put an ad in a local Manchester newspaper asking people who had known her to get in touch (see Morrow 2000). A newspaper clipping of the ad is remediated at the beginning of the film: "Carol Morley Film Project. Please contact me if you knew me between 1982–1987. Box No. 348/1." During the film the director revisits friends and lovers from 1980s Manchester and makes them share their recollections of the person they used to know as "Carol Morley". Morley interviews, among others, *The Jesus and Mary Chain* bassist Douglas Hart, Vini Reilly of *The Durutti Column*, promoter and Nico's former manager Alan Wise, singer-songwriter and musician Stella Grundy, Dave Haslam, Debby Turner of *ToT* as well as Tony Wilson, broadcaster and founder of Factory records.[116]

Defying the alleged positivism of documentary film images, the film becomes an epistemological tool to foreground the construction of cultural memory around 1980s post-punk Manchester. To illustrate, a comparison with the aesthetic strategy of *Control* might be useful. Although *Control* is a fiction film, it has been praised for its "authenticity". Corbijn's biopic draws both on the look of photographs of the time and re-enacts televised performances. In contrast, *The Alcohol Years* does not attempt to create an 'authentic look' of the past. *Control* epitomizes Bolter and Grusin's (2000) notion of the "double logic" of remediation, since it uses hypermediacy as a means to create immediacy and the impression of "mnemonic authenticity" (Erll 2011a, 165).[117] While *The Alcohol Years* uses both re-enactments and point-of-view shorts, unlike *Control* it does not try to represent history "how it really was" (Ranke). Instead it presents different subjective accounts, which form a kaleidoscope of reminiscences. *The Alcohol Years* deconstructs the dominant modes of visual representations of music culture which we find in band documentaries, for example, with their collage of talking heads and archival footage of the band's live performances. Rather than employing archival footage Morley uses contemporary footage of the Manchester city spaces, of rainy streets and night clubs on a Friday or Saturday night, thus linking the past and the present.

---

116 The film features music by Morley's own band ToT, Stella Grundy, New Order, The Durutti Column, Pete Shelley, Vini Reilly and The Fall's Spencer Birtwistle.
117 To illustrate, for the film's re-enactment of the televised performances of Joy Division's *Transmission* two live performances were amalgamated in order to convey an authentic representation: "the September 1978 performance of 'Shadowplay' on Tony Wilson's *Granada Reports*, and the September 1979 performance of 'Transmission' [...] on BBC2's *Something Else*" (Fauteux 2009, 25).

The Alcohol Years, which due to its anti-positivist stand can be conceptualised as an essay film, could also be contextualized within the tradition of autobiographical documentary filmmaking, of personal filmmaking (Rascaroli 2009) and of the "Cinema of Me", as Alissa Lebow (2012) has termed the first-person documentary (see also Renov 2008).[118] Employing filmmaking as an instrument of self-inscription, Carol Morley embarks on a "journey of the self", to use Catherine Russell's (1999: 275) term. Morley's film is an original intervention into recent trends within autobiographical filmmaking: it is a confession video without a confessor and a first person film without the "I". In fact, Morley's film is an act of confession, but this act is not exerted by herself, but by others. Therefore, her approach differs from first person documentaries such as Jonathan Caouette's *Tarnation* (2003) or Gwen Haworth *She's a Boy I Knew* (2007). The self-inscription performed in *The Alcohol Years* is based on the dialectics of presence and absence: Carol Morley is mostly absent in the film's visual representation while she is omnipresent throughout. The presence of the filmmaker is not only evoked via the narratives of the interviewees, but also through inserted photographs, scenes of re-enactment as well as through the talking heads addressing the person behind the camera. Moreover, the film undermines the modes of conventional documentary film-making by abstaining from a coherent voice-over which would evoke the impression of an "authentic" I-narrator. In the following paragraphs I would like to examine the aesthetic strategies employed in the film by looking at the use of re-enactment scenes, voice-over and talking heads. My aim is to show how their unconventional use in *The Alcohol Years* foregrounds both the mediation of memory and the power relations involved in the process of its construction.

Although Morley constructs herself as an absence, *The Alcohol Years* is characterized by a strong auteurial agency. Therefore Carol Morley's film can also be viewed in the context of feminist body art, such as the works by Carolee Schneemann, Valie Export, Cindy Sherman or Marina Abramović. However, while these artists deliberately use their bodies as the centre of their performances, the female body in Morley's film remains a blank space. While the film foregrounds male desire on the female body, the female protagonist is never exhibited, thus undermining a possible male gaze objectifying the female body (Mulvey 1989).[119] In this sense, Morley's approach is reminiscent of Tracey Emin's instal-

---

[118] Lebow prefers the term "cinema of me" because not all the films she examines are autobiographical.
[119] Laura Mulvey's pioneering article "Visual Pleasure and Narrative Cinema", published in *Screen* in 1975 (see Mulvey 1989), can be regarded as the starting point for the emergence of psychoanalytically inspired feminist film theory. Although some of the blind spots in Mulvey's

lation *Everyone I Have Ever Slept With 1963 – 1995* (1995), showing a quilted list of the people the artist has slept with. In Emin's art project the "I" remains strangely absent. Morley's film can be said to engage in a dialogue with Emin's work in constructing the "I" as absent while placing it at the centre of the act of remembrance. Instead, Morley's film uses point-of view-shots in which only the gaze of the camera is represented. Morley's strategy forms an interesting contrast to the one applied by Pratibha Parmar in *Khush* (1991). In *Khush* Parmar intertwines autobiographical oral history accounts of South Asian lesbians and gay men with *tableaux vivants* and archive footage. In one scene a staged scenario of two South Asian women is intercut with a dance scene from a Bollywood film, from which the objectifying gaze of the male characters watching the female dancer is edited out. Parmar's aesthetic strategy employed in *Khush* subverts the male gaze on (exoticized) female bodies in favour of celebrating lesbian desire and granting "visual pleasure" to a lesbian gaze. In contrast to Parmar's film, though, *The Alcohol Years* never exhibits the female body as a potential object of desire, not even in the scenes of re-enactment.

The scenes of re-enactment in Morley's film are not extensive dramatisations, but brief scenes of reconstructions without dialogue. While reconstructions in documentaries can be used to compensate for the lack of archival footage of specific events and to add to the film's alleged authenticity, their use in *The Alcohol Years* is more ambivalent. Rather than enacting scenes with dialogues and specific characters, they provide impressionistic glimpses of Carol in and around the Haçienda. These reconstructions concentrate on emblematic details mentioned in the interviews, such as Carol Morley's alter ego in a fur coat or drawing a plastic duck behind her. As such they confirm the narratives provided in the interview. However, if we regard the film as an epistemological tool, this reading of the reconstruction scenes must remain superficial. Recreating the scenes of her own past can also be regarded as a way of the filmmaker to create a distance between the accounts provided by the interviewees and her own memory, or her moments of amnesia. Trying to fill these gaps remains impossible because the memory of Carol's past is characterised by the way others define her – and not by her own recollections. The subject of the film is not an "I", a "Me", but an individual as seen by others.

In documentaries the voice-over is one of the most efficient means of intervention on the part of the filmmaker.[120] However, Morley abstains from employ-

---

theorisations have subsequently been criticised, her notion of the 'male gaze' on the female body in Classic Hollywood Cinema has lost none of its relevance and can be found in today's music videos, advertising or contemporary cinema alike. See also Brunow 2013b.

[120] For a discussion of the voice in documentary filmmaking, see Bruzzi 2000, 40 – 65.

ing a voice-over which would impose authority on the autobiographical narrator and her version of the events. The voice-over can also be used to create a coherent narrative structure within the film. As Michael Renov has pointed out, for a filmmaker such as Michael Moore the voice is the "primary agent of Moore's subjectivity – that supervenes and restores order" (Renov 2008, 48). Apart from these functions the voice-over commentary can also invite identification and empathy. Drawing on the works by Cameroonian filmmaker Jean-Marie Teno, Renov claims, that "the voice of the filmmaker [...] underscores the ways that subjectivity, the 'I' of the writing self, can lead the way, personalize the subject matter and soften up the audience for a greater receptivity" (Renov 2008, 49). Morley defies the various uses of voice-over commentary in documentary filmmaking: not only does she dismiss the voice-of-God commentary used for the purposes of creating authority, but also the personal voice-over often used in autobiographical filmmaking to invite empathy, as well as the polyphonic "I" in voice-overs in the essay film.[121] Rejecting the possibilities a voice-over commentary provides, Morley abstains from trying to correct or modify the statements of the interviewees. Unlike mediated acts of remembrance setting out to present the "true story" about the Manchester scene (e. g. Lawson 1998, Middles 2002), Morley's film refrains from disambiguating the version of events given by the interviewees. This strategy contributes to exposing the interviewees by foregrounding the manner in which they construct their memory of Carol Morley.

The use of talking heads in *The Alcohol Years* challenges the conventional role of testimonial witnesses in documentaries.[122] Although talking heads are one of the most commonly used devices in documentary filmmaking not only in conventional documentaries, but also in webcam footage or in genres such as confession videos or video diaries, they have been researched only rarely within documentary film theory.[123] Generally we have to distinguish between

---

121 See Nichols 1991 for the notion of the "voice-of-God commentary" and Lupton 2011 on the heteroglossic voice-over in the essay film.
122 Morley's film undermines the notion of testimonial witnesses in documentaries as what Louise Spence and Aslı Kotaman Avcı in another context have described as forging "an implicit contract with the audience that is based on our desire for the real and our good faith. They knit us into a moral community of 'we', a collective we who are united by our compassion." (Spence and Avcı 2013, 300)
123 For the notion of 'testimonial witnesses' see Keilbach 2008, 2012, Hallas 2009, Spence and Avcı 2013. As Keilbach (2012) has pointed out, we can observe an increasing tendency to use testimonial witnesses as a means to enhance the film's affective value in "history television". In the German context the discursive construct of the "Zeitzeuge" gained prominence after 1945 in the aftermath of the Holocaust (see Frei and Sabrow 2012 as well as Kansteiner 2012). Moreover, Judith Keilbach's studies on the representation of testimonial witnesses of National

'talking heads' and 'testimonial witnesses'. While the term 'talking heads' refers to a stylistic means used in documentaries, the term 'testimonial witnesses' (Zeitzeugen) designates the function ascribed to a person featured in the film. Not all talking heads are testimonial witnesses – some might be interviewed in their role as 'experts', for example, whereas not all testimonial witnesses will be edited into the film as talking heads.[124] Although the use of witness accounts is supposed to convey the impression of "authenticity", Hito Steyerl warns us of making witnesses guarantors of historical truth. She suggests that it is important to reflect on the subjectivity and rhetoric of the witness testimonies (Steyerl 2008, 19). Despite such concerns, talking heads have become a convention in documentary filmmaking, connoting authenticity and the mediation of subjective experiences. While talking heads occurred as early as the 1930s with Harry Watts' *Housing Problems* (1935), they became a convention in the age of television documentary. In television documentaries on historical events testimonial witnesses are often staged in such a way that they provide evidence for the documentaries' overall thesis, for example in the so-called 'history television' ('Geschichtsfernsehen') on German public service television. The talking head is "deeply implicated in the disciplinary function of dominant media representation", as Hallas maintains (2009, 37). This convention regulates the representation of the body, but also the right to speak, and the mode of addressing the interviewer. In most cases the interviewees cannot control the repercussions unfavourable lighting or framing might have for their representation in the film. Moreover, they cannot decide how much of the footage is edited out, what is left in the final clip, how the interviewer already sets an agenda by asking specific questions on a topic he/she has chosen beforehand. While the editing process highlights or side-lines the utterances of the interviewees, close-ups might be used to stir emotions in the viewer.[125]

The Alcohol Years challenges the use of talking heads as a means of authentication. As such *The Alcohol Years* can be inscribed into the tradition of self-reflexive documentaries exploring the use of talking head and witness accounts, such as, for instance, Trinh T. Minh-ha's *Surname Viet, Given Name Nam*

Socialism offer valuable theoretical and methodological considerations on the analysis of witness accounts in historical documentaries (see Keilbach 2007, 2008).

124 Another common filmic device is to have testimonial witnesses walk around sites and locations of biographical relevance, for instance childhood streets or the remnants of a concentration camp (as in Claude Lanzmann's *Shoah*). Moreover, testimonial witnesses could also be incorporated into the film by having them speak the voice-over commentary.

125 For instance, the use of tears has become a conventional means to evoke empathy among the audience members.

(1989) or Errol Morris' *The Thin Blue Line* (1988).[126] Like these films *The Alcohol Years* questions the truth claims of the witness accounts. It sets out "to document the witness, the witnesses' memory of events, and the transmission of this memory – not the events", as James E. Young (1988, 166) claims in another context. Rather than taking the narratives of the interviewees for granted, Morley's film explores the power relations at work in the mediation of cultural memory. By constructing herself as an absence, the film's protagonist Carol Morley becomes the film's 'slippery signifier' exposing the patriarchal discourses which run through the recollections and in which Morley's sexual activity is pathologised while she is described as a 'freak'. As Fiona Morrow (2000) sums up: "The film pushes even the most liberated among us to confront our own boundaries of what is, and is not, acceptable behaviour." As such, Morley's film reflects on the construction of cultural memory by pointing at the power structures involved in carving out a discursive space for the versions of the past being remediated. *The Alcohol Years* also points at the questions of who has the prerogative of definition over the past and whose versions will be circulated. The seriality of the witness accounts does not represent a polyphony of narratives, but foregrounds how the versions echo each other through their constant repetition of patriarchal views on female sexuality.

The film's feminist perspective foregrounds the construction of hegemonic cultural memory with its inherent male homosociality, its stereotypical representation of women as wives, girlfriends or groupies, and its heteronormative stance. Instead of offering a "herstory" which would add yet another recollection of the past to the patriarchal "master narrative", an approach typical for accounts on women in rock music[127], Carol Morley's film sets out to deconstruct hegemonic pop-historiography. In avoiding essentialist subject positions the film addresses the modes of exclusion prevalent in post-punk historiography. It shows how cultural memory is constructed as a homosocial (male) sphere, marginalising norm-critical and non-heteronormative practices. Offering a place for both the enunciation of bisexuality and of non-normative female sexual behaviour, such as often changing sexual partners, the film carves out a discursive space for non-hegemonic articulations of sexuality. *The Alcohol Years* is both an intervention into the audiovisual archive of the city and part of the retro culture around the memorialisation of 1980s Manchester.

---

126 Bill Nichols would term these films 'reflexive filmmaking' or 'performative filmmaking' (see Nichols 2001). However, my goal is not to sort films into already established categories. For a critique of Nichols' classification see Bruzzi (2000, 2006).
127 See, for example Gaar 1992.

3.2.3 Translating cultural memory: gentrification and subcultural nostalgia

The example of The *Alcohol Years* points at the gendered power dimensions inherent in the construction of a city's cultural memory.[128] The film's feminist approach challenges the representation of hegemonic masculinities prevalent in filmic acts of remembrance. As such Morley's film stands not only in contrast to the male flâneries of Patrick Keiller's *London* (1994) and *Robinson in Space* (1997) and to the male gay perspective in Terence Davies' *Of Time and the City* (2008), the director's autobiographical elegy on the Liverpool of the 1950s and 1960s. Each of these films intervenes into the city's audiovisual archive by expanding and reworking it. Along with other remediations they become plurimedia constellations which create a psychogeography of the city. This mapping of the city is accomplished through place-making via travel guides, city tours, audio walks, tourist amateur photography, selfies in front of iconic buildings, but also through fan culture, such as uploads on YouTube or the practice of sharing digital memories of the city on Flickr or Instagram. In the following paragraphs I would like to look at the multidirectionality of the cultural memory of a city. I will examine remediation as a project of place-making and its role for the city's culture-led regeneration. Thereby, I will keep a critical eye on the way Manchester's post-punk memories are appropriated by neoliberal politics of city branding.

Today, Manchester is promoted as "the rock'n'goal capital of the world!"[129]. This slogan draws on the heritage of popular culture the city is known for: music and football. Leaving the aspect of football aside, one could say that Manchester epitomizes the kind of music city which we find in Liverpool in the early 1960s, in Seattle's 90s grunge, in 1960s Motown Detroit, in 1990s Bristol with the Bristol sound of *Massive Attack*, *Portishead* and *Tricky*. In all of these cities the cultural memory of the city's musical past creates a spatial-temporal dimension which in turn contributes to merging past and present and which develops a certain sense of locality for a music culture with a transnational reception. Through countless remediations Manchester's local music culture has been fashioned in opposition to London's political and economic power. These rhetorics can be found in many books and films on post-punk Manchester in which this scene is described as a subculture inspired by punk's do-it-yourself spirit, opposing the commercialism

---

128 Moreover, all of these films construct whiteness as hegemonic. A notable exception would be Reece Auguiste's *Twilight City* (1988) in which the racial dimension of urban mapping is addressed. See Eshun 2004a who proposes to read *Twilight City*, a collaborative project by the Black Audio Film Collective, as a filmic psychogeography of London.
129 http://www.prideofmanchester.com/ (19 November 2010).

of London's big record labels. When analysing the way these discourses have developed over the years, we can observe that they have come to take on the characteristics of a rock museum, which Simon Reynolds describes as presenting "music with the battle lines erased, everything wrapped up in a warm blanket of acceptance and appreciation" (Reynolds 2011, 7). In contrast, Hebdige has famously claimed that the emergence of subcultures "has signalled in a spectacular fashion the breakdown of consensus in the post-war period." (Hebdige 1996, 17). Thus, the impact of retro culture and nostalgia on cultural memory has re-established the consensus previously challenged by the diversity of subculture.

The notion of "a warm blanket of acceptance and appreciation" (Reynolds 2011, 7) can be seen in the use of the pop cultural heritage for re-branding the city. Internal conflicts are set aside in favour of creating an "imagined community" (Anderson 1991).[130] Dave Haslam's account *Manchester, England. The story of the pop cult city*, originally published in 1999, is in itself part of the discourse on Manchester's rebirth after its industrial decline. He describes how Manchester, "the first industrial city in the world" (Haslam 1999, x), "known for two things: pop music and football" (Haslam 1999, xxv), has changed from an industrial to a creative city, from Cottonopolis to Madchester. In the introductory chapter "Manchester: Past Imperfect, Present Tense, Future Uncertain" Haslam (2000, xi) anthropomorphises the city when stating: "Manchester, like England, is now re-creating itself, looking for a new role, a life without manufacturing industry. Like a middle-aged man made redundant after a lifetime in a factory, Manchester is either facing years drawing charity, welfare and government handouts, or it's going to retrain, reorganise, and find something to keep it occupied." Through this rhetorical device the city's transcultural complexity becomes unified and homogenized. Benedict Anderson's notion of the "imagined community", in being translated from a national into a transcultural framework, offers a useful narrative formula – or premediation – to be employed for the purposes of city branding.

Drawing on the works by Jane Jacobs on neighbourhoods and Sharon Zukin on New York's loft culture during the 1980s, Thomas Elsaesser (2005, 85) defines city branding as part of cultural clustering and its interaction between culture and commerce "in today's mixed economy of leisure, culture and creativity", with a tendency to "re-valorise location and emplacement". Renewal and regeneration of inner cities and industrial areas are "to infuse new life into the urban

---

130 See also Redfern (2005, 286) who has pointed out how the region has increasingly been conceptualised as a cultural space and a state of mind creating relationships between groups and places.

fabric (often neglected over the previous half century, or victim of the private motor car, the suburbs and centralized planning)" (Elsaesser 2005, 85). As Elsaesser has shown, former industrial cities such as Rotterdam have been relaunched as post-industrial, cultural cities, for example by positioning themselves as capitals of cultures or by becoming the site of international film festivals. Other cities, such as Liverpool, have instead used their musical heritage of The Beatles and Merseybeat for city branding (see Cohen 2007; Roberts 2012b). The cultural memory of 1980s and 90s Manchester has been utilized in order to relaunch the city as modern and innovative, drawing on both nostalgia and the current trend towards retro culture. As Redfern (2005, 290) states: "The physical landscape of the city was transformed through the regeneration of declining industrial areas as rehearsal spaces, performances spaces and nightclubs (e. g., the Haçienda, Sankey's Soap), design and retail spaces (e. g., Affleck's Palace), or as clearly defined cultural areas (e. g., the "Northern Quarter)." Instead of being limited to the regeneration of urban space, city branding also exploits the 'cultural capital' (Bourdieu) the city has accumulated via remediating its cultural memory. Remediated local music history, for instance, is used as a way to shape a cultural memory of the city. In this process transnational popular music becomes narrowed down to a cultural memory rooted in a site-specific locality and a specific region with the aim to attract international visitors or global investors. Popular music heritage is spatially embedded in order to relaunch Manchester as a city of culture. While Brabazon (2005) perceives Manchester as "a touristic musical space that is able to market its past", Bottà (2006) claims that efforts to use popular music for the purpose of city branding "have often failed or have even been harmful." (Bottà 2006, 122) However, I am not interested in whether Manchester's strategies of city branding and cultural clustering strategies are successful or not – what is crucial here is to examine how cultural memory translates into different contexts.

Manchester's past fame as an industrial city declined gradually from the 1960s to the 1980s. Ironically enough, the IRA bombing in 1996, devastating great parts of the city centre, created new opportunities for city planning. Since the mid-1990s huge investments have been made and cultural attractions led to an increase in tourism. For our purposes of discussing the way transcultural memory travels, Justin O'Connor's and Derek Wynne's (1996) findings can be useful. For instance, the narrative formula used in relaunching the city shifted the emphasis from industrial to urbanistic innovation, employing popular culture as a symbol of vibrancy and creativity. It is based on long standing narratives of Manchester as the first global city, as entrepreneurial and open to change. In order to coordinate such efforts the agency 'Marketing Manchester' was founded, a private-public partnership of the City Council and Manchester

Airport (Haslam 2000), aiming to attract investors and tourists. "A Manchester brand identity had been created in 1998" (Julier 2005, 881), commissioned by 'Marketing Manchester'. This brand identity included "a 'Manchester font' that was intended to reflect Manchester's unrivalled skill at merging the old and the new, from Stockport's towering railway viaduct to the new, organic form of Urbis" (Julier 2005, 881). As the website of 'Marketing Manchester' states: "We aim to develop the Manchester city-region into a leading leisure, learning and business destination for domestic and international visitors, enhance the national and international reputation of the city-region and promote sustainable economic development and growth."[131] In 2004 Peter Saville, co-founder of Factory Records who had designed the iconic record covers for Joy Division and New Order, became the creative director of the City of Manchester. Saville's tasks included the conceptualisation of international exhibitions and festivals, the city's cultural strategy and the design for Metrolink. As Julier maintains, "Saville is implicated into the mythology of Manchester's most-known popular cultural history" (Julier 2005, 882). In the same year, in 2004, Urbis also showcased a retrospective of Peter Saville's works. The exhibition space Urbis, funded by the Millennium Commission and Manchester City Council, was part of the regeneration project in the aftermath of the 1996 IRA bombing. "Saville's hand is deployed across the city's designscape, not just through the Urbis exhibition but, for example, through his historical association with Factory Records, to inflect this tradition of modernity with the desired notions of 'attitude' and 'edge'." (Julier 2005, 882) This personal continuity from post-punk Manchester to contemporary city branding is also epitomized in Tony Wilson, founder of Factory records and the Haçienda, who was a board member of "Elevate East Lancashire", "one of the government's 'market renewal' agencies" (Minton 2009, 37).

Independent culture, ultimately commodified, has been incorporated into neoliberal ideas of the creative city, as launched prominently by Richard Florida (2002) in his *The Rise of the Creative Class*. According to Richard Florida, in the first decade of the new millennium Manchester became the most creative and enterprising city in the UK (Minton 2009, 39). Another potential factor in city branding is fan culture. Even if individual fans might oppose gentrification, fan culture is complicit in neoliberal politics of culture-led regeneration.

Fan culture involves a number of place-making projects which contribute to the mapping of urban space. City walks and tours visit sites and locations which have played a role in the history of Manchester's music scene. For instance Inspiral Carpets drummer Craig Gill is now offering tours promoted by the official

---

[131] http://www.marketingmanchester.com/who-we-are.aspx (8 June 2014).

website for Manchester tourism.¹³² His company, Manchester Music Tours, nominated for *The Tourism Star* award (Manchester Tourism Awards 2012), was founded in 2005.¹³³ What had initially started as a walking tour to significant sites of the local music scene has since developed into five driving tours, four of them centering on individual bands (*The Smiths, Joy Division, Oasis, The Stone Roses*) *while a fifth is dedicated to the label Factory Records. On the website the tours are promoted as follows:* "[Y]ou can now see and experience all the sights of the city and beyond that inspired the Manchester music scene, hear how the city has produced so many great bands over the last 40 years it has become the envy of the world."¹³⁴ Fan culture, triggered by nostalgia and 'retromania', both relocates cultural memories in the city space, but also dislocates or deterritorializes them. Remediated transcultural memories oscillate between locatedness and deterritorialization. This oscillation is characteristic for digital memories.

Fan practice on the internet, for instance the sharing of photographs or videos, creates transnational digital memories which in turn contribute to urban mapping. They create a psychogeography of the city which eventually evolves into a chronotope. One example of such a remediation which shows how urban mapping and cultural memory are related is the case of the Salford Lad's Club. A photograph of The Smiths' by Stephen Wright, which shows the band standing in front of the Salford Lad's Club, at the entrance to the red brick building, was used on the inner sleeve of the band's single "The Queen is Dead" in 1986 and has since achieved iconic status. A quick search on Google reveals innumerable amateur photographs of tourists and Smiths-fans posing in front of the building, almost all of them imitating the camera angle of the original shot. The motif is so embedded within the cultural memory of his generation that even David Cameron tried to profit from its popularity by posing in front of the building during his election campaign before he became the British prime minister.¹³⁵

Photographs, such as the amateur shots of the Salford Lad's Club or the legendary photographs by Kevin Cummins, published in the music press and on record sleeves during the late 1970s and 1980s, have created a psychogeography of

---

132 http://www.visitmanchester.com/articles/video/craig-gill-mcr11-interview/ (8 June 2014).
133 http://www.manchestermusictours.com/ (8 June 2014).
134 http://www.manchestermusictours.com/about-us (8 June 2014).
135 After the incident The Smiths' guitarist Johnny Marr publicly protested on Twitter against Cameron's effort to profit from the pop cultural memory related to the Salford Lad's Club. http://www.theguardian.com/music/2010/dec/06/morrissey-johnny-marr-david-cameron (23 July 2014).

the city (see Cummins 2009).[136] These images create an imaginary cartography of the city's subcultural spaces, constructing a transnational memory of urban spaces. However, not only visual culture has contributed to the mapping of the city – the same can be said for songs and their various remediations as well as narratives and mythmaking evolving around specific geographical places. According to Haslam, during the late 1980s the Madchester era's "thriving sub-culture" epitomized a crucial turning point for the rebuilding and refashioning of Manchester, symbolising that "the city was no longer carrying the baggage of a hundred and fifty years of preconceptions, about the weather, the environment, the misery. Manchester's talent [...] embodied an attitude which struck a chord worldwide." (Haslam 2000, 250). In contrast, the city's official heritage politics of turning Castlefield into the UK's first "Urban Heritage Park" is described by Haslam as "death sentence heritage. It was as if we were all destined to no better future than re-creating a tourist version of the old days; Manchester as hygienic industrial theme park" (Haslam 2000, 250). Of course, we have to read Haslam's statement as highly performative in the sense that he is trying to contribute to a new 'master narrative' of Manchester as the "pop cult city", as his book is subtitled. In his evaluation of the development he characterizes official heritage politics as inefficient, while the true impulses for the city's redevelopment stem from its subcultures: "It has now become accepted that shopping and tourism have key roles in the future prosperity of the city. For the young, especially, Manchester is becoming a must-see city, a cult pop city, and it was probably the Madchester era that brought the first big influx of tourists." (Haslam 2000, 254) For instance, a concert by the Stone Roses with an audience of almost thirty thousand drew people from the whole of Europe and overseas. While Haslam's book was written before the massive Manchester 'memory boom', it is interesting to see how the chronotope of Manchester music city has been broadened out from 1990s "Madchester" to include late 1970s punk and 1980s postpunk. According to Redfern (2005, 303) *24 Hour Party People* "sees the Manchester punk and rave scene as building on the city's proud history, and specifically demonstrates an awareness of this history. It seeks to build on a tradition of progressiveness that is projected as the antithesis of 'death sentence heritage'." Redfern describes *24 Hour Party People* as "a nostalgic tour through the 'ripped backsides' of Hulme, Little Hulton, and Castlefield, and the film celebrates the

---

[136] Kevin Cummins' work "Manchester. Looking for the Light through the Pouring Rain" (2009) has been marketed as the "definitive photographic history of Manchester pop from 1976 to today."

marginal status of these places beyond London, but also beyond the official discourses of nostalgia and heritage in the North" (Redfern 2005, 300).

Furthermore, these findings underline the need to rethink the notion of space as culturally constructed and therefore as a *product* of cultural memory. Space is not just "out there", waiting to be mediated and memorialized, but it is constructed through a variety of place-making projects. Manchester's brand identity could profit from the "subcultural city branding" conducted via the self-fashioning of 1980s post-punk culture. On the one hand, as Redfern points out, Manchester developed its "own cultural networks with the creation of independent record labels, fanzines, and venues that deliberately steered clear of the mainstream, and, in doing so, created a powerful voice for those outside London" (Redfern 2005, 289). London was "associated with an artistic conservatism and political Conservatism that Manchester subverts" (Redfern 2005, 299–300).[137] Manchester's culture-led urban regeneration draws on long-standing narrative formula which premediate future remediations. The North (of England) has become a 'mnemotope' (Erll 2010, 309) through *longue durée* processes and plurimedia networks of cultural memory, from Elizabeth Gaskell's novel *North and South* via the works of the "Angry Young Men", the working-class writers in the Northwest, to the television series *Coronation Street* and *24 Hour Party People*. Such overlapping references, layered like a palimpsest and encompassing different geographical spheres, provide narrative schemata for future remediations. Premediations were discursive concepts of 'Northernness', based on the North-South-divide. Drawing on these discourses in the process of city branding allowed Manchester, as Redfern (2005, 290) states, "to re-create itself as an innovative centre of culture that was modernising and forward-looking rather than provincial." The premediations were reworked, and the notion of 'Northernness', for example, "was refracted through an avant-gardism to create not a nostalgic view of the North as 'working-class', but as [...] 'working-class bohemianism'" (Redfern 2005, 290–291). This interaction of premediation and remediation shows how certain narrative templates are used, but instead of remaining unchanged and stable, they are reworked in the process of remediation. At the same time these premediations contribute to mapping the region and function as a method of place-making.

Just like other media such as photography, travel writing, biographies or songs, filmmaking is a method of place-making. In *24 Hour Party People* Manchester is represented as a cultural region, Redfern argues. "This [music]

---

[137] This development could be observed in other cities as well, such as Liverpool and Coventry, for example.

scene is associated with an ambivalent attitude to Northern identity, with new cultural spaces in the city that develop free of the centralising influences of the London-based music industry, and where the distinction between producers and consumers of cultural products is blurred." (Redfern 2005, 287). In contrast, *The Alcohol Years* does not contribute to place-making projects which can be employed for contemporary city planning. The contemporary footage employed in the film does not evoke the iconic images of Manchester constantly remediated in a plurality of media. Instead, the Mancunian street scenes could easily take place anytime and anywhere and point at the contemporary relevance of the film's feminist criticism: nothing seems to have changed.

While not much seems to have changed when it come to the representation of gender, the representation of sexuality in the cultural memory of the city might currently undergo some alterations. Manchester illustrates a trend within city planning in which previously marginalised LGBT memories are being employed in city branding. According to Richard Florida's study on urban regeneration, *The Rise of the Creative Class* (2002), creativity and a good 'gay index' prove fertile ground for the city's economic growth. The gay index indicates "an area's openness to different kinds of people and ideas" (Florida 2002, 255–258). Manchester's queer cultural memory has long been absent from the locations associated with post-punk memory, such as the Haçienda. Despite the fact that the nightclub "Flesh" at the Haçienda played a pioneering role for Manchester's LGBT culture during the 1990s, with its slogans "Queer as Fuck" and "Practice makes Pervert" being advertised citywide, the cultural memory of LGBT culture is not located around the iconic post-punk spaces, but around Canal Street.[138] In the memory of the city, LGBT memories have long been relegated to the Canal Street area, which has become immensely popularised (and mainstreamed) through TV series such as *Bob and Rose* (ITV 2001) and *Queer as Folk* (Channel 4, 1999–2000, since then also remade into a US version).[139]

It seems that the discourse on "Gaychester" within Manchester's post-punk memory had narrowed down during the first decade of the millennium before opening up again only a couple of years ago. While in his 1999 book *Manchester*

---

[138] For LGBT memories of the Haçienda, see the website http://www.lgf.org.uk/news/Haçienda-memories/ (25 July 2012).

[139] Today, Manchester's "gay village" around Canal Street is one of the city's major tourist attractions and marketed by the city as such. This was not always the case. During the 1980s the former red light district was subjected to massive surveillance by the police. The attitude towards LGBT culture only changed during the 1990s, when Canal Street was recognized by Manchester City Council.

England Haslam (2000, 199–201) briefly mentions the resurgence of a gay scene in the early 1990s, it then seems to have gradually disappeared from the city's subcultural memory for over a decade. Only recently memory projects of queer Manchester surfaced with the "Queer Noise" project on the website of the Manchester District Music Archive, introduced by highly influential music journalist Jon Savage.[140] Furthermore, in 2013 the Museum of Science and Industry, which also owns the archive of Factory Records, showcased the community exhibition "Behind The Scene; Stories from Manchester's LGBT Communities". It is one of the paradoxes that, until now, LGBT memories have hardly had any discursive space in subcultural memory, while they have been smoothly included into the neoliberal repurposing of memory for city branding.[141] These paradoxes cannot be solved in this study, but call for further examination. The cultural memory of 1980s post-punk has had the tendency to close rather than open up any discursive spaces for the construction of memories by feminists, queers or Black or Asian Britons. Carol Morley's *The Alcohol Years* is a notable exception.

As we have seen, the cultural memory of post-punk Manchester translates and travels into different context. However, this development should not be perceived as a linear or even teleological process. The cultural memory of post-punk was not at first a subcultural memory which then entered the mainstream. Instead both developments coincided, creating a tension in which the cultural memory of 1980s Manchester and its retro culture would engage with the discourse of urban regeneration in various ways. The example of such commodification of subcultural aesthetics and memory shows that popular memories are not automatically subversive, but can become part of a city's neoliberal regeneration politics by being incorporated into the local heritage industry. Cultural practice, once perceived as oppositional or alternative, is never fixed and stable, but can be translated and appropriated for a variety of purposes. Transcultural memory travels not only in a geographical sense, but also between different discursive framings.

3.2.4 Conclusion: multidirectional memories and the notion of transculturality

The case of post-punk Manchester shows that popular, subcultural or countermemory is not automatically emancipatory, but can be translated, transformed

---

140 http://www.mdmarchive.co.uk/exhibition/id/77/QUEER_NOISE.html (8 June 2014).
141 The tendency to include gay memories into the official narrative of the city can also be observed in Liverpool, where Terence Davies' film *Of Time and the City* was commissioned as part of the European City of Culture celebrations in 2008.

and appropriated. For instance, memory can be translated from being a subcultural memory into becoming an official one, utilized for neoliberal city planning. The case confirms the assumption, now established in cultural memory studies, that memory does not belong to specific groups alone. Instead, it can be adapted, reworked and appropriated within multiple contexts. These memories are travelling memories, both in a geographical sense (they are transnational and are reworked by global audiences), but also in the sense that they are adapted into a new discursive framework, that of the city's neoliberal regeneration politics, which incorporates them into the local heritage industry. In view of Richard Florida's notion of the 'gay index' one might even find the neoliberal discourse more open to the inclusion of LGBT memories than the subcultural independent discourse which excludes or marginalizes female and queer participants. The transcultural memories emerging around the same chronotopes are topicalised in different, albeit often overlapping, manners for various purposes and in a number of contexts: as forms of nostalgia, retro culture, as generational memory (plus personal memory and communicative memory), as 'official' memory in the context of city branding, as cultural memory connected to specific urban spaces (for the purposes of tourism, for example in the form of travel guides on The Smiths' Manchester). Therefore the multidirectionality of cultural memory challenges the division between "official" and "subcultural" or "counter"-memory.

Transculturality is defined by the routes, not the roots of cultural memory. Its various translations and appropriations turn cultural memory into transcultural memory. Merely using the concept of 'transcultural memory' to refer to national or ethnic belonging would reduce its possibilities in an essentialist manner – it would rather turn around and undermine its original intention, which was to get away from the limitations of a national perspective, prevalent in a lot of research within memory studies departing from Nora's notion of the *lieux de mémoire*. Rather than using the concept of 'transcultural memory' in reference to transnational memory, including different nationalities or ethnicities, this chapter has shown how the term can be employed to designate different cultural practices within the same (g)local space. This mode of referring to the processes of translation and adaptation of cultural memory would not run the risk of essentialising groups of people, but could rather allow for a critical perspective taking the intersections of power relations into account. Categories such as gender, race, class, sexuality and ability could be included in the analysis without ending up in essentialist notions of identity.

4. Reworking the archive

The aim of this chapter is to highlight the importance of the archive for cultural memory studies. In merging theorizations of media specificity of the archive and its function as an instrument of power it attempts to show the discursive aspect of the mediation of memory and its media specificity. The following two case studies examine the possibilities of contemporising and reworking the archive. The first study addresses the interdependence of the archive's materiality and discursivity by examining the work and contemporary archival practice of video collectives. The second example reflects on filmmaking as an intervention into the audiovisual archive, both by carving out traces of the past and by recoding images with the help of new contextualisations. Both sub-chapters give rise to questions of canon formation and film historiography, thereby reconsidering Aleida Assmann's distinction between 'storage archive' and 'functional archive' (Assmann 1999). In 4.1 the role of the curator as a 'memory agent' will be highlighted whereas chapter 4.2 focuses on the filmmaking process as a theoretical tool for a critical investigation into archival stock. Artists use archive footage as vehicles for exploring the relation of past and present and for negotiating cultural memory. Their work can address and foreground the "problematic of relying upon or understanding an archive collection as a reliable or complete source of historical or contemporary 'evidence'" (Lanyon 2006, 4). Such a critical perspective on the archive can be found in *Handsworth Songs* (Akomfrah, 1986) by the Black Audio Film Collective which will be analysed in chapter 4.2. I will show how the film's self-reflexive aesthetics entails a number of functions which could be conceptualised in view of an anti-essentialist perspective within cultural memory studies. The essay film as an archival intervention shows the capacity of self-reflexive filmmaking to foreground the politics and history of representation and to address gaps and absences in the master narrative of the nation. Therefore, it can be regarded as an epistemological tool investigating the workings of cultural memory and its mediation.

Filmmaking as a way of reworking the audiovisual archive is not a recent phenomenon, but a practice going back to early compilation films as well as the tradition of experimental filmmaking (Sjöberg 2001; Blümlinger 2009). Sjöberg (2001) regards compilation films as "performative archives", whereas Blümlinger uses the term "second hand cinema" for describing the practice of appropriating archival footage. From early cinema's recycling of stock footage – for example Edwin S. Porter's use of Edison stock footage for the fire scenes in *The Life of an American Fireman* (1902), mentioned by Jay Leyda (1964) in his seminal study on the compilation film[142] – to the collages of stock footage and/or found footage in experimental and avant-garde filmmaking, archival footage has been employed for a variety of purposes: it has been a means of authentication as well as a way to foreground the politics of representation. Compilation films or "second hand films", from Esfir Shub's *The Fall of the Romanov Dynasty* (1927) or Dziga Vertov's *The Man With a Movie Camera* (1929) to the found footage works by Matthias Müller (*Home Stories*, 1990) or Lisl Ponger (*Passagen*, 1996), can offer various forms of self-reflexive investigation into the medium film and its capacity to capture 'reality'. Throughout the history of filmmaking the positivist truth claim of film images has been challenged. For some filmmakers, the use of film images for the purposes of propaganda resulted in a disbelief in the image and its alleged status of visible evidence. Moreover, the question of how atrocities such as the Holocaust could be represented gave rise to aesthetic as well as social and ethical considerations. During the 1950s European filmmakers experimented with essayistic approaches to filmmaking: French auteurs such as Alain Resnais (*Night and Fog*, 1955), Chris Marker, Agnès Varda and Jean-Luc Godard in turn inspired German filmmakers such as Alexander Kluge, Harun Farocki or Hartmut Bitomsky. Their films, setting out to interrogate the image and the politics of image making, have been conceptualised as essay films. Such an approach to filmmaking as a theoretical investigation can be found in the works by two Black British film collectives whose members embarked on their filmmaking careers in 1980s London: Sankofa and the Black Audio Film Collective. The latter's seminal 1986 essay film *Handsworth Songs* will serve as an example for filmmaking as an intervention into the audio-visual archive.

Theorising about issues of representation, memory, the film's materiality and the archive via filmmaking is characteristic for the essay film, a term embraced by Sergej Eisenstein, Hans Richter and Pier Paolo Pasolini alike and theorized among others by Christa Blümlinger (1992), Thomas Tode (1992), Laura Rascaroli (2009) and Tim Corrigan (2011).[143] While it has been discussed to what extent the essay film can be regarded as a specific genre, it is generally agreed upon that it forms a distinct category.[144] Despite its refusal to be pigeonholed, the essay film, paradoxically enough, has more often than not been domi-

---

142 See Blümlinger 2009.
143 The most recent contribution is the edited collection by Kramer and Tode 2011.
144 Despite their transgressive form, essay films are often conceptualized as documentaries, both in academia and, for example, in film festival programming.

nated by an auteurist perspective, focussing on textual analysis.[145] So far, theoretical studies of the essay film have been a fairly new phenomenon in an Anglo-American context, while looking back at a longer tradition in France and Germany.[146] The dominant focus on French and German filmmaking has had crucial consequences for the conceptualisation of the essay film: studies on essay films are to a great extent guided by the notion of the auteur. Film critic Frieda Grafe has called the essay film "documentary filmmaking's auteur film"[147]. Indeed, both auteur theory and essay film theory draw on the same text for legitimising their approach: Alexandre Astruc's 1948 "The Birth of the New Avant-Garde: The Caméra-Stylo" (Astruc 1999), in which Astruc conceptualises cinema as an art form with the same importance as painting and the novel. Comparable to literary texts, film language offers "a form in which and by which the artist can express his [sic!] thoughts, however abstract they may be, or translate his obsessions exactly as he does in the contemporary essay or novel" (Astruc 1999, 65). Thus, the cinema as an art form can express abstract ideas and is not limited to the 'visible world'. Astruc's pupil André Bazin became another influence for both auteur theory and essay film theory, for the latter especially through his text on Chris Marker's *Letter from Siberia* (1958), reprinted in Blümlinger and Wulff (1992), in which he conceptualises Marker's film as an essay film.

The common theoretical ground which inspired both essay film theory and auteur theory influenced the formation of essay film research during the decades: the auteurist perspective on the essay film has led to a focus on white male filmmaking, thereby perpetuating Romanticism's patriarchal, logocentric myth of the (male) genius. As a result, works by female filmmakers have been sidelined. Moreover, a predominantly white perspective in essay film research

---

145 However, Christa Blümlinger's 2011 article (in Kramer and Tode 2011) paves the way for a new perspective on the essay film, when she examines the shift from the black box to the white cube in Harun Farocki's installation *Gegen-Musik (Contre-Chant, 2004)*. With her focus on exhibition practice Blümlinger broadens the scope from textuality to aspects of production, distribution (for example programming and the role of film festivals) and exhibition.

146 For German-speaking scholars Christa Blümlinger's and Constantin Wulff's anthology *Schreiben, Bilder Sprechen* (1992) has proved to be the most influential conceptualisation of the essay film – along with Christina Scherer's ground-breaking study on memory, *Erinnerung im Essayfilm* (2001). Recent efforts at a systematic approach to the essay film are Laura Rascaroli's *The Personal Camera* (2009) as well as Timothy Corrigan's *The Essay Film* (2011) and the edited collection *Der Essayfilm*, which includes both English and German-language contributions (see Kramer and Tode 2011).

147 ["der Autorenfilm des Dokumentargenres"] (Frieda Grafe in Blümlinger and Wulff 1992, 139).

has tended to exclude diasporic filmmakers or filmmaking from countries outside Western Europe. Furthermore, the auteur perspective with its focus on a single filmmaker has also lead to a marginalisation of the works by film collectives. Therefore I suggest to expand the concept of filmmaking as an epistemological tool away from the "usual suspects", such as Jean-Luc Godard, Chris Marker or Harun Farocki, to the works of Hito Steyerl, Angela Melitopoulos and Petra Bauer, Yvonne Rainer, Chantal Akerman or Trinh T. Minh-ha as well as the works by Sankofa or the Black Audio Film Collective. In fact, the essayistic works by the Black Audio Film Collective, such as *Handsworth Songs* or *Twilight City*, can be regarded as a predecessors of recent works by Harun Farocki (*Respite*, 2007), Hito Steyerl (*November*, 2004), Philip Scheffner (*Halfmoon Files*, 2007) or The Otolith Group (*Otolith I–III*, 2003–2009).[148]

In the following I will examine *Handsworth Songs* from a perspective of 'strategic auteurism', adapting Gayatri Spivak's notion of 'strategic essentialism' (Spivak 2006). Conceptualising a film as an essay film can liberate it from a reductive critical reception as an expression of a minoritarian position, for instance being categorised as a social-realist representation of Black experiences. A director's status as an auteur is still crucial for his or her critical reception, and as a result, for canon formation and for being included in film historiography. The auteur perspective can also be employed in a strategic manner, I argue, for the purpose of a 'strategic auteurism', even if the author, as in this case, is a collective which defies essentialist notions of community, as I will show.

We can currently observe a tendency in the funding politics of digitization whereby the focus is placed on analogue film gauge, such as 35 mm films, in favour of the different video formats. The notion of film heritage needs to reconsider its criteria of selecting the films preserved for future generations. The question therefore is how to make the notion of film heritage more polyvocal in terms of contents and filmmakers as well as with regards to different formats. Video, I argue in this study, as a media specific form of minor cinema, contains the cultural memory of a variety of alternative media practice. Today video is not only threatened by material decay, it currently tends to be forgotten by audiences, curators, programmers, by restorers, official funders, government politics and by municipal cultural politics alike. The first chapter (4.1.) argues for the need to preserve the cultural heritage of video. As Giovanna Fossati states, the digitization of video tapes is both urgent and relatively easy to accomplish: "the quality of a video image is relatively low and can be digitized without any loss and at a

---

[148] Also the Sankofa films *Territories* and *Looking for Langston* could be conceptualised as essay films.

reasonably low cost." (Fossati 2009, 68). However, as the chapter will show, not only these economical aspects are crucial. In the wake of digitization, preservational politics have increasingly been transformed into politics of access. Therefore, archives need to reflect upon their choices of selection and critically re-examine the role of the curator(s) in this process.

Drawing on the example of the practice of video collectives, the first case study looks at the impact of media specificity and its discursive frameworks on memory. It also addresses the repercussions for the works' canonization, their role within film historiography and their way of challenging the notion of the auteur. To a large extent, collective filmmaking practice in Germany is still unresearched. This is all the more astonishing since independent filmmakers established a nationwide network of film and video workshops in the Federal Republic of Germany, Austria and Switzerland during the 1970s and 1980s. An important context was the burgeoning social movements of the New Left, such as the workers' movement, the peace movement, the women's movement and the struggles against nuclear power. The video collectives aimed at intervening in ongoing political conflicts, at empowering the 'people affected', appropriating Sergej Tretyakov's notion of operative art practice, thereby creating a counter public sphere as theorized by Oskar Negt and Alexander Kluge (see Negt and Kluge 1993). In their attempt to create a new, anti-bourgeois aesthetics, the filmmakers drew on avant-garde practice, experimental filmmaking traditions as well as influences from *agit-prop*, Direct Cinema and *cinéma vérité*.

During the 1970s the workshops would deliberately use video technology instead of film in order to distance themselves from the aesthetics of conventional TV documentary and from the dependencies that arise out of TV funding.[149] The comparably cheap storage medium video allowed them to copy tapes, to disseminate and archive them to a greater extent than had been possible before. By 1983 over 40 media cooperatives and video groups existed in the Germanophone countries. In Hamburg the most important ones were the *Medienpädagogikzentrum (mpz)*, *die thede* and *bildwechsel*, outside Hamburg the most influential were the *Medienwerkstatt Freiburg* and the *Videoladen Zurich*. They were creating, distributing and archiving hundreds of videos.[150] In this respect the video collectives can be regarded as predecessors of contemporary activists' films on *Indymedia* or *YouTube*. Today, the thousands of videos and films stored in the

---

[149] According to Rees (1999, 88) the British workshops did not conceptualize themselves in opposition to television.
[150] Other groups existed in Berlin, Bremen, Hannover, Duisburg, Essen, Oberhausen, Dortmund, Bielefeld, Cologne, Wuppertal, Eppelheim, Stuttgart, Freiburg, Nuremberg, Offenbach, Erlangen and Vienna (cf. *Medienzentren und Videogruppen in der BRD*, eds. 1984).

archives of the media collectives contain the cultural and collective memory of the social movements of recent decades and, as such, form an important source for historians, political scientists and sociologists, and not least for research into film studies or media and communication studies. Both the state of the tapes as well as their contents opens up questions of the archive. While the tapes can be said to contain the cultural memory of the social movements of the last 30 years, the question remains: what if this cultural memory is falling apart?

4.1 Archival interventions: excavating the cultural memory of video art and activism[151]

While video was promoted as the 'mobile memory' during the 1970s, many video activists had to face the fact that the videotapes disintegrated much sooner than expected. In the early 1980s the first generation of videotapes produced by brand leader Sony suffered from the 'sticky-tape syndrome'. The tape would disintegrate and jerk during playback in a VCR. To compensate for this, Sony offered the video workshops a cleaning machine to copy the tapes.[152] However, the workshops would not get one machine each, but had to share one among them. During this time-consuming procedure the members of the video collectives selected the tapes that should survive. The workshops were therefore compelled to sort out their stock and to quickly decide which tapes to preserve and which ones to sacrifice and throw away. As a consequence, a large amount of original footage disappeared, for examples hours of uncut material of political discussions that from today's perspective would be regarded as an invaluable historical source. The experimental, self-reflexive video "Aus Lust am Schauen" (dir. Bau and Oppermann 1983), produced by *die thede* film collective, depicts the decay of video material and highlights the impact of material disintegration which will result in the loss of visual information. In foregrounding the materiality of the video tape, "Aus Lust am Schauen", merging art and activism, self-reflexivity and agit-prop, addresses issues of cultural memory and the archive as a discursive construct, but also in terms of media-specificity.

If we perceive the archive as the foundation from which history is being written, the archival holdings of video workshops and film collectives are important

---

[151] An earlier version of this chapter has been published as: "Before YouTube and Indymedia: Cultural memory and the archive of video collectives in Germany in the 1970s and 1980s". *Studies in European Cinema*. Special issue "Film collectives", (8) 3, May 2012, 171–182.

[152] The decay of the videotapes forced several video collectives to change to the more expensive format U-matic.

sources for historians. If these moving images fade away, so does important source material, as Marita Sturken has emphasized: "Without this work we only have the mainstream media's view of a movement that was conceived precisely in opposition to that monolithic view-point" (Sturken 1990, 114). In their attempt to create a counter public sphere, the video collectives gave an alternative view on political events. Therefore, the films and videos created during the 1970s and 1980s are important sources for research, since they give a unique insight into the aesthetics and politics of alternative, independent filmmaking. The works by the video collectives complicate the hegemonic media representation and allow us to get another perspective on political conflicts. Moreover, the production of the workshops and collectives can add to the polyvocality of cultural memory.[153]

As the cultural heritage of video collectives is in danger, reflecting on these aspects has become an urgent, though hitherto neglected question. Today archived videos are facing severe problems concerning preservation: the video tapes slowly disintegrate,[154] formats cannot be played any longer or only on specific machines which are rare and need to be preserved as well (U-matic for example). As Giovanna Fossati has pointed out: "[V]ideo tapes of all sorts are poor preservation carriers as they are much more perishable than film and there is not much that can be done to slow down their decay" (Fossati 2009, 68). As a consequence, the memory of the various media practices of the last decades is fading away. As digitization is costly and time-consuming, many video productions will not survive. This has repercussions not only for (left-wing) historiography, but also for the audiovisual archive. The materiality of the video tapes is one aspect which has repercussions on cultural memory. The other one is related to the concept Aleida Assmann discusses along with the notion of the archive: the canon. Assmann's concept of the 'canon' allows to refracture the discursive and material aspects of the archive into questions of film historiography, the role of the curator, of distribution, exhibition, preservation and funding. Therefore, today's remaining video collectives encounter a number of challenges: the most urgent issue being the restoration and preservation of the decaying analogue video material. Another question to be faced is the aspect of digitization and its need of permanent migration. Would digitization be the solution to ob-

---

[153] I follow Andersson and Sundholm's (2010) usage of the term 'polyvocality', derived from Robert F. Berkhofer and appropriated by Patricia Zimmermann (2007) for her study on the home movie.

[154] The *Kompendium der Bildstörungen beim analogen Video* (Gfeller, et al. 2013, 49) lists twenty-eight image errors in analogue video, for example tape misalignment, loss of colour lock, scratches and tape wear, dihedral maladjustment or crumpled tape.

tain a long-standing preservation of the footage? Nobody knows to what extent digitization might be a better option than analogue stock. Finally, the collectives will have to find ways of transforming the assembled "storage memory" into functional memory again. In this process curatorial decisions have an impact on the dissemination of archival stock.

This chapter is divided into two sections. The first section gives an overview over the practice of three video collectives in Hamburg. Examining the archival practice of three workshops in Hamburg – the mpz (Medienpädagogikzentrum, 1973–), *bildwechsel*, the feminist video workshop and archive for female artists (1979–), and thede (1980–) – the aim is twofold: First I will outline the media specificity of video and its impact on the political and aesthetic practice of the workshops. Rather than delving into textual analysis, I am going to give an overview over the industrial context: the modes of production, distribution and exhibition. Second, I will give an overview over the archival practices of the three workshops. How do they deal with the economics of disappearance? Moreover, this study is a memory work in itself. In highlighting a neglected field within film studies the research process becomes an act of remembrance in itself. Another aim of this section is therefore to contribute to the historiography of these workshops which have been excluded from German film historiography. In doing so, I argue for shifting from a predominantly national towards a transnational perspective. Furthermore, the chapter aims at complicating the division between video art and activism.

The first section also addresses the function of video as a medium. Why was it chosen? How was it used? How were the films distributed and exhibited? Video practice clearly shows the conceptual limitations of a national perspective on film historiography. Video art and activism is a highly transnational practice, involving international collaborations, global inspirations as well as transnational modes of distribution, such as international the role of video and film festivals for the circulation of the works. The chapter shows what impact media specificity has on cultural memory. It then sums up its findings by arguing that the decay of these videos will be an irretrievable loss of important memories which would add new images and perspectives to the visual archive of the 1970s and 1980s. The second section looks at the mnemonic practices of the workshops themselves. How do they try to turn the archives from a 'storage archive' to a 'functional archive' (A. Assmann)? What are the archival practices of preserving, restoring and exhibiting the material? What is the impact of digitization? I will look at today's archival practice, which means my brief overview is limited to the last three or four years, because my focus lies on the possibilities, but also the limitations, of digitization for preserving and distributing alternative memories. This case study examines the aesthetic, political and archival practice of three workshops in Hamburg which still exist: the *mpz/Medienpädagogikzentrum* (*Centre for Media Pedagogy*), the longest-lived video collective in Germany; *bildwechsel*, an umbrella organisation for women in media, culture and art, whose archive is unique throughout the world, and *die thede*, an association of documentary filmmakers.[155]

The following case study of three Hamburg video collectives aims at challenging the dichotomy of art versus politics prevalent in current research on video. In order to bridge the division between experimental/avant-garde and documentary/political filmmaking, the term 'minor cinema', based on the notion of 'minor literature' developed by Deleuze and Guattari (1986) and introduced into film studies by Tom Gunning (1989–1990), proves particularly fruitful. Moreover, the concept of 'minor cinema' is useful since it not only focuses on the films' aesthetics, but includes both the cinematic apparatus and the economic context as well as aspects of distribution and exhibition which will be dealt with in this chapter. In this sense this overview will not offer any textual analysis, but can hopefully provide valuable insights that may prove useful for film and media studies, archivology, archival studies, gender studies, sociology and history alike. While the terminology varies from 'media centre' and 'media group' to 'video workshop', the different collectives, at least initially, aspired to the same ideals: To be politically and economically independent, to guarantee open access to the media, to promote self-activity and self-guided learning, to erase the division of labour in favour of a collective, anti-hierarchical mode of practice, to support the social movements and to take their side (Kinter 1994, 208). Carving out a discursive space for the articulation of otherwise neglected subject positions would be another, more poststructuralist inflected way to describe the ambition of the video workshops. However, their endeavour has so far not been adequately acknowledged in film historiography. This neglect, I argue, has repercussions on future funding policies and is therefore in need of further examination.

---

[155] Other collectives in Hamburg were the *Medienladen*, the *Medienzentrum Fuhlsbüttel*, the *Stadtjournal* and *Video Ex*. Margaret Dickinson distinguishes 'access workshops', such as the London Film-Makers' Co-op from 'collectives' that 'consisted of fewer members who worked together as a team' (Dickinson, 1999: 41). In this understanding, the *Medienladen* (1974–78) can be called an access workshop, while *die thede* would be classified a collective. The *mpz* and *bildwechsel* were both.

4.1.1 The cultural legacy of video collectives: film historiography as memory work

One of the reasons why the cultural memory of the video workshops is in danger is their marginal status in film historiography. Despite their massive output, the independent film and video workshops in Germany have hardly been researched in film studies.[156] The reasons are several: 1) the impact of auteurism, 2) the politics of canon formation, 3) the choice of video and the self-fashioning of the workshops, as well as 4) the lack of access to most of the works. First, in spite of the impact of the New Film History, the notion of the auteur still dominates film historiography, thus sidelining collective filmmaking. The marginalization of collective filmmaking practice is not limited to German film historiography, but also true for Britain and its film collectives, such as Amber, Berwick Street Collective or Cinema Action, to name but a few. In the German case, the auteurist perspective dominating the notion of 'New German Cinema' tends to prevail in film historical accounts. Second, the prevalent mechanisms of canonisation prioritise video art and artists' video over a filmmaking practice considered as activism (cf. Rees 1999, Spielmann 2008). As Marita Sturken sums up: "The marginal way with which the collectives are treated in video history is indicative of the way in which socially concerned work was simply written out of the art-historical agenda for video set forth in its museumization." (Sturken 1990: 113) Third, the workshops themselves contributed to a marginalisation of their work since mainstream media was eyed with suspicion, especially during the 1970s. As *bildwechsel* founder Durbahn (1996) has remarked, positive coverage would have prompted the activists to review their practice. Finally, the lack of research is also due to the limited access to most of the work by video collectives, as the films have only rarely been remediated and hardly ever been released for commercial distribution on video or DVD.[157]

Collective film practice in Germany in the 1970s and 1980s is sidelined in both national and international accounts on experimental or avant-garde filmmaking.[158] In this respect, a lot of research still needs to be done to complicate the predominant focus on the United States and Britain. This overview is a first attempt to map the field. However, a perspective on national cinemas proves only partly useful, I argue, for example as the distribution network also included

---

[156] Exceptions are unpublished degree dissertations, such as Does (1997), or articles by former activists, cf. Stickel (1990) and Kinter (1994).
[157] The video archives can be accessed in the premises of the workshops during opening hours.
[158] For example Drew (2007), Rees (1999) and Reekie (2007).

Austria and Switzerland. Therefore, a transnational perspective might be more suitable for acknowledging international co-operations and inspirations. This approach will also help to complicate the perception of European workshops as generally based on the model of the New York Film-Makers' Cooperative. Especially in the case of Germany with its decentralised film funding, a national perspective might overlook important distinctions between the collectives in different cities and their attitude towards state funding. Therefore, I follow recent trends in avant-garde film historiography, of focussing on cities and of network practices such as publishing or festivals as nodal points for cinema cultures (Hagener 2007). Hamburg will be the focus of my case study, since after the student upheavals of the late 1960s and the subsequent rise of social movements the city became a stronghold for experimental and avant-garde filmmaking in Germany. While attempts have been made to bridge the gap between art and politics in filmmaking and video culture (cf. Wollen 1982, Marshall 1985), the division still haunts film historiography.

The thriving independent film culture in Hamburg was triggered off after the 'film-in' in October 1967, when Underground films from London, New York, Tokyo, Amsterdam and Hamburg were screened non-stop for three nights. This film happening as well as the first and second 'Hamburger Filmschau' in 1968 and 1969, an alternative film festival for contemporary avant-garde and experimental filmmaking, established Hamburg as a site for *'Das andere Kino'*/'The Other Cinema' (Töteberg 1997, 204). In spring 1968 the *Hamburger Filmmacher-Cooperative* (Hamburg Filmmakers' Coop) was set up, modelled after the Filmmakers' Coop in New York. Contacts had been established when P. Adams Sitney toured Germany and introduced the New American Cinema in a series of sold-out screenings at the America House in Hamburg in 1967, showing films such Andy Warhol's *Harlot* (1964) as well as Stan Brakhage's *The Art of Vision* (1961–65), Jonas Mekas' *Circus Notebook* (1967) and various works by Harry Smith and Gregory Markopoulos. With its catalogue of 100 films the Hamburg Filmmakers' Coop became the most important independent distributor in Europe apart from the London Filmmakers' Co-op. After 1969 the Hamburg Coop fell apart, mostly due to the emerging conflict between avant-garde, experimental filmmakers and documentarists who would dedicate themselves to explicit political filmmaking.[159]

---

159 According to Michael Töteberg (1997, 207) the 'revolutionaries' reproached the 'cineastes' for merely dedicating themselves to individualistic filmmaking. In September 1970 the Hamburg Filmmaker's Coop published their distribution catalogue, as a special issue, using a red cover and a picture of Mao Tse-tung on the back. From now on, the Co-op announced, they would issue two different distribution catalogues: *'Das Andere Kino'* ('The Other Cinema') and *'Sozialis-*

In contrast to the Hamburg Filmmakers' Coop and its professional approach to filmmaking, the video collectives defied the notion of auteurism. The coop was in fact an access workshop and films were credited to individual directors. While New York was the model for the Hamburg Coop, the video collectives had other inspirations: international video groups, such as Video-Inn in Vancouver or Meatball in Den Haag, who would use the cable TV network as a means of distribution. Yet, since the situation was different in Germany, where public service television had a monopoly until 1984, other modes of distribution had to be found, leading to the creation of a nationwide network of video distribution.[160]

Video technology became a means to subvert hegemonic media representation. Drawing on conceptualisations of the counter public sphere, video was regarded as an egalitarian medium as opposed to 16 mm filmmaking associated with professional television productions. Video technology also allowed the workshops to be independent from film laboratories. Moreover, the availability of synchronous sound made the editing process much easier and smoother, especially in interview sequences. The possibility to immediately view the recorded footage was another advantage which not only speeded up the production process, but also enabled the filmed people to interfere, participate and contribute to a hitherto unknown extent. For these reasons video technology was regarded as a Brechtian means to disrupt the boundaries between producer and recipient

---

tische Filmarbeit' ('Socialist film practice') (cf. Töteberg 1997, 207). Even earlier, in 1968, the gap between political and less politically dedicated filmmaking became visible when the second Hamburger Filmschau took place on the very same weekend (17–18 June 1968) as the 'Internationale Vietnam-Kongress' at the TU Berlin, organised by the Socialist Student Union (SDS). In a pre-conference letter to Hellmuth Costard, Holger Meins, later to become a legendary member of the West German militant group Red Army Faction (RAF), explained the reason why he and his filmmaking colleagues would not come to Hamburg. According to Meins, they found the Hamburg Coop and the Filmschau irrelevant since the Hamburg filmmakers were 'running the wrong, the capitalist path', affirming and reproducing the hegemonic system (Bock and Jacobsen 1998: 30–31).

160 In his influential 1985 essay "Video: From Art to Independence: A Short History of a New Technology", published in Screen, Stuart Marshall points at the long lasting ideological differences between "independent video communities/video artists and social action/agit-prop video workers" which are "now beginning to close as community video workers increasingly question dominant televisual forms and video artists loosen their historical ties with modernism and begin to embrace issues of social and political relevance." At the same time independent filmmakers and video producers are approaching each other after realising "that many of the debates within the independent film community have also taken place within the video community." Marshall finds this development especially important in view of the cuts in state funding for the independent sector and the "political scrutiny" it is increasingly subjected to (Marshall 1985, 70–71).

(see Brecht 1992). Being a faster and cheaper medium than 16 mm film, video was used as a quick intervention into ongoing political struggles. *bildwechsel* co-founder Durbahn (1996, 17) stresses the anarchic qualities of video with is immediate access to events. Since video images were regarded as more objective, video provided an opportunity to move away from written texts because writing was suspiciously eyed as a subjective mode of representation (Durbahn 1996, 18). For female filmmakers video was an interesting option. Since access to filmmaking proved to be difficult for women, video practice in media workshops provided a good start while also allowing control over the entire film process from recording to cutting to exhibition (see Durbahn 1996).

4.1.2 The practice of the video collectives: production, distribution and exhibition

In their attempt to create a new aesthetics, the video activists and filmmakers drew on avant-garde practice, experimental filmmaking traditions as well as influences from agit-prop, Direct Cinema and cinéma vérité. Inspired by Sergei Tretyakov's notion of operative practice, filmmaking was seen as an intervention into political struggles and, moreover, as a mode to create a counter public sphere in the sense of Oskar Negt and Alexander Kluge. This approach, however, was not shared by all workshops. Some, such as *bildwechsel*, defied the idea of the counter public sphere. While video technology was regarded as a useful tool in undermining hegemonic media representation, a nationwide network of video collectives was established in which festivals, magazines, screenings and meetings would form nodal points. In this section I am going to outline the practice of the three Hamburg video collectives examined in this chapter, by focussing on the industrial context of production, distribution and exhibition.

The *mpz* was set up by a group of teacher training students from the Academy of Fine Arts in Hamburg (HfbK) in 1973. The goal was to support political activities among teachers and pupils and to empower them according to Tretyakov's concept of self-organisation. Soon political activist groups from the left-wing social movements became involved: housing action groups, campaigners against nuclear power, oppositional groups within trade unions and companies, women's groups as well as initiatives for youth centres. In cooperation with these groups, collaborative film projects were realised on topics such as community work in the neighbourhood, about dockers' strikes, squatters, the environmental movement and the women's movement.[161] For the *mpz* it was important not only to provide access to the technical equipment, but also to make production, post-production, distribution and reception a collective process while encouraging self-activity.[162] Thanks to the activity of the various social movements, the years 1976–1992 became the heyday of the *mpz*. As part of the operative notion, the *mpz* did not confine its political practices to filmmaking, but would also produce exhibitions, for example on labour in the port of Hamburg. Due to the changing political climate since the 1990s with its decline of the social movements, the team decreased from between 15 to 25 members in the early years down to 8 members in 2010. As a consequence, activities were scaled back: fewer film projects were realised, the opening hours were reduced and the number of video loans peaked off.[163] In recent years, individual members of the *mpz* have produced films in cooperation with the *Museum der Arbeit* (Museum of Work), the Concentration Camp Memorial in Neuengamme or the *Geschichtswerkstatt Barmbek* (History Workshop Barmbek). The films cover a wide range of topics, such as forced labour during the Nazi period, the first generation of Spanish migrants in Hamburg, the Oaxaca rebellion in Mexico, or the drugs policy in the local neighbourhood of the Schanzenviertel. These cooperations also mark a shift in the notion of collectivity, since the films realised for these institutions specify the names of the director and the film crew while no longer claiming to be a collective "*mpz* production". Some of these productions, though without a commercial distributor, are available on DVD through the local library network.

Unlike many video groups in the United States and in Britain, the Hamburg film collectives had a highly theoretical approach. As part of their integrated practice the *mpz* published a series of theoretical writings on media practice, the *mpz-Materialien*, and edited the magazine *Medienarbeit* (1975–1986), while the *Video-Magazin* (1976–1980) was issued by the video collective *Medienladen* in Hamburg. These magazines had a nationwide distribution and were usually published as special issues on theoretical questions of media practice, for example, the counter public sphere or new media.[164] Re-editions of classic film theory,

---

161 For a complete list of *mpz* productions, see http://mpz-hamburg.de/neu/?page_id=19 (10 January 2011).
162 In contrast, the Hamburg video collective *Medienladen* enabled the realisation of numerous video projects, while it only produced two films as the *Medienladen* collective.
163 To illustrate, until the mid-1980s the *mpz* recorded on average 500 video loans per year, in 1984 even more than 700 (personal communication).
164 For a list of publications, see http://mpz-hamburg.de/projekte/publikationen/ (19 July 2014).

for example, were published by the *Medienladen* who owned a printing press. These publications, along with the video catalogues each workshop issued, helped to create a wide-ranging distribution network covering Germany, Austria and Switzerland.

Once a year the video collectives would organise a festival to meet up, screen their work and exchange video copies. In order to facilitate the mutual exchange between the German media collectives, a distribution catalogue was published. In 1982 *Cut-in* was founded as a collective monthly magazine for independent film and video news. Via the alternative non-commercial network videos could be disseminated quickly. The works would usually be shown at political gatherings, in pubs, at trade union meetings or workplaces opposing the solitary activity of television viewing. The collectives would target specific groups of audiences as the goal was not to reach out to the masses, but to activate the public. Therefore, feedback was highly encouraged, which is why the screening was usually followed by a discussion. In the early years the videos would be screened on TV monitors, later, in the 1980s, large-screen projectors were used.[165] While many of the video collectives focussed on an interventionist media practice, producing activist videos, other collectives departed from this notion in order to contextualise themselves in feminist art practice (*bildwechsel*), or to dedicate themselves to various forms of documentary and experimental filmmaking, such as *die thede* whose members mostly consisted of film class students of the Academy of Fine Arts in Hamburg.

The artist-run organisation *bildwechsel* is a good example why the distinction between art and activism is problematic. Co-founder Durbahn, who is still an active member, had been part of the *Medienladen* (1974–1978) film collective. The emergence of *bildwechsel* as a nodal point for feminist visual artists in 1979 attracted filmmakers such as Monika Treut and Claudia Wilke, photographers and other artists from all over Germany. Inspired by *Vidéo-femmes* in Quebec, *bildwechsel* situates itself in the context of feminist collectives, which aim at empowering female artists in order to increase the number of women in filmmaking and media practice. In the early years *bildwechsel* provided female filmmakers with access to equipment, but also produced films collectively – about 50 to 60 productions, ranging from experimental works to documentaries about female filmmakers. In 1986 *bildwechsel* was restructured to become an umbrella organisation for a variety of projects, such as the archive for female artists

---

[165] Exceptions occurred, for example, when the *mpz* decided to blow up their video about an alternative children's daycare centre onto 16 mm film in order to reach a wide audience (personal communication). *Kinderhaus – wir machen weiter* (Producers: *mpz* and Kinderhaus Heinrichstraße. 1977, 50 min.)

and the video museum. To date sister organisations exist in Glasgow and Berlin, Warsaw, Basel and Chicago. Networking, providing scholarships for female artists, film programming and archival practice are the focus of *bildwechsel's* collective practices today.

Unlike their Scandinavian counterparts, the Hamburg workshops did not receive any state funding.[166] To be independent from state funding was a political strategy. In order to preserve its critical stance, the *mpz* developed a model of self-financing. As a consequence, none of the staff has a salaried position. Instead the members finance the collective with the help of their salaries from their day jobs, while bigger purchases, such as new technical equipment, were financed, for example, by collectively taking out a loan. The self-financing model was adopted by other workshops in Hamburg, whereas media collectives in other cities were less sceptical towards state funding during the 1970s and 1980s. Since its inception *bildwechsel* has conceptualised itself as a project without salaried positions and institutionalised funding. The running costs are covered by regular contributions from *bildwechsel* supporters, individual donations and revenues from charity events. Yet, over the years the mode of financing changed from exclusive self-financing to project-based funding provided by the *Filmförderung Hamburg* (Film Fund Hamburg) or the Hamburg Cultural Authority.[167] The Film Fund, however, would only support selected film projects, but not video productions.

In a 1984 brochure summarising ten years of collective video practice, the authors conclude that video quickly became a popular medium, though unfortunately not in the way that the video collectives aspired to (see Medienzentren und Videogruppen in der BRD 1984, 7). Instead of a being an emancipatory practice, the writers bemoan, video had not only developed into an ubiquitous instrument of surveillance, but also led to a flood of depoliticized home movies and video pornography. Therefore, quite paradoxically, the video boom had caused independent video practice to plunge into a crisis. From their 'minor' position, while remaining on the margin, the video workshops were not able to revolutionize filmmaking. As a consequence, many collectives turned away from interventionist media practice, favouring historical subjects instead, such as anti-fas-

---

166 *Filmworkshoppen* in Denmark (established in 1970) and *Filmverkstan* in Sweden (1973–2001) were funded by national television and the national Film Fund. See Andersson, et al. (2010).
167 For many years the independent filmmakers in Hamburg negotiated with the Film Fund (set up in 1979) to acknowledge video as a medium of expression, not just as a storage medium. However, negotiations failed and video funding was never institutionalised. Another problem was that film funding was usually targeted at individual auteurs, not at collectives.

cism, the Spanish Civil War, revolutions, strikes and other working-class upheavals. The crisis of video activism in turn lead to a discussion about the formal and stylistic means it employed. The initial assumption, according to which political movements would develop their own cultural forms of expression, was now met with scepticism. Moreover, the subjective role of the auteur was to be reconsidered. These changes can be tracked in the development of film collective *die thede*.

die thede was founded in 1980 by a group of filmmakers, most of them film students at the Academy of Fine Arts in Hamburg, among them Maria Hemmleb, Manfred Oppermann and Nina Rippel, with the goal of pursuing an emancipatory media practice. Inspirations were not least the London-based film collective *Cinema Action*, which *thede* co-founder Christian Bau collaborated with during his stay in London in 1971/72. The first works by *die thede* were interventionist videos about squatting and local urban changes in regeneration areas, co-produced with the *mpz*.[168] Soon more experimental works were realised. When *die thede* showed their early works at a video festival in 1981, the films received very positive feedback because they were perceived to be aesthetically more innovative than a lot of the video productions available.

In the early 1980s *die thede*, like the *mpz* and *bildwechsel*, was still reluctant to work for television or apply for funding. Furthermore, the video material used in the early 1980s, Japan half-inch standard 1, was not used by TV stations. In the early 1980s *die thede* produced the first of a range of videos documenting collective squatting actions.[169] *Irgendetwas wird schon hängenbleiben* (video, b/w, 65 min) is a video about the media representation of the demonstration against the nuclear power plant Brokdorf on 28 February 1981. The film team which called themselves the "Filmgruppe Spratzer" described their motivations as a result of the misrepresentation of the protests in television news coverage: "We made this film out of rage. Out of rage against the TV screens on which the world is turned upside down by the news coverage."[170] However, video was not only used in terms of sudden intervention, but also as documentations of 1980s urban regeneration in the local district of Altona. The *Thedebadfilm* (1981–1985, video, b/w 30 min, dir. Christian Bau and Jürgen Mainausch) was

---

[168] A survey of the history of *die thede* is given in thede (1996).
[169] The titles were usually derived from the address of the squat: *Hospitalstrasse 6 (1980, b/w, 45 min.)*, *Billrothstrasse 55* (1981, b/w, 10 minutes) or *Amandastrasse 73* (1981, b/w, 15 min, co-production: *die thede, mpz*, Stadtjournal).
[170] My translation. The original statement goes: "Wir, eine Gruppe von AKW Gegnern, haben diesen Film gemacht, weil uns die Wut gepackt hat. Die Wut beim Blick auf den Fernsehschirm, wo die Berichterstattung die Welt auf den Kopf stellt" (thede 1996, 119).

a long-term documentation of the Thede swimming bath and its users, following the protests against the closing down of the bath in a Direct Cinema style. One of the first videos to be funded by the Filmbüro Hamburg was *Hamburg Altona, Ein starkes Stück* (1983, video, b/w, 90 min, collective work by the members of *die thede*) which dealt with urban regeneration. Nina Rippel's prize-winning experimental video *Drei Unterwasserstücke mit Cello* (1985, colour, 6 min.) could be categorized as video art. A media specific experiment was Gerda Lampalzer and Nina Rippel's *Cadavre Exquisit* (1989, U-matic, colour, 7 min.) which is based on the video tape being sent back and forth between Hamburg and Vienna, compiling video footage filmed in both cities. These examples show that the boundaries between art and activism within the collective are blurred.

However, the focus on video was abolished especially after Barbara Metzlaff joined *die thede* in 1987. Metzlaff, a cinematographer, introduced the collective to 16 mm film which was to become the dominant film format for the collective. From now on a variety of productions were realised, some of them co-produced by TV stations, such as NDR or arte.[171] As a result, *die thede* founded their own production company, *die thede filmproduktion,* in 1999. By then *die thede* had left interventionist media practice behind in order to produce films with a wider range of aesthetic approaches. Some of the documentaries were highly reflexive while those co-produced for television would often be more conventional.[172] One strand in *die thede's* productions consists of films on history and visual arts. *Rendezvous der Freunde* (Maria Hemmleb and Christian Bau, 1992) traces the story of Max Ernst's painting *Rendezvous der Freunde* (1922) and how its collectors, the filmmaker's parents, rescued it during the Nazi period. *Zwiebelfische Jimmy Ernst, Glückstadt – New York* (Christian Bau and Artur Dieckhoff, 2010) merges the story of Jimmy Ernst, son of Max Ernst and Luise Straus, with a North German print shop. *Die kritische Masse* (dir. Christian Bau, 1998) revisits the members of the Hamburg Filmmakers Coop, while Jens Huckeriede's *Return of the Tüdelband* describes the story of two popular Jewish music hall artists, the Wolf brothers,

---

171 Some of *die thede* films were co-produced by television. For instance, *Schuss ins Blau* (Bau 2004) is a coproduction by arte and the ZDF, funded by Filmförderung Hamburg as well as the Filmstiftung NRW. *Duell auf dem Eis* (Gramatke and Hemmleb, 2005) was produced for arte and *Eisfieber* (Hemmleb, 2004) was also shown on Finnish television (YLE Teema) in January 2005.
172 Examples of more self-reflexive work would be *Dialogzeichen* (dir. Maria Hemmleb, 1987). The 6–minute long video shows two artists drawing while the camera leaves its observational position and eventually becomes a part of the drawing itself. *Lubitsch junior* (dir. Christian Bau and Jens Huckeriede, 1990) explores questions of authenticity and truth, transgressing the boundaries of fiction filmmaking and documentary. *Der geflüsterte Film* (dir. Nina Rippel, 1992) uses the perception of blind people as a point of departure for an exploration of non-visual senses via filmmaking.

who had to emigrate to the United States during national socialism. *die thede* is the only Hamburg workshop to have issued some of their works on DVD, for example *The Return of the Tüdelband, Die kritische Masse, Zwiebelfische, Das Ding am Deich* (dir. Hubert 2012) or *20 Geigen auf St. Pauli* (Barbara Metzlaff and Alexandra Gramatke 2011). However, distribution is still an issue for *die thede*, as those of their films that are not broadcast on television often only reach small audiences.

4.1.3 Archival practice in times of digitization

Preserving the films from the archive, expanding the collection and disseminating it are the main archival practices for the workshops. In this section I will focus on the archival politics of *bildwechsel*, because their curatorial practice is by far the most complex of the three video workshops examined in this chapter. Its practice differs from the archival politics of the *mpz* and *die thede*, which I will briefly outline here by way of comparison. The *mpz* archive consists of several thousands of video tapes, both *mpz* productions as well as videos by other media collectives and filmmakers. Occasionally retrospectives are arranged in collaboration with local cinemas, while more recent film projects are screened in repertory cinemas, at local libraries or in the premises of the *mpz*. A series of workshops on visual politics, the *Filmwerkstatt Bildpolitik* (2008–2009), critically analysed the formal-aesthetic means of political filmmaking and highlighted the role of film as a mediator of history, memory, and representation. A hesitant attitude towards online exhibition formats characterizes the archival practice of the *mpz*. The goal is not to reach out into the mainstream, but to address target audiences. Passive media consumption is rejected in favour of exhibiting the films in political and pedagogical contexts, accompanied by a discussion. Therefore channels such as YouTube are also rejected, since they perpetuate passive media consumption according to the *mpz*.[173]

Die thede has archived all of its film and video footage at the Stiftung Kinemathek in Berlin. This includes both the negatives and the projection copies on 16 and 35 mm, while the videos have been transferred to Digi Beta. Their films are shown at repertory cinemas or at local history workshops, while recently early

---

[173] Some of the *mpz* productions can be found online, though, for example the videos of the occupied buildings at Hafenstrasse, as they have been uploaded with some of the former collaborators. In contrast to the post-1968 video collectives, more recent interventionist media projects, such as Feuerlöscher TV, set up in Hamburg in 2004, or AK Kraak, founded in Berlin in 1990, explicitly use the internet for the distribution and exhibition of their works.

interventionist videos on squatting and urban regeneration have been screened at political gatherings against gentrification. Some of their films have become performative archives since they remediate older archival footage with only limited accessibility. Examples would be the above mentioned *Die kritische Masse* as well as *Das Ding am Deich* by *die thede*'s youngest member Antje Hubert, which uses video material shot by *die thede* and the *mpz* about the local struggle against a nuclear power plant. Another original example of film as a performative archive is Jens Huckeriede's *Return of the Tüdelband* in which the director invites artists to present cover versions of songs by the Gebrüder Wolf. While all of these films can be considered acts of remembrance in their specific ways, they offer different approaches to questions of cultural memory. Antje Hubert's *Das Ding am Deich* deals with issues of forgetting and the legacies of lost political struggles. *Return of the Tüdelband* is representative for Jens Huckeriede's reflexive approach to the relationship of film and cultural memory, which he further explores in *Ab nach Rio. Die Akte Guggenheim* (2009) and *Sounds in the Silence* (2013).

The case of *bildwechsel*'s archival practice is more complex for a variety of reasons. First, it is an umbrella organisation which also houses other video collections besides its own. Second, it regards archival practice as an artistic practice in its own right. Third, it is sceptical about online publishing, but has decided to experiment with it. All of these factors imply a number of challenges for *bildwechsel* in terms of property rights and personality rights, questions of selection as well as the role of metadata and paratexts in the context of online publication. All of the archive stock has been received from the filmmakers themselves and includes performance videos, documentaries, home videos, video diaries, video essays, fiction films and video art. While initially the collection consisted of videotapes only, since 1993 the original formats have been archived as well, including a diverse range of video systems, 16 mm film, Super-8 and slide shows.[174] Still, most of the 7000 titles in the archive exist on time-worn videotape alone.

As an umbrella organisation for female art practice, *bildwechsel* hosts one of the world's first video collections of feminist filmmaking, from independent film to art cinema. The organization does therefore not only house its own archival collections, but also several collections donated by other feminist collectives[175]: for example the "cinenova collection", comprising early films from the distribu-

---

[174] Half inch, u-matic (Sony), betacam, beta sp, vhs, s-vhs, video8, hi8, mini dv, dv-cam http://videomuseum.bildwechsel.org/?p=85 (23 June 2014).
[175] For a whole list of collections see http://*bildwechsel*.org/info/en/collections.html (13 September 2013).

tion catalogue of the UK feminist film distribution collective *cinenova* [176]. Another example is the "feminale collection" consisting of videos submitted to the Cologne-based women's film festival *feminale* from 1999 until 2006[177], while the "Pelze collection" encompasses visual art and texts on "pelze multimedia", a West-Berlin art space for feminist artists between 1986 and 1990. In addition, *bildwechsel* hosts the collection of the open access tv-show "Lesben in Sicht" ("Lesbians in sight"), broadcast on Hamburg's Open Channel from 1994–98, as well as archival material from the follow-up show "Lesben-TV", broadcast from 1998–2001, including uncut video footage.[178]

bildwechsel also provides a steadily growing collection of works from the international queer, trans and intersex art scene – a fact which contextualises *bildwechsel* within the tradition of lesbian herstory archives, although it exceeds this notion through the scope of its collections and through its focus on the works by female artists, no matter what their sexual orientation might be. Its collections include video documentations of events at the "Frauenkneipe", a crucial meeting point for feminists and lesbians in Hamburg during the 1980s and 1990s. In documenting these events, for instance a "country and western night" or a "karaoke night" in the early 1990s, the videos contribute to the rare visual archive of lesbian urban culture. As such, the collections of *bildwechsel* can also be regarded as an archive of feelings, to use the notion which Ann Cvetkovich has developed in view of LGBT archives. *bildwechsel* thus constitutes an important archive of artists' work and alternative media practice, trying to create different images which challenge and undermine the dominant media representation of women, and, more specifically, lesbians. Therefore, it can be regarded as part of a counter public sphere [Gegenöffentlichkeit], while at the same time challenging its homogenic notion which more often than not has excluded women and LGBTs. The concept of the counter public sphere has only rarely created a discursive space for the articulation of LGBT experiences. The archive at *bildwechsel* is therefore important on several levels: a) it offers plurimedia memories of artist practice, b) it enables interventions into the audiovisual archive, providing the cultural memory of alternative media representation and of alternative media practice based on video technology, and c) it contributes to rework-

---

[176] Cinenova was established in 1991 as the merger of two feminist distributors, Circles and Cinema of Women.
[177] In 2006, due to cuts in public funding, the *feminale* merged with the international women's film festival Dortmund. The collaboration lasted until 2009.
[178] *bildwechsel* also houses a collection of the early videos of political movements in Germany (1974–85), among them most notably the remnants of another video collective, the "Medienladen", from which *bildwechsel* emerged.

ing the cultural memory of various feminist projects (libraries, archives, film projects) by showing the diversity and the multitude of feminist practices from the late 1970s until today.

Digitization is currently one of the prime challenges for *bildwechsel's* archival practice. In 2006 *bildwechsel* inaugurated its project 'video museum' in order to digitize selected films by a number of filmmakers, such as Monika Treut, Elfi Mikesch, Claudia Richarz, Maria Lang or Bev Zalcock. In this process VHS and S-VHS tapes are digitized onto DVD or mini-DV or DV-cam. Another focus of the video museum, which up to now has digitized hundreds of videos, are works on feminist filmmaking practice, including portraits of or interviews with Ulrike Ottinger, Pipilotti Rist, Margarethe von Trotta or Mariola Brillowska. Also artist's videos by, for example, Martha Rosler, have been restored. *bildwechsel* topicalises films from their archive by curating film series for festivals or cinemathèque screening, but has long been reluctant to publish the digitized versions online out of consideration for the artists' intellectual property rights. In an interview, Durbahn rejected the notion that artistic expression should be accessible for easy consumption (personal communication). Moreover, *bildwechsel* is critical of YouTube because of the channel's erratic interference into the uploaded material. Online publication involves legal and ethical aspects which need to be considered. These include copyright infringements, for instance the music used in the films/played in the background, but also ethical considerations about the personality rights of the individuals featuring in the videos. Therefore, to stay in control, *bildwechsel* has decided to experiment with own online platforms providing access to selected works from the archives.

For *bildwechsel* archival practice is regarded as an artistic practice. This highly self-reflexive artistic practice takes place on several levels, which include the person of *bildwechsel* co-founder Durbahn, activist and visual artist, as well as the design of the archive's rooms.[179] However, I will focus on the process of archivization as an artistic intervention and on the role of curatorial practice. In my understanding these two aspects are deeply interrelated. One such artistic intervention is a tent, called "video-denkarium" (video-pensive) which, thanks to its mobility, can be reconstructed at various locations outside the premises of *bildwechsel*. In this tent videos are digitized in real time (as is the case for all analogue stock), while the film images are projected on one of the screens of the tent and can be watched by the audience assembling outside the tent. The "video-denkarium" was inaugurated at the Hamburg art space "Westwerk" in

---

179 For example, the entry hall of *bildwechsel* serves as an "info box" showcasing changing exhibitions and the display of new material acquired for the collections.

2011. This mobile space invites the public to reflect on archival politics, and on questions of selection and preservation. It foregrounds the otherwise secret, hidden work of preservation, usually confined to the premises of the archive.

In the remaining section of this chapter I would like to take a look at *bildwechsel*'s access practice and outline some of the consequences for theorising the notion of the archive in cultural memory studies. For this purpose, I will draw on Giovanna Fossati (2009) who has divided access practice into three categories: "[A]ccess by the broader public via video or digital reproductions, cinema distribution to audiences, outside the archive, and cinema exhibition to audiences inside the archive." (Fossati 2009, 24) For the case of *bildwechsel* I would like to abridge these and rearrange their order into 1) distribution to audiences outside the archive, via cinema, in an arts context or in the public space; 2) exhibition to audiences inside the archive; 3) access online. This chapter will not be able to document all of the activities, which is why I will briefly look into the three areas, illustrating *bildwechsel's* access politics with a few examples, before outlining the conclusions we could draw from the *bildwechsel* case. I would like to use the collaborative curating processes at *bildwechsel* as an example in order to highlight the role of curating for the shift from 'storage memory' to 'functional memory'. My hypothesis is that curators, programmers and archivists can turn storage memory into functional memory because they can trigger remediation, exhibition and distribution.

1) The first examples of *bildwechsel's* access politics refer to presenting items from the collections to audiences outside the organisation's own premises, for example through screenings at the Hamburg Cinémathèque, at the Hamburg Queer Film Festival or other festivals dedicated to visual arts. Thereby *bildwechsel* either contributes to existing festivals with a selection of their archival holdings, often in collaboration with the respective festival curators, or they host their own film series or video festivals. Open calls for festival programmes invite filmmakers to either produce or submit works for screening and eventual archivization. For example, during the Hamburg Ladyfest in 2003 *bildwechsel* invited queer-feminist filmmakers to submit their work to an open screening, while for the 2014 Hamburg LaDYIfest *bildwechsel* issued call for autobiographical films on Do-It-Yourself practice. *bildwechsel* has regularly collaborated with the Hamburg Queer Film Festival and with the Hamburg Cinémathèque to arrange cinema screenings of the archival collections. In October 2010 *bildwechsel* collaborated with nine independent art spaces and the Hamburg Cinematheque to launch a decentralised video festival, entitled "Parole Hochformat". The festival screened films especially produced for this event, but also films from the archive which were chosen for of their engagement with the specific art space or community building in which they were screened. Which films can be shown outside

the *bildwechsel* premises is the result of negotiations with the filmmakers or the right holders, but depends also on the *bildwechsel* curators' judgment, for instance when it comes to personality rights of those individuals represented in the archival material.

2) Since *bildwechsel* is a feminist separatist space, access is usually limited to female-identified or transgender persons. However, rather than being a limitation, these politics allow for a wider access to the collections compared to the public screenings outside the premises because the impact of property or personality rights might be of lesser consequence. In 2013 *bildwechsel* inaugurated a new screening format, the so-called "swarm viewing" [Schwarmsichtung], for which video artists and filmmakers were invited to produce video letters about their current work. On the premises of *bildwechsel* DVD copies were available to the individual audience members who were equipped with a mobile DVD player. Acknowledging the changes in film exhibition from cinema screens to mobile screens, the mode of reception shifted from a collective to an individual mode of reception, while encouraging the mutual exchange among the audience members. Although the filmmakers were not present for a Q&A session, the spectators would engage in conversations about the films, recommending films to each other and discussing the works. Contrary to the concerns expressed by some members of the *Medienpägogikzentrum*, the example shows that dispersed viewing does not necessarily imply an isolated reception context. For the Hamburg International Queer Film Festival in 2014 *bildwechsel* has digitized about 30 short films from the festival archive, most of them submitted on video formats in the early years of the festival. The films, both prize winners and controversial works, were re-screened during the festival at a *bildwechsel* "Schwarmsichtung". This project opens up questions about remediation and the factors which trigger it, about film historiography and the impact of curatorial processes on functional memory.

3) While digitization enables online access, not every digitized video can be published online, for legal or ethical reasons. In recent years *bildwechsel* has experimented with a number of approaches to online publication. For example, in 2012 *bildwechsel* launched an online project called "50 windows" to grant online access to 50 selected artists' videos. This exhibition project was initiated as a way to prepare future digital online access. The project "50 windows" invites reflection on aspects of remediation and the impact of paratextual information in the context of exhibition. In analogue times the video would have been introduced by the curator or a member of the video collective (which is the approach still favoured by the *mpz*), who would give contextual information about the production of the video. In contrast, digital online publication often provides this information through short textual descriptions. Here, the curator needs to consider

what information can be published (and, for instance in the case of political interventionist filmmaking, what information cannot). An upcoming project, derived from the experiences made with the "50 windows" website, is the "video castle". It consists of three sections combining different approaches, while the artist can decide which mode she prefers for the presentation of her work. First, the "video castle" contains virtual rooms in which films are screened online. Second, it contains exemplary videos of various female artists. Third, it provides the user with a list of links to artists' websites.

The case of *bildwechsel*'s archival practice indicates how curatorial practice can turn 'storage memory' into 'functional memory'. Furthermore, it shows how this practice consists of a variety of tasks: selecting archival material and developing new forms and concepts of presenting archival stock. These tasks include negotiating about property rights, reflecting on personality rights as well as making the audience aware of the work of an archive, for instance digitising analogue video footage. *bildwechsel* illustrates how some of those challenges film and video archives have to face in the near future can be dealt with.

4.1.4 Conclusion: video collectives, archival politics and digitization

This chapter has shown that the case study of Hamburg complicates the divisions of art versus politics and avant-garde versus agit-prop. Especially the aesthetic politics of *bildwechsel* and *die thede* challenge this predominant notion in film historiography on video collectives.

These conclusions of the case study point at three aspects relevant for archival practice: first, the need to rethink national archiving politics – in order to include the works by the media collectives. Second, the need to consider the materiality and media specificity – because technology is not only to be considered within the framework of technological progress, but also regarding its ideological implications. Finally, third, the need to readdress canon formation and film historiography. This chapter has shown that more film historical research is needed, but also that a more thorough examination of the archival practice of the workshops is necessary, for example with the help of participant observation. My methodological and theoretical approach to the history and practice of the three workshops has been rather eclectic, but with this first attempt to map the field I wanted to carve out new research perspectives, inviting rather than preventing further research.

In 2011, when the research for this study was started, the *mpz* had only digitized 10 per cent of its archive while *bildwechsel* had restored 300 of its over 7000 titles.[180] The impact of funding becomes apparent in the very different financial possibilities of the Hamburg collectives compared to their Swiss counterpart, the *Videoladen Zürich*, which was able to digitize its archive thanks to considerable funding. Contrary to the German situation, state-funded initiatives to digitize video footage have been started in both Switzerland and Austria. In 1997 Swiss *memoriav* started a project to preserve videos on the youth movement in the 1980s and to make parts of its archive accessible online.[181] In July 2014 the "Mediathek", the Austrian archive for historical sound recordings and videos, initiated a project to digitize amateur videos recording public events. The project "Viennese Video Recorder" (Wiener Video Rekorder), financed by the "Wiener Wissenschaft-, Forschungs- und Technologiefonds", sets out to collect recordings by individuals on condition that these were filmed for private purposes, not aimed for publication. This approach sets aside the works by video collectives or semi-professional filmmakers. This chapter, however, has shown that for German video workshops – also those not mentioned here – the need for sustainable preservation is urgent, even for those who are not active anymore, such as the *Medienladen*. Preserving the cultural memory of the video collectives would not be complicated or expensive at all. Because of their low resolution, the video images are less costly and less time-consuming to digitize than analogue film. Alexander Horwath, director of the Austrian Film Museum, points at an important aspect: "through curatorial work, archives and museums can strengthen their role. The value of an institution is then not only the fictional value of the thousands of prints that they want us to assess, but the capacity and competence of the institution to create 'stories' and draw knowledge out of that repository, to produce a cultural history." (Cherchi Usai, et al. 2008, 96) As the chapter has shown, curatorial decisions and remediation can have a crucial impact on rescuing an important contribution to the polyvocality of cultural memory under threat of oblivion.

---

180 Only in 2014, another 700 titles were added when *bildwechsel* received the archival holdings of the former feminist film festival *Feminale* in Köln.
181 Meanwhile, the activist video *Züri brännt* (1981), praised for its avant-garde style and its experimental filmmaking qualities, is so far their only production available on DVD.

4.2 Filmmaking as archival intervention – reworking cultural memory in the essay film (*Handsworth Songs*)[182]

On the occasion of the wave of social unrest which spread from London to various other British cities in August 2011, Tate Britain presented a screening of a 35-year-old film experiment which still impresses with its innovative stand towards issues of representation, political media practice and politics of the image: *Handsworth Songs*, the seminal essay film by the Black Audio Film Collective, directed by John Akomfrah in 1986.[183] In 2008 Tate Britain had acquired *Handsworth Songs* for its collection, along with two earlier works, the tape slide installations *Expeditions One: Signs of Empire* (1984) and *Expeditions Two: Images of Nationality* (1984). An important factor for a renewed interest in *Handsworth Songs* was its selection for the 2002 Documenta XI in Kassel, curated by Okwui Enwezor. Thanks to the 'documentary turn' in the arts, *Handsworth Songs* was all of a sudden able to experience a renaissance 25 years after its premiere.[184] Following on from the critical reception the film received at the Documenta, the retrospective of the Black Audio Film Collective, shown at FACT in Liverpool in 2007 and curated by Kodwo Eshun and Anjalika Sagar (see Eshun and Sagar 2007), paved the way for a renewed critical interest in the film. Recently it has been exhibited at Tate Britain on various occasions, among others as part of the 2012 exhibition "Migrations", and in a number of shifting contexts at Tate Modern.

Handsworth Songs' reconceptualisation within the art world (Akomfrah 2002, Eshun and Sagar 2007) has increased the scholarly and curatorial interest in the film as an essay film (see Eshun 2011, Brunow 2011a).[185] I would go so far as to

---

[182] An earlier version of this chapter has been published as: "Deconstructing Essentialism and Revising Historiography: The Function of Metareference in Black British Filmmaking." *The Metareferential Turn in Contemporary Arts and Media: Forms, Functions, Attempts at Explanation.* Eds. Werner Wolf in collaboration with Katharina Bantleon and Jeff Thoss. Amsterdam/New York: Rodopi, 2011, 341–355.

[183] The Black Audio Film Collective was set up in 1982 and existed for sixteen years. Its members were John Akomfrah, Lina Gopaul, Reece Auguiste, Avril Johnson, Trevor Mathison, Edward George, David Lawson (from 1985) and Clare Joseph (until 1985). In 1998 Akomfrah, Gopaul and Lawson established the film and television production company Smoking Dogs Films, which still exists.

[184] In 2006 it was part of the exhibition "Making History, Art and Documentary in Britain from 1929 to Now" at Tate Liverpool.

[185] Previously *Handsworth Songs* has been conceptualised, among others, in the context of diasporic filmmaking (Mercer 1988b), avant-garde filmmaking (Diawara 1993b, Hill 1999), documentary filmmaking (Corner 1996), found footage film (Russell 1999) or intercultural cinema

argue that *Handsworth Songs* has been of fundamental importance for establishing the concept of the essay film in the UK. The UK reception of the essay film ties in with both the publication of the first Anglo-American studies on the essay film (Rascaroli 2009, Corrigan 2011) and with the reconceptualisation of *Handsworth Songs* in the art world and within film studies. Reconceptualising *Handsworth Songs* as an essay film has allowed for new curatorial contexts. For instance, in August 2013 *Handsworth Songs* was screened as part of the BFI Southbank's film season "Thought in Action: The Art of the Essay Film". Instead of being programmed as 'Black British filmmaking' or 'ethnic filmmaking', *Handsworth Songs* was screened alongside Humphrey Jennings' *A Diary for Timothy* (1945) in a double feature entitled "Listen to Britain". The season was curated by Kieron Corless of *Sight and Sound* magazine (see Sandhu 2013) which also accompanied the film programmes with a special dossier on the essay film. The film has thus returned from 'storage memory' to 'functional memory' as a result of curatorial decisions which have allowed it to re-enter the art circuit, and eventually the cinema circuit.[186]

Essay films are 'film as theory', a notion I have adopted from Volker Pantenburg's (2006) work on Godard and Farocki.[187] Reading the film in the context of essay filmmaking, this chapter will examine the aesthetic and conceptual strategies at work in *Handsworth Songs*. My focus will be on the self-reflexivity of the essay film and its function as an archival intervention. Defying the alleged positivism of (documentary) film images, essay films at times even manage to carve out a discursive space for utopian visions.[188] I would therefore like to conceptualise the essay film as an emancipatory practice which can open up discursive

---

(Marks 2000). The film has never been published for sale on video or DVD. When I started researching the Black Audio Film Collective I had to watch *Handsworth Songs* on an old VHS tape at the BFI archives.

186 This move away from conceptualisations as 'ethnic filmmaking' can also be observed in the film's critical reception. For instance, in the 2011 volume *Der Essayfilm*, edited by Sven Kramer and Thomas Tode *Handsworth Songs* is now contextualised along Chris Marker and Alexander Kluge instead of being classified in terms of ethnicity. See Eshun (2011), an article commissioned especially for this volume. The question remains, though, how the film's critical reception can challenge notions of hegemonic whiteness in essay film research without 'othering' the film again.

187 In his contribution to the exhibition catalogue which accompanies the retrospective dedicated to the Black Audio Film Collective in 2007, Okwui Enwezor also conceptualises *Handsworth Songs* as a work of theory when he argues that the film is "a classic of 1980s cultural analysis alongside such works as The Centre for Contemporary Cultural Studies collectively authored *The Empire Strikes Back* (1982) and Paul Gilroy's *There Ain't No Black in the Union Jack* (1987)" (Enwezor 2007, 120).

188 See chapter 5.2. on Isaac Julien's *Looking for Langston*.

spaces in which cultural memory is reworked. The question remains, though, how this can be achieved without lapsing into essentialism. In other words: how can the essay film challenge essentialist understandings of "container cultures", "memory collectives" or "counter practice"?

In the chapter I argue that the self-reflexivity of the essay film can be employed as an anti-essentialist strategy. By foregrounding the apparatus and by an innovative use of sound and music, essay films can offer a theoretical reflection on visual and sonic representation. Reworking the archive goes beyond merely incorporating archive footage into a film as a means of authentication, as in conventional documentary film-making. A self-reflexive aesthetics implies that archival footage can be dislocated from its original context and recontextualised, for instance through montage techniques or a new soundtrack. In her contemporary review of *Handsworth Songs* Pam Cook states: "Variously described as a 'documentary' and a 'film essay' on race and civil disorder in Britain today, [*Handsworth Songs*] owes more to poetic structures than to didactic exposition. Familiar TV and newspaper reportage is juxtaposed with opaque, elusive imagery, newsreel and archive material is reworked, and sound is pitted against image to release a multitude of unanswered questions about the underlying causes of 'racial unrest'." (Cook 1987, 77) This approach differs from that of filmmakers such as Michael Moore, whose work Laura Rascaroli (2009, 42) has described as texts which are "not open, but closed: at all times, the spectator is clearly told where to be, what to feel, how to react, what to find out, what to believe." Characteristic for the essayistic approach is the scepticism about a fixed meaning of the image. Essay films point at the provisional character of film images which are subject to constant revision, and thereby liberated from their alleged function as visible evidence. Self-reflexive means can express this scepticism, but are not a means to its end, as Erll's re-reading of Bolter and Grusin (2000) has shown (see Erll 2011d). Focussing on the double logic of remediation, Bolter and Grusin only considered a single function of hypermediacy as a means of authentication. However, *Handsworth Songs* can be regarded as an example of 'aggressive remediation', foregrounding remediation and thereby defying notions of authenticity and verisimilitude. In the following chapter I will look at this practice and its function for cultural memory, but I will rather use the more widespread term 'self-reflexivity'.[189]

---

[189] The term 'self-reflexivity' is not uncontested. For instance, Werner Wolf (2011) prefers the term 'metareference'. In this chapter I use both terms as synonyms, but have chosen 'self-reflexivity' because it connotes a historical and discursive context of being conceptualised within a political, Brechtian framework.

4.2 Filmmaking as archival intervention — 129

This chapter will explore the notion of self-reflexivity in *Handsworth Songs* as an aesthetic and political practice, while specifically focussing on its role in the mediation of cultural memory and remembrance. Self-reflexivity is any "device which reveals the film's enunciation, or [...] any device which reminds the audience that they are watching a film" (Limoges 2009: 391). Limoges (2009) differentiates between reflexivity in film, i.e. film within the film, and self-reflexivity, exhibiting the filmic apparatus. Similarly, Meyer (2005) makes a distinction between self-reflexivity and self-referentiality, the latter not being a device used consciously by the director, but other factors that might direct the attention of the audience to the fact that they are currently watching a film, e.g. black stripes on the filmstrip. According to Jay Ruby (2005, 35), being reflexive means that the producer deliberately and intentionally reveals to his audience the underlying epistemological assumptions that caused him to formulate a set of questions in a particular way, to seek answers to those questions in a particular way, and finally to present his findings in a particular way. Since the initial starting point for my research was to complicate Stuart Hall's outline of strategies for subverting racist stereotypes in the media (Hall 1997, 269–276), the relation between self-reflexivity and subversion should be briefly reflected upon. I agree with Dana B. Polan (1985) and Robert Stam (1992, 16) that self-reflexivity does not automatically mean subversion. Back in the 1970s Jay Ruby (2005) came to the conclusion that self-reflexivity was more common in fiction film than in documentary, whereas today self-reflexivity has become a conventional means in TV series and in post-classical Hollywood cinema. Jane Chapman notes: "Reflexive techniques are now so widespread [...] that the boundaries are blurred between the truly reflexive and the mimetic" (2009, 115). However, during the 1970s, with the impact of structuralism and Marxism, self-reflexivity was theorised in terms of counter cinema practice (see Wollen 2002) and as an anti-positivist critique of conventional documentary filmmaking with its alleged objectivity and neutrality. Self-reflexivity can be a way of undermining the emphasis on verisimilitude in documentary filmmaking: "we are moving away from the positivist notion that meaning resides in the world and human beings should strive to discover the inherent, objectively true meaning of things" (Ruby 2005, 36). Therefore, I would like to suggest that in the black British context (which neither Stam nor Polan take into account) self-reflexivity serves as a Brechtian device which subverts conventional modes of narration and invites the audience to reflect on the ontology of the image and its inherent power structures.

For the Black Audio Film Collective "the archive constitutes a privileged terrain of knowledge", as BAFC member Reece Auguiste has emphasized (Auguiste 2007a, 156). *Handsworth Songs* questions the alleged status of archive footage as visible evidence, as a source of factual, positivist knowledge. The example of

Handsworth Songs shows how film can rework the archive on various levels. The film uses the social unrest in 1980s British inner cities as a point of departure for its archival intervention. As Kobena Mercer describes the film: "Instead of 'nowness', the film reaches for historical depth, creating a space of critical reverie, which counteracts the active ideological forgetting of England's colonial past in media discourses on Handsworth to articulate an alternative 'archaeological' account" (Mercer 1988b, 55). Employing footage from various television archives and libraries[190] the filmmakers set out to first decontextualise the images before rearranging them into a highly self-reflexive collage of archive footage, photography and stills, which address colonialism as well as the lost hopes of the first post-war generation of West Indian immigrants. This aesthetic practice was guided by three endeavours: first, to deal with the hegemonic media representation of Black Britons[191], second, to explore forgotten relations between the white and the black working classes and common moments of resistance and, third, to look for lost moments of a Black British presence in the archive.[192] Taken together, these efforts invite us to ask what kind of (and whose) cultural memory has been suppressed by the hegemonic audiovisual archive in Britain.

In the following I will show how on the one hand the film reworks contemporary archival footage in order to question the hegemonic media representation of Black Britons, and how on the other hand it excavates images from the archives which might point at forgotten connections and genealogies. Such an intervention into the archive sets out to decontextualise the images from their former context(s) and, by deconstructing them, to challenge former meanings adhered to the images. I will first outline the way *Handsworth Songs* reworks hegemonic media images and will therefore start with an overview of the industrial

---

190 *Handsworth Songs* reworks footage from the following archives: Archive Film Agency, Birmingham Central Library, BBC, British Movietonenews, Central Independent Television, Granada Television, Pathe Film Library and Yorkshire Television.

191 This approach is echoed in the motto Chris Marker chose for his essay film *The Last Bolshevik/Le tombeau d'Alexandre* (1993): "It's not the past that dominates us, but images of the past". Marker's assemblage of newsreels, archival footage and interviews interrogating Soviet cinema's construction of history might well have been influenced by *Handsworth Songs*.

192 Reece Auguiste describes the challenges the filmmakers faced during the making of *Handsworth Songs* as an attempt "[t]o bring alive those nervous reflexes, to capture and reconstitute the sensibilities of those who were forever 30 years voiceless or those who were given a voice when the BBC or other television companies said 'You may now speak, but don't forget our narrator holds in his left hand a sword and in the right hand the winning card'. In other words, 'we shall articulate your emotions, we shall define your sense of belonging or displacement.' Our task was to find a structure and a form which would allow us the space to deconstruct the hegemonic voices of British television newsreels." (Auguiste 2007a, 157)

context for the film's archival inquiry. Since the dimension of sound has long been overlooked in film studies, and especially in essay film studies, I will examine the role of the soundtrack both in terms of self-reflexivity and as an intervention into the archive. Finally, I will take a look at the role of archival images as an inventory before addressing aspects of canon formation and film historiography.

4.2.1 Recoding news footage: television, whiteness and national memory

In post-war Britain television became the prime medium to establish consent and to create the 'imagined community' (Anderson 1991) of the nation.[193] As an agenda-setting and opinion-forming medium ("Leitmedium") television thus had an impact on the definition of Britishness. Television was characterised by a white hegemony, allowing ethnic minorities only limited access (see Hall 1990b, Malik 2002). Televised racist attitudes and racifying representations on national television affected the population's sense of (un)belonging to the 'imagined community'.[194] In 1983 the Black Audio Film Collective observed how hegemonic media were grounded in racist and colonial discourses: "It is now widely accepted that the media play a crucial role in the production and reproduction of 'common-sense assumptions' and we know that race and racist ideologies figure prominently in these assumptions" (quoted in Eshun and Sagar 2007, 145). For a short period of time during the 1980s, institutional changes permitted Black and Asian filmmakers to challenge these assumptions and gain access to film production. These changed politics were the result of the disturbances in the inner cities, which were usually represented as 'race riots' in the media. (Herridge 1983).

Inner city social unrest during the late 70s and early 80s (Notting Hill 1976, Brixton 1981, Toxteth 1981) triggered institutional reactions, among them the idea to provide funding for Black cultural work. According to BAFC co-founder Lina

---

193 See Edgerton and Rollins (2001), Bell and Gray (2010).
194 A significant contributor to the sense of (un)belonging was Enoch Powell's notorious "Rivers of Blood" speech which he gave in Birmingham on 20 April 1968 and which received widespread media attention. In 1978, the year before she was elected prime minister, Margaret Thatcher expressed her racist views during a television interview with Granada TV. It contained passages such as this one, which is inserted in *Handsworth Songs:* "I think it means that people are really afraid that this country might be swamped by people of a different culture. The British character has done so much for democracy, for law, and done so much throughout the world that if there is any fear that it might be swamped, then people are going to be rather hostile to those coming in. [...] the moment the minority threatens to become a big one, people get frightened." (qtd. Diawara 1993b, 147)

Gopaul, the Black Audio Film Collective would not have been possible without the 1981 riots which "created a space for our intervention in the media" (Gopaul 2007, 146). The increased access of Black filmmakers to production and distribution was made possible by two key agents: the Greater London Council (GLC), which was eventually abolished by Margaret Thatcher's Tory government in 1986, and the newly founded TV station Channel 4, which became noted for its innovative programming and for paving the way for 1980s New British Cinema with films such as *My Beautiful Laundrette* (Frears, 1985), *Letter to Brezhnev* (Bernard, 1985) and *High Hopes* (Leigh, 1988). Moreover, after coming to power in 1981, Ken Livingstone's Labour-run GLC developed a new funding policy, focussing on 'community' and 'ethnic' arts. Within only a few years the budget for ethnic arts increased from 30,000 to over 2 million GBP (cf. Hill 1999: 219). While the Greater London Council provided the finances, Channel 4 facilitated the access to the public sphere. To illustrate this: As provided in the Broadcasting Acts 1980 and 1981, Channel 4 was obliged to "encourage innovation and experiment in the form and content of programmes" (Hill 1999, 54). Therefore, it franchised independent workshop units such as the Black Audio Film Collective, Sankofa or Ceddo which were commissioned to produce experimental TV programmes, and in addition required to carry out community work. *Handsworth Songs* was not only screened in repertory cinemas and at film festivals, but was able to reach a nationwide audience when it was broadcast on Channel 4 in July 1987.[195]

Within this industrial context, which gave the Black Audio Film Collective access to television archives, *Handsworth Songs* sets out to critically examine television images in a self-reflexive manner. The title of the film refers to Birmingham's inner city area Handsworth, which had been the site of social unrest sev-

---

[195] This specific funding practice ends in the 1990s, after only five years (see Alexander 2000). As a result of the cuts in public funding John Akomfrah's films *Last Angel of History* (1995) and *Memory Room 451* (1997) were co-produced by German television, as part of the ZDF series "Das kleine Fernsehspiel". Other works were commissioned by the BBC: *Dark Side of Black* (1994), *Seven Songs for Malcolm X* (1993), *Martin Luther King: Days of Hope* (1997) and *Gangsta Gangsta – The Tragedy of Tupac Shakur* (1998). In fact, *Handsworth Songs* came about before the BAFC received any funding as a workshop. Only at the end of the production process the BAFC was able to invest 2500 GBP of GLC research funding into the film (Dickinson 1999, 311). Before the Channel 4 broadcast *Handsworth Songs* in its series "The Lie of the Land" in July 1987, the film had a limited theatrical release, mainly in London. In subsequent years *Handsworth Songs* was also screened at repertory cinemas and at film festivals in London, Havana, Berlin, Toronto, Burkina Faso, Melbourne and Oberhausen (Eshun and Sagar 2007, 218). In December 1987 it was included in the exhibition "The Elusive Sign: British Avant-Garde Film and Video 1977 – 1987" at the Tate Gallery in London. "The Elusive Sign" toured various European cities, such as Graz, Rotterdam, Osnabrück, Belgrade und Zagreb (Eshun and Sagar 2007).

eral years earlier, on July 10th 1981. Since then, the place had served as a topos in a long tradition of racifying and criminalising in media discourses. When the Black Audio Film Collective refers to the symbolic location in the title of the film, they make use of the fact that "Handsworth" has already become a metaphor for "race riots" – a notion which the film sets out to deconstruct.[196] In 1985, from 9 to 11 September, protests and street fights broke out in Birmingham, in the neighbourhood of Lozells Road in the district of Handsworth, after a man was arrested. In the course of the events two British-Asian men lost their lives.[197] At that time, images of young Black men as agents of social unrest in 1980s London (Brixton, Tottenham, Peckham), Liverpool (Toxteth) or Birmingham were constantly remediated, thereby cementing the notion of the younger generation of Black Britons as potential troublemakers in an otherwise peaceful British society. "This widely accepted view of a green and pleasant land torn apart by unwelcome violence, innocent victim of conflicts internal to ethnic communities, conveniently locates the 'problem' elsewhere", Pam Cook points out (1987, 78). Although the 1985 upheavals did not occur in Handsworth in the first place, but in the neighbouring Lozells area, they were continually referred to as "Handsworth riots" in the media. However, as John Akomfrah notes in his text for the *Documenta* catalogue, *Handsworth Songs* does not locate the problem in the contemporary situation of social unrest, but "in the annals of post-war news reportage of race in Britain, transformed in the film into an archive of black (un) belonging, in the expression of hopes of belonging brutally deferred" (Akomfrah 2002, 553). When reworking 'riot footage' the film does not limit itself to the contemporary situation, but uses it as a point of departure for elaborating on the gaps and fissures in cultural memory.

Instead of merely adding the hitherto marginalised "Black" perspective as an alternative perspective to dominant media representation, the idea was to rework the visual archive in such a way that the strategies of media representation would be foregrounded. As Coco Fusco states: "by the time of the 1985 riots, an established and limited visual vocabulary about Blacks in Britain was in place"

---

[196] "Handsworth" also figured in the name of the 1978 album "Handsworth Revolution" by the Birmingham reggae band Steel Pulse. In 1984 Handsworth had became the site of Birmingham's first Caribbean inspired carnival. Thus, the district has been remediated as a symbol of multiethnic Britain, continually contesting and renegotiating the cultural memory constructed around the place.

[197] In late September 1985 social unrest broke out in Brixton in London after the police shot Dorothy "Cherry" Groce during a raid at her home. Only weeks later, in October, the death of Cynthia Jarrett during a raid at her house in Tottenham in London triggered the Broadwater Farm riots, which led to another fatality when the white policeman Keith Blakelock was killed. Archival footage of both events is remediated in *Handsworth Songs*.

(Fusco 1988, 18). *Handsworth Songs* challenges the racifying media representation about the upheavals and its metonymic use of the topos of the violent Black male. "A black thug stalks a Birmingham street with hate in his eyes and a petrol bomb in his hand" writes the *The Sun* on 11 September 1985, while the *Daily Telegraph* uses the same imagery in its coverage: "He walks with a chilling swagger, a petrol bomb in hand and hate burning in his heart." [198] In view of this kind of hegemonic media representation, the Black Audio Film Collective set itself the task to open a visual space in their films which would allow them to deconstruct common media images. In order to acknowledge the role of mass media in the production and reproduction of common sense, the focus in Black British filmmaking should not merely lie on developing alternative filmmaking practices, but on contesting the dominant regimes of representation.

Setting out to foreground the processes of image making and the politics of representation, *Handsworth Songs* employs a highly self-reflexive aesthetics. Self-reflexivity occurs when the continuity of the film is dissociated through montage, when the apparatus is exhibited while the gaze of the camera and its discursive framing is foregrounded, or when artificial spaces are created through the means of stylisation and defamiliarization (e.g. in the use of tableaux vivants). In his text "Handsworth Songs: Some Background Notes" Reece Auguiste describes how the archival footage was reworked: "In order to bring emotions, uncertainties and anxieties alive we had to poeticise that which was captured during the lens of the BBC and other newsreel units – by poeticising every image we were able to succeed in recasting the binary opposition between myth and history, imagination, and experiential states of occasional violence." (Auguiste 2007a, 157). Furthermore, intermediality in the appropriation of photography and painting as well as the foregrounding of the materiality of the film through the use of archive footage and photographs reflect on the construction of reality through the media.

Handsworth Songs, in articulating itself as an intervention into the hegemonic discourse, uses self-reflexivity as a Brechtian device of defamiliarization. For example, the filmic apparatus is constantly exhibited. Instead of showing 'riot footage', the film presents scenes showing cameras filming the upheavals. In the rare cases where the film shows footage from the upheavals, it is defamiliarised, for example through the use of slow-motion. Moreover, the role of the media in creating the public perception of the social unrest is foregrounded by newspaper headlines inserted in stop motion. The stop motion technique,

---

[198] Quoted in Solomos and Back 1995, 82.

which recalls, for example, the surreal animation sequences of *Monty Python's Flying Circus* (1969–1974), contributes to mocking the sensationalist coverage in the press. Thus, the newspaper inserts can be said to function as a parody. These self-reflexive practices lay bare the construction of reality through media images and point at the ideological framing.

In the process of image making, power structures are at work, as Susan Sontag (1977) has observed. *Handsworth Songs* critically examines the racifying and colonial structures of image making by highlighting and foregrounding the filmic apparatus and the modes of image production. In one scene in *Handsworth Songs* the camera approaches a group of white and Black children, focussing on different children, before circling around a little Black boy in an extreme close-up which transfers the uncanny feeling of the camera's object to the viewers. The objectifying gaze of the camera, being foregrounded in the moment of the boy's reaction, echoes nineteenth-century photography's practice of classifying people into 'types' through police photography, but also photography as a racifying practice used for medical or anthropological purposes. This connection between photography and bio-political issues, under the influence of positivism, was observed in the mid-1980s by Alan Sekula, among others, in his study of the photographs from Alphonse Bertillon's Paris police archives and the work of Francis Galton who was an advocate of eugenics (cf. Sekula 2003). The insertion of archival footage can therefore foreground the 'white gaze' on the racial Other (Hall, 1990b). In one scene the camera follows two Asian women who obviously want to avoid being filmed. Although the women clearly appear to be disturbed by the presence of the camera, its gaze is persistent. All of a sudden the women turn around and strike back with their handbags. This scene exemplifies a practice of looking back – we witness how the gaze of the camera on Asian subjects is rejected. By foregrounding the filmic apparatus and its inherent racism, the archival footage is not employed as a means of authenticity, of "as it really was" in the sense of Ranke, but as a reflection about the ontology of historical images. *Handsworth Songs* questions contemporary media images of Black Britons by pointing at their construction through the media – by foregrounding the apparatus. We see cameras, journalists and TV teams recording the events, while, in other cases, the images are defamiliarized. For example, archive footage of a Rastafarian being hunted and beaten up by the police is shown twice in different contexts, the second time in slow-motion. Through the changed projection speed the scene becomes "part of a project to look again, more closely, at everyday images usually taken for granted" (Cook 1987, 78).

According to Kobena Mercer the aim of Black British filmmaking practice is to perform "a critical function in providing a counter-discourse against those versions of reality produced by dominant voices and discourses in British film and media" (1988b: 52). However, both the Black Audio Film Collective and Sankofa were critical of the notions of counter practice based on essentialist understandings of identity. Their refusal to merely add positive images to the reductive media representation might have been influenced by Homi Bhabha's *1983* article "The Other Question", published in *Screen*. Bhabha (1983) adds the dimension of 'race' to the debate on representation, which had been dominated by issues of gender and sexuality in the wake of Laura Mulvey's influential 1975 *Screen* article "Visual Pleasure and Narrative Cinema" (Mulvey 1989). He argues that the colonial discourse finds its legitimisation in the "concept of 'fixity' in the ideological construction of otherness" (Bhabha 1983, 18). To stabilize itself, the discourse uses stereotypes which are continuously repeated (or remediated). The stereotype, Bhabha points out, should not be understood as a 'negative' or 'positive' image in relation to 'reality'. Instead it is enunciated within a complex discursive framework. Bhabha challenges the notion that the stereotype offers "at any one time, a secure point in identification" (Bhabha 1983, 22). This would not allow for alternative readings of the stereotype, in other historical constellations or contexts. Stuart Hall's (1997a) rejection of 'positive stereotypes' might be grounded in Bhabha's considerations. Accordingly, Hall suggests to rather examine the politics of representation itself, which is exactly what *Handsworth Songs* sets out to do.

Television's structural racism – of which stereotypes are merely one possible articulation – is foregrounded in one scene in *Handsworth Songs* which remediates a piece of archival footage from Thames Television, until then unpublished. The footage shows the preparations for a live television broadcast of a discussion with representatives from Handsworth. On the soundtrack we hear the dialogue between a producer and the floor manager, which sound artist Trevor Mathison had overheard during the preparations and had been able to record:

PRODUCER: Can I see the audience?
FLOOR MANAGER: Yes, from here.
PRODUCER: Is it slightly dark or light?
FLOOR MANAGER: I don't think so. You are worried that there are not too many whites, obviously there.
PRODUCER: No, in lighting terms I'm talking about. It just looks a bit down, especially in the front.
FLOOR MANAGER: I have my friend, Mr Lafamin here who says that the reason is the colour of their skins. (Qtd. Eshun and Sagar 2007: 88)

The scene demonstrates the power structures at work in the British media discourse of that time. Richard Dyer uses this example in *White* (1997) to discuss the role of photography and film in normalising 'whiteness'.[199] Dyer argues that both photography and cinema, in their historical development have "len[t] themselves to privileging white people." (Dyer 1997, 83) The technological developments of the material used for analogue visual media played a crucial role in constructing whiteness as norm, since the properties of analogue film stock would not accommodate black skin tones.[200]

By drawing on a media practice which reflects on the modes of representation, instead of trying to convey 'the suppressed truth', *Handsworth Songs* defies media concepts of the counter public sphere as developed by Negt and Kluge (1993) in their critique of Habermas (1989).[201] Rather than presenting a mere counter history to the dominant media discourse, *Handsworth Songs* questions media images and their function in constructing 'reality' while at the same time defying notions of truth and authenticity. *Handsworth Songs* can therefore be regarded as an example of interventionist media concepts developed by critical media theorists during the 1980s and 1990s in their attempt to question the presuppositions of Negt and Kluge. While the concept of the counter public sphere is based on notions of homogeneity and authenticity, theorists such as Geert Lovink (see 1992) have highlighted the pitfalls of this approach. The idea of a counter public sphere perpetuates the hierarchy implied between the public sphere and its alternative counterpart. Instead, Lovink suggests an interventionist media practice that points at the inherent power structures at work in the hegemonic media discourse[202].

In contrast to many of their contemporaries on the left, the *Black Audio Film Collective* and *Sankofa* did not intend to create a counter public sphere and to make suppressed voices heard. The aim was not to become a mouthpiece for the community or to function as a megaphone for the growing protest movement. Instead, they set out to develop a new film language which would be able to capture the complexity of Black diasporic experience in Britain. As Isaac Julien, then a member of *Sankofa*, states: "Previous riots had paradoxically enfranchised a whole section of the black community, releasing funds for what I

---

199 Previously Dyer had written an article on whiteness in mainstream cinema for Screen in 1988, for the "Last issue on race", edited by Kobena Mercer and Isaac Julien.
200 See also Akomfrah 2010, in which he discusses the impact of digital technology on black filmmaking.
201 My reading of the film differs from the one offered by Okwui Enwezor (2007, 121) who conceptualises *Handsworth Songs* in terms of Negt and Kluge's concept of proletarian publicity.
202 Alternative media of the oppositional public sphere are based on the idea that the hegemonic media discourse ('bourgeois media') has to be completed and corrected. The bourgeois media leave the masses in ignorance while suppressing 'proper' information whereas the oppositional media provide access to the oppressed truth. Lovink criticises this approach.

call 'social work-type' projects. At this time both Black Audio and *Sankofa* were insisting on our rights to a full range of artistic expression – black film-makers should not be restricted to the ghetto of realism." (Julien and Nash: 1996, 481) In their attempt to create a new cinematic language with the ability to reflect on the complexity of Black British experiences, the Black Audio Film Collective defied the social realism of the so-called race-relations-films of the 1970s and of fellow film collectives whose practice was guided by ideas of the counter public sphere. Pratibha Parmar has described the risks of certain tendencies within 1970s and early 1980s Black filmmaking in Britain thus: "one of the dangers with this has been the way in which perceptions of the black communities as a homogenous group have been reinforced. Differences of class, culture, ethnicity, sexuality, and gender became subjugated, and the black communities were represented as an undifferentiated mass. Diversity, the multiplicity of our histories, experiences, and identities were reduced to 'typical' and 'representative' stereotypes" (Parmar 1993, 7).

This refusal to confine themselves to realist filmmaking and to use images as visible evidence becomes obvious if one compares the aesthetic practice of the Black Audio Film Collective to that of another Black film collective: Ceddo.[203] The comparison is revealing because *Handsworth Songs* employs archival footage filmed by Ceddo.[204] During the social upheavals in Handsworth, Tottenham or Brixton, Ceddo had filmed on location in order to document the actions taken by the police against the protesters (cf. Diawara 1993). As Karen Alexander notes, the use of oppositional media by Blacks in Britain "has usually been at the level of content – i.e. using independent film and video facilities for documenting events or producing campaign films or tapes with clear agit-prop intentions, for specific political struggles." (Alexander 1983, 27) Yet, the Black Audio Film Collective does not employ this footage as a strategy of conveying the 'truth' in order to show 'how it really was'. Instead, it poeticises and defamiliarizes the material. As Kobena Mercer has pointed out, conveying the impression of authenticity and immediacy would be problematic insofar "as a given 'type' of black person or experience is made to 'speak for' black people as a whole.

---

[203] The members of the Ceddo Film and Video Workshop included Menelik Shabazz, Milton Bryan and Imruh Bakari Caesar, among others.
[204] Commissioned by Channel 4, *Ceddo* produced the documentary *The People's Account* (1985) about the social unrest at Broadwater Farm in Tottenham. The scheduled broadcast, however, never happened, because the *Independent Broadcasting Authority* criticised the film's representation of the police as racist and violent and, moreover, it did not accept the interpretation of the unrest as an act of self defence. As a consequence, Channel 4 chose not to broadcast the documentary which to date has never been shown on British television (see Diawara 1993).

Not only does this reduce the diversity of black experiences and opinions to a single perspective assumed to be 'typical', it may reinforce the tokenistic idea that a single film can be regarded as 'representative' of every black person's perception of reality." (Mercer 1994, 58). In contrast to such an approach, the self-reflexive aesthetics of *Handsworth Songs* "offers no comfort zones, no free rides [...] for those who might somehow expect BAFC to 'speak' for them or to 'tell' their stories." (Chambers 2006, 30). Instead of using the footage in the sense of an alternative media practice based on the idea of the counter public sphere, such as Ceddo had intended, *Handsworth Songs* employs the images in order to show the racifying structures of hegemonic media representation.[205]

Black British avant-garde filmmaking can thus be seen as an attempt "to try and develop a different kind of expressive cinematic language that begins to open up hitherto neglected aspects of black people's experiences" (Pines 1991, 10).[206] In order to counter the social-realist trend in Black British filmmaking, the BAFC drew on both Third Cinema and European Art Cinema practice. According to BAFC member Reece Auguiste the task for Black independent filmmakers would be to radically depart from conventional artistic forms in order to create "desired inflections, new forms and new narrative structures in cinema" (Auguiste 2007, 152). Influential were both the Brazilian Cinema Novo and the Argentinean Grupo Cine Liberación, co-founded by Fernando Solanas and Octavio Getino, as well as European formalist political filmmaking and essay films, such as Dziga Vertov's *Man with a Movie Camera* (1928), Jean-Luc Godard's films from the 1970s, Alexander Kluge's *Die Patriotin* (1979) and Chris Marker's *Sans soleil* (1983). An inspiration for the collaborative mode of filmmaking were film collectives such as Chris Marker's SLON as well as Godard and Gorin's Groupe Dziga Vertov in Paris and the political filmmaking practice by Cinema Action or the Berwick Street Collective in London.

---

205 In contrast to *Ceddo* who conceptualised itself as part of the community and positioned itself on the side of the protesters, the members of the Black Audio Film Collective would only travel to Birmingham during the shooting of *Handsworth Songs* in order to film a few interview sequences with some of the locals.
206 See also Mercer 1994.

4.2.2 Sonic interventions – remixing cultural memory[207]

Volker Pantenburg (2006) suggests not to define the essay film via the image/sound-relation, since this separation underestimates the political and theoretical potential of the film image. Instead, research should depart from the montage and its metonymic order of images. Yet, I would like to stress the importance of the soundtrack, and its use of commentary, sounds and music.[208] I argue that *Handsworth Songs*, in creating a dialectical relation between sound and images, uses the soundtrack as another means of defamiliarisation and self-reflexivity.

Abstaining from a coherent voice-over can both "eschew the notion of the singular, authentic, homogenous Black voice" (Chambers 2006, 24) and become a means to recontextualise the audiovisual archive. Instead of privileging "any one voice, or community of voices" (Chambers 2006, 29), the film's commentary consists of a polyphony of voices (sensu Bakhtin 1981) which, along with the music on the soundtrack, connects the collage of archival fragments through the creation of sound-bridges.[209] Most of the archival footage is inserted into the film without its original voice-over. Bill Nichols's describes how the 'voice-of-God' commentary in documentaries, for example in news programmes, sets out to represent "a broader, institutional source of authority" (Nichols 1991:37). However, Nichols does not address the way this voice, usually spoken by a white speaker of Oxford English, helps to establish a 'common-sense' which perpetuates hegemonic whiteness and patriarchal (upper) middle-class values. In freeing the archival footage from its 'voice-of-God' commentary so prevalent in newsreels and conventional documentaries, the images are (at least partly) liberated from the objectifying gaze on Black Britons.

Unlike a conventional 'voice-of-God' commentary, the polyphonic voice-over in *Handsworth Songs* does not explain the images to the viewers, it is at times detached from the film images, at times poetic or ironic. One scene, for example,

---

[207] The term 'sonic archive' is derived from the notion of the 'audiovisual archive' for merely heuristic purposes. The following paragraphs set out to foreground the meaning of the soundtrack, since the impact of the voice-over commentary, sound or music is too often neglected in analyses of audiovisual media.

[208] The importance of the soundtrack is slowly gaining more attention within essay film research. See also the contributions to Kramer and Tode's edited volume *Der Essayfilm* by Catherine Lupton (2011) on sound and heteroglossia in the essay film and by Nora Alter (2011) on the importance of music for essay filmmaking. None of them mentions *Handsworth Songs*, though.

[209] In *Handsworth Songs* the voice-overs are spoken by Pervais Khan, Meera Syal and Yvonne Weekes.

shows footage of the British home secretary Douglas Hurd visiting the site of the upheavals. Surrounded by journalists he speaks into a microphone. However, on the soundtrack his voice is not represented. Instead we hear a female voice-over (Meera Syal) taking an ironic stand, when she states that one has heard Hurd talk to the press and say: "These are senseless occasions, completely without reasons", whereupon a voice from the crowd said: "The higher the monkey climb, the more he will expose". In this scene the relation between sound and image is a dialectical one, whereas in other sequences of the film the indexical bond between sound and image, characteristic of documentary filmmaking in the wake of the Direct Cinema and its possibilities of synchronous sound recordings, can be disrupted. Kodwo Eshun (2011) has analysed in detail how *Handsworth Songs* reworks and reorganizes nine scenes from the television documentary *The Colony* (1964), directed by Birmingham filmmaker Philip Donellan. Only in one scene the original voice-over by one of the immigrants being interviewed, a bus conductor from Jamaica, is retained. In the other scenes the voice is separated from the body while new voice-overs are employed to "articulate 'a secret history of dissatisfaction' and 'an archive of (un)belonging'" (Eshun 2011, 253, quoting Akomfrah 2002). The belief in the possibility of an 'authentic' articulation is undermined.

The reluctance to provide the space for an 'authentic' enunciation is also expressed through the film's sound design by BAFC co-founder Trevor Mathison. The soundtrack's electronic score was inspired by the industrial noise of post-punk bands such as Test Department. Inserted into Mathison's own compositions are intermedial references such as Mark Stewart and the Maffia's version of Hubert Parry's composition "Jerusalem" (1915/16), reworking the sonic archive by deconstructing the classical anthem of English patriotism in a punk-like fashion. The original hymn "Jerusalem" enjoys iconic status, being played both at the wedding of Prince William and Kate Middleton and in Danny Boyle's opening ceremony of the London Olympics in 2012. "Jerusalem" is in itself a remediation, being based on William Blake's poem "And did those feet in ancient time" from 1820. In the poem Blake creates an antithesis between "Jerusalem in England's green and pleasant land" and the "dark Satanic mills" of the Industrial Revolution. At first glance, the use of "Jerusalem" in *Handsworth Songs* could be regarded as a means of contrast: of opposing the pastoral space of "England's green and pleasant land" and Handsworth's derelict inner city area. However, this reading would be fairly obvious. "Jerusalem" is a song evoking the imagined community (Anderson 1991) of the English nation. As such, it was reappropriated in various political contexts and campaigns drawing deliberately on this "national treasure". In 1918 the hymn was sung in the Royal Albert Hall during the "Fight for your Right" movement and its campaign for "Votes for Women" (cf

Aitken and Zonn 1994). The suffragettes have thus used the song as a political strategy to claim that women suffrage is a matter of national interest. On the one hand the use of "Jerusalem" in *Handsworth Songs* can be regarded as a means to deconstruct a national myth, on the other hand it can be regarded as a reappropriation in order to reinscribe oneself into the notion of Englishness and thus into the audiovisual archive of the nation. Moreover, the use of Mark Stewart and the Maffia's remix of "Jerusalem" also alludes to several British cinema classics. Lindsay Anderson has employed "Jerusalem" in *If* (1969), a satire on the British class system. The intersections of class and nation were also foregrounded by the use of the song in Tony Richardson's *The Loneliness of the Long Distance Runner* (1962), a film adaptation of Alan Sillitoe's short novel, which came about within the context of the "Angry Young Men", a group of working-class writers in the industrial Northwest. For contemporary audiences, though, the allusion to the award-winning *Chariots of Fire* (Hudson, 1981) might have been the most obvious one. The film paved the way for the New British Cinema, which in turn lead to a debate about Britishness (see Elsaesser 2005). Through the remediation of the well-known motif from "Jerusalem" on the soundtrack, *Handsworth Songs* inscribes itself both into contemporary discourses around Britishness and into national film historiography.[210]

4.2.3 The archive as inventory: traces and links

Reworking the archive is both a self-reflexive process and an archaeological excavation: it is a means of laying bare submerged cultural memory by recontextualising the images and liberating them from layers of meaning previously assigned to them. At the same time the reworking of the archive also implies a "return to the inventory of black presences in this country", as John Akomfrah notes (Eshun and Sagar 2007, 131). By looking for traces of a Black presence in the archive, it revives lost moments which have been sidelined or forgotten in cultural memory. In one sequence of *Handsworth Songs*, works by Black Birmingham photographer Vanley Burke are inserted, among them the famous *Boy with a Flag* (1975), which portrays a proud Black boy standing next to his bicycle, a Union Jack fastened to its handlebars. As if to defy Paul Gilroy's book title *There Ain't No Black in the Union Jack* (1987/2002), Burke's photographs, many

---

[210] Further remediations of the songs are its parodic use in the first season of *Monty Python's Flying Circus* (episode 4) (1969) as well as adaptations by, among others, Emerson, Lake & Palmer (1973), Billy Bragg (1988) and Bad Religion (1990).

of them taken in Handsworth, are not only traces of a Black presence in Britain, but also demonstrate a normality of Black British everyday life.[211] Stuart Hall (1993) has compared Burke's importance for the Black community in Birmingham with the one of James Van Der Zee (1886–1983) in Harlem during the 1920s and 1930s.[212] According to Hall, Burke's photographs show how for "the first time an intimate, insider's 'portrait' – as opposed to a sociological study – of a settled British 'colony' and its way of life had found its way into print in the form of a memorable set of images" (Hall 1993: 12f.). However, in *Handsworth Songs* Burke's pictures are not merely inserted through montage, they are also defamiliarised in a formalist manner by being exhibited as artefacts in a highly self-reflexive way, reproduced on huge screens. Moreover, the media specificity of the static photographs is foregrounded through the moving camera.

While Vanley Burke's political project was based on the notion of representation, of showing reality 'as it is' in order to defy the stereotypical representation of Blacks, the use of his photographs in *Handsworth Songs* becomes a self-conscious mediation rather than a mere representation. The self-reflexive use of the photographs defamiliarises representation in order to reflect on it. Self-reflexivity in this case points at the discursive space of Blacks in Britain. Thus, the photographs show British identities who claim their sense of belonging in a discourse of 'un-belonging' – they are identities 'in becoming'. Paraphrasing Judith Butler's notion of 'doing gender' as a performative act (sensu Butler 1990), the strategy could be called 'doing Britishness', performing a normality, a sense of belonging, claiming a space in the national discourse on Britishness. The intermedial reference to Burke's photography creates a genealogy of Black British identity, while at the same time reflecting on the politics of representation through its self-reflexive use.

Handsworth Songs and its project of archival intervention may have been inspired by another photo project which sets out to deconstruct the dominant media representation of Handsworth, with the purpose of celebrating the presence of its multicultural population. In 1979 the three photographers Derek Bishton, John Reardon and Brian Homer challenged the documentary style within Black photography by creating an interactive performative project entitled the *Handsworth Self-Portrait*. During this project – which could be called an early "selfie" project – Handsworth locals were invited to take self-portraits in front

---

[211] An exhibition of Vanley Burke's Handsworth photographs, entitled "Handsworth From The Inside", was shown at the Ikon Gallery Birmingham and the Commonwealth Institute London in 1983. It was his first major retrospective.
[212] For a discussion of the remediation of James Van Der Zee's photographs in Isaac Julien's *Looking for Langston*, see also chapter 5.2.

of a white screen using a delayed-action shutter release. By allowing the participants to stay in control over the image making process, this setting challenged the opposition between photographer and the photographed object, thus undermining the power relations inherent in image making. Moreover, it was possible to represent the inhabitants of the district outside the derelict urban spaces which dominated the hegemonic media images on Handsworth (Courtman 2006). Both the photographs by Vanley Burke and the *Handsworth Self-Portrait* project are artistic interventions into the visual archive, as they challenge and rework its dominant mode of representation. Even though the Black Audio Film Collective chose to quote Vanley Burke's photography, but not the *Handsworth Self-Portrait* project, its archival intervention was undoubtedly inspired by the discussions about Black British documentary photography in the influential journal *Ten.8* (1979–1994), which was founded by Bishton, Homer and Reardon in 1979.[213] However, while the *Handsworth Self-Portrait* project sets out to create 'positive images' of Blacks, attempting to counter the stereotypical representation in hegemonic media, *Handsworth Songs* decontextualises existing footage in order to recode it.

Intertextual and intermedial references and allusions can contribute to both challenging dominant historiography and reinscribing oneself into it. This seemingly paradoxical strategy plays out a dialectics that on the one hand undermines or deconstructs hegemonic narratives while on the other hand being part of an auteurial strategy through which the filmmakers set out to inscribe themselves into film historiography. In *Handsworth Songs* the archive footage used in a sequence at the end of the film consists of clear references to the British documentary tradition of the 1930s and 1940s. Yet, the footage contains an image of a Black worker, absent from the films of Humphrey Jennings and the Grierson school. Although the footage of the Black worker resonates with images of the miners in Alberto Cavalcanti's *Coal Face* (1935), there is a difference: In *Coal Face* all the workers are white. The image of the Black worker can be regarded as a means of highlighting the performativity of the 1930s Griersonian documentaries, which in their "creative treatment of actuality" (Grierson 1966: 13) attempt to create an "imagined community" (Anderson 1991), the British nation, which is imagined as white. In contrast to this, *Handsworth Songs* adds a Black presence to the imagined white community while at the same time defying dominant media image of Blacks as 'in need', as social problems and trouble-

---

[213] Along with the journals *Screen* or *Framework*, *Ten.8* was one of the most influential arenas in Britain for contemporary debates about documentary images and the politics of representation.

makers.²¹⁴ Archival footage is thus used as an intertextual reference to renegotiate dominant media images and to reflect on their role in the construction of the national visual archive and of hegemonic historiography. At the same time the footage captures an archival moment, seemingly forgotten in the master narrative of post-war Caribbean immigration to Britain as the start for a multi-cultural society. The archival images place the Black worker in the context of the 1930s or 1940s, thus acknowledging a Black presence in Britain prior to the end of the Second World War and before the arrival of the Afro-Caribbean immigrants of the so-called "Windrush generation".

Handsworth Songs readdresses the notion of the archive as a storehouse of traces from the past, as a visible evidence of a Black presence, and as a system of power which has been trying to suppress or delete these moments of being and becoming. These are aspects overlooked by Salman Rushdie when he criticized the film in *The Guardian*, causing a debate between himself, Stuart Hall and Darcus Howe, then editor of *Race Today*. While Rushdie criticised *Handsworth Songs* for merely showing "riot footage", Hall, in defending the film, pointed at the aesthetic strategies employed.²¹⁵ In this context the title of the film "Handsworth Songs" and its allusion to film titles such as Basil Wright's *Song of Ceylon* (1935) and Humphrey Jennings' *Listen to Britain* (1942) can be regarded as a means of self-inauguration for the collective. These intertextual references could be seen as an attempt to reinscribe oneself into the tradition of British Documentary filmmaking from the 1930s. At the same time, in alluding to Dziga Vertov's *Three Songs of Lenin* (1934) the title expresses a versioning, a mode also found in the title by another BAFC-film: *Seven Songs for Malcolm X*.²¹⁶

---

214 Reece Auguiste notes that "*Handsworth Songs* was made in a Griersonian spirit with our own diasporic inflection adding substance on it." (Auguiste 2007a, 157)
215 In his reply to Rushdie, Stuart Hall emphasizes the film's originality and its formal innovation: "What I don't understand is how anyone watching the film could have missed the struggle which it represents, precisely, to find a new language." (Hall 1987). Hall concludes that Rushdie "seems to assume that *his* songs are not only different but better." Kobena Mercer in turn retrospectively criticizes Rushdie for enacting "an authoritarian practice of 'interpretation' which assumes a priori that one version of reality, his political analysis of Handsworth, has more validity, legitimacy and authority than another, the version put forward in the film. What is at stake here is the fact that there is no shared framework for a viable practice of black cultural criticism, something both acknowledged and disavowed by Darcus Howe's defence of Rushdie's polemic" (Mercer 1994, 55). According to Eshun and Sagar (2007, 142) the critical reception of *Handsworth Songs* shows the degree to which "BAFC had offended the mainstream black British norms of *The Voice*, the putatively radical black British norms of *Race Today* and the liberal Asian fictional norms of Salman Rushdie."
216 According to the Black Audio Film Collective the term "songs" is meant to connote "the lamentations from the dramas of industrial decline; the elegies of an increasingly dissatisfied

The use of the film title indicates the various functions of relating to the archive: the archive as a means of carving out a genealogy, but also as a means of finding more "songs", more versions of a narrative, more soundings than have been perceived before.

4.2.4 Conclusion: essay filmmaking, auteurism and canon formation

As the example of *Handsworth Songs* has served to show, the filmic practice of reworking the archive can have different functions. Remediating archival footage, as in the example of *Handsworth Songs*, can be a way to counter the hegemonic media representation of Black Britons. However, deconstructing hegemonic media images and foregrounding dominant politics of representation through the use of self-reflexive means is only one dimension of the poetic reworking of archival footage. Filmmaking as an intervention into the archive can also help to address the way media-specificity is interrelated with the construction of 'race', and the interplay of experiences of migration and diaspora in the media. Moreover, the film's 'archival impulse' (Hal Foster) re-establishes the broken links of political struggles, but above all it can observe the disrupted connection between the white and black working class in Britain. The footage is a way to interrogate the past "to document periods of recent British history, moments of celebration as well as protest" (Attille 1988:54), as Martina Attille, co-founder of the Sankofa film collective, has stated.[217] "Negationists have already shown that to deny what has happened, it isn't necessary to deny fact after fact: denying the links that run through them and give them the weight of history is enough." (Rancière 2006, 158) In this sense, *Handsworth Songs* re-establishes the links that are denied by hegemonic historiography. At the same time, it remediates archival footage which functions as traces of the Black presence in Britain. The film becomes an archive of images in itself. Another artistic strategy that can be singled out is the filmmakers' attempt to reinscribe themselves into film history. Finally, *Handsworth Songs* carves out a discursive space for addressing issues of race without being limited to questions of identity. Since "the official discourse insisted on narrativising black lives as migrant lives, insisted on treating black subjectivity as simply either criminal or pathological or sociological", John Akomfrah

---

'surplus' class; the falling debris of shattered hopes and broken dreams" (quoted in Dickinson 1999, 316).

217 Sankofa was founded by Isaac Julien, Martina Attille, Maureen Blackwood, Nadine Marsh-Edwards and Robert Crusz in 1983 and was active until the late 1990s.

4.2 Filmmaking as archival intervention — 147

explains, "the recourse to memory was, for us, a way of sidestepping that" (Eshun and Sagar 2007, 132).

By using memory as a point of departure, the collective widened the discursive possibilities for its filmmaking practice instead of merely trying to, for example, provide 'positive images' or convey 'the true story' of the events. In doing so, the film refuses to become part of alternative media practice which is based on the idea of the counter public sphere. The homogenising mode of Negt and Kluge's concept of the counter sphere is undermined by the Black Audio Film Collective's use of self-reflexive means which defy an essentialist speaking position. For example, a polyphonic soundtrack and a dialectical relation between sound and image undermine homogenising notions of speaking for a 'community'. Thus, *Handsworth Songs* challenges ideas of container cultures in favour of an anti-essentialist understanding of cultural identity, as outlined in the theorisation by Stuart Hall within the context of Black British Cultural Studies.

To conclude, five functions of self-reflexivity can be outlined – bearing in mind that this division into five functions is merely heuristic, as they are often entangled and their purposes overlap. First, self-reflexivity can be perceived as a way of dealing with the gaps, fissures and absences in Britain's visual archive and of questioning the master narrative of British historiography (see Lyotard 1979). Second, it is used as a way of transgressing the boundaries of representation and of escaping the fruitless debate about negative and positive stereotypes (see Hall 1997). Third, self-reflexivity is an artistic means of inscribing oneself as an auteur into film historiography. Fourth, it can be regarded as a means of escaping the critical label of the social realist filmmaker who deals with the representation of black experiences. Finally, self-reflexivity contributes to a reconceptualisation of the works in terms of both media theory and the essay film. While the works analysed move away from concepts of the counter public sphere towards an understanding of media as an interventionist practice, the notion of the essay film in a tradition of Chris Marker, Alain Resnais or Agnès Varda can foreground the process of filmmaking as an epistemological process (see Scherer 2001, Eshun 2011). Often, the various functions of self-reflexivity overlap and cannot be separated from one another.

The example of *Handsworth Songs* addresses an aspect of remediation which has barely been acknowledged until now. Remediation theory, while taking the notion of self-reflexivity – termed hypermediacy – into account, has hardly analysed the functions of remediation apart from conveying the impression of immediacy. *Handsworth Songs* shows how remediation involves hypermediacy, though not with the result of obtaining immediacy, but as a way of foregrounding the politics of representation. The case study of *Handsworth Songs* has also pointed at the risk of dehistoricising cultural practice and of generalising one's findings. Moreover, memory scholars ought to be aware that filmmaking by minorities is more than merely an attempt to create a specific 'community's' social or collective memory. *Handsworth Songs* critically challenges the notion of coherent, homogenic communities. The film deconstructs cultural memory by taking a critical stand against the archival image as 'evidence', while at the same time celebrating its function as a 'trace'. This method of both pointing at the gaps and absences in the audiovisual archive and carving out forgotten genealogies has been further developed by John Akomfrah in his more recent works such as *The Nine Muses* (2010) or *The Stuart Hall Project* (2013). As "projects of critical revision" (Mercer 2001) essay films such as *Handsworth Songs* or *The Nine Muses* are critical interrogations of the archive, challenging hegemonic representation as well as questioning the colonial and Eurocentric mode of canonisation. Reflecting on the construction and mediatization of cultural memory without lapsing into essentialism, essay films can offer emancipatory potential instead of stabilising essentialist notions of belonging. In the next section these two aspects will be further examined.

5. Remediation: reappropriations in digital media and in the essay film

The example of *Handsworth Songs* (chapter 4.2) has shown how the remediation of archival footage can be a way to rework a colonial and Eurocentric perspective. Critical interrogations into the archive can create alternative and vernacular memories which might offer emancipatory potential instead of stabilising essentialist notions of belonging. This perspective could allow cultural memory studies to get away from essentialising concepts of cultural or transcultural memory as based on the notions of container cultures.

In this chapter I will take a closer look at the remediation of the Windrush-footage and the ways it is being reappropriated. In what ways can archival footage be used in order to acknowledge the Black past in Britain and to carve out discursive spaces for Black British cultural memory? Looking at the way archival footage is translated, reclaimed and remixed, is also a way to grant agency to subjects, in this case migrants, whose access to dominant media production has been limited. The aim of this sub-chapter is twofold: first, to contribute to theorising about the mediation of migrant memory and the role of documentary images and archival footage. Second, to further conceptualize the notion of remediation. The chapter sets out to examine in what ways the archival footage – or the iconic status of the Windrush – can be used, appropriated or reworked in order to diversify the cultural memory of the nation and to acknowledge the legacy of Black immigration and its impact on contemporary Britain. In looking at various remediations of the footage available on YouTube, I am going to take the media specificity of the cultural memory of migration and its different forms of mediation (mediatization) into account. Yet, I argue that we not only have to analyse the media specificity of these visual representations and their roles as performative acts, but also their specific discursive context. Only then can we get away from concepts of cultural or transcultural memory as static and fix, as based on the notions of container culture and belonging to one specific group. Instead, I would like to show how mediated memories of migration travel (Erll 2011b), how new layers of meaning are added to them and how they can be translated, reclaimed, reworked and reappropriated.

Remediation has been defined as "the ongoing transcription of a 'memory matter' into different media" (Erll 2011a, 141). However, I argue that remediation not always concerns a 'memory matter'. Using the example of Isaac Julien's film *Looking for Langston* which does not depict or rework a specific historical event, I would like to complicate the notion of remediation while examining the uses and function of intermediality in the film. The second case study offers a new perspective on *Looking for Langston* in contextualising the film within memory studies and intermediality. *Looking for Langston* (1989) came about at the heyday of psychoanalytically inspired feminist film theory and its focus on looking relations and the gaze and was clearly conceptualized under this influence. In what way can the insights from intermediality studies contribute to a further theorization of the concept of 'remediation' in order to acknowledge media specificity? I argue that the film uses intermedial references as a self-reflexive device in order to carve out a discursive space which allows for hitherto neglected subject positions to reinscribe themselves into cultural memory.

The concept of remediation within memory studies needs to be reconsidered from two perspectives: first we need to take its industrial and discursive context into account, and second, we have to critically examine the notion that it refers to the remediation of a "memory matter". Remediation and its diverse distribution contexts provide images with additional meanings to be decoded in newly created reception contexts. Earlier discursive frameworks have positioned the images within the public sphere – in which their meaning has been established, contested and re-negotiated (see Hall 1991) – and every new positioning/circulation creates new modes of re-negotiation the meaning of the photograph (or film image). My ambition to rethink the notion of 'remediation' has been inspired by Stuart Hall's article "Reconstruction work" (Hall 1991). Hall sets out to examine "the difficulties inherent in reconstructing those histories from existing photographic texts, which are themselves extremely diverse." (Hall 1991, 152) Hall points out that one of the difficulties in using photographs from the post-war Black immigration as a source, lies in the fact that many of these images have already been published in various contexts. Each new publication adds a new layer of meaning to the photograph. According to him, a photograph does not have an inherent meaning, it does not convey an essential truth, or an original meaning, but is the result of a set of practices within a specific discursive framework. Each new dissemination creates new meanings. Thus, photographs (and the same goes for archival film footage) are polyvocal, "multiaccentual": "No such previously natural moment of true meaning, untouched by the codes and social relations of production and reading, and transcending historical time, exists." (Hall 1991, 152)

5.1 Remediating the cultural memory of migration: reappropriating the audiovisual archive of the Windrush[218]

The arrival of the SS Empire Windrush in Britain in June 1948 is now commonly regarded as the starting point of post-war immigration to Britain and has been described as a foundation myth of multi-cultural Britain (Mead 2007).[219] Today "the Windrush generation" has become a household term, commonly denoting what is thought to be the 'first generation' of Black immigrants to Britain.[220] This has not always been the case, as Korte and Pirker (2011, 27) point out: "before the late 1990s, the Windrush had practically slipped from Britain's historical consciousness".

Meanwhile the archival footage of the Windrush can be accessed via YouTube and has been remediated widely. On board of the Windrush the Trinidadian calypso singer Lord Kitchener had composed a tune which he sang a cappella for the cameras which met the arriving migrants at the Tilbury Docks: "I am glad to

---

[218] An earlier version of this chapter has been published as: "Rethinking Remediation and Reworking the Archive. Transcultural Reappropriations of Documentary Images of Migration." In: *ISTME (In Search of a Transcultural Memory in Europe) Working Paper* 2/2013. Lund: Centre for European Studies.

[219] On its homebound voyage from Australia the SS Empire Windrush had passed the Caribbean where 492 cheap tickets had been sold to West Indians looking for a job in the 'mother-country', many of them ex-servicemen who had fought for Britain during the Second World War. In those days immigration was not policed: before the Commonwealth Immigration Act was imposed in 1962 to restrict further immigration of Black and Asian Britons, the citizens of the colonies of the British Empire held British passports which allowed them to settle in the British 'motherland'. Still, the authorities were alarmed by reports of several hundred Black Caribbeans coming to Britain and reports about the Windrush resulted in racist attacks by some politicians (Phillips and Phillips 1998, Dabydeen, et al. 2007). For a discussion of the number 492, see Mead 2009. On board were also around 50 displaced persons, mostly Polish women. Their presence is usually unobserved within the cultural memory of the Windrush.

[220] The iconic status of the Windrush, however, is not unproblematic since its lack of a diachronic perspective tends to neglect the long-standing Black presence in Britain which dates back to the 15th century. Since then Black communities have existed in London, Cardiff, Bristol and Liverpool, among others. As Barnor Hesse criticizes: "the prevailing narratives of contemporary Black settlement in Britain tend to relegate the earlier part of the twentieth century to the shelf of curiosity studies, while suggesting that matters of real historical interest take place in the middle to late twentieth century." (Hesse 2000, 103) The Windrush topos has also been criticized for marginalising the fact that ten thousands of Caribbeans volunteered to fight for Britain in the two World Wars (cf. Procter, Gilroy). Moreover, the Windrush was not even the first ship to bring Black workers to Britain. In 1947 the Ormonde had hundreds of Caribbeans labour migrants on board, but went completely unnoticed by the media (cf. Korte and Pirker 2011, 27, fn. 15).

know my Mother Country", Lord Kitchener sang. "I've been travelling to countries years ago, but this is the place I wanted to know, London is the place for me." The archival footage of Lord Kitchener has been remediated on various occasions: in *Handsworth Songs* by the Black Audio Film Collective, during the exhibition "The West Indian Front Room. Memories and Impressions of Black British Homes" (October 2005–February 2006) at The Geffrye Museum in the London East End or during the opening exhibition "London is the Place for Me" at Rivington Place in the London district of Shoreditch (October – November 2007). Lord Kitchener's calypso "London is the Place for Me" is also played on the soundtrack at the end of the feature film *Wondrous Oblivion* (dir. Paul Morrison, 2003) and features prominently in the CD-series "London is the Place for Me" (Honest Jon's Records), of which the first volume is dedicated to "Trinidadian Calypso in London, 1950–1956".

Through its remediation, its recurrent circulation in various media formats, the Windrush topos has entered cultural memory: Over the years it was employed in exhibitions and musicals as well as in televised crime series, such as *Foyles War* (ITV 2002) and *Jericho* (ITV 2005), or in Andrea Levy's bestselling novel *Small Island* (2004), which in turn was adapted into a popular television drama in 2009 (see Korte and Pirker 2011, 183–250), or in Danny Boyle's opening ceremony of the 2012 London Olympics. Among others it has been included in documentaries, both for mainstream television, community channels or for user-generated videos uploaded on YouTube. In the beginning, however, was the newsreel.

5.1.1 Media specificity and the construction of the nation: The Pathé newsreel of the arrival of the Windrush (1948) and its Eurocentrism

The 1948 British Pathé footage of the arrival of the SS Empire Windrush in Tilbury is about one minute long, but it comes in a package with a newsreel clip on Ingrid Bergman's visit to Britain under the title "Pathe Reporter Meets". Very likely the two news stories have been screened in the order presented in this complation, having the Bergman clip precede the Windrush story. In those years before the introduction of television, newsreels would be screened in the cinemas before the main feature film. A newsreel would consist of short clips about specific political and historical events, sports events and some entertainment. Pathé was one of the leading companies at that time, producing newsreels in several countries to be screened at Pathé-owned cinema chains.[221] For many decades, until digitised film footage could be uploaded on the internet, the access to the newsreel footage stored in the Pathé archives was restricted. It was mainly targeted at professionals who would have to pay for the use of the footage. Due to these circumstances the remediation of the Windrush footage was limited and its impact on the cultural memory of migration can be said to have been fairly minimal. Instead, the visual archive of migration was dominated by photographs of West Indian migrants circulating in newspapers and magazines (see Hall 1991). Since the digitisation of the British Pathé archives in 2002 the Windrush newsreel footage has been available online, both on the Pathé website and on YouTube.[222] The footage of the arrival of the Windrush starts with a long shot of the ship in a harbour and continues using long shots showing crowds of immigrants onboard, standing crammed along the rails. The establishing shots are followed by a sequence in which a white reporter conducts interviews with three of the passengers. [223] In a classical "voice-of-God"-manner the authoritarian male voice-over, speaking standard English, would comment on the pictures, thereby framing their reception by directing the audience towards a 'dominant reading' (Hall) as he is offering an interpretation of the images. The perspective of the clip creates an imagined community of white Britons.

The Windrush footage is preceded by a newsreel clip on Ingrid Bergman's visit to Britain. The clip contains a dialogue sequence between director Alfred Hitchcock and his star in which Hitchcock conducts an interview with Bergman. The clip ends with a close-up of Bergman's face, while the voice-over states: "The Swedish-born actress wearing no make-up, yet being lovelier than Hollywood has pictured her, has come over here to star in a British film." The close up is intercut with a long shot of a ship in a harbour. Without a break the voice-over continues, now accompanying footage of the arrival of the Windrush at Tilbury: "Arrivals at Tilbury. The Empire Windrush brings to Britain 500 Jamaicans [sic!]. Many are ex-servicemen who know England. They served this country well. In Jamaica they couldn't find work. Discouraged, but full of hope, they sailed for

---

[221] The production company Pathé, founded in Paris in 1896, opened a branch in London in 1902, while acquiring a chain of cinemas as well.

[222] The title of the clip is "Pathe Reporter Meets". In 2002 the the complete Pathé archive, holding newsreels, cinemagazines and documentaries produced by Pathé News from 1910 to 1970 was digitized and has since been available online via its own website. Since 2014 it has been remediated via its own YouTube Channel.

[223] A description of the clip "Pathe Reporter Meets" can be found on the Pathé website. The given length of 169 seconds includes the Bergman-Hitchcock-sequence.

Britain. Citizens of the British Empire coming to the mother country with good intent. [...] Our reporter asks them what they want to do." Reporter: "Now, why do you come to England?" Migrant: "To seek a job." Reporter: "And what sort of job do you want?" Migrant: "Any type as long as I get a good pay." Then the voice-over continues: "Some will go into industry, others intend to rejoin the services." An interview with an ex-serviceman follows. The voice-over states: "Some intend to return to Jamaica when conditions improve." Another interview features a West Indian man who explains that he came to England to support his family. Finally, the reporter interviews calypso singer Lord Kitchener, the only interviewee who is mentioned by name. The dialogue develops as follows: Reporter: "May I ask your name?" Lord Kitchener: "Lord Kitchener." Reporter: "Lord Kitchener. Now I am told that you are really the king of Calypso singers. Is that right?" Lord Kitchener: [barely understandable as the reporter keeps on talking] "Yes, that's true." Reporter: "Will you sing for us?" Lord Kitchener: "Right now?" Reporter: "Yes." [Lord Kitchener sings an a capella version of his calypso "London is the Place for Me" before the clip stops.]

The modes of 'othering' at work in the Windrush clip become even more obvious in contrast with the previous newsreel clip showing Ingrid Bergman meeting Hitchcock on arrival in Britain. While Ingrid Bergman is represented as an individual whose coming to Britain is justified by her professional role as an actress, the passengers of the Windrush are represented as a homogenous group, as "500 Jamaicans", according to the voice-over.[224] The use of long shots lumps the most diverse individuals together into seemingly homogenous groups, while having the tendency to distance the spectators from the immigrants. Despite the change from long shots to medium shots in the subsequent dialogue sequences the interviewees are not named, with the exception of Lord Kitchener. Looking at the politics of representation from a historical perspective, we can state that Lord Kitchener singing into the camera being asked by a white person to do so ties into a long legacy of colonial images.[225]

---

[224] As historical research has shown, neither the number of the immigrants stated here nor their geographical origins are accurate. See Mead 2007, Dabydeen, et al. 2007, Schwarz 2007, Mead 2009.

[225] As Bill Schwarz suggests: "The first social act in Windrush Britain is for a white man to ask a black man to sing" (Schwarz 2007, 7) and in 1988 Reece Auguiste, member of the Black Audio Film Collective, who reworked the footage in the essay film *Handsworth Songs*, describes the scene such: "The sad irony of Lord Kitchener's words 'London is the place for me'. Kitchener standing on the deck, nervous, shaking, but desperately trying to keep the calypso rhythm together; Prospero want to hear so Caliban must continue to sing it." (Auguiste 2007a, 157).

Overall, the interviewees are confined to the limitations of the interview situation, having to react to the question asked by the reporter. Most likely the interviews have been rehearsed beforehand. As film stock was expensive, talks would occur prior to the shooting of the scene with the purpose of selecting potential interviewees, briefing both them and the reporter. Especially the interview sequence with Lord Kitchener shows that the reporter has obtained some information in advance: "Now I am told that you are really *the* king of Calypso singers." No discursive space for a possible self-representation is carved out: the migrant cannot tell his own story, but has to articulate himself within an already given (Eurocentric) framework in which his role is reduced to an extra. Hence, the following questions arise: how can remediation contribute to translating the footage into other contexts? How have the archival images been reclaimed by different groups? Have the images – at least partly – been liberated from their white Eurocentric perspective? Before I look at examples of reworking archival footage, we will have to take a closer look at the notion of remediation and its preconditions.

5.1.2 Premediation and the discursive context of remediation

In my attempt to find out which factors might prompt processes of remediation I am going to readdress the notion of premediation (iconography and narrative) and discursive changes as a condition for remediation. In the years following the arrival of the SS Empire Windrush the number of Caribbean immigrants remained comparably low. The British media soon lost interest in the Black migrants whose struggle with everyday racism went unnoticed within the predominantly white public sphere (cf. Phillips and Phillips 1998). During the 1950s, however, despite its low numbers, immigration from the Commonwealth countries was increasingly regarded as a problem in the public discourse, culminating in the Commonwealth Immigrants Act of 1962 which regulated immigration from the colonies. As Barnor Hesse (2000, 98) notes, "[f]or forty-nine years *Windrush* signified in the public sphere the problem of 'race' and the racialized other." The debate on immigration was guided by a white British perspective, from which Black or Asian migration would be described as a potential threat. For instance, migrants would be referred to in numbers, combining these (increasing numbers) with rhetoric of 'flood' or 'waves', culminating in Enoch Powell's "Rivers of Blood" speech on 20 April 1968 and in Margaret Thatcher's notorious 1978 television interview for Granada TV's current affairs programme *World in Action* about Britain being "swamped" by immigrants. While these racist discourses still exist today, most outspokenly in populist right-wing rhetoric, a discursive shift has occurred in hegemonic politics since New Labour's proclamation of Britain as a multicultural society.[226]

Since the late 1990s the Windrush footage has been remediated widely, thus turning the Windrush into an icon.[227] Fifty years after the arrival of the Windrush oral history interviews with former passengers were recorded for both book publicatios and TV series. In 1998 the BBC series "Windrush" was one of the first media events which brought the experiences of the 'Windrush generation' into the public sphere and reached broader audiences. The series assembles testimonial interviews with historical witnesses, but also with Black British historians and cultural critics (such as Stuart Hall), as well as archival footage. Both the highly popular series and the accompanying book *Windrush. The Irresistible Rise of Multi-Racial Britain* by Mike and Trevor Phillips (Phillips and Phillips 1998) created a 'plurimedial constellation' (Erll) which helped to carve out a discursive space for migrant memory. In the same year, Channel 4 aired its series *The Windrush Years*. The Museum of London celebrated the 50th anniversary of the arrival of the Windrush in the exhibition "Windrush – Sea Change" in 1998.[228] The exhibition included contemporary film footage, most probably the Pathé newsreel. In 1998 The Essex Record Office created an entry in their sound archive called "Radio recordings: Windrush Archive".[229] 1998 also saw the publication of another oral history account: *With Hope in their Eyes*, edited by Vivian Francis, is a collection of interviews with Windrush passengers. Thus, it took almost five decades for the memories of the Windrush generation to be preserved and rescued from the road to oblivion. How come the Windrush topos all of a sudden proved so suitable for remediation? We can explain this

---

226 Of course the notion of multi-culturalism is highly problematic, especially if it is based on a concept of container cultures, which are homogenous and clearly demarcated and which are to co-exist in a given society. However, I will not discuss the concept of multi-culturalism and its pitfalls here, but would like to stress that the British (New Labour) conceptualisation of multi-culturalism might also be understood in terms of hybridity rather than 'cultures', and of a multitude of heterogeneous cultural practices, not connected to an essentialist understanding of 'nation' or 'race', but one which takes the various intersections of identity into account.

227 For several decades the footage would only rarely be employed in films or exhibitions. One notable exception would be the essay-film *Handsworth Songs* by the Black Audio Film Collective in 1986 (see also Brunow 2011). According to Spence and Navarro (2011, 50), the Lord Kitchener sequence was also included in a documentary on calypso "One Hand Don't Clap" by Kavery Dutta (1989).

228 For the first time the passenger list, now held at the Public Record Office, was on display.

229 It is 19 minutes 47 seconds long and consists of six recordings, among them sound files from British Pathé. It uses the index terms "Migration" and "Racism" under the reference code: SA 1/1962/1. The copyright is held by BBC Essex 1998.

phenomenon, at least partly, with the help of the concept of premediation, put forward by Astrid Erll (Erll 2009).

The Windrush could become an iconic symbol because it has been premediated via another national icon with symbolic value: the white cliffs of Dover, famously depicted in Ford Madox Brown's painting *The Last of England* (which in turn gave the title to Derek Jarman's 1987 film). The painting, which shows a couple in a small vessel facing the spectator while the white cliffs of Dover can be spotted in the background, was created in the years 1852 to 1855, "at the height of a period of mass emigration from the British Isles to the British colonies" (Kuhn 2002, 130). As such, the Windrush footage becomes emblematic for a reversal in the national self-understanding: from emigration to immigration.[230] Immigration, usually sidelined and marginalised in national historiography, is now part of the national master narrative in Britain. One of the latest examples of including the Windrush into the national master narrative would be Danny Boyle's opening ceremony for the 2012 Olympics in London. During the show a huge model of the Windrush entered the stage, accompanied by numerous extras dressed in the iconic outfit of the Windrush generation: smart dresses and gloves, suits and hats. Thus, the Windrush topos, being a symbol for multi-cultural Britain, is adding a new dimension to the notion of heritage in which British identity is imagined as solely white and homogenous.

Remediation cannot be explained by premediation alone, though. The reason why the arrival of the Windrush became iconic cannot be found solely in its iconic and narratological conditions. For example, in the 1984 television series "A Passage to Britain" (Channel 4), the Windrush is not even mentioned (see Korte and Pirker 2011, 35). There has to be a "readiness" in the hegemonic discourse to allow these images to enter the public arena and thus into the visual archive. New Labour's redefinition of Britain as a multi-cultural society helped pave the way for this development, although it is not the only reason for the discursive shift from regarding migration as a problem to acknowledging multi-cultural Britain. Especially since the late 1980s Black Britons have been negotiating their identity as Black AND British in many sectors (literature, audiovisual media, music). Therefore the discursive shift did not come out of thin air. From the mid-1990s the idea of Britain as a multicultural society has gained a wider appeal within the public sphere. While both everyday racism, racist attacks in the streets as well as structural racism, for example within the police

---

[230] Although the Windrush did not dock in Dover, but in Tilbury, I would claim that the notion of Britain as an island, with its coastline as the border, is a topos which capitalizes on the symbolic value of the white cliffs of Dover.

and other authorities, are still part of reality, various measures have been taken to acknowledge the diversity within the British population.[231] For example, school curricula would be changed, museum and galleries would change their permanent exhibitions, libraries would expand their stock, the book market would increasingly publish literature by Black British or Asian British writers and the media (both radio and television) would represent multicultural Britain to a higher degree than ever before. No matter if some of these measures have been due to social engineering (school curricula) and others merely the result of market considerations (publishing) or both (museum politics) – in effect, the hegemonic discourse in Britain tends to acknowledge the existence of a multicultural society. The 50th anniversary triggered remediations of the Windrush, and so did the 60th, and most recently the 65th anniversary. Yet, the fact that the Windrush anniversaries are celebrated is also a result of political changes in Britain's historical programme, towards promoting 'multiethnicity' (cf. Korte and Pirker 2011).

5.1.3 Digital archives of migration: reappropriating and reworking mediated memories on YouTube

I will use the example of YouTube as a digital archive of migration, because in contrast to official archives, such as the archive(s) of the British Film Institute or the archives of the BBC, Channel 4 or ITV, it allows for user-generated material to be uploaded and reworked to a greater extent. While its impact on cultural memory might be lower – obviously, a YouTube clip with 5000 hits has a lesser impact than a TV series broadcast on the BBC, with an audience of a million – YouTube as a digital archive contains remediations of the Windrush footage which (might) allow for a higher degree of self-representation than the footage contained in official film and television archives due to the limited access of Black Britons to media production (see Malik 2002). Although the notion of self-representation is not unproblematic per se, the user-generated clips can tell us a great deal about the ways cultural memory travels and how it is reworked and remediated.

Despite the fact that YouTube lacks some of an archive's most important tasks, such as preservation and restoration, it is commonly perceived as an ar-

---

[231] This is remarkable insofar as this discursive shift has not yet happened in other Western European countries, for instance in Germany.

chive and can teach us about the workings of archives in general.[232] Indeed, the video platform is not sustainable and its politics of preservation are highly erratic. All of a sudden a clip might disappear, being removed by the users for personal reasons or due to alleged copyright infringements or other legal reasons. Therefore, the content on YouTube is in constant flux, is continuously reworked and re-edited. Nevertheless, YouTube is not only a video platform, it is indeed an archive, giving access to hitherto forgotten or inaccessible TV shows, children's programmes, music video clips, bootlegged concert recordings or interviews. It allows users to digitise their old videos (VHS or other formats) and to make them accessible – at least for a certain period of time. YouTube is also an archive of first person filmmaking, of confessional videos, make-up tutorials and manuals, as well as an archive of viral videos and their remixes, illustrating the transnational and transcultural translations and appropriations of global media.

The YouTube clips I look at are not only those which rework the Windrush newsreel footage. Some of the examples I will mention set out to preserve the cultural memory of the Windrush generation. Without using the archival footage, they record testimonial witness interviews which they then disseminate via YouTube. Although the clips examined are all available on YouTube (at least at the time writing in 2013), their modes of production and previous forms of dissemination differ to a great extent: the Windrush remediations are both TV series, clips from open access broadcasting, documentations of oral history interviews, stop-motion animations, etc. Some have been previously broadcast on public-service television, some on a (local) community channel with fairly limited audiences, others use YouTube to make school-related activities accessible to wider audiences. Therefore, the look of the clips can range from professional to amateur quality of camera or sound, some have undergone a complex process of postproduction, others would merely record a testimonial witness interview. All these different modes of production and previous distribution need to be taken into account if we analyse the mediation of cultural memory. In addition, it is important to consider that reception takes place in different sociohistorical contexts: mediated memories are actualised on a regional, local or national level. The film clips might be viewed differently by audiences in Jamaica in 1974 and in 2013, and differently again by audiences in other countries. In short, the reception of a specific film clip will vary according to the age, gender, ethnicity and personal experiences of the viewers as well as the specific emotional state that they find themselves in when watching the clip. The following

---

[232] See Snickars and Vonderau 2009, especially the contributions by Kessler and Schäfer, Prelinger, Snickars and Schröter.

paragraphs are dedicated to some of the remediations of both the Windrush footage and the topos accessible on YouTube.

Uploading a user-generated YouTube video can be regarded as an intervention into the audiovisual archive. Reworking the Pathé newsreel can for example result in a video which liberates the archival footage from its Eurocentric perspective. The "Windrush Story", a short (2 min. 40sec.) clip uploaded in October 2009, is a collage of archival film footage, photographs and text frames.[233] On the soundtrack Lord Kitchener's calypso "London is the Place for Me" can be heard for the duration of the whole clip. While the voice-over of the Pathé footage is deleted, the clip uses text inserts, such as "Where was this ship from?" and "Why were these people on board?" It argues that many West Indians, who had fought alongside white Britons during WWII, would have to face racism while settling in Britain. In a didactic manner the video ends with questions such as "Why were these British men and women treated in this way?" or "What were their experiences of coming to Britain?" The "Windrush story" is not restricted to an exclusively Black speaking position. It abstains from referring to the immigrants in terms of "us" or "our ancestors", instead it uses terms such as "these people" which both distance the viewer from the migrants, while at the same time providing a broader scope of spectatorship positions. The use of Lord Kitchener's cheerful calypso "London is the Place for Me" (this time not employing the a cappella version, but the studio recording) clearly gives the West Indian immigrants a form of agency by creating a 'point of audition' ('point d'écoute', Chion 1999) based on Black cultural practice. This mode of empowerment, however, is undermined by the textual commentary which deprives the immigrants of their agency by making them mere victims of British racism.

An example of a user-generated upload which stems from a VHS-recording of a TV programme is the short (01:11) clip entitled "Kitch ~ 'London'......".[234] The clip consists mainly of an excerpt from the Channel 4 documentary "The Great Black British Invasion", originally broadcast in a prime time slot, on Saturday, 5 August 2006 at 7.25 pm. The first nine seconds of the clip consist of a user-gen-

---

[233] The video was uploaded by the signature "mrgreen1066" who has published 300 videos online, most of them on historical topics. With over 15,000 hits in August 2013, the "Windrush Story" is clearly one of the most successful of his uploads. http://www.youtube.com/watch?v=LZfOHnnT6ZE (7 November 2013)

[234] "Kitch ~ 'London'"…..": http://www.youtube.com/watch?v=TReqIteRp7c (7 November 2013). The clip was uploaded by the signature "TVybe" on December 11th, 2008. The description reads: "Lord Kitchener a master of his craft, one of my favourite Calypsonians. [T]his clip is lifted from the superb Great British Black Invasion documentary aired on Channel 4 in 2006. (My first VHS post!!!) (Plenty more to follow....) Enjoy (:"

erated title sequence (white letters on a blue background) announcing "Lord Kitchener – King of Calypso", before we hear a cheerful female voice-over stating: "The Afro-Caribbean servicemen who found a new life in Britain soon wrote home telling others there was plenty of work here. In the late 40s a steady stream of young men began to arrive from all the islands, but it was no surprise who stole the limelight..." Now the Lord Kitchener clip from the Pathé newsreel is inserted. His a capella rendition of the calypso "London is the Place for Me" is fading over to the recorded version which plays on during an animated sequence in which the route of a Trinidadian entertainer from the Caribbean to Britain is shown on a map. The mickey-mousing on the soundtrack, while the drawn figure of the entertainer is speedily moved from Trinidad to Britain, adds to the cheerful atmosphere. The voice-over continues: "entertainers, many from Trinidad, would be the next migrants. They brought with them enough colour, excitement and style to make Britain smile again." In this clip the newsreel footage is reappropriated in order to rework the narrative of Black migration to Britain. Instead of migrants being depicted as a social problem or a potential threat, the clip establishes a story of migration which sees the Caribbean presence in Britain as an asset (bringing "colour, excitement and style" and uplifting the desolate nation).

This new version of the Windrush myth can be regarded as a result of the changed political discourse in the late 1990s which has brought about changes in pedagogy and in politics of diversity. Another example does not use any of the Pathé footage, but looks at the journey of the Windrush as a means to carve out a discursive space that allows for diversity. In this YouTube clip the Windrush generation is constructed as a common reference point for school children with a diverse multi-ethnic background. The short (02:10) clip entitled "The Empire Windrush – The Deighton Centre Animations"[235] is described as follows: "To celebrate Black History Month, children at the Deighton Centre, Huddersfield, made short stop-motion animation films of influential Black role-models, as part of the PBCA workshop – 'Director for a Day'." This short animation opens up the point of identification by integrating local and regional memories (Yorkshire) as well as global sounds (salsa) into the narrative.[236] The clip is a mixture of black and white archival photographs as well as color landscape photography, showing both iconic tropical landscapes (beach, palm-trees) and English scenery

---

235 "The Empire Windrush – The Deighton Centre Animations": http://www.youtube.com/watch?v=MOVuXMMl2kc [7 November 2013].
236 Since its upload on 18 November 2011 it has reached about 2000 hits. It was uploaded by a user called Barry Skillin, who seems to works with stop-motion animation commissioned by different schools because his other uploads deal with the same subject. Obviously he uses his uploads, at least partly, for the purpose of public relations.

(Yorkshire) as well as stop-motion animation with plasticine figures. The Deighton Centre is a multi-purpose centre, situated in Huddersfield, West Yorkshire, which might explain the use of landscape photography in which "England" equals the Yorkshire dales. In the intro we see photographic stills of a tropical landscape which we cannot locate exactly, dubbed with Salsa music. The use of salsa, which might be the result of Eurocentrism, indicates that the point obviously has not been to create a notion of authenticity. The clip does not use any voice-over commentary. Instead intertitles briefly explain the context before we hear children's voices dubbing the figures in an animated sequence with a number of clay figures, using one of the photographs in the background. On the soundtrack we hear a short dialogue sequence: "It's lovely and warm here", "Why are we going to England?", "To get a wide education obviously" (spoken in contemporary urban English). The figures disperse. After another intertitle the cheerful salsa fades out and gives way to a more melancholic music accompanying a sequence of black and white photographs of the Windrush generation. Inserted are animated scenes showing a boat on the sea, a map pointing out the route from the Caribbean to Tilbury. Another text frame explains that the Empire Windrush landed in Tilbury carrying 492 passengers "wishing to start a new life in the UK". The style of the animated figures differs strongly from the elegant style of the Caribbean migrant. In their hippie outfits the plasticine figures rather look like characters from a 1970s Ken Russell film than the well-dressed men in their suits and hats from the newsreel footage. After dubbing the figures with the voices of school children exclaiming "It's so cold", "Hoo!", "Really cold" and "Wish I were back in Jamaica", the clip ends with a sequence of landscape images showing Yorkshire. Choosing the genre of animation film for the mediation of migrant experiences has enabled a less Eurocentric perspective on the cultural memory of migration. Unlike the Pathé newsreel the animation reduces the migrant narrative not only to the moment of arrival in Britain, but includes depictions of the home countries which are represented as attractive locations reminiscent of iconic holiday images rather than of poverty and decay. The text insert "The MV Empire is a ship that is an important part of multiracialism in the UK" indicates the discursive framework in which the clip has been produced, categorising the MS Windrush as a metaphor for the birth of multicultural Britain. Also the names of the three young filmmakers listed in the credits – Komal Bains, Jasmin Collins and Usma Javaid – suggest how the Windrush topos is now used as a pedagogical tool towards diversity. The clip shows how today's politics of diversity set out to include pupils from various cultural backgrounds, not only those of Caribbean descent, but also, as in this case, British Asian children. Moreover, this clip is an example how the Black History Month, which has been celebrated in Britain since 1987, can prompt the remediation of the cultural memory of migration.

Not only initiatives, such as the Black History Month, but also anniversaries of the arrival of the Windrush can initiate the production of different media formats to commemorate the event. The clip "SS Windrush – Mr Chong's Story" is an example of a mediatized oral history project created in the wake of anniversaries.[237] It shows former Windrush passenger Mr. Chong, who came to Britain as a nineteen-year-old, sharing his migrant memories with pupils at a British school. The clip which is half an hour long has so far only received 170 hits. Its static camera records the visit in a Direct Cinema manner, without any use of voice-over commentary of extra texts. It is described as follows: "Mr Chong came to speak with some of our Year 8 students as part of Nottingham Histories rich task in which the students are studying the famous SS Windrush story." The video illustrates how the mediatization of witness testimonies is more often than not grounded in institutional frameworks.

An example for televised memory triggered by anniversaries would be the YouTube-clip "Sixty years on – the Windrush legacy". It was uploaded by BBC Midlands Today, which is the YouTube channel of the BBC's regional news programme for the West Midlands, based in Birmingham. The short clip (02:44 min), uploaded on 23 June 2008, has had over 7000 hits.[238] On the YouTube channel it has been announced as follows: "It was a momentous moment in history. 22 June 1948 saw nearly 500 West Indians arrive for a new life in Britain. Some of the passengers on board the Empire Windrush would settle here in the West Midlands. Sixty years on, Genelle Aldred has been assessing how much life has changed for Black Britons – and what the future may hold." The reggae music employed in the clip situates the point of audition within Black cultural practice, and, unlike calypso, addresses several generations, including younger urban audience.

Remediating footage as an archival intervention with the purpose of creating a space for articulating the cultural memory of Black Britain is exemplified in the YouTube-clip "Black Britain – A Brief Overview"[239]. Describing the Windrush as a vessel which brought "a few hundred brothers and sisters from the Caribbean" the male voice-over opens up a space of enunciation for a Black perspective. The clip does not include the Pathé newsreel footage, but it inserts photographs

---

237 The clip was uploaded on 13 October 2011.
238 The number of hits refers to the time of writing, that is August 2013. "Sixty Years on – The Windrush Legacy": http://www.youtube.com/watch?v=ycNTamNlGog [17 November 2013]
239 "Black Britain: A Brief Overview": https://www.youtube.com/watch?v=RiPvOF7fukk [last access: 12–11–13].

from other contexts to illustrate the arrival of the migrants. Today the iconic photographs of Black Caribbeans arriving at London's Waterloo station in 1956, almost a decade later than the arrival of the Windrush, have come to stand for the "Windrush generation". The clip acknowledges the generational memory of the Windrush passengers and their children ("Their children now experienced a different kind of reality, because they were born here in the UK, they were British citizens") and addresses issues such as economic downturn, unemployment and discrimination both at the workplace and from the police, as well as racist violence and the upcoming of far right fascist groups. However, the clip also includes aspects of empowerment: it describes possibilities of militancy, the rasta movement, the impact of the US Black Power movement on British youth in the 1970s, as well as upheavals in inner cities as a result of dissatisfaction and frustration. Moreover, the narrator adds his own experiences as the son of a family migrating to Britain from Uganda in the late 1970s due to the turmoil in the East African country. According to the voice-over commentary African migrants, many of them coming from Nigeria and Ghana, were often met with hostility from the Caribbeans. It was "not cool at all to be African, not cool to have an African accent". During the 1990s Muslim migrants from Somalia "added a whole new kind of perspective" since "their worldview was quite different". The narrator classifies Black migration into different national backgrounds, but he sidelines categories of class, gender and sexuality. His effort is thus partly anti-essentialist in showing the different experiences of Black migration to Britain, but it essentializes the variety of memories by homogenising them as experiences primarily grounded in national belonging.

These selected examples show the different ways material uploaded on YouTube can be regarded as an intervention into the audiovisual archive of migration. Some the clips are the result of anniversaries, of the Black History Month, or of changed school curricula and pedagogical ambitions. We find televised clips or user-generated material, or clips from television recordings with additional user-generated material. However, we should not only ask what motivated the production of these films or videos, but also what motivated their upload on YouTube. Motivations can range from pedagogical, didactic interest to advertising or the wish to share experiences which have hitherto not been acknowledged, such as an outspokenly Christian perspective.[240] And, of course,

---

[240] An example for the latter would be the clip called "Windrush Legacy" which was uploaded 30.06.2013 and has reached 15 hits by August 2013. It is described as follows: "On 22nd June 1948 the Windrush docked at Tilbury. Now many of those who arrived in that era are in their late 70s + and in the next decade many of them will die taking their history with them. The white British people who saw the Windrush generation arrive are similarly well advanced in years

all of these reasons might overlap. YouTube provides us with an archive of different versions of cultural memory and allows us, at least partly, to develop an analytical perspective on the most recent changes in the audiovisual archive, especially within the last decade.

5.1.4 Remediation and its discursive frameworks

The impact of the discursive context for allowing certain narratives to become part of dominant narratives (or even the master narrative) has been shown by Korte and Pirker (2011) in their study on Britain's historical programme around two commemorative events: the bicentenary of the abolition of slavery in Britain (1807) and the 60th anniversary of the Windrush (1948). While historical research on Black Britons had existed before the 1990s as a result of educational activities or the work in decentralised community centres, "it had never reached the mainstream before because it did not 'fit' the earlier master narratives of British historical culture" (Korte and Pirker 2011, 24). Even an inclusive approach to the multicultural past is the result of a process of selection, being "biased towards themes, icons, and figures that suit current interpretative needs better than others" (Korte and Pirker 2011, 25). For example, South Asian British history has not entered the mainstream in the same way as Black British history, which in turn focusses "on the Anglo-Caribbean, a cultural space that seems less 'other' from its former mother country than the multi-lingual and religiously 'foreign' subcontintent. Of course, the Raj is an essential part of the history of the Empire [...], but the history of Asian migration to Britain in the twentieth century is only in the first stages of being redefined as a part of the national historical imaginary." (Korte and Pirker 2011, 25) Instead, the new master narrative of Black British history is characterised by two dominant themes: slavery, or rather its abolition, and the Windrush. While the history of slavery is met with "guilt and shame" by White Britons, abolition can more easily celebrated, Korte and Pirker (2011, 29) argue, "since abolition was a collaborative effort of whites and blacks, its narrative offers the sort of 'racial healing' needed for the new story of the diverse society".

---

and they too will die and take their history with them. While numerous book and documentaries have been made about the Windrush generation and response of the white British to their arrival, as far as I am aware no visual resource exists documenting the experience of Caribbeans and White British people from a Christian perspective." The clip shows testimonial witnesses who express the importance of Christian faith in order to endure the hardships of the migrant experience. http://www.youtube.com/watch?v=_JwoT5u5GJI (07–11–2013)

To conclude, remediation seems to be a precondition for images to become part of working cultural memory. Yet, remediation does not occur haphazardly, but is the result of changing discourses which might carve out a space for the articulation of certain memories. The case study has shown how (p)remediation needs to be examined not only from the perspective of iconography, narrative or genre, but that the discursive context has to be reconsidered as well: a readiness to let these images become part of the audiovisual archive and thus part of cultural memory. One important incentive for remediation can stem from the institutional context defined by political interests which initiate commemorative events. Both a general and political interest in acknowledging and celebrating these commemorative events, which for instance are triggered by anniversaries, can lead to increased funding for documentaries, especially TV productions, and exhibitions, but also for the publication of non-fiction, novels, or the staging of plays. For instance, the institutionalisation of anniversaries usually results in a broader media coverage. The increased production and circulation of film and other media in turn will most likely lead to more remediations which will keep the cultural memory alive.

The second aspect looks at the reworking of colonial/Eurocentric modes of the archive. As this case study has shown, the remediation of archival footage can function as a critical interrogation into the visual archive. The same footage can be used to tie into completely different narratives: from illustrating a threat to the nation to becoming a symbol for celebrating multicultural Britain. For many Black Britons (and others) the footage had another meaning than the one prescribed: despite being employed in racifying discourses, the footage could at the same time be interpreted as an archival trace of Black life in Britain. Reworking the archive can contribute to challenging hegemonic representation, but also to questioning colonial and Eurocentric perspectives. The archive has been translated and reworked in order to fulfil two functions which are interrelated: a) to become part of a national narrative promoting diversity and celebrating Britain as a multi-cultural society, and b) carving out a discursive space for the story and legacy of Black Britain in order to compensate for the absences of images and stories in the archive of Black life in Britain.

5.2 Remediation and intermediality: media specificity and the discursive context (*Looking for Langston*)

The following case study sets out to explore the notion of 'remediation' from the perspective of intermediality studies. Intermediality studies have recently offered a variety of theoretical and methodological considerations which might be useful for memory studies attempting to acknowledge the media specificity of memory. The use of intermediality in the film has different functions, some of which will be outlined throughout this chapter. I agree with Irina Rajewsky who maintains that "intermediality is not bound to a uniform, fixed function" (Rajewsky 2005, 51) Rajewsky outlines three subcategories: "medial transposition" (film adaptations, "the transformation of a given media product [...] into another medium"[241]), "media combination" (opera, film, theatre, multimedia) and "intermedial references" (cf. 2005, 51). I will concentrate on the last function. The analysis of Isaac Julien's *Looking for Langston* is therefore primarily a study of "intermediality as a critical category" (Rajewsky 2005, 47) since it examines intermedial relations within a single text. However, the division is merely heuristic since all three modes of intermedial practices are present in *Looking for Langston:* first, 'medial transposition' can be found in the appropriation of photography into film, via *tableaux vivants* and *tableaux vivants animé*; second, media combination can be found in the medium film's mixed-media character, and third, Julien's film includes references to a number of literary texts, films and photographs.

Irina Rajewsky reminds us that "in dealing with medial configurations, we never encounter 'the medium' as such, for instance, film as medium or writing as medium, but only specific individual films, individual text, and so on" (Rajewsky 2010, 53). Therefore, I find it highly useful to take a specific film, Isaac Julien's *Looking for Langston,* as an example to explore intermedial relations and their function. No matter which use of terminology we agree upon within intermedia studies, we should be aware that "we always only encounter concrete medial forms of articulation, which moreover are characterized by a multilayered and multimodal complex mediality" (Rajewsky 2010, 53–54). Instead of contributing to the ongoing attempt to create a coherent terminology within intermedia studies (see Ellestrōm 2010), my ambition here is to look at one specific medial form of articulation: a film which employs a number of intermedial references. The aim of this chapter is to both outline their functions and to complicate the notion of coherent, homogenous communities. Following on from the analysis of self-reflexivity in *Handsworth Songs* by the Black Audio Film Collective, intermediality and intertextuality will be conceptualised here as self-reflexive traits.

---

241 "This category is a production-oriented, 'genetic' conception of intermediality" – 'source' and its formation "based on a media-specific [...] transformation process". (Rajewsky 2005, 51)

Looking for Langston is a film project by the Black British film workshop Sankofa Film and Video, directed by Isaac Julien.[242] *Looking for Langston* was produced by Channel 4, and broadcast in the gay and lesbian series "Out on Tuesday" in the spring of 1989. It gained international attention after winning the Teddy award at the 1989 Berlinale. Sankofa's 1980s work can be placed in a context of contemporary British filmmaking with feature films such as *My Beautiful Laundrette* and *Sammy and Rosie Get Laid*, which managed to address issues of national, ethnic and sexual identity and still cross over into the mainstream. Yet, while these films "still remain within the ambit of traditional 'art cinema' and its fusion of narrative and expressive concerns", as John Hill notes, the films of Sankofa and the Black Audio Film Collective move beyond this in favour of formal experimentation in an avant-garde tradition, combining "political with aesthetic radicalism" (Hill 1999, 220). Sankofa's films offer an intersectionalist perspective which allows for an anti-essentialist understanding of Black Britishness, as can be found in the theorisations of Stuart Hall or Paul Gilroy.[243]

Looking for Langston by Isaac Julien/Sankofa is a multi-layered complex work, an assemblage of intermedial references. According to Muñoz, *Looking for Langston* "displays other modes of black queer cultural production such as music, performance, poetry, prose, cultural criticism, and photography" (Muñoz 1999, 57). The film thus turns into an archive of black cultural production across the Black Atlantic. It focusses on two nodal points, one in the US, the other one in Britain: the Harlem Renaissance (1919–34) and 1980s British club culture. *Looking for Langston* creates a vast network of references, including silent cinema, European art cinema and US-American underground film. Moreover, it appropriates visual art, such as photography, alludes to paintings and reworks archival footage. Its soundtrack, an assemblage of quotations, voices and songs from different genres and decades, contains a multitude of intermedial references which will be examined in this chapter. One guiding question is: how to create a genealogy of affiliations without ethnic self-essentialisation?

As the previous chapter on the remediation of the Windrush footage has shown, remediation can refer to the adaptation and reworking of a 'memory mat-

---

242 The name Sankofa was "given to us by our friend Kobena Mercer; it symbolised a bird flying into the future with its head turning back, looking at the past." (Julien 2001, 177).
243 Before *Looking for Langston* Sankofa had produced *The Passion of Remembrance* (1986), co-directed by Maureen Blackwood and Isaac Julien, as well as *Territories* (1984). *The Passion of Remembrance* addresses feminist and queer issues within the Black British community, highlighting the intersection of race, gender and sexuality. The film does not target white audiences in the first place, but foregrounds conflicting positions within a Black British family, thereby pointing at the differences amongst Blacks in Britain while also celebrating their diversity.

ter'. The Windrush example illustrates how remediation can be conceptualised as an archival intervention in order to create a sense of history, belonging, and genealogy. The example of *Looking for Langston* sets out to complicate this notion. While the remediation of the Windrush myth can be regarded as a contribution to a 'Black' or 'Black British' historiography, we ought to keep in mind that neither the notion of Blackness nor of Black Britishness are homogenous. Such a homogenising approach might entail the risk of excluding a number of individuals, for example LGBT persons. To illustrate, in the narrative(s) around the Windrush generation, gay voices are completely absent. Filmmaking as memory work can reflect on these gaps and absences. *Looking for Langston* not only addresses gaps within heteronormative Black history, but also within LGBT history and its white hegemony. Through the use of a variety of archival footage the film becomes an archive in itself while at the same time reworking the audiovisual archive of Black and/or gay cultural memory.

Although the film uses re-enactment, it is devoid of dialogue. Instead it works with looks and the gaze which expresses gay desire. Just like archives housed in buildings, such as the *Black Gay and Lesbian Archive* based in New York, *Looking for Langston* can be regarded as a performative archive of Black (gay) cultural practice: it collects archival footage which it makes accessible again, it reappropriates gay photography and reworks the white gaze on black bodies, thereby freeing the Black bodies in the pictures from being 'othered'. It carves out spaces for Black gay desire – spaces which have been hidden, which have been forgotten, marginalised or overwritten. Other queer films, such as Greta Schiller's *Before Stonewall* (1985), also rework archival footage in order to create a genealogy of gay and lesbian culture and activism during the twentieth century before the Stonewall uprising. Unlike *Before Stonewall*, however, *Looking for Langston* does not attempt to create an LGBT historiography, but rather carves out a space in which Black gay desire and art can be articulated and remembered. For Schiller, art, for instance in 1920s and 1930s Harlem, serves as a mode of empowerment, as a way to gain agency. Julien is less utilitarian in his understanding of art. He celebrates art and artistic practice which sets out to broaden the scope, to transgress the limitations of time and space. Other films which reflect on the Black visual archive are Cheryl Dunye's *Watermelon Woman* (1996), a highly self-reflexive mockumentary, which addresses issues of representation from the perspective of Black lesbian history. A feminist historiography of African-Americans if offered by Julie Dash in her fiction film *Daughters of the Dust* (1991). Filmmaking can therefore be regarded as a way of creating audiovisual archives which provide a space for Black cultural memory. Both *Daughters of the Dust* and *Watermelon Woman* show that even fictionalised memory, re-enactments or mockumentaries can function in this way.

Looking for Langston's way of dealing with memory can be compared to the aesthetic strategy used in Chris Marker's *The Last Bolshevik*, which Jacques Rancière describes in his *Film Fables* as follows: "The point, then, isn't to preserve Medvedkin's memory, but to create it." (Rancière 2006, 157) And he goes on: "Memory is not the store of recollections of a particular consciousness, else the very notion of a collective memory would be devoid of sense. Memory is an orderly collection, a certain agreement of signs, traces, monuments" (Rancière 2006, 157). However, the cultural memory reworked in Julien's film is not an "orderly collection". Therefore *Looking for Langston* is not merely to be understood as a historical research project, in terms of creating a revisionary historiography or reworking the history of the Harlem Renaissance. No doubt, the film can be characterised as Julien's "heritage project". Yet, while Julien acknowledges gay interracial desire in the Harlem Renaissance, his intermedial reworking of the archive connects to contemporary debates. *Looking for Langston* engages in a dialogue with contemporary Black queer (or gay) theorising, along debates around or efforts of carving out black gay subject positions, especially in literary projects, around the discourse of "black men loving black men", placing itself deliberately in the context of the Aids crisis and the homophobia which became more prevalent in its course.[244]

Isaac Julien's *Looking for Langston* creates a transtemporal network of gay desire and reflects on black masculinity, reworking icons of Black culture, such as Langston Hughes and James Baldwin. The film's transtemporal dialogue is created by a complexity of layered intermedial references, which encompass film extracts from Oscar Micheaux, footage of Bessie Smith's "St. Louis Blues", old Blues recordings, photographs of Countee Cullen and James Baldwin, as well as archival footage from television programmes showing Langston Hughes reciting his poems. While *Looking for Langston* has received some critical attention within film studies or related disciplines (see for example Mercer 1994, Muñoz 1999, Wallenberg 2002, Grönstad 2007, Kirstein 2002, Silverman 1996, Bravman 1993, Dickel 2011), most of the studies are based on a theoretical framework grounded in psychoanalysis, feminism and cultural studies, focussing on issues of Blackness, gay identity, masculinity, the gaze. Despite the fact that

---

[244] The Aids crisis has resulted in policing gay desire even further. In his interview with bell hooks Julien states: "with the advent of this new pseudo-black nationalism there's a closing off or policing of those different discourses that make it difficult to articulate those desires." (Julien in hooks 1991, 178).

the film employs a wide network of intermedial references, it has so far never been discussed in the context of the burgeoning field of intermediality studies.[245]

Intermediality studies, as noted by Bruhn (2010), have had a formalistic tendency. He therefore suggests to broaden intermediality studies so as to get away from pure formalism, towards acknowledging the ideological aspects. He sets out to promote a concept of intermediality (or 'heteromediality', as he calls it) that should include "ideological questions of gender, class, race or struggles between different aesthetic positions" (Bruhn 2010, 232).[246] However, while Bruhn's suggestion is useful, we should be aware of its risks. As Hall (1996a) has argued, binary constructions such as 'black' or 'white' are not natural, not a-historical, but created through and within historically specific discourses. Therefore, it is crucial not to speak merely of "Black" cultural practice, for this would naturalize Blackness. In his essay "The Question of Cultural Identity" Stuart Hall points out the importance to take an intersectionalist perspective into account: "this 'black' identity [...] continues to exist alongside a range of other differences" (1992:309) – such as gender, class or generation. Films such as *Territories* (1984) and *The Passion of Remembrance* (1986) by the Sankofa film and video collective, but also the Frears-Kureishi collaborations *My Beautiful Laundrette* and *Sammy and Rosie Get Laid,* show "that the question of the black subject cannot be represented without reference to the dimensions of class, gender, sexuality, and ethnicity" (Hall 1996a, 167). As Stuart Hall has famously claimed in his article "New Ethnicities", based on a paper at the influential conference "Black Film/British Cinema" at the ICA in London (see Mercer 1988a): "What is at issue here is the recognition of the extraordinary diversity of subjective positions, social experiences, and cultural identities which compose the category 'black'; that is, the recognition that 'black' is essentially a politically and culturally *constructed* category, which cannot be grounded in a set of fixed, trans-cultural or transcendental racial categories and which therefore has no guarantees in Nature" (Hall 1996a, 166). Instead, we need to acknowledge "the immense diversity and differ-

---

[245] Notable exceptions are Mercer and Darke 2001 who point out some of the intertextual relations used in the film. Many authors discuss Mapplethorpe (Muñoz) or the presence of the cultural practitioners of the Harlem Renaissance, but as far as I know, the media specificity of the film's archival remediations has not been discussed. (Brunow 2011a briefly mentions *Looking for Langston* and the use of *tableaux vivants* in looking at the use of self-reflexivity in some of Black British 1980s filmmaking).

[246] One of the ways formalism and ideology can be brought together is the use of self-reflexivity within Black British filmmaking. Intertextuality and intermediality are two self-reflexive devices. For a study on intermedial references and their self-reflexive function in Black British filmmaking of the 1980s, see also Brunow 2011a.

entiation of the historical and cultural experience of black subjects" (Hall 1996a, 166). *Looking for Langston* is the result of acknowledging such intersectionality.

From the perspective of film studies scholarship I would argue that an intersectionalist research perspective (race/class/gender) is not specific enough, because it might contribute to de-historicising artists' practice by treating the works purely in terms of sociology and overlooking the artists' creativity. While Bruhn's suggestion entails the risk of essentialising artworks created from a minoritarian position, I would like to use this case study to both point at this risk and to offer ways of minimising it. Therefore, this study challenges an essentialist understanding of 'culture', even of 'Black culture'. Isaac Julien points at the problems of essentialist understandings of Blackness for LGBT persons. In his article "'Black Is, Black Ain't': Notes on De-Essentialising Black Identities", which was inspired by Charles Nero's essay "Towards a Black Gay Aesthetic" and by Ralph Ellison who in *Invisible Man* outlines a relational (not essential) understanding of Blackness, Isaac Julien (1992) argues for the need to de-essentialise Black identities. Nero's, Ellison's and Julien's texts all address the issue of homophobia within Black popular culture, reaching from African-American religious communities to the Nation of Islam and from Afrocentrism to rap. Within (and through) these diverse cultural practices masculinity has been constructed as exclusively heterosexual whereas gay Black men have been conceived of as "traitors of the race". My aim is therefore to show that cultural adaptations and appropriations should not be conceptualised in terms of a general understanding of "Black cultural practice", but ought to be contextualised in the specific discursive and aesthetic context with which they engage in a media-specific manner.

During the 1980s Black gay men have increasingly addressed this in their cultural production, in both writings, photography, art and filmmaking. Inspirational were, among others, filmmaker Marlon Briggs (*Tongues Untied*, 1989), poet Essex Hemphill, the singer Blackberri, novelists Melvin Dixon and Samuel Delaney in the US as well as in Britain the photographers Rotimi Fani-Kayode and Ajamu and Kobena Mercer's theorisations on diasporic art and filmmaking practice. These artists and cultural critics do not form a school or share aesthetic or formal traits. Muñoz sums up what these practitioners are trying to accomplish: "the (re)telling of elided histories that need to be both excavated and (re)imagined, over and above the task of bearing the burden of representing an identity that is challenged and contested by various forces, including, but not limited to, states that blindly neglect the suffering of bodies of men caught within a plague[247], the explosion of 'hate crime' violence that targets black and gay bodies, and a reactionary media power structure" (Muñoz 1999, 57).

For Isaac Julien, "it was the construction of race, memory, and desire, the closet in black popular culture, that needed to be explored filmically" (Julien 1992, 259). In this context Julien describes *Looking for Langston* as his "project of demarginalising and recentering black literary figures" (Julien 1992, 258).[248] While it was known that Langston Hughes was gay, he was not officially out. Therefore Julien had to meet the challenge of realising his filmic project around the icon Langston Hughes within the existent discourses of Black masculinity while at the same time trying to traverse them.[249] After its critical acclaim, winning the Teddy Award at the Berlin Film Festival, two further screenings – at the International Film Festival in Washington, DC and the San Francisco International Lesbian and Gay Film Festival 1989 – had to be cancelled at short notice due to a legal dispute with the Langston Hughes Estate who had only granted the rights on Hughes' material for the European market. At the New York Film Festival *Looking for Langston* was only shown in a censored version in October 1989 (see Hemphill 1991a, 183). Two archival sequences of Hughes reciting his poetry were shown without the accompanying sound. As the estate did not want Langston Hughes to be associated with homosexuality, more sequences of the soundtrack featuring Hughes poetry had to be re-edited (see Julien 1992, 259). The reception of the film seems like an ironic commentary on the film's effort to carve out a discursive space for queer black male sexuality. The silence during the film screening and the omission of Hughes' gayness is symptomatic for the silence around homosexuality in black masculinity.

To carve out this discursive space *Looking for Langston* employs a self-reflexive aesthetic (see Brunow 2011a) which works in a different manner than the one employed by the Black Audio Film Collective for *Handsworth Songs*. In contrast to the Sankofa films, *Handsworth Songs* is devoid of an intersectionalist perspective. While Pam Cook (1987) has criticised it for its lack of a feminist perspective, I would add that the relation between race, gender and sexuality is not explored in the film, as a result of which heteronormativity is naturalized and perpetuated. Isaac Julien's approach is grounded in the earlier works by the Sankofa film and video collective, especially in films such as *The Passion of Remembrance* or *Territories*.

---

[247] The "plague" refers to the ongoing Aids crisis.
[248] On a similar note José Arroyo states that in Isaac Julien's 1980s films "the otherwise marginal is made central. They make a subject of various forms of Otherness." (Arroyo 1995, 321)
[249] "The repicturing of an iconic figure like Hughes trespassed across the essentialist battle line of blackness." (Julien 1992, 259).

This chapter outlines two points of argument. First, the case study will follow the idea outlined in the previous chapter that remediation is always situated within a specific discursive framework. I argue that focussing on the situatedness will help to minimize the risk of essentialism. Second, the case study sets out to show that remediation is not only about translating 'memory matters' into different media. I would argue that the scope of the concept of remediation can be broadened out, to encompass not only transmitting specific events but also the creation of discursive spaces of commemoration which allow for an exploration of memory, desire and identity. Rather than mediating a historical event through plurimedia constellations, the use of 'remediation' within memory studies might also be expanded towards a utopian dimension.[250] Therefore, the chapter is divided into three parts. First, I will examine how intermediality has been used as a deliberate artistic device in Isaac Julien's *Looking for Langston*. My thesis is that intermediality can be used as an aesthetic strategy to open the discursive space for various subject positions, to rework the canon and to renegotiate the audiovisual archive. Second, I will look at the appropriation of photography in the film and third, discuss these findings in the context of 1980s discourses on Black gay male identity. In closing, I will outline several functions of intermediality in the context of cultural memory and its remediation.

The primary aim is not to contribute to the burgeoning field of intermediality studies. However, I will take up Bruhn's suggestion who calls for more social/political contextualisation in intermediality studies. At the same time we should be aware of the power relations and exclusions at work in film historiography. The auteur perspective and its alleged universality is obviously still necessary to canonize a director's work and to enter it into film historiography. Julien's film shows how a filmmaker can both serve the auteur perspective while at the same time embedding one's film in a specific discourse, which, however, is not the only reading the film invites.

---

250 The utopian dimension of *Looking for Langston* is echoed in the fact that Julien had intended to include sections of Langston Hughes' essay "The Negro Artist and the Racial Mountain" into his film, but was not allowed to do so. In an interview with Paul Gilroy Julien quotes the final sentences of Hughes' text: "We younger negro artists who create now intend to express our individual dark-skinned selves without fear or shame. If white people are pleased we are glad. If they are not, it doesn't matter. We know we are beautiful. And ugly too. The tom-tom cries and the tom-tom laughs. If coloured people are pleased we are glad. If they are not, their displeasure doesn't matter either. We build our temples for tomorrow, strong as we know how, and we stand on top of the mountain, free within ourselves." (quoted in Gilroy 1993, 172).

5.2.1 Contemporising the past: intermediality and transtemporal dialogue

Looking for Langston is a complex film with an extremely dense net of intermedial references, of allusions and appropriations. Among them are allusions to films by Kenneth Anger, Jean Cocteau and Jean Genet, excerpts from texts by Bruce Nugent, Langston Hughes and Essex Hemphill and the voices of James Baldwin, Langston Hughes, Toni Morrison and Stuart Hall. According to John Hill *Looking for Langston* can be regarded as "an act of historical recovery, a bringing to the surface of what had been previously 'hidden from history'" (Hill 1999, 231) Yet, as I would argue, *Looking for Langston* is more than a mere archaeological excavation of hidden histories and hidden voices. The film reworks the archive and contemporizes it. In this chapter I argue that the film, by employing a variety of intermedial references, creates a "transtemporal dialogue" (Henry Gates jr). The transtemporal dialogue is created through the montage of various sources of images and sound: fiction film, documentary footage, TV programmes, radio recordings, recorded songs, voice-overs. Moreover, it is therefore able to construct a new, deterritorialised discursive space for the articulation of hitherto unacknowledged subject positions. In this section of my study I am going to focus on filmmaking as a means to reappropriate the audiovisual archive and to rework it – both with the purpose to create a genealogy of Black cultural practice and also to topicalize the past (Benjamin) in order to develop a utopian dimension.[251]

More than any previous Sankofa film, *Looking for Langston* explores the notion of fantasy. With its focus on fantasy Julien inscribes the film into the tradition of surrealist filmmaking, from Germaine Dulac and Luis Buñuel to Jean Cocteau or Jean Genet, but also into the contemporary trend within British experimental filmmaking: the New Romantics. I would argue that these intermedial references contribute to creating new utopian spaces for desire ("Möglichkeitsräume"). According to Julien, desire is the notion along which discourses of cultural policing unfold. As bell hooks has claimed in an interview with Isaac Julien: "There's a kind of absolutism in this resurgence of black cultural nationalism, and desire is one of the arenas that it polices." (hooks 1991, 174). In representing Black gay desire, *Looking for Langston* expresses 'impossible desires' (Gopinath 2005), to use a term Gayatri Gopinath has coined referring to queer readings of South Asian cinema. In the context of colonialism and racism,

---

[251] My understanding of genealogy is derived from Foucault who defines genealogy as "an examination of descent", focussing here on resonances and affiliations, which "permit the discovery, under the unique aspect of a trait or a concept, of the myriad events through which – thanks to which, against which – they were formed." (Foucault 1977, 146).

queer desire does not remain peripheral, but moves into the centre: "there is no queer desire without these histories, not can these histories be told or remembered without simultaneously revealing an erotics of power", as Gopinath states, drawing on *My Beautiful Laundrette* (2005, 2). Looking for Langston creates an archive of this 'impossible' desire.

José Arroyo (1995) is one of the critics who have pointed at Julien's aesthetic practice of resignifying. Drawing on Trinh T. Minh-ha's essay "There is a Third World in every First World" (1986), Arroyo argues that "'looking back' and ‚talking back' form a necessary step to the unsaying of what has been said and concealed". (Arroyo 1995, 329). According to Arroyo, in Isaac Julien's films the practice of "looking back" is central in order "to unearth and reconstruct a history of black British culture" (Arroyo 1995, 329).[252] This collage of archival footage contributes to creating a network of Black creativity on the one hand and a deterritorialised Black queer history archive on the other hand. Archival footage of LGBT history, as is found in Greta Schiller's *Before Stonewall* (1985) for example, can create a genealogy of LGBT lives, cultural practice and political activism. In remediating the footage, the film(s) can themselves become deterritorialised archives of LGBT memory (a memory which has traditionally only rarely left the private sphere). In this sense, one of the functions of remediation (intermediality) in *Looking for Langston* is the creation of an audiovisual archive of Black gay culture (omitting lesbian, bisexual and transgender subject positions, though). In contrast, Schiller's approach is more inclusive towards lesbian or transgender histories. Julien's film, however, enters into a dialogue with a specific contemporary debate on black (male) gay identity. Along with the DVD release in 2005 a special box set was published including a selection of 26 stills by Sunil Gupta. Photographs from the film, by Isaac Julien and Sunil Gupta, were exhibited at the Rudenstine Gallery of the W.E.B. Du Bois Institute for African and African American Research at Harvard University in the spring of 2007. Moreover, screenings of *Looking for Langston* occur repeatedly in both cinematic and arts contexts, for example in 2011 in Berlin under the umbrella of the Robert Mapplethorpe exhibition which toured different European cities. Thus, the film's archival intervention was not only temporary – through its renewed circulation the film becomes a performative archive in itself.

Looking for Langston contemporizes the past through a network of intermedial references. One example are the film's allusions to Jean Cocteau's film *Orphée* (1950) and *Orfeo Negro/Black Orpheus* (Brazil 1959) by Marcel Camus. Julien

---

[252] José Esteban Muñoz conceptualises this relation in terms of the Black cultural practice of 'call-and-response' (see Muñoz 1999, 61–62).

appropriates the Orpheus myth by relocating it into the new deterritorialised filmic space he creates, a space which combines both the memory of the Black Harlem Renaissance and the contemporary queer pop scene of 80s London. Not only are parts of *Looking for Langston* shot at the back of the legendary gay nightclub "Heaven" in London, but the film also stars Jimmy Somerville, singer of the 1980s band Bronski Beat, who was known for his falsetto voice and queer appeal. Somerville also briefly appears in Sally Potter's *Orlando* (1992), the filmic adaptation of Virginia Woolf's 1928 novel, in itself a work of transgenerational memory and queer desire.[253] Another intermedial reference concerns Somerville's role as an angel in *Looking for Langston*, alluding to both the kitsch and camp works of French photographers Pierre et Gilles as well as Walter Benjamin's notion of the 'angel of history'. However, the appropriation of the image from Cocteau's *Orphée* can be read as a means not only of inscribing *Looking for Langston* into the canon of European Art cinema, but also of reinscribing Blackness into contemporary pop culture. A film still showing Jean Marais in *Orphée* was used by the 1980s Manchester band The Smiths for their single cover of "This Charming Man" (Rough Trade), released in October 1983. Carving out spaces for Black British identity that are informed by 1980s popular culture, such as club culture and soul, is a project Isaac Julien continued in his feature *Young Soul Rebels*.

The link with The Smiths in turn leads on to Derek Jarman, whose super 8 productions and New Romanticism had inspired Julien. Jarman had been commissioned to create a number of music videos for The Smiths, both for their single "Ask" as well as a three-song compilation video, employing super 8 footage, "The Queen is Dead" (1986), including "The Queen is Dead", "There's a Light that Never Goes Out" and "Panic".[254] In his film *Derek* (2008), Julien delivers a portrait of the artist, and he was also the curator for the Derek Jarman exhibition "Brutal Beauty" at the Serpentine's Gallery in London 2008, where the film was screened in an ongoing loop. In *Derek* Julien inscribes himself into the film by inserting a film sequence showing him walking around in an archive. A similar strategy of inscribing himself into the film, though in a different manner, is employed in *Looking for Langston*. In the funeral scene we see Isaac Julien himself lying in the casket. This can be understood as a pun on the notion of "the death

---

[253] Intertextual or intermedial references are here understood in Kristeva's dialogical sense, transgressing linear chronologies.

[254] Derek Jarman had already started to direct music videos before MTV was established. Commissioned by Island Records, he produced a 12 minute album taster for three songs from Marianne Faithfull's new wave record *Broken English* (1979). Jarman also directed videos for the Pet Shop Boys and Throbbing Gristle (*"Psychic Rally In Heaven"*, 1981).

of the author", drawing on Barthes and Foucault, as Julien states in the commentary to the DVD edition. However, it can also be regarded as a self-fashioning as an auteur, as a performative move towards becoming an auteur. At that time Julien was about to leave the Sankofa collective behind, and *Looking for Langston*, despite being a Sankofa production, is today more often than not credited as an Isaac Julien film. Drawing on the findings in the chapter on *Handsworth Songs*, I would argue that this 'strategic essentialism' in terms of auteur-ising oneself might be a way to re-inscribe oneself into film historiography.[255]

Isaac Julien employs a number of auteurist strategies, both within the filmic text and in its paratext. For example, he accompanies his film(s) with interviews, own writings in magazines and exhibition catalogues or DVD commentaries. Thus, he creates a plurimedial constellation through which he can put forward his views and arguments to critics and audiences alike. Another auteurist strategy is the self-fashioning within a cultural context. Julien states that he was inspired by "Henry Louis Gates, Jr., Houston A. Baker Jr., bell hooks, Gayatri Spivak, Paul Gilroy, Stuart Hall, Homi K. Bhabha, Kobena Mercer, Cornel West, and Kwame Anthony Appiah" (Julien 1992, 258). I quote this list at length because it can be seen as a performative move by Julien to contextualise himself in an intellectual network of Black cultural critics, all of whom have attacked essentialism. In this context the choice of Langston Hughes becomes a self-reflexive comment on the self-fashioning of a Black artist in relation to his community. According to Isaac Julien, Hughes was chosen as "a symbol not just of the issue of the sexuality within the race but for the experience of the black artist" (Gilroy 1993b, 170) (see also Hemphill 1991b, 175). Essex Hemphill describes Julien's work as follows: "By creating *Looking for Langston*, Julien gives us the first gay film to articulate black gay desire and assert the experience of black gay men into a 'sacred' historic context – the Harlem Renaissance" (Hemphill 1991c, 182)[256]. Mercer conceptualizes *Looking for Langston* as "archaeological inquiry": "The film excavates what has been hidden from history" (Mercer 1993a,

---

[255] We can observe the same tendency in the career of John Akomfrah who nowadays is credited as the director of the works produced by Smoking Dogs Films, which, apart from Akomfrah, consists of Lina Gopaul and David Lawson.

[256] Characterising the role of 1920s and 1930s Harlem in *Looking for Langston* as a site of creativity, of utopian visions, of desire, Bakhtin's concept of the 'chronotope' and Foucault's notion of 'heterotopia' might be useful. The notion of the Harlem Renaissance as a heterotopia can also be seen in Greta Schiller's influential documentary *Before Stonewall* (1984) which carves out a genealogy of LGBT lives in the US.

249).²⁵⁷ Yet, *Looking for Langston* not only creates a network of Black gay literary practice, but also broadens the scope towards a larger perspective on Black creativity.

Looking for Langston's project to excavate a network of Black creativity is demonstrated in the opening of the film. The title sequence, which shows intertitles recalling silent film, introduces the film as "A Mediation on Langston Hughes and the Harlem Renaissance". While the film has occasionally been misunderstood to be a documentary *about* Langston Hughes, the term 'mediation' indicates a wider scope than a focus on a single individual. The context of the Harlem Renaissance is of crucial importance for the film: In contrast to the Middle Passage and plantation, Harlem can be regarded as the first *lieu de mémoire* with positive connotations for African-Americans, as Dorothea Löbbermann (2002) states. Moreover, "the fact that the Harlem Renaissance was as gay as it was black" (Mercer 1993a), with many of its key figures known to be queer (Claude McKay, Alain Locke, Countee Cullen, Wallace Thurman, Bruce Nugent), positions Hughes within a context of black gay cultural practice. The second intertitle "With the poetry of Essex Hemphill and Bruce Nugent (1906–1987)" continues to establish a network of Black (gay) literary practice. Bruce Nugent died in 1987, the year *Looking for Langston* was filmed. In the same year, another Black (gay) author passed away: James Baldwin. The third intertitle "In Memory of James Baldwin (1924–1987)" widens the scope of references still further. Instead of limiting itself to Langston Hughes, the film's title sequence carves out a context and a network of Black (queer) literary practice. Thus, the title sequence leaves the sphere of the individual in order to broaden the scope towards a larger perspective on Black creativity. This will be enhanced in the course of the film.

The use of archival footage in *Looking for Langston* defies the conventional approach, which employs such material in historical documentaries as a means of creating the impression of historical authenticity by connecting image and sound to the same historical era. One scene in *Looking for Langston* consists of a piece of black and white archival footage from the 1929 short film *St. Louis Blues*, showing bisexual Bessie Smith sitting at a bar and singing the song of the same name, composed by W.C. Handy in 1914. The line "My man's

---

257 As Julien states in his interview with Essex Hemphill: "If you are talking about black gay identities, you're talking about identities that are never whole in the sense that there is always a desire to make them whole, but in real life, experiences are always fragmentary and contradictory. So basically, this is a hybrid of different material coming from different moments in history. You can't really seriously try to tackle black gay identities and not find yourself drawing from one historical moment to a more contemporary moment." (Julien in Hemphill 1991b, 178)

got a heart like a rock cast in the sea" fades into a track by contemporary singer Blackberri ("Blues for Langston"), as if both artists were singing a duet. Muñoz (1999, 62) has described the scene as "something uncanny about these voices resonating; the resonance produces a smooth superimposition that is visually impossible." I argue that one of the functions of this aesthetic strategy is to create a transtemporal chronotope of black queer cultural production with the help of intermedial references. The clips engage in a transtemporal dialogue in which different media, decades and spaces engage with each other.

At the same time the montage acknowledges the intersection of 'race' and sexuality. In the commentary for the DVD edition of *Looking for Langston* Julien explains that he found the clip at the MoMa in New York, and that he regards blues as one of the first cultural expressions of the articulation of a queer desire (see also Hemphill 1991b). The blues does not merely refer to a Black cultural tradition in the United States, but, more specifically, to queer desire. One example of this on the soundtrack is George Hannah's 1930 version of the "Freakish Man Blues", displaying Black bisexual desire. Later on in the film the "Sissy Man Blues" is another expression of queer desire. Thus Julien did not simply choose random blues tracks, but two songs which both create a genealogy of Black queer desire while at the same time containing references to a specific historical context.[258]

One example of how time and space is merged via the chronotope of the Harlem Renaissance is the funeral scene in the beginning of the film. We see a scene set in a space above the speakeasy. In one long, unbroken shot the panning camera connects different temporal dimensions, echoing both Deleuze's concept of *space-time* (Deleuze 1989) and, for instance, its use in Tarkovskij's films, especially *The Mirror* (1974). Mourners surround an open casket. While one would expect the scene to re-enact the funeral of Langston Hughes, especially since his death was announced in the previous sequence, this is not the case: on the soundtrack, we hear the voice of Toni Morrison reading her obituary of James Baldwin.[259] The audio footage was recorded at Baldwin's funeral which Julien at-

---

[258] The lyrics of "Freakish Man Blues" go: "She called me a freakish man, what more was there to do? / Just 'cause she said I was strange that did not make it true. / I sent her to the mill to have her coffee ground./'Cause my wheel was broke and my grinder could not be found. / You mix ink with water, bound to turn it black. / You run around with funny people, you'll get a streak of it up your back. / There was a time when I was alone, my freakish ways to treat. / But they're so common now, you get one every day of the week. / Had a strange feeling this morning, well, I've had it all day. / I wake up one of these mornings, that feeling will be here to stay."

[259] Toni Morrison is the editor of the two volume editions of Baldwin in the Library of America edition.

tended in 1987.²⁶⁰ Thus, Baldwin and Hughes melt into each other. As John Hill (1999) has observed, the funeral is set in the 1960s, but the clothes worn by the mourners are designed in the style of the 1920s. Moreover, by having Isaac Julien perform the dead body to be mourned, this scene layers at least three eras: the Harlem Renaissance of the 1920s, the late 1960s and the 1980s. The 1920s are not only alluded to by the costumes, but also by the visual style of the sequence, for which Julien was inspired by the black and white aesthetics of Harlem photographer James Van Der Zee, especially the images collected in "The Harlem Book of the Dead" re-published in 1978.²⁶¹ At the same time the 1980s are evoked, both by the presence of Julien himself, contemporising the past, but also by alluding to the ongoing Aids crisis and the increasing number of deaths. One of these was Joseph Beam, editor of a pioneering anthology of black gay literature, *In the Life* (1986), who died in 1988. Essex Hemphill's 1991 anthology *Brother to Brother. New Writing by Black Gay Men*, which follows Beam's endeavours of carving out a discursive space for gay black desire, is dedicated to him.

Isaac Julien inscribing himself into the film scene is not merely, as Hill (1999) has suggested, comparable to a pun such as Alfred Hitchcock's cameo appearances in his own movies. Instead, it can also be understood as a look forward into the future (his own death) and his artistic legacy and the question what will happen to it. For instance, when Essex Hemphill, whose voice features prominently in the film, died in 1995, his works were held back from publication or even destroyed by his homophobic family. Isaac Julien decided to make *Looking for Langston* after having attended James Baldwin's memorial meeting, as he told Paul Gilroy in an interview: "The power of the official histories that can form around the memory of the black artist is something that I fear." (Julien in Gilroy 1993b, 172) In this sense the film can be understood in relation to LGBT history

---

260 Toni Morrison quotes Baldwin in her speech. The extract we hear in the film goes: "[...]'who are the only people in the world who know anything about them who may be, indeed, the only people in the world who really care anything about them.' When that unassailable combination of mind and heart, of intellect and passion was on display it guided us through treacherous landscape as it did when you wrote these words – words every rebel, every dissident, revolutionary, every practicing artist from Capetown to Poland, from Waycross to Dublin memorized: 'A person does not lightly elect to oppose his society. One would much rather be at home among one's compatriots than be mocked and detested by them. And there is a level on which the mockery of the people, even their hatred, is moving, because it is so blind [...]'." Quoted in: http://www.nytimes.com/books/98/03/29/specials/baldwin-morrison.html [12–03–14]
261 The genre of funeral photography remediates "the colonial American tradition of 'mourning paintings'", as Muñoz (1999 65) notes in his discussion of Van Der Zee's photographs in *The Harlem Book of the Dead*, several of which were reworked for the funeral scene in *Looking for Langston*.

archives, whose role is often not simply to provide access to the material collected by LGBT persons, but primarily to save it from destruction and annihilation by homophobic families in the first place. Because their material is so laden with shame, LGBT archives complicate the contemporary debate about digitisation and access: They require us to rethink the material from the perspective of affects, such as shame (see Cvetkovich 2003). In these cases providing access to the archived material cannot be the highest priority, when acquisition and collection are so bound up with affects and have therefore long been confined to the realms of (relative) privacy. This raises important questions about how to deal with archival material which could potentially contribute to a self-representation by LGBTs.

These examples illustrate how multi-layered the use of intermedial references can be. I would outline three preliminary functions. First, to create a transtemporal, but also a transnational space, This "transhistorical crosscutting" (Muñoz 1999, 60) creates a transtemporal dialogue (Gates). Second, to inscribe oneself (as an artist) into the canon. Third, to create a transnational dialogue between different discourses on Blackness and Black creativity in the US and in Britain during the 1980s. Merging chronotopes of US and UK practice, the film engages with the notion of the Black Atlantic in the sense of Paul Gilroy. It both deterritorialises Blackness, while at the same time locating it within specific discourses. *Looking for Langston* does not only contain references to US culture, but also to Black British culture. Moreover, cross-cutting these references can be seen as an anti-essentialist strategy to offer an alternative to the African-American dominance within Black culture through Black British cultural practice (see Dent 1992). With these functions in mind, I would now like to examine the way the film reworks specific media forms. I will look at a couple of examples in which photography is appropriated into film. The film not only becomes an archive of this photography, but reworks it and translates it into the cultural practice of a different era or a different discursive context. The cultural memory around these photographs travels into another discursive framework, but also into another medium: film.

5.2.2 The discursive frameworks of media specificity: reworking photography

I will now take a closer look at some of the modes *Looking for Langston* employs to rework photography, especially by James Van Der Zee, Robert Mapplethorpe,

George Platt Lynes and Carl Van Vechten.[262] Looking at the reappropriations of photography in the film, I will examine the different strategies employed by Julien which might be able to foreground functions of intermediality.

Photographs are appropriated in a variety of ways throughout the film. Mostly they are transformed into *tableaux vivants*. The use of *tableaux vivants* became a common aesthetic strategy in Black British avant-garde filmmaking for carving out new discursive spaces, for example in Pratibha Parmar's *Khush* (1991) or in *Looking for Langston*. Yet, I would like to argue that the use of *tableaux vivants* as a self-reflexive device differs from film to film and should not only be analysed individually for each work but also within specific works. At times, the *tableaux vivants* are 'intertextual' references to other films as in John Akomfrah's *Seven Songs for Malcolm X* (1993) which alludes to Sergei Paradjanov's 1968 film *The Color of Pomegranates*, whereas in other cases the *tableaux vivants* are based on intermedial appropriations of either photography, as in *Looking for Langston*, or of paintings, for example in Isaac Julien's *The Attendant* (1993). In the *tableaux vivants* in *Looking for Langston* Isaac Julien appropriates photographic works by Carl Van Vechten, George Platt Lynes and Robert Mapplethorpe. At times *Looking for Langston* plays out the tension – and the medial difference – between the referencing medium (film) and the medium referred to (photography). Intermedial references to photography in *Looking for Langston* are created as quotations of photography (the angels holding framed photographs of Hughes or Baldwin), as appropriations of photographs in *tableux vivants*, quoting the visual style of photographers (Van Der Zee, Mapplethorpe), allusions to photographers (a character leafing through Robert Mapplethorpe's *Black Book*) or impersonating photographers.

One intermedial reference in the film is to Carl Van Vechten who is alluded to by the character "Karl". Carl Van Vechten (1880–1964) was the author of the 1926 novel *Nigger Heaven*, the publication of which was surrounded by controversy. The title *Nigger Heaven* "referred to the upper gallery in a theatre where blacks were forced to sit" (Smalls 2006, 48). The novel represents Harlem as a segregated space, "a geographical locale above or at the north of Manhattan, where black culture flourished" (Smalls 2006, 48). The novel, set in nightlife Harlem, was targeted by critics such as Countee Cullen and Alain Locke. "For many African-American readers, *Nigger Heaven* promoted Harlem as a cultural, sexual and exotic fictional space where one played out and played through racial and sexual fantasy roles", James Smalls states (2006, 48). W.E.B. DuBois denounced

---

[262] A photograph by Van Der Zee is discussed by Barthes in *Camera Lucida*, however, as Muñoz (1999) notes, Barthes' commentary "is flawed by a petty racism."

it as "filth" in the official NAACP-magazine "The Crisis", while Alain Locke described it as a "affront to the hospitality of black folks and to the intelligence of white" (quoted in Smalls 2006). The novel was defended by Nella Larsen, Langston Hughes and Wallace Thurman (see Smalls 2006). Van Vechten, who later became the literary executor of Gertrude Stein, was a central figure of the Harlem Renaissance and as such part of a network of queer creativity. The film's reference to him addresses questions of (literary) historiography and of canonisation.

Apart from remediating or quoting photographic works the film enacts the tension between film and photography. In several scenes the film engages in the dialectics of movement and stillness. For example when the camera pans over a *tableau vivant* or when the camera stands still and shows a scene which looks like a freeze-frame of male couples dancing in a speakeasy, but in fact is a *tableau vivant* of dancers frozen in their movements. As Irina Rajewsky (2005) points out: "Intermedial references, then, can be distinguished from intramedial (and thus intertextual) ones by the fact that a given media product cannot *use* or genuinely *reproduce* elements or structures of a different medial system through its own media-specific means; it can only *evoke* or *imitate* them. Consequently, an intermedial reference can only generate an *illusion* of another medium's specific practices." I would like to qualify Rajewsky's statement and argue that intermedial references to photography in *Looking for Langston*, rather than merely evoking or imitating works of photography, in a self-reflexive manner play out the tension between photography, film still, *tableau vivant* and moving image. Moreover, the pastness of photography, its implied absence, is contrasted with the present tense of the medium film and its presence. Merging the past and the present creates a transgenerational memory which grants present or future generations access to the cultural memory of their predecessors. Through intermedial references a network of black gay cultural practice is created.

In one scene we see angels standing in a night-time graveyard, holding up photographs of Langston Hughes and James Baldwin. This self-reflexive use of the medium photography in the film differs from what Lars Ellestöm (2010) describes as "smooth" mediation, "that is, when the material, the sensorial and the spatiotemporal modalities do not cause any friction in the mediating procedure." (Ellestöm 2010, 32)[263] In contrast, the intermedial references in *Looking for Lang-*

---

[263] Ellestöm (2010, 32) explains this using the example of a photograph of a landscape painting: "when asked what the photograph represents one is inclined to say 'a landscape' whereas it actually represents a painting: the photograph mediates a painting that represents a landscape." Going back to the example of *Handsworth Songs* in this study (chapter 4), the self-reflexive use of

ston do cause friction in the mediating procedure. This strategy defamiliarizes the inserted photographic images. In *The Threshold of the Visible World* Kaja Silverman described it as follows: "These photographs have been unrolled, as if they were sacred texts written on parchment [...] The effect is precisely what Benjamin would call a 'ceremonial image'." (Silverman 1996, 107). We have here, I would argue, a self-reflexive use of photography which creates a genealogy and a performative site of mourning. According to Silverman the writers Hughes and Baldwin "are given to us not only as cinematic representations, but also as cinematic representations of photographic images. As such, they have none of that illusory three-dimensionality for which cinema is celebrated." (Silverman 1996, 107) Thus, this reworking of photography does not imply a transformation of the media specificity, but keeps the media specificity of photography intact. However, I would like to argue that we ought to look more closely at the media specific translations Julien undertakes.

Another example of the archival reworkings in *Looking for Langston* is the appropriation of James Van Der Zee's photography. James Van Der Zee is a photographer whose work stood out stylistically from that of his contemporary colleagues. His mode of stylization, of creating *tableaux vivants* with the help of backdrops and costumes, remediates trends within Victorian photography. Kobena Mercer (2002) has shown how Van Der Zee's photographs transgress the mere social realist trend within documentary photography. According to Mercer (2002, 8) his photographs show the influence of cinema with their way of combining print techniques, photomontage, double exposures and superimpositions as well as editing in scenes – a use of aesthetic devices which points both into the past and the future. For example, Van Der Zee used to combine different negatives to create a montage. His funeral photograph "The Death of a Great Man" (1925) contains a number of intermedial references: Van Der Zee inserted both another photograph and a newspaper clipping with a poem. Here we can draw a parallel to the intermedial references employed in *Looking for Langston*, for instance in the funeral scene referring to Hughes, Baldwin and the Aids crisis, employing the voice-over by Toni Morrison on the soundtrack. Just like Van Der Zee incorporates different time layers in one single photograph, *Looking for Langston* transforms these into one single film image or into a single film scene. A couple of years before Julien conceptualised *Looking for Langston*, Van Der Zee

---

Vanley Burke's photographs in the film causes friction in the mediating procedure by foregrounding their media specificity in the process of remediation. Rather than claiming that the remediation of photographs in Akomfrah's film results in a representation of Black life in Britain, the politics of visual representation themselves, the process of image making and its power structures, are foregrounded.

had experienced a renaissance, especially with the publication of the collection of his funeral photography in *The Harlem Book of the Dead* in 1978, with a foreword by Toni Morrison.[264] Also in 1978, his portrait was part of a series of commemorative stamps called "Black Heritage Covers". During the early 1980s Van Der Zee would return to portrait photography, capturing among others Muhammed Ali and artist Jean-Michel Basquiat, who died in 1988. Therefore, I would argue that Van Der Zee's photographic practice impacted on the aesthetics in *Looking for Langston*, not only due to its visual style, but also in the way it works as a genealogy of Black creativity and creates a transgenerational memory for African-American cultural practice in New York and, specifically, in Harlem.

The use of photography in *Looking for Langston* allows on the one hand for inter-medial tensions to be played out while on the other hand allowing for their assimiliation through the appropriation by another medium: film. For instance, the film reworks photographs by Robert Mapplethorpe, but also alludes to him by directly quoting his *Black Book*. The intermedial references to Robert Mapplethorpe in *Looking for Langston* are twofold: on the one hand the film's black and white chiaroscuro echoes Mapplethorpe's visual style, and on the other hand the film employs a direct intermedial reference by quoting Mapplethorpe's 1986 *Black Book*. In the film we see a man leafing through the collection of photographs which gained prominence because of its pictures of Black male nudes. This representation of Black bodies triggered a controversy among Black critics, and the film's reference to the *Black Book* engages with Kobena Mercer's criticism of Mapplethorpe's white gaze on the black body and with his revised opinion about Mapplethorpe (Mercer 2004). Drawing on feminist cultural theory, Mercer criticised Mapplethorpe for aestheticising and eroticising the Black male body. Mercer also points at the way the photograph establishes looking relations which stabilize the subjectivitiy of the white spectator while objectifying the Black body. Moreover, the Black male body is fetishised, and the male genitals are a synechdoche for a Black individual. After Mapplethorpe's photography became part of a debate in the US in 1989 and 1990, Mercer revised his initial reading of the work. As a result of a senator's campaign against national funding of what he claimed to be "indecent and obscene materials", Mapplethorpe's work gained widespread attention, just before his death from an Aids-related illness in 1989. Mercer outlines how the political climate had changed towards cultural re-

---

[264] After the decline of portrait photography in the 1950s Van Der Zee was rediscovered during the controversial Moma exhibition "Harlem on My Mind" in 1969, which triggered a debate about race and the politics of representation (see Mercer 2003).

pression.²⁶⁵ According to Mercer, the New Right "successfully hijacked and appropriated elements of the feminist antipornography argument" while feminists allied themselves with "the law-and-order state" (Mercer 1994, 280–281). In 1990, for instance, a Mapplethorpe retrospective in Cincinnati was closed down after feminists had joined forces with the police department against the exhibition violating "community standards". Such "antidemocratic politics of censorship and cultural closure" (Mercer 1994, 281) made Mercer change his mind. As a consequence, in view of the changed discursive context around the dissemination and exhibition of Mapplethorpe's work, Mercer highlights the visual pleasure the eroticized and aestheticised photographs of male nudes might imply for a black gay spectator. The example shows how shifting discursive contexts have an impact on the changing critical reception of a work and its reconceptualisation.

Looking for Langston depicts a dark empty space, without any markers locating it, in which images from Mapplethorpe's *Black Book* are projected onto panels of transparent white fabric. The sensual, three-dimensional impression conveyed by the projection of the photographs is increased by the character Karl (aka Carl Van Vechten) walking through them, caressing them. The images are accompanied by extracts from Essex Hemphill's poem "If His Name Were Mandingo" which describes an encounter between a white gay man who pays a younger black man after their sexual encounter. "Your paths cross the next day, you don't acknowledge him but/He remembers his semen dilutes in your blood/ [...] To you he's only visible in the dark." In the following *tableau vivant* the scene describing the money being handed over is re-enacted.

Exploring the fetishising gaze of a white gay man on black male bodies, echoes the debate which Mapplethorpe's works had triggered among Black British cultural critics during the late 1980s.²⁶⁶ In their 1986 article "True Confessions", originally published in the journal *Ten8*, Isaac Julien and Kobena Mercer contend that debates about sexuality have been "colonized" by white persons, gay or straight alike. Whereas 'race' is slowly becoming an issue among white

---

265 Other victims of "policing and prosecution of cultural practitioners" were performance artist Karen Finley and the black rap group 2 Live Crew.
266 Jose Esteban Muñoz (1999) uses the debate around Mapplethorpe's photographs to develop his concept of disidentification which has become a widely applied notion within Queer Theory. Reminiscent of Stuart Hall's term "negotiated reading", disidentification attempts to capture the ambivalences and contradictions Mapplethorpe's images might trigger in a spectator. Unlike Hall's notion of 'negotiated reading', which is one of three modes of reception (with dominant and oppositional reading), however, disidentification is not limited to reception, but can refer to production as well. In reworking his reading of Mapplethorpe, Julien's artistic production has been influenced by disidentification, Muñoz argues (see 1999, 71–72).

feminists, "white gay men retain a deafening silence on race" (Julien and Mercer 1991, 167). This lack of racial awareness has been diagnosed both in the sexual politics of gay culture and in the cultural politics of gay artists. Although black struggle inspired gay liberation in the late 1960s, this heritage is not acknowledged. Julien and Mercer name photography as a contested field for the representation of desire and pleasure. While many feminists have rejected eroticised images of women as pornography, and therefore condemned them, in the gay movement porn has been defended, overlooking the racial privileges calling for a right to choose according to one's desire. Julien and Mercer claim that this position is indicative of hegemonic whiteness: "As black men, we are implicated in the same landscape of stereotypes which is dominated and organized around the needs, demands and desires of white males." (Julien and Mercer 1991, 169). Drawing on the notion of 'colonial fantasy' developed by Homi Bhabha (1983) in his Screen article "The Other Question: The Stereotype and Colonial Discourse" Julien and Mercer maintain that colonial fantasies, remediated and perpetuated in gay porn, reduce the discursive space for Black gay males to stereotypical images of "the supersexual stud and the sexual 'savage' on one hand or the delicate, fragile and exotic 'oriental' on the other." (Julien and Mercer 1991, 169) From the perspective of these Eurocentric representational politics, Julien and Mercer discuss Robert Mapplethorpe's catalogue "Black Males" (1982): by appropriating "porn's racialized codes of representation, and by abstracting its stereotypes into 'art', he makes racism's phantasms of desire respectable", they contend (Julien and Mercer 1991, 169). Being framed in a manner reminiscent of porn photography the black body is fragmented and fetishized. Drawing on a reading of Frantz Fanon's "Black Skin, White Mask", Julien and Mercer argue that the politics of representation in Mapplethorpe's photographs, especially in "Man in a Polyester Suit" (1980), reproduces colonial myths, fantasies and anxieties about aggressive Black male sexuality. However, considering the need for representations of homosexual desire, the authors find themselves in an ambivalence of being attracted while being alienated at the same time: *"we want to look, but don't always find the images we want to see"* (Julien and Mercer 1991, 170, italics in the original). Yet, black viewers are able to reappropriate those colonial fantasies in the process of reception for the purpose of affirming a black gay subject position. In this sense, despite their stereotypical quality, these images can function as 'visible evidence', and can be understood as a trace of black gay sexualities.

Mapplethorpe's photography has also been discussed within the context of Black British cultural studies of the 1980s. In his 1988 essay "New Ethnicities" Stuart Hall draws on the debate around Mapplethorpe to point at the intersection of race, gender and sexuality: "This continuous circling around Mapplethorpe's work [for example in *Ten.8*], is not exhausted by being able to place him as the white fetishistic gay photographer; and this is because it is also marked by the surreptitious return of desire" (Hall 1996a, 168). Hall points at the ambivalence of Black cultural politics and its misapprehension that "the categories of gender and sexuality would stay the same and remain fixed and secured" (Hall 1996a, 168).

Looking for Langston also appropriates works by the photographer George Platt Lynes (1907–1955), among them "John Leaphart and Buddy Mc Cartny" (1952). Platt Lynes' work had experienced a renaissance at the 1977 *documenta* in Kassel. During his lifetime only his closest friends would know about his nude photographs. In the film the photographs are staged as *tableaux vivants*. As Irina Rajewsky (2010, 58) points out with regards to photorealist painting: "it is not two or more different forms of medial articulation that are present in their own materiality." Instead, another medium "is 'brought into play'". In the *tableaux vivants* appropriating George Platt Lynes' work in *Looking for Langston*, photography does not manifest itself materially. It is performed and at the same time its materiality is transgressed and its material limitations overcome. The photograph, in being re-enacted, 'comes to life', while at the same time the media specificity of analogue black and white film and its chiaroscuro lighting is being foregrounded: through the slow panning shot over the male nude and the play of shadows on the body. As Rajewsky points out, again referring to photorealist painting, the effect of foregrounding media specificity is accomplished through referencing "to another medial system: with the medium's own specific means and instruments, elements and/or structures of another conventionally distinct medium are thematized, evoked or [...] simulated" (Rajewsky 2010, 58). In another scene, not alluding to a specific photograph, the dancers in the speakeasy are frozen into a *tableaux vivant*, at first glance easily mistaken for a still. However, the rising smoke points at the fact that this is not a still photograph, but a moving image. At the same time, the rising smoke repeats the movement of the tilting camera towards the upper floor, the site of the funeral, thus pointing at the off-screen space where another time layer (that of the 1980s) is situated.

Intermedial references to different photographers also symbolize different ways of looking at the black (male) body. *Looking for Langston* foregrounds the medium of photography by not merely editing Platt Lynes' photograph "John Leaphart and Buddy Mc Cartny" (1952) into the film, but by showing a black hand holding the picture in the left frame of the image, belonging to a spectator who is situated in the off-screen space. It is this gaze (of a black person) into which the spectators of the film (both blacks and whites alike) are sutured. However, while the "interracial chiaroscuro" (Mercer and Darke 2001, 16) of the photograph is achieved through the contrasting skin colours, in the filmic version it obtains a "strange quality of sameness", as Mercer and Darke maintain (2001, 16). The same effect can be observed in a film scene, based on another Platt Lynes photograph, showing two men undressing each other. The interracial desire in Platt Lynes' photographs is disambiguated in the film. In re-enacting the works by the white gay photographers with exclusively black actors, Isaac Julien deconstructs the fetishising white male gaze on black male bodies. He disambiguates interracial desire and propagates a politics of black men loving black men (see Dickel 2008). However, in his later films *Young Soul Rebels* (1991) or *The Attendant* (1993) Isaac Julien abandons this stance, in favour of employing the motif of the interracial male couple which can be found in the films by Fassbinder, in the paintings by Duncan Grant and in literary works by James Baldwin, for example (see Mercer and Darke 2001, 8), but also in the British avant-garde film *Borderline* (1930), directed by Kenneth MacPherson, starring Paul Robeson and British white poet H.D.

5.2.3 Discursive frameworks: the context of the 1980s

Looking for Langston does not attempt to recreate a specific historical period such as the Harlem Renaissance, but it constructs the cultural memory of specific discursive debates, such as the 1980s debate about essentialism within Black practice and its heteronormative understanding of Black masculinity. While Julien acknowledges gay interracial desire within the Harlem Renaissance, his intermedial reworking of the archive connects to contemporary debates. I would like to illustrate the "end of the essential black subject" (Hall 1996a, 166) by Isaac Julien's shift in his politics from the strategic essentialism of "black men loving black men" towards an anti-essentialist understanding of gay masculinity and desire. As we have seen in chapter 5.2.2. *Looking for Langston* is dedicated to the politics expressed by the motto "black men loving black men is the revolutionary act of the 1980s", coined by Joseph Beam in his essay "Brother to Brother. Words from the Heart" (cf. Dickel 2011, 32). Hemphill's anthology in turn takes its title from Beam's essay, and uses the following extract as its motto: "Black men loving Black men is a call to action, an acknowledgement of responsibility. We take care of our own kind when the night grows cold and silent. These days the nights are cold-blooded and the silence echoes with complicity" (quoted in Hemphill 1991, vi).

Dickel (2011) has examined how Isaac Julien has appropriated the intermedial reference to Bruce Nugent's modernist short story *Smoke, Lilies and Jade* (1926). The story deals with a black bisexual man's polyamorous relationship

5.2 Remediation and intermediality — 191

with a white man and a Black woman. In *Looking for Langston* the story is transformed from "an interracial bisexual narrative [...] to a black male homosexual narrative", as Simon Dickel (2011, 133) has observed. In the film the white character Beauty is turned into a black man while the black female protagonist is omitted. Dickel (2011, 134–35) also notes how the excerpts read from the story by the voice-over are altered as a means to disambiguate the narrative. Dickel supports his argument by analysing the way Julien has adapted the short story and by the way the film reworks the photographs of Robert Mapplethorpe. He argues that "the racial and sexual ambiguity of 'Smoke, Lilies and Jade' is changed to a rather unambiguous narrative" (Dickel 2011, 134). According to Dickel this appropriation ties in with the notion of "black men loving black men". The intermedial references include reworkings of George Platt Lynes' photograph "John Leaphart and Buddy Mc Cartny" (1952). The filmic adaptation of the portrait of an interracial couple to a scene showing two Black men is a reappropriation "from a black gay perspective", as Simon Dickel (2011, 133) states. Dickel then sets out to contextualize this reappropriation within the context of 1980s debates on black gay identity. With this reading Dickel challenges previous critics who have "argued that Julien's film [...] takes an anti-essentialist approach to the categories of blackness and gayness" (Dickel 2011, 133). However, I argue that the intermedial references do not solely tie into notions of 'black men loving black men', but transgress it. In *Looking for Langston* the reworking of the photographic archive can be understood not only as a move towards an essentialist understanding of Black masculinity, but as a form of a strategic essentialism emphasising the importance of connecting and belonging among black gay men in times of homophobia during the Aids crisis.

In his 1991 interview with bell hooks Julien questions the slogan "Black men loving black men is *the* revolutionary act of the 1980", which he finds results in "a kind of closure around racial representation and anything that aims to be slightly ambivalent" (Julien in hooks 1991, 174). By the time of his essay "Confessions of a Snow Queen" (1993) Isaac Julien had distanced himself from this approach. In using the slang expression "snow queen", which refers to black men who prefer white men as their partners, Julien's text "draws attention to the fact of black desire for the white subject and contests pathologised racial identities, the products of afrocentric readings." (Julien 2000, 82) Accordingly, Julien gave up the politics of "black men loving black men" in his short film project *The Attendant* (1993). *The Attendant* complicates Julien's exploration of black male queer desire by depicting the "forbidden pleasures" (Orgeron 2000, 33) of S/M. *The Attendant*, set at an art museum, appropriates François-Auguste Biard's oil painting "Slaves of the West Coast of Africa" (ca. 1833), which depicts scenes at a slave market. The painting shows black characters being treated in a degrading manner by white colonizers, naked black bodies being submitted to the power of white men. Julien re-enacts the main scene in the painting as a sado-masochistic interracial sex scene with a Black man lying in the centre in a submissive position, being dominated by other men, both black and white. As Isaac Julien explains in "Confessions of a Black Snow Queen" (Julien 2000) his aesthetic choice is a way of carving out the discursive space for black gay subject position – and especially black masochism in the light of colonial power structures and the legacy of slavery.

This example shows that intermedial references and remediation are not only a matter of 'reworking' and 'appropriation' from a perspective characterised as "Black". The case study has shown the complexity of that category. Instead, in order to avoid an essentialist perspective on the reworkings, it has proven fruitful for their understanding to situate them in specific, at times even conflicting, discourses. As Jan Distelmeyer (2005) has convincingly argued, examining the works by Oliver Stone, the auteur should not merely be understood as an isolated character embodying universal traits, but also in his or her discursive context. Media memory scholars should therefore reflect on their own practice of possibly essentialising cultural practice by minorities instead of regarding it as a means of self-fashioning of an auteur or, as in Isaac Julien's but also John Akomfrah's case, an auteur in becoming.

5.2.4 Remediating cultural memory: from 'memory matter' to mnemonic discourses

This chapter has set out to outline an anti-essentialist perspective on practices of adaptation, appropriation or reappropriation. Julien's appropriation of the work of white photographers is not merely a way of 'returning the gaze', of deconstructing the white gaze directed towards a black body. Such a reading would be fairly a-historical and run the risk of essentialising the process of reappropriation as grounded in identity politics alone. Instead, it can be related to specific discursive moments with which the artist engages in a dialogue through the practice of reappropriation. The example of *Looking for Langston* has shown that remediation is not always about a 'memory matter'. It can be highly self-reflexive and can therefore use the specificity of different media for its project of carving out a black gay discursive space. The film does not depict or rework a specific historical event, but instead uses intermedial references as a self-reflexive device to reinscribe themselves into cultural memory. In contrast to models of cultural memory which see art as an act of remembrance for a community, *Looking for Langston* explores new ways of thinking about the construction of cultural memory through filmmaking: filmmaking is not a means to store or represent the memory of a community or group, but it is highly performative in the sense that it opens up a utopian space. Unlike site-specific (topographical and geographical) spaces of memory provided by memorials, *Looking for Langston* creates metaphorical, deterritorialized spaces of remembrance, informed by the chronotope of the Harlem Renaissance and London's 1980s club culture. The transtemporal dialogue created in the film not only shows "how the queer racialized body becomes a historical archive" (Gopinath 2005, 1)[267], it also reminds us, as Isaac Julien and Kobena Mercer (1991, 173) contend, "that our pleasures are political and that our politics can be pleasurable".

This chapter has dealt with the different functions of intermediality. On a textual level intermediality can be perceived as a form of recoding. The texts reflect other works and recode their arguments and (aesthetic) standpoints. As we have seen, four functions of intermediality can be outlined: 1) it is employed as a means to create a transnational transgenerational dialogue to create a genealogy of LGBT knowledge, 2) as a means to reinscribe oneself into the canon of European art cinema as well as into contemporary popular culture, 3) it also reinscribes the Black subject into geography and history, and 4) reflects on historiography and on the modes of representation. Through these intermedial references *Looking for Langston* creates an archive of Black (queer) cultural practice in the twentieth century. As such, it is both an act of empowerment and an intervention into the literary and art historical canon(s) of modernism and postmodernism in which Black art is systematically excluded.

With regards to cultural memory studies, in what way can intermediality studies contribute to refining the notion of remediation? Intermediality studies force us to reflect on the notion of the medium, on mediatisation. They show the interrelatedness, the mutual influences of different artefacts not only from a diachronic perspective, but also as a way of contemporising the past. Intermediality studies therefore contribute to contemporary theorisations around the dynamics of cultural memory, of travelling memory or entangled memories. A cultural memory perspective, in turn, could add more nuances to intermediality studies and include social and political aspects to its aesthetic concerns (see Bruhn 2010). It could also offer theoretical considerations to the transcultural and transnational modes of translation, reappropriation and reworking.

---

[267] Gayatri Gopinath refers here to *My Beautiful Laundrette*.

6. Conclusion – Mediated cultural memory in a digital age

Memory studies have only recently turned their attention to the media specificity and the mediatization of cultural memory. In this study I have suggested a number of avenues that might be taken by media memory studies. This study has drawn on ideas of the performativity of cultural memory, its multidirectionality and its capacity to travel from one context to another. Drawing on selected case studies, model analyses provide useful tools for media memory studies. I have argued for the need to take the mediation of memories into account and to provide a textual analysis which is not limited to the representation of content or thematic issues, but which looks at the formal-aesthetic means employed in specific media texts. The case studies have shown how media is not merely a vessel for memory, but actively constructs cultural memory, through aesthetic means such as framing and lighting, the use of music or the use of interviews, talking heads and testimonial witnesses. This study has also shown the importance of the power relations at work within the dynamics of memory. These power relations find their expressions in the discursive framework and in the industrial context (the production, distribution and exhibition) of mediated memories. Moreover, this thesis has addressed questions of canonization and film historiography. It suggests to employ the notion of 'minor cinema' for two reasons: as a way to foreground the power aspects involved in the construction of cultural memory and as a possibility to bridge the gap between political and artist video practice.

This study has theorized three notions relevant for the study of mediatized cultural memory: Transculturality, the archive and remediation. This study is a contribution to media memory studies setting out to direct their attention from fiction film to documentary film images. Due to their alleged objectivity and neutrality, documentary images need to be critically examined. I have argued that the essay film can contribute to challenging positivist notions about the documentary image as 'visible evidence'. Each section includes the case study of an essay film (*Handsworth Songs, Looking for Langston, The Alcohol Years*) which is used as a theoretical tool to examine the politics of representation. The self-reflexivity of the essay films allows for such an examination of the workings of representation, but it also provides insights into a number of other aspects related to cultural memory. Essay films and documentary filmmaking are here understood as an intervention into the audiovisual archive, which I have defined as the circulation of images, narratives and sounds in a specific society at a specific historical moment. In addition, this understanding entails a diachronic dimension, which allows for a historical perspective on representation politics. Filmmaking is regarded as an act of remembrance, as a 'memory work' and as an act of agency for minoritized persons. This study has pointed at the risk to 'other' these works in the process of reception, for instance within cultural memory studies or film studies, but also in the context of production and distribution. Based on the concept of "film as theory" (Pantenburg 2006), essay films can be regarded as epistemological tools to explore questions of representation, memory and identity. Therefore, thanks to their self-reflexive aesthetics these films have been able to offer fruitful insights into the workings of mediated cultural memory.

6.1 Transculturality

In view of the current 'transcultural' and 'transnational turn' within memory studies this study points at the risk of re-essentialising concepts of 'culture', which notions of transnationality and transculturality set out to challenge. The first section (*3. Mediatized memories in a global age: the transcultural turn?*) argues in favour of distinguishing 'transcultural' and 'transnational' memory. Using the concept of transculturality merely in relation to nationality and ethnicity would reduce its possibilities without any conceptual gain. In fact, if we regard 'cultural memory' as travelling, multidirectional memory, it has a transcultural dimension, since it situates itself within different cultural contexts and practices. At the same time, this study points at the risk of neglecting the impact of a national framework. The current focus on transcultural and transnational processes of memory is also due to the prevalence of Nora's concept of the *lieux de mémoire* and can be seen as a critical reaction, setting out to challenge the dominance of the nation-state perspective within memory scholars' reception of Nora. However, the example of migrant memories shows that neglecting the national perspective entails two risks: first, to exclude migrants from the 'imagined community' (Anderson) of the nation, and second, to overlook the impact of the national framework on discourses of migration. Conceptualising migrant or diasporic memory as 'transcultural' entails the risk of 'othering' cultural practices which are considered to be different from those of the country of arrival. Such a perspective would sideline the complexity of cultural practices as well as their modes of production and reception. Instead, this study argues to employ the concept of transculturality in the sense of multiple overlapping cultural practices.

Chapter 3.2. *Transcultural memories – post-punk Manchester in times of urban regeneration* has shown how transculturality can be used to describe a number of different cultural practices within the same (g)local space. Such an approach helps to avoid an essentialising perspective and allows for an intersectional, anti-essentialist understanding of memory. Drawing on the example of subcultural memory around 1980s post-punk Manchester, the multidirectional contemporary translations of memory within different discursive contexts have been examined. On the one hand, the case study has shown how subcultural memory is used within neoliberal politics of urban regeneration. On the other hand it has critically analysed that concepts of 'counter memory' are not automatically subversive and emancipatory. Therefore, it suggests to challenge and overcome the binarism inherent in conceptualisations of alternative memories, such as vernacular, popular or counter memories. If we understand cultural memory as "travelling" (Erll 2011b) and "multidirectional" (Rothberg 2009), these binary divisions cannot be upheld, as they will not be able to grasp the complexity of cultural practices involved in the translation of memory through the most diverse discursive spaces.

Using Fatih Akin's autobiographical documentary *We Forgot to Go Back* (2001) (see chapter 3.1. *Mediating the cultural memory of Turkish-German labour migration)* as an example, this study examines the mediatization of migrant memories, analysing its aesthetic practices and including the film's industrial context. Conceptualising the film as an act of remembrance which foregrounds the marginalisation of migrant memory in hegemonic historiography, I have argued that Akin's film does not set out to complete the master narrative from the perspective of a specific community. Instead, Akin's film refrains from situating itself within identity politics by employing a number of anti-essentialist strategies: emphasising the situatedness of knowledge, challenging the alleged interrelatedness of identity, belonging, ethnicity and territory through the construction of transnational film spaces or the anti-essentialist use of music. Akin's film carves out a discursive space for articulating different experiences of Turkish-German labour migration, thus acknowledging the diversity of historical experiences in today's multicultural societies. The chapter also points at the paradox that the film's aesthetics deconstruct essentialist notions of identity, while its industrial context of production, distribution and reception entails the risk of re-essentialising the film, for instance through practices of programming or film criticism. Therefore a textual analysis proves to be insufficient. This insight opens up new research perspectives for film and memory scholars alike: a film's multiple discursive and industrial frameworks need to be taken into account. These frameworks are situated at a regional, national as well as transnational level, all of which interact, but have specific repercussions for the creation of mediatized cultural memory. Therefore, this study argues to not loose sight of the national perspective, while at the same time promoting a transnational perspective which liberates minor cinema from its position as the 'other' within national film culture. A transnational approach also opens up new modes of canonization or conceptualisation, for instance in terms of genre cinema (e.g. a road movie) or within the context of autobiographical filmmaking.

6.2 The archive

In this study I have suggested to rethink the notion of the 'archive' from the perspective of media memory studies and to employ a theoretical perspective which combines the archive's material and discursive aspects. Section 4. *Reworking the archive* has shown that media specificity and its discursive frameworks are crucial factors for the diversification of audiovisual heritage. Therefore, their repercussions on archival practices, politics of preservation and funding decisions need to be taken into account. In order to complicate Assmann's division of storage and functional memory, I developed the concept of the 'audiovisual archive', referring to the sounds, images and narratives circulating within a specific socio-historical context.

Chapter 4.1 *Archival interventions: excavating the cultural memory of video art and activism* on the archival practice of Hamburg's video workshops shows that debates about the preservation of the audiovisual heritage need to include the medium video in all its formats and genres, instead of being limited to a number of canonized films or selected pieces of video art alone. The chapter illustrates the media specificity of video as a dispositif in its own right and highlights the role of the curator for the formation of functional memory. Moreover, drawing on the example of the Hamburg collective *bildwechsel*, the chapter has been able to show the complexity of the challenges archives have to meet in view of digitisation. While digitisation may not lead to a sustainable preservation of archival footage, it is important to reflect on both archival practices and modes of granting access to the collections. Therefore, the chapter has shown the need to examine the criteria according to which the archival stock is selected for preservation. Moreover, the role of the archivist and curator need to be further examined, as programming decisions may have repercussions on digitisation, canonisation and, likely, film historiography. Looking at the archival practice of the video collective ties in with recent trends in archival studies to focus on the use of the archive rather than on the archive as an institution. In this understanding archives are not merely sites or containers of storage, but the sum of activities related to their everyday use (see Friedrich 2013, 17). Such a user-related approach centres on specific moments of archival practice, which describes the practical work within the archive and the process of archiving. Another result of this study, which presents a first mapping of the field of German video collectives and their audiovisual heritage, is the insight that the hegemonic dichotomy between video art and political video cannot be upheld.

Drawing on the example of *Handsworth Songs*, chapter 4.2 *Filmmaking as archival intervention – reworking cultural memory in the essay film* has dealt with the self-reflexivity of the essay film and has outlined five functions of the film's self-reflexive aesthetics. First, the remediation of archival footage challenges hegemonic representations of, for instance, Black Britons. Second, with the help of self-reflexive means an essay film is able to foreground the media-specific construction of discourses about nation, race, and Britishness. Third, homogenising and essentialising notions of counter practice and the counter public sphere are undermined. Self-reflexive means, such as the use of the voice-over or of music, can become anti-essentialist strategies aiming at the subversion of notions of container-cultures and the homogenisation of communities. Fourth, the intervention into the audiovisual archive serves to excavate political alliances neglected in hegemonic historiography, for instance the links between the predominantly white working-class movements in Britain and the antiracist struggle. Finally, fifth, the archival intervention can contribute to showing traces of a Black presence in Britain. As such, the film in itself has been transformed into a deterritorialised image bank. To conclude, modes of self-reflexivity within the archival intervention also serve in terms of the self-fashioning of the filmmakers, reinscribing their works into a film historical tradition. It is an act of agency which sets out to influence processes of canonization and film historiography.

6.3 Remediation

The final section of this study, chapter *5. Remediation: reappropriations in digital media and in the essay film*, discusses the theoretical challenges and limitations inherent in the concept of remediation, introduced by Bolter/Grusin (2000) into media studies and by Erll and Rigney (2009) into memory studies. As opposed to Bolter/Grusin, who neither consider the industrial context nor the power relations involved in remediation, this study suggests to broaden the understanding of the notion of 'remediation' in order to take both those aspects into account. Including both specific discursive as well as media-specific contexts into the analysis, I argue, helps to avoid a de-historicising, essentialising research perspective.

A close analysis of remediation of the Windrush myth on YouTube (chapter 5.1 *Remediating the cultural memory of migration: reappropriating the audiovisual archive of the Windrush*) has shown how new media enable the transnational recirculation of analogue archival footage, allowing it to re-enter the audiovisual archive. The chapter also discusses the discursive changes that can lead to such a recirculation, for instance the debate about Britishness and multiculturalism in the wake of New Labour during the late 1990s. During these years, Britain's self-fashioning as a multicultural society began to evolve. Official politics encouraged or institutionalized the celebration of anniversaries (such as the 50th and 60th anniversary of the arrival of the Windrush in 1948), commemorative events (e. g. Black History Month in Britain) as well as reworked school curricula as a result of political programmes aiming at diversity and inclusion. In order to understand the dynamics of remediation, we therefore have to look at a number of interrelated factors: 1) the mediation/mediatization of memory, its media specificity and its genre; 2) the politics of representation at work and 3) the industrial context of production, distribution and exhibition.

The example *Looking for Langston* (5.2 *Remediation and intermediality: media specificity and the discursive context*) has shown that remediation is not only the transformation of a memory matter into different media formats. Instead, I suggest to widen the scope of the concept of remediation and to include a discursive aspect. However, the discursive framework should always be contextualised within the specific industrial context as well as the materiality of the medium. To avoid essentialising practices of adaptation, appropriation and translation in the research process, media memory scholars need to take the dialectics of materiality and discourse into account. Therefore the chapter suggests to make use of recent trends within intermediality studies for memory studies. At the same time this study warns against de-historicising transnational adaptations. Altogether, I argue that Bolter and Grusin's (2000) concept of remediation is too limiting for the study of mediated cultural memories, since a diachronic perspective is needed and the industrial context ought to be taken into account. Moreover, in Bolter and Grusin's understanding of remediation the notion of the archive is not addressed. For them remediation is conceptualised within terms of 'old' and 'new' media, whereas the relation between storage and functional memory is not taken into account. This study argues that this relation is of crucial importance for understanding the workings of canon and film (or literary or art) historiography. It is only through them that we can study the impact of curatorial practice on the audiovisual archive, and thus the circulation of a work. Therefore, this study has looked at the repercussions of remediation on the audiovisual archive. Moreover, it suggests to gain insights into media specificity from the burgeoning field of intermediality studies. Chapter 5.2 has looked at the remediation of archival footage and the appropriation of photography in the essay film. Examining the self-reflexive way of foregrounding the media specificity of archival footage as a way of reworking the archive, Isaac Julien's *Look-*

ing for Langston indicates that this reworking of the archive must not be homogenized and essentialised in terms of generalising categories, such as "Black practice" or "queer practice". Instead, filmmaking as an intervention into the audiovisual archive takes place within a specific discursive framework and engages with contemporary debates. In the case of *Looking for Langston* some of the discursive contexts include the debates about 1980s Black gay male cultural practice and the politics of "Black men loving Black men", developments within Black documentary photography in Britain during the 1980s, the emergence of Black British historiography as well as the anti-essentialist theorizations within the Birmingham Centre for Cultural Studies. Such debates need to be taken into account when analysing archival interventions via filmmaking or remediation in general.

6.4 Outlook

Rethinking the mediatization of cultural memory by merging film and media studies with memory studies offers multiple theoretical and methodological approaches for historians, art historians, social scientists, librarians or archivists, curators and festival programmers alike. Through its case studies this book gives an insight into the mediatization of cultural memory. Yet, further research needs to be done on the specificity and materiality of various media formats and their impact on cultural memory. In this respect Judith Keilbach's study of the media specificity of interviews with Holocaust witnesses can prove influential due to its inclusion of the industrial context (Keilbach 2012). My study also offers new avenues of thinking for museum studies and the use of audiovisual media, both analogue and digital, within historical exhibitions. Since the iconic turn we can observe a burgeoning trend to focus on archival moving images as well as photographs not only for the purposes of illustration, but as sources in their own right. Examples would be the Holocaust exhibition at the Imperial War Museum in London or the relaunched permanent exhibition at Bergen-Belsen.

Moreover, debates about diversity and inclusion have had repercussions on contemporary exhibition practices, especially in Great Britain. Acknowledging today's multi-ethnic population as well as the experiences of LGBT persons implies challenges for museums and other exhibition practices, but also for national film archives and their online platforms. Therefore, I suggest that film and media studies can offer useful theoretical and methodological insights for acknowledging the polyvocality and diversity of cultural memory. For example, this study has pointed at ways of dealing with archival footage without taking up essentialist notions of identity and without 'othering' the persons represented in the footage once again. A critical perspective on the audiovisual archive, its politics and history of representation is highly necessary in the works of museums, archives and exhibitions. This study also suggests to reflect on questions of diversity and inclusion in national museums and archives as well as in national or European film archives. Acknowledging the role of the archive as an agent in its own right also means to reflect on the processes of selection in film archives, the role of the curator and the impact of these decisions for the audiovisual archive and its functional memory.

The concept of 'remediation' offers a number of approaches for research. Media memory studies need to address both the industrial and the discursive context of mediated memories. Such an approach can also enrich media studies on convergence culture. Digitisation has crucial repercussions on the construction of cultural memory. However, the digital turn should not be understood as a complete departure from analogue media, but rather in terms of a continuity, as yet another dispositif for the remediation and dissemination of cultural memory. This study also offers impulses for the burgeoning field of intermediality studies. It suggests to conceptualise intermedial references not merely from a formal-aesthetic perspective, but also in the context of their discursivity and materiality. Moreover, it may be fruitful to develop an anti-essentialist perspective on artist practice, such as the (re)appropriation of archival footage, within adaptation studies and remake studies. This perspective can avoid the classification of works by minoritized artists in terms of their author's ethnicity or nationality. Such an approach would also be useful within transnational film studies, especially within World Cinema. Transnational film studies are another point of departure for further research. When studying transnational remakes or adaptations, scholars need to be aware of the risk of essentialism inherent in conceptualisations such as "Indian"/"Turkish" reappropriation (of, for instance, Shakespeare or Star Trek). Classifying Akira Kurosawa's adaptation of Shakespeare's *Macbeth* simply as a "Japanese adaptation" entails both a Eurocentric perspective and the risk of essentialism. Kurosawa's *Macbeth* is not solely to be studied in terms of categories based on national identity or ethnicity, but as a media-specific reworking which is the result of a specific historical, materialistic dispositif. Researchers therefore need to reflect upon the risk of de-historicising art practice by aligning it with essentialist notions of national belonging or ethnicity. These insights offer fruitful methodological avenues for intermediality studies, adaptation studies and remake studies alike.

Another area for further research are audience and reception studies. While they were not included in this study, its anti-essentialist approach would also prove fruitful for empirical reception studies and its classifications and categorizations of audiences. This study invites to reflect critically on the risk of homogenising and essentialising diverse individuals from the perspective of ethnicity or national belonging (as, for instance, in studies on 'British Asian women' and their media reception of Bollywood). Furthermore, this study also encourages further research within fan culture. To add, user-generated remediations, such as fan fiction, mash-ups or remixes, could provide material for further case studies and methodological considerations.

This work offers useful inspirations for the field of trauma research as well. Its focus on memory "written into the body" poses new challenges for the theorization of mediatized memory and its media specificity. This work's anti-essentialist approach can provide impulses for trauma research in conceptualising affects and emotions as culturally constructed. Useful approaches are provided by affect theory, for instance the works by Sara Ahmed, Ann Cvetkovich or Lauren Berlant. Their writings offer an anti-essentialist approach to affects and emotions. Instead of understanding these as 'authentic' expressions of individual 'bodies', they can be regarded as culturally constructed, situated within a specific historical context and intertwined by medial, political and economical discourses.

To sum up, this study has complicated the notion of coherent memory communities. It has also shown the problems inherent in the concept of transcultural memory. Furthermore, it has argued to widen the scope of the term 'remediation' towards including the discursive and industrial context into its theorizations. This study has reintroduced the notion of the archive into cultural memory studies. Thereby it has pointed at the need to think of its materiality and discursivity in conjunction. Inspired by media archaeology, it has examined the archive as an agent by itself. Looking at the archival practice of a specific video archive, it has opened new avenues for research within archival memory studies. To conclude, my work regards itself as a contribution to a dynamic field of interdisciplinary research which will have to face the challenge of not necessarily unifying its diversity of theoretical and methodological approaches, but instead articulating their applicability for scholars from other research areas. Film and media studies could offer valuable insights for memory scholars, especially the research undertaken in the wake of New Film History, the before mentioned audience and reception studies, adaptation and remake studies as well as the burgeoning fields of production studies, film festival studies and fan studies. This is just the beginning.

Bibliography

Achinger, Christine, and Dagmar Brunow, and Janina Jentz, and Regina Mühlhäuser. "Engendering Airwaves. Zur Konstruktion von Geschlecht im Radio." *Radio-Kultur und Hör-Kunst*. Ed. Andreas Stuhlmann. Würzburg: Königshausen & Neumann, 2001. 24–37.
Adorno, Theodor W. *Noten zur Literatur*. Frankfurt am Main: Suhrkamp, 1981.
Agnew, Vanessa. "History's Affective Turn." *Rethinking History* 11.3 (2007): 299–312.
Aitken, Stuart C., and Leo E. Zonn, eds. *Place, Power, Situation and Spectacle: A Geography of Film*. Lanham: Rowman & Littlefield, 1994.
Akomfrah, John. "Black Independent Filmmaking." *Artrage* 3–4 (1983): 29–30.
Akomfrah, John. "'Handsworth Songs': Audiences/Aesthetics/Independence. Interview with the Black Audio Film Collective." *Framework* 35 (1988): 9–17.
Akomfrah, John. "Sneaking Ghosts through the Back Door." *Black Film Bulletin* 1.1 (1993a): 3.
Akomfrah, John. "Wishful Filming." *Black Film Bulletin* 1.2 (1993b): 14.
Akomfrah, John. "Black Audio Film Collective." *Documenta 11, Platform 5: Ausstellung*. Ed. Gerti Fietzek. Ostfildern-Ruit: Hatje Cantz, 2002. 553.
Akomfrah, John. "Black Independent Filmmaking: A Statement by the Black Audio Film Collective [1983]." *The Ghosts of Songs. The Film Art of the Black Audio Film Collective 1982–1998*. Eds. Kodwo Eshun & Anjalika Sagar. Liverpool: Liverpool University Press and FACT 2007. 144–145.
Akomfrah, John. "Digitopa and the Specters of Diaspora." *Journal of Media Practice* 11.1 (2010): 21–29.
Alavi, Bettina. "Geschichtsschulbücher als Erinnerungsorte. Ein Gedächtnis für die Einwanderungsgesellschaft?" *Geschichte und Gedächtnis in der Einwanderungsgesellschaft. Migration zwischen historischer Rekonstruktion und Erinnerungspolitik*. Eds. Jan Motte and Rainer Ohliger. Essen: Klartext, 2004. 199–212.
Alexander, Karen. "'Film and Video Workshops' – Production and Images." *Artrage* 3–4 (1983): 27–28.
Alexander, Karen. "Black British Cinema in the 90s: Going Going Gone." *British Cinema of the 90s*. Ed. Robert Murphy. London: BFI Publishing, 2000. 109–114.
Allen, Graham. *Intertextuality*. London and New York: Routledge, 2000.
Allen, Jeanne. "Self-reflexivity in Documentary." *Explorations in Film Theory: Selected Essays from Ciné-Tracts*. Ed. Rod Burnett. Bloomington: Indiana University Press, 1991. 103–110.
Allen, Robert C., and Douglas Gomery. *Film History: Theory and Practice*. York: Knopf, 1985.
Alphen, Ernst von. "Imagined Homelands: Re-mapping Cultural Identity." *Mobilising Place, Placing Mobility: The Politics of Representation in a Globalized World*. Eds. Ginette Verstraate and Tim Cresswell. Amsterdam: Rodopi, 2002. 53–70.
Alter, Nora. "Second Thought: Hearing the Essay." *Der Essayfilm: Ästhetik und Aktualität*. Eds. Sven Kramer and Thomas Tode. Konstanz: UVK, 2011. 175–188.
Anderson, Benedict. *Imagined Communities: Reflections on the Origin and Spread of Nationalism*. London: Verso, 1991.
Andersson, Lars Gustaf, and John Sundholm, and Astrid Söderbergh Widding. *History of Swedish Experimental Film Culture: From Early Animation to Video Art*. Stockholm: National Library of Sweden, 2010.

Andersson, Lars Gustaf, and John Sundholm. "Film Workshops as Polyvocal Public Spheres. Minor Cinemas in Sweden." *Canadian Journal of Film Studies* 19.2 (2010): 66–81.
Appudarai, Arjun. *Modernity at Large: Cultural Dimensions of Globalization*. Minneapolis: University of Minnesota Press, 1995.
Araeen, Rasheed, ed. *The Other Story: Afro-Asian Artists in Post-War Britain*. London: Hayward Gallery, 1989.
Araaen, Rasheed, and Sean Cubitt, and Ziauddin Sardar. *The Third Text Reader on Art, Culture and Theory*. London and New York: Continuum, 2002.
Armatage, Kay. "Fashions in Feminist Programming." *There She Goes: Feminist Filmmaking and Beyond*. Eds. Corinn Columpar and Sophie Mayer. Ann Arbor: University of Michigan Press, 2010. 92–104.
Arroyo, José. "The Films of Isaac Julien. Talk Back and Look Back." *Cinemas of the Black Diaspora: Diversity, Dependence and Oppositionality*. Ed. Michael T. Martin. Detroit: Wayne State University Press, 1995. 318–338.
Ashby, Justine, and Andrew Higson, eds. *British Cinema, Past and Present*. London and New York: Routledge, 2000.
Ashcroft, Bill, and Gareth Griffiths, and Helen Tiffin. *The Empire Writes Back: Theory and Practice in Post-Colonial Literature*. New York/London: Routledge, 1989.
Aspinall, Sue. "The Space for Innovation and Experiment." *Screen* 25.6 (1984): 73–87.
Assmann, Aleida. "Texts, Traces, Trash: The Changing Media of Cultural Memory." *Representations* 56 (1996): 123–134.
Assmann, Aleida. *Erinnerungsräume: Formen und Wandlungen des kulturellen Gedächtnisses*. München: Beck, 1999.
Assmann, Aleida. "Das Archiv und die neuen Medien des kulturellen Gedächtnisses." *Schnittstelle: Medien und Kulturwissenschaften*. Eds. Georg Stanitzek and Wilhelm Vosskamp. Köln: DuMont, 2001. 268–281.
Assmann, Aleida. *Der lange Schatten der Vergangenheit: Erinnerungskultur und Geschichtspolitik*. München: Beck, 2006.
Assmann, Aleida. "Canon and Archive." *Cultural Memory Studies: An International and Interdisciplinary Handbook*. Eds. Astrid Erll and Ansgar Nünning. Berlin: de Gruyter, 2008. 97–107.
Assmann, Aleida. *Cultural Memory and Western Civilization: Functions, Media, Archives*. Cambridge: Cambridge University Press, 2011.
Assmann, Aleida, and Sebastian Conrad, eds. *Memory in a Global Age: Discourses, Practices and Trajectories*. Basingstoke: Palgrave Macmillan, 2010.
Assmann, Jan. "Kollektives Gedächtnis und kulturelle Identität." *Kultur und Gedächtnis*. Eds. Jan Assmann and Tonio Hölscher. Frankfurt/M.: Suhrkamp, 1988a. 9–19.
Assmann, Jan. "Stein und Zeit. Das 'monumentale' Gedächtnis der altägyptischen Kultur." *Kultur und Gedächtnis*. Eds. Jan Assmann and Tonio Hölscher. Frankfurt/M.: Suhrkamp, 1988b. 87–114.
Assmann, Jan. *Das kulturelle Gedächtnis: Schrift, Erinnerung und politische Identität in frühen Hochkulturen*. München: Beck, 1992.
Assmann, Jan. "Collective Memory and Cultural Identity." *New German Critique* 65 (1995): 125–133.
Assmann, Jan. *Moses the Egyptian. The Memory of Egypt in Western Monotheism*. Cambridge, Mass/London: Harvard University Press, 1997.
Assmann, Jan. *Religion und kulturelles Gedächtnis: Zehn Studien*. München: Beck, 2000.

Astruc, Alexandre. "The Birth of the New Avant-Garde: The Caméra-Stylo" [1948]. *Film and Literature: An Introduction and Reader.* Ed. Timothy Corrigan. Upper Saddle River: Prentice Hall, 1999. 158–162.

Attille, Martina. "The Passion of Remembrance: Background." *ICA documents 7, Black Film, British Cinema* 1988. 53–54.

Auguiste, Reece/Black Audio Film Collective. "Black Independents and Third Cinema: The British Context." *Questions of Third Cinema.* Ed. Jim Pines and Paul Willemen. London: BFI Publishing 1989. 212–217.

Auguiste, Reece. "Handsworth Songs: Some Background Notes" [1988]. *The Ghosts of Songs: The Film Art of the Black Audio Film Collective 1982–1998.* Ed. Kodwo Eshun and Anjalika Sagar. Liverpool: Liverpool University Press and FACT, 2007a. 156–157.

Auguiste, Reece. "Black Cinema, Poetics and New World Aesthetics" [1988]. *The Ghosts of Songs: The Film Art of the Black Audio Film Collective 1982–1998.* Ed. Kodwo Eshun and Anjalika Sagar. Liverpool: Liverpool University Press and FACT, 2007b. 152–155.

Austin, J.L.: *Philosophical Papers.* Oxford: Oxford University Press, 1979.

Austin, Thomas, and Wilme de Jong, Wilma, eds. *Rethinking Documentary: New Perspectives, New Practices.* Maidenhead: Open University Press, 2008.

Auty, Martin, and Nick Roddick, eds. *British Cinema Now.* London: BFI Publishing, 1985.

Bailey, David A., and Stuart Hall. "The Vertigo of Displacement." *Ten 8* 2.3 (1992): 15–23.

Bailey, David A., and Ian Baucom, and Sonia Boyce, eds. *Shades of Black. Assembling Black Arts in 1980s Britain.* Durham, NC and London: Duke University Press/inIVA and Aavaa, 2005.

Bakari, Imruh. "A Journey from the Cold. Rethinking Black Film-making in Britain." *Black British Culture and Society: A Text Reader.* Ed. Kwesi Owusu London and New York: Routledge, 2000. 230–238.

Baker, Houston A., Jr., and Manthia Diawara, and Ruth H. Lindeborg, eds. *Black British Cultural Studies: A Reader.* Chicago and London: The University of Chicago Press, 1996.

Bakhtin, Mikhail M. *Problems of Dostoevsky's Poetics.* Ann Arbor: Ardis 1973.

Bakhtin, Mikhail M. "Forms of Time and of the Chronotope in the Novel." *The Dialogic Imagination: Four Essays by M.M. Bakhtin.* Ed. Michael Holquist. Austin: University of Texas Press, 1981. 84–258.

Bal, Mieke, and Jonathan Crewe, and Leo Spitzer, eds. *Acts of Memory: Cultural Recall in the Present.* Hanover, NH: University Press of New England, 1999.

Barthes, Roland. *Camera Lucida.* London: Vintage, 1982.

Barton, Joe. "'Welcome to Manchester': Heritage, Urban Regeneration, and Michael Winterbottom's *24 Hour Party People*." *Frames Cinema Journal* 2 (2012).

Baur, Joachim. *Die Musealisierung der Migration: Einwanderungsmuseen und die Inszenierung der multikulturellen Nation.* Bielefeld: Transcript, 2009.

Bazin, André. *What is Cinema?* Vol. I. Berkeley, CA: University of California Press, 1967.

Bell, Erin, and Ann Gray, eds. *Televising History: Mediating the Past in Postwar Europe.* Basingstoke: Palgrave Macmillan, 2010.

Benjamin, Walter. *Illuminations: Essays and Reflections.* Edited and with an introduction by Hannah Arendt. Translated by Harry Zohn. New York: Schocken, 1968.

Benjamin, Walter. *Sprache und Geschichte: Philosophische Essays.* Stuttgart: Reclam, 1992.

Berghahn, Daniela, and Claudia Sternberg, eds. *European Cinema in Motion Migrant and Diasporic Film in Contemporary Europe.* Basingstoke: Palgrave Macmillan, 2010.

Bergfelder, Tim. "National, Transnational or Supranational Cinema? Rethinking European Film Studies." *Media Culture Society* (27) 2005: 315–331.
Bhabha, Homi. "The Other Question ... The Stereotype and Colonial Discourse." *Screen* 24.6 (1983): 18–36.
Bhabha, Homi. "DissemiNation: Time, Narrative, and the Margins of the Modern Nation." *Nation and Narration.* Ed. Homi Bhabha. London and New York: Routledge, 1990, 291–322.
Bhabha, Homi. *The Location of Culture.* New York/London: Routledge, 1994.
Bijsterveld, Karin, and José van Dijck, eds. *Sound Souvenirs: Audio Technologies, Memory and Cultural Practices.* Amsterdam: Amsterdam University Press, 2009.
Bjerg, Helle, and Claudia Lenz. ""If Only Grandfather Were Here to Tell Us...". Gender as a Category in the Culture of Memory of the Occupation in Denmark and Norway." *Gendering Memory.* Eds. Sylvia Paletschek and Sylvia Schraut. New York: Campus, 2008, 221–236.
Bleicher, Joan Kristin. "The Old in the New: Forms and Functions of Archive Material in the Presentation of Television History on Television." *Self-Reference in the Media.* Eds. Winfried Nöth and Nina Bishara. Berlin: de Gruyter 2007, 183–194.
Bleicher, Joan Kristin. "Digitales Fernsehen: YouTube als Supermedium im Spiegel der Forschung." *Videoportale: Broadcast Yourself? Versprechen und Enttäuschung.* Eds. Julia Schumacher and Andreas Stuhlmann. Hamburg: Hamburger Hefte zur Medienkultur 12 (2011): 13–27.
Blouin, Frances X, jr., and William G. Rosenberg. *Processing the Past: Contesting Authority in History and the Archives.* Oxford: Oxford University Press, 2011.
Blümlinger, Christa, ed. *Sprung im Spiegel: Filmisches Wahrnehmen zwischen Fiktion und Wirklichkeit.* Wien: Sonderzahl, 1990a.
Blümlinger, Christa. "Blick auf das Bilder-Machen: Zur Reflexivität im dokumentarischen Film." *Sprung im Spiegel: Filmisches Wahrnehmen zwischen Fiktion und Wirklichkeit.* Ed. Christa Blümlinger. Wien: Sonderzahl, 1990b. 193–208.
Blümlinger, Christa, and Constantin Wulff, eds. *Schreiben Bilder Sprechen: Texte zum essayistischen Film.* Wien: Sonderzahl, 1992.
Blümlinger, Christa. "Sichtbares und Sagbares: Modalitäten historischer Diskursivität im Archivkunstfilm." *Die Gegenwart der Vergangenheit: Dokumentarfilm, Fernsehen und Geschichte.* Eds. Eva Hohenberger and Judith Keilbach. Berlin: Vorwerk8, 2003. 82–97.
Blümlinger, Christa. *Kino aus zweiter Hand: Zur Ästhetik materieller Aneignung im Film und in der Medienkunst.* Berlin: Vorwerk8, 2009.
Bodnar, John. *Remaking America: Public Memory Commemoration and Patriotism in the Twentieth Century.* Princeton: Princeton University Press, 1992.
Bösch, Frank. "Holokaust mit ‚K': Audiovisuelle Narrative in neueren Fernsehdokumentationen." *Visual History: Ein Studienbuch.* Ed. Gerhard Paul. Göttingen: Vandenhoeck und Ruprecht, 2006. 317–323.
Bohn, Anna. *Denkmal Film. Band 1: Der Film als Kulturerbe.* Wien, Köln, Weimar: Böhlau, 2013a.
Bohn, Anna. *Denkmal Film. Band 2: Kulturlexikon Filmerbe.* Wien, Köln, Weimar: Böhlau, 2013b.
Bolter, Jay David, and Richard Grusin. *Remediation: Understanding New Media.* Cambridge, Mass.: MIT Press, 2000.

Bottà, Giacomo. "Pop Music, Cultural Sensibilities and Places: Manchester 1976–1997." Paper from the ESF-LiU Conference "Cities and Media: Cultural Perspectives on Urban Identities in a Mediatized World", Vadstena 25–29 October, 2006 www.ep.liu.se/ecp/020/ (11 October 2013).

Bouchard, Donald F. 1977. "Preface." In: Michel Foucault: *Language, Counter-Memory, Practic: Selected Essays and Interviews*. Ithaca, NY: Cornell University Press, 1977. 7–9.

Bourdieu, Pierre. *Eine illegitime Kunst: Die sozialen Gebrauchsweisen der Photographie*. Frankfurt/M.: Suhrkamp, 1983.

Bourne, Stephen. *Black in the British Frame: The Black Experience in British Film and Television*. London and New York: Continuum, 2001.

Boym, Svetlana. *The Future of Nostalgia*. New York: Basic Books, 2001.

Boym, Svetlana. "Nostalgia and its discontent." *The Hedgehog Review*. Summer (2007): 7–18.

Brabazon, Tara. *From Revolution to Revelation: Generation X, Popular Memory and Cultural Studies*. Aldershot: Ashgate, 2005.

Bradshaw, Peter. "*Control*. Directed by Anton Corbijn (review)". *The Guardian*, 18 May 2007. Online: http://www.guardian.co.uk/film/2007/may/18/cannes2007.cannesfilmfestival1 (3 April 2014)

Brah, Avtar. *Cartographies of Diaspora: Contesting Identities*. London and New York: Routledge, 1996.

Braidotti, Rosi. *Nomadic Subjects: Embodiment and Sexual Difference in Contemporary Feminist Theory*. New York: Columbia University Press, 1994.

Brauerhoch, Annette. "Wahrnehmung und Medium: Theoretische und ästhetische Fragen der Film- und Medienwissenschaft." *Frauen und Film* 64 (2004): 27–41.

Bravmann, Scott. "Isaac Julien's 'Looking for Langston': Hughes, biography and queer(ed) history." *Cultural Studies* 7.2 (1993): 311–323.

Brecht, Bertolt. *Schriften zum Theater: Über eine nicht-aristotelische Dramatik*. Frankfurt/M.: Suhrkamp, 1957.

Brubaker, Rogers. *Citizenship and Nationhood in France and Germany*. Cambridge: Harvard University Press, 1992.

Bruhn, Jörgen. "Heteromediality." *Media Borders, Intermediality and Multimodality*. Ed. Lars Elleström. Basingstoke: Palgrave Macmillan, 2010. 225–236.

Brunow, Dagmar. "Representation and Performativity – Methodological Considerations on Film and Historiography: The Example of Baader-Meinhof." *Historier: Arton- och nittonhundratalets skönlitteratur som historisk källa*. Eds. Christer Ahlberger (et al.). Gothenburg: Gothenburg University Press, 2009. 44–56.

Brunow, Dagmar. "Deconstructing Essentialism and Revising Historiography: The Function of Metareference in Black British Filmmaking." *The Metareferential Turn in Contemporary Arts and Media: Forms, Functions, Attempts at Explanation. Studies in Intermediality 5*. Ed. Werner Wolf, in collaboration with Katharina Bantleon and Jeff Thoss. Amsterdam/New York: Rodopi, 2011a. 341–355.

Brunow, Dagmar 2011b. "Film als kulturelles Gedächtnis der Arbeitsmigration: Fatih Akins 'Wir haben vergessen zurückzukehren'". *50 Jahre türkische Arbeitsmigration in Deutschland*. Eds. Şeyda Ozil, Michael Hofmann and Yasemin Dayioglu-Yücel. Göttingen: V&R Unipress, 2011b. 183–204.

Brunow, Dagmar. "Soundscapes als akustisches Gedächtnis der Stadt: Künstlerische Strategien gegen Gentrifizierung." *Testcard. Beiträge zur Popgeschichte* 20 (2011c): 37–41.

Brunow, Dagmar. "Before YouTube and Indymedia: Cultural Memory and the Archive of Video Collectives in Germany in the 1970s and 1980s". *Studies in European Cinema* 8.3 (2012a): 171–182.

Brunow, Dagmar. "Film als Historiographie: 'Handsworth Songs' als Dekonstruktion kolonialer Geschichtsschreibung". *"All We Ever Wanted…" Eine Kulturgeschichte europäischer Protestbewegungen der 1980er Jahre*. Eds. Hanno Balz and Jan-Henrik Friedrichs. Berlin: Dietz, 2012b. 107–119.

Brunow, Dagmar. "Amateur Home Movies and the Archive of Migration: Sandhya Suri's I for India (UK, 2005)". *Tourist and Nomads: Amateur Images of Migration*. Eds. Sonja Kmec and Viviane Thill. Marburg: Jonas, 2012c. 153–160.

Brunow, Dagmar. "Western. Zwischen nationalem Kino und transnationaler Hybridkultur." *Filmwissenschaftliche Genreanalyse. Eine Einführung*. Ed. Markus Kuhn, Irina Scheidgen and Nicola Valeska Weber. Berlin: deGruyter, 2013a. 39–61.

Brunow, Dagmar. "Mulvey Reloaded: Den manliga blicken och feministiskt filmskapande." *Tidskrift för genusvetenskap* 4 (2013b): 64–67.

Bruzzi, Stella. *New Documentary: A Critical Introduction*. London and New York: Routledge, 2000.

Bruzzi, Stella. *New Documentary*. 2. ed. London and New York: Routledge, 2006.

Bruzzi, Stella. "The Performing Film-maker and the Acting Subject." *The Documentary Film Book*. Ed. Brian Winston. London: BFI/Palgrave Macmillan 2013, 48–58.

Burgin, Victor. "Something about Photography Theory." *Screen* 25.1 (1984): 61–66.

Burgoyne, Robert. *Film Nation: Hollywood Looks at U.S. History*. Revised Edition. Minneapolis/London: University of Minneapolis Press, 2010.

Burke, Peter. *Eyewitnessing: The Uses of Images as Historical Evidence*. Ithaca, NY: Cornell University Press, 2001.

Burns, Rob. "Turkish-German Cinema: From Cultural Resistance to Transnational Cinema?" *German Cinema Since Unification*. Ed. David Clarke. London and New York: Continuum, 2006. 127–149.

Butler, Judith. *Gender Trouble: Feminism and the Subversion of Identity*. London and New York: Routledge, 1990.

Butler, Judith. *Bodies That Matter: On the Discursive Limits of 'Sex'*. London and New York: Routledge, 1993.

Butler, Judith. *Excitable Speech: A Politics of the Performative*. London and New York: Routledge, 1997.

Casteel, Sarah. *Second Arrivals: Landscape and Belonging in Contemporary Writing of the Americas*. Charlottesville and London: University of Virginia Press, 2007.

CCCS. *The Empire Strikes Back. Race and Racism in 70s Britain*. London: Hutchinson, 1982.

Cham, Mbye, and Claire Andrade-Watkins, eds. *Blackframes: Critical Perspectives on Black Independent Cinema*. Cambridge, MA: MIT Press, 1988.

Chambers, Eddie. "'Handsworth Songs' and the Archival Image." *Ghosting: The Role of the Archive within Contemporary Artists' Film and Video*. Eds. Jane Connarty and Josephine Lanyon. Bristol: Picture This, 2006. 24–33.

Chapman, Jane. *Issues in Contemporary Documentary*. Cambridge and Malden, MA: Polity, 2009.

Cherchi Usai, Paolo. *Silent Cinema: An Introduction*. London BFI Publishing, 2000.
Cherchi Usai, Paolo, David Francis, Alexander Horwath, and Michael Loebenstein, eds. *Film Curatorship. Archives, Museums, and the Digital Marketplace*. Wien: Österreichisches Filmmuseum/SYNEMA, 2008.
Chion, Michel. *The Voice in the Cinema*. New York: Columbia University Press, 1999.
Clark, Dylan. "The Death and Life of Punk, The Last Subculture." *The Post-Subcultures Reader*. Eds. David Muggleton and Rupert Weinzierl. Oxford: Berg, 2003. 223–236.
Cleaver, Eldridge. *Soul on Ice*. New York: McGraw-Hill, 1968.
Clifford, James. *Routes: Travel and Translation in the Late Twentieth Century*. Cambridge, Mass: Harvard University Press, 1997.
Cohen, Sara. *Decline, Renewal and the City in Popular Music Culture: Beyond the Beatles*. Aldershot: Ashgate, 2007.
Jean-Luc Comolli, and Jean Narboni. "Cinéma – idéologie – critique". *Cahiers du cinéma* 216 (1969): 11–15.
Confino, Alon. "Collective Memory and Cultural History: Problems of Method." *The American Historical Review* 102.5 (1997): 1386–1403.
Confino, Alon and Peter Fritzsche. "Introduction." *The Work of Memory: New Directions in the Study of German Society and Culture*. Eds. Alon Confino and Peter Fritzsche. Chicago: University of Illinois Pess, 2002. 1–24.
Connarty, Jane, and Josephine Lanyon, eds. *Ghosting: The Role of the Archive within Contemporary Artists' Film and Video*. Bristol: Picture This, 2006.
Connerton, Paul. *How Societies Remember*. Cambridge: Cambridge University Press, 1989.
Cook, Pam. "Handsworth Songs (review)". *Monthly Film Bulletin* 54.637 (1987): 77–78.
Cook, Pam. *Screening the Past: Memory and Nostalgia in Cinema*. New York: Routledge, 2005.
Corner, John, and Sylvia Harvey, eds. *Enterprise and Heritage: Crosscurrents of National Culture*. London and New York: Routledge, 1991.
Corner, John. *The Art of Record: A Critical Introduction to Documentary*. Manchester: Manchester University Press, 1996.
Corrigan, Timothy. *The Essay Film: From Montaigne, After Marker*. Oxford: Oxford University Press, 2011.
Courtman, Sandra. "A Journey through the Imperial Gaze: Birmingham's Photographic Collections and its Caribbean Nexus." *Visual Culture and Decolonisation in Britain*. Eds. Simon Faulkner and Anandi Ramamurthy. Aldershot: Ashgate, 2006. 127–152.
Craps, Stef, and Michael Rothberg. "Introduction: Transcultural Negotiation of Holocaust Memory." *Criticism*, 53.4 (2011): 517–521.
Creet, Julia, and Andreas Kitzmann, eds. *Memory and Migration: Multidisciplinary Approaches to Memory Studies*. Toronto: University of Toronto Press, 2011.
Crenshaw, Kimberlé. "Mapping the Margins: Intersectionality, Identity Politics, and Violence Against Women of Color." *Identities: race, class, gender, and nationality*. Ed. Linda Martin Alcoff and Eduarto Mendieta. Malden, Mass: Blackwell, 2003. 175–200.
Crofts, Stephen. "Concepts of National Cinema". *Oxford Guide to Film Studies*. Ed. John Hill and Pamela Church Gibson. New York: Oxford University Press 1998. 385–394.
Crownshaw, Richard. "Introduction." *parallax* 17.4 (2011): 1–3.
Crusz, Robert. "Black Cinemas, Film Theory and Dependent Knowledge." *Screen* 26.3–4 (1985): 152–156.

Cruz, Amada, ed. *The Film Art of Isaac Julien*. New York: Center for Curational Studies, Bard College, 2000.
Cubitt, Sean. *Timeshift: On Video Culture*. London: Routledge, 1991.
Cubitt, Sean. *Videography: Video Media as Art and Culture*. Basingstoke: Macmillan, 1993.
Cubitt, Sean. *The Cinema Effect*. Cambridge, Mass/London: The MIT Press, 2004.
Cummins, Kevin. *Manchester: Looking for the Light through the Pouring Rain*. London: faber and faber, 2009.
Curtis, Deborah. *Touching from a Distance: Ian Curtis and Joy Division*. London: faber and faber, 2007.
Curtis, Robin. *Conscientious Viscerality: The Autobiographical Stance in German Film and Video*. Berlin: Edition Imorde, 2006.
Cvetkovich, Ann. *An Archive of Feelings: Trauma, Sexuality, and Lesbian Public Cultures*. Durham, NC/London: Duke University Press, 2003.
Dabydeen, David, John Gilmore and Cecily Jones, eds. *The Oxford Companion to Black British History*. Oxford: Oxford University Press, 2007.
Danbolt, Mathias. "We're here! We're queer? Activist archives and archival activism", *lambda nordica* 15.3–4 (2010): 90–118.
Dasgupta, Sudeep and Esther Peeren, eds. *Constellations of the Transnational: Modernity, Culture, Critique*. Amsterdam: Rodopi, 2007.
Davenport, Neil. "A Joyless Depiction of the Post-Punk Era." [Review of *Control*, dir. Anton Corbijn]. *Spiked* 8, October 2007. Online: http://www.spiked-online.com/index.php/site/article/3943/ (12 October 2013).
Dayan, Daniel, and Elihu Katz. *Media Events: The Live Broadcasting of History*. Cambridge, MA: Harvard University Press, 1992.
DeLauretis, Teresa. *Technologies of Gender. Essays on Theory, Film, and Fiction*. Bloomington: Indiana University Press, 1987.
Deleuze, Gilles. *Cinema 1: The Movement-Image*. London: Athlone, 1986.
Deleuze, Gilles. *Cinema 2: The Time-Image*. London: Athlone, 1989.
Deleuze, Gilles, and Félix Guattari. *Kafka: Toward a Minor Literature*. Minneapolis: University of Minnesota Press, 1986.
Den Boer, Pim Heinz Durchhardt, Heinz and Georg Kreis, eds. *Europäische Erinnerungsorte 1. Mythen und Grundbegriffe des europäischen Selbstverständnisses*. München: Oldenbourg, 2011.
Den Boer, Pim, Heinz Durchhardt, Heinz and Georg Kreis, eds. *Europäische Erinnerungsorte 2. Das Haus Europa*. München: Oldenbourg, 2012a.
Den Boer, Pim, Heinz Durchhardt, Heinz and Georg Kreis, eds. *Europäische Erinnerungsorte 3. Europa und die Welt*. München: Oldenbourg, 2012b.
Dent, Gina, ed. *Black Popular Culture*. (Dia Center for the Arts, Discussions in Popular Culture, Number 8). Seattle: Bay Press, 1992.
Derrida, Jacques. *Archive Fever: A Freudian Impression*. *Diacritics* 25. 2 (1995): 9–63.
Derrida, Jacques. *Archive Fever: A Freudian Impression*. Translated by Eric Prenowitz. Chicago: University of Chicago Press 1998.
Diawara, Manthia. "The Absent One: The Avant-Garde and the Black Imaginary in Looking for Langston." *Wide Angle* 13.3–4 (1991): 96–109.
Diawara, Manthia. "Power and Territory: The Emergence of Black British Film Collectives." *British Film and Thatcherism: Fires We Started*. Ed. Lester Friedman. London: UCL Press, 1993.147–160.

Diawara, Manthia. "Black British Cinema: Spectatorship and Identity Formation in Territories." *Black British Cultural Studies. A Reader*. Eds. Houston A. Baker, Jr., Manthia Diawara and Ruth H. Lindeborg. Chicago/London: The University of Chicago Press, 1996. 293–305.
Dickel, Simon. "Black Men Loving Black Men and Other Revolutionary Acts. Positionen zu Begehren und Sexualität in schwarzer schwuler Kultur." *Testcard. Beiträge zur Popgeschichte 17. Sex* (2008): 172–177.
Dickel, Simon. *Black/Gay: The Harlem Renaissance, the Protest Era, and Constructions of Black Gay Identity*. Münster, LIT, 2011.
Dickhaut, Kirsten. "Intermedialität und Gedächtnis." *Gedächtniskonzepte in der Literaturwissenschaft*. Eds. Astrid Erll and Ansgar Nünning. Berlin: de Gruyter, 2005. 203–226.
Dickinson, Margaret, ed. *Rogue Reels: Oppositional Film in Britain, 1945–1990*. London: BFI Publishing, 1999.
Didi-Huberman, Georges. *Bilder trotz allem*. München: Fink, 2007.
Dijck, José van. *Mediated Memories in the Digital Age*. Stanford, Cal.: Stanford University Press, 2007.
Dillon, Robert. *History on British Television: Constructing Nation, Nationality and Collective Memory*. Manchester and New York: Manchester University Press, 2010.
Distelmeyer, Jan. *Autor Macht Geschichte: Oliver Stone, seine Filme und die Werksgeschichtsschreibung*. München: edition text und kritik, 2005.
Distelmeyer, Jan, ed. *Babylon in FilmEuropa: Mehrsprachen-Versionen der 1930er Jahre*. München: edition text und kritik, 2006.
Distelmeyer, Jan. *Das flexible Kino: Ästhetik und Dispositiv der DVD & Blu-ray*. Berlin: Bertz +Fischer, 2012.
Does, Christoph. *Bilder der Bewegung: Bilder, die bewegen? Strategien und Interventionsmöglichkeiten ‚alternativer' Video- und Fernsehgruppen in den neunziger Jahren*. MSc-Thesis, Berlin, 1997.
Douglas, Lawrence. "Film as Witness: Screening Nazi Concentration Camps before the Nuremberg Tribunal." *The Yale Law Journal* 105.2 (1995): 449–481.
Doulis, Mario, and Peter Ott, eds. *Remediate: An den Rändern von Film, Netz und Archiv*. München: Fink, 2013.
Doy, Gen. *Black Visual Culture: Modernism and Postmodernism*. London and New York: Tauris, 2000.
Drew, Jesse. "The Collective Camcorder in Art and Activism." *Collectivism after Modernism*. Eds. Blake Stimson and Gregory Sholette. University of Minnesota: Minneapolis, 2007. 95–113.
Durbahn. 'Unser Begriff von "Medienzentren"'. *die thede 1980–1990*. Ed. die thede. Hamburg: Schwarze Kunst, 1996. 17–23.
Ďurovičová, Nataša, and Kathleen Newman, eds. *World Cinemas, Transnational Perspectives*. New York, NY: Routledge, 2010.
Dyer, Richard. "White." *Screen* 29.4 (1988): 44–65.
Dyer, Richard. *White*. London and New York: Routledge, 1997.
Ebbrecht, Tobias. *Geschichtsbilder im medialen Gedächtnis: Filmische Narrationen des Holocaust*. Bielefeld: Transcript, 2011.
Ebeling, Knut, and Stephan Günzel. *Archivologie: Theorien des Archivs in Philosophie, Medien und Künsten*. Berlin: Kulturverlag Kadmos, 2009.

Eckstein, Lars. *Re-membering the Black Atlantic: On the Poetics and Politics of Literary Memory*. Amsterdam: Rodopi, 2006.

Eco, Umberto. *The Role of the Reader*. Bloomington: Indiana University Press, 1979.

Eder, Angelika, ed. *"Wir sind auch da!" Über das Leben von und mit Migranten in europäischen Großstädten*. Hamburg: Dölling und Galitz, 2003.

Edgerton, Gary R., and Peter C. Rollins. *Television Histories: Shaping Collective Memory in the Media Age*. Lexington: The University Press of Kentucky, 2001.

El-Tayeb, Fatima. "The Archive, the Activist, and the Audience, or Black European Studies: A Comparative Interdisciplinary Study of Identities, Positionalities and Differences." *Transit. Migration, Culture, and the Nation State* 1.1 (2005). Online: http://escholarship.org/uc/item/4tc204x4 (21 August 2014).

Eliot, T.S. *Notes Towards the Definition of Culture*. London: faber and faber, 1991.

Elleström, Lars. "The Modalities of Media: A Model for Understanding Intermedial Relations." *Media Borders, Multimodality and Intermediality*. Ed. Lars Elleström. Basingstoke: Palgrave Macmillan, 2010. 11–48.

Elsaesser, Thomas. "The New Film History." In: *Sight and Sound* (55.4) 1986: 246–251.

Elsaesser, Thomas. "Subject Positions, Speaking Positions: From Holocaust, Our Hitler, and Heimat to Shoah and Schindler's List." *The Persistence of History. Cinema, Television and the Modern Event*. Ed. Vivian Sobchack. New York and London: Routledge, 1996. 145–183.

Elsaesser, Thomas. "One Train May Be Hiding Another: History, Memory, Identity and the Visual Image." *Topologies of Trauma: Essays on the Limit of Knowledge and Memory*. Eds. Linda Belau and Petar Ramadanovic. New York: Other Press, 2002. 61–71.

Elsaesser, Thomas. *European Cinema: Face to Face with Hollywood*. Amsterdam: Amsterdam University Press, 2005.

Enwezor, Okwui. "Coalition Building: Black Audio Film Collective and Transnational Post-Colonialism." *The Ghosts of Songs: The Film Art of the Black Audio Film Collective 1982–1998*. Eds. Kodwo Eshun and Anjalika Sagar. Liverpool: Liverpool University Press and FACT, 2007. 106–123.

Enwezor, Okwui. "Documentary/Vérité: Bio-Politics, Human Rights, and the Figure of 'Truth' in Contemporary Art". *The Green Room: Reconsidering the Documentary and Contemporary Art 1*. Eds. Maria Lind and Hito Steyerl. Berlin/Annondale-on-Hudson, NY: Sternberg-Press, 2008. 62–102.

Enwezor, Okwui. *Archive Fever: Uses of the Document in Contemporary Art*. New York: International Center of Photography/Steidl, 2008.

Erll, Astrid. *Kollektives Gedächtnis und Erinnerungskulturen*. Stuttgart, Weimar: Metzler, 2005.

Erll, Astrid. "Literature, Film, and the Mediality of Cultural Memory." *Cultural Memory Studies: An International and Interdisciplinary Handbook*. Eds. Astrid Erll and Ansgar Nünning. Berlin and New York: de Gruyter, 2008a. 389–398.

Erll, Astrid. "Cultural Memory Studies: An Introduction." *Cultural Memory Studies: An International and Interdisciplinary Handbook*. Eds. Astrid Erll and Ansgar Nünning. Berlin and New York: de Gruyter, 2008b. 1–15.

Erll, Astrid. "Remembering across Time, Space and Cultures: Premediation, Remediation and the 'Indian Mutiny'." *Mediation, Remediation, and the Dynamics of Cultural Memory*. Eds. Astrid Erll and Ann Rigney. Berlin and New York: de Gruyter. 109–138.

Erll, Astrid. "Regional Integration and (Trans)cultural Memory." *Asia Europe Journal* 8.3 (2010): 305–315.

Erll, Astrid. *Memory in Culture*. Basingstoke: Palgrave Macmillan, 2011a.
Erll, Astrid. "Travelling Memory." *Parallax* 17.4 (2011b): 4–18.
Erll, Astrid. "Traumatic Pasts, Literary Afterlives, and Transcultural Memory: New Directions of Literary and Media Memory Studies." *Journal of Aesthetics & Culture* (3) 2011c: [not paginated].
Erll, Astrid. "Odysseus' Reisen: Remediation und transkulturelle Erinnerung." *Gedächtnisstrategien und Medien im interkulturellen Dialog*. Eds. Sonja Klein, Vivian Liska, Karl Solibakke and Bernd Witte. Würzburg: Königshausen & Neumann, 2011d. 125–144.
Erll, Astrid. "War, Film and Collective Memory: Plurimedial Constellations." *Journal of Scandinavian Cinema* 2.3 (2012): 231–235.
Erll, Astrid, and Ansgar Nünning, in collaboration with Hanne Birk, Birgit Neumann und Patrick Schmidt, eds. *Medien des kollektiven Gedächtnisses. Konstruktivität – Historizität – Kulturspezifität*. Berlin/New York: de Gruyter, 2004.
Erll, Astrid, and Ansgar Nünning, in collaboration with Hanne Birk and Birgit Neumann, eds. *Gedächtniskonzepte der Literaturwissenschaft: Theoretische Grundlegung und Anwendungsperspektiven*. Berlin/New York: de Gruyter, 2005.
Erll, Astrid, and Ansgar Nünning, eds. *Cultural Memory Studies: An International and Interdisciplinary Handbook*. Berlin/New York: de Gruyter, 2008.
Erll, Astrid, and Stephanie Wodianka, eds. *Film und kulturelle Erinnerung: Plurimediale Konstellationen*. Berlin/New York: de Gruyter, 2008.
Erll, Astrid, and Ann Rigney. *Mediation, Remediation, and the Dynamics of Cultural Memory*. Berlin/New York: de Gruyter. 2009.
Ernst, Wolfgang. *Das Rumoren der Archive: Ordnung aus Unordnung*. Berlin: Merve, 2002.
Ernst, Wolfgang. *Das Gesetz des Gedächtnisses: Medien und Archive am Ende (des 20. Jahrhunderts)*. Berlin: Kulturverlag Kadmos, 2007.
Ernst, Wolfgang. *Digital Memory and the Archive*. Minneapolis, MN: University of Minnesota Press, 2013.
Eshun, Kodwo. "Further Considerations on Afrofuturism." *The New Centennial Review* 3.2 (2003): 287–302
Eshun, Kodwo. "Twilight City: Outline for an Archaeopsychic Geography of New London." *Wasafiri* 43 (2004a): 7–13.
Eshun, Kodwo. "Untimely Meditations: Reflections on the Black Audio Film Collective." *Nka: Journal of Contemporary African Art* 19 (2004b): 38–45.
Eshun, Kodwo and Anjalika Sagar, eds. *The Ghosts of Songs: The Film Art of the Black Audio Film Collective 1982–1998*. Liverpool: Liverpool University Press and FACT, 2007.
Eshun, Kodwo. "Drawing the Forms of Things Unknown." *The Ghosts of Songs: The Film Art of the Black Audio Film Collective 1982–1998*. Eds. Kodwo Eshun and Anjalika Sagar. Liverpool: Liverpool University Press and FACT, 74–105.
Eshun, Kodwo. "The Disenchantments of Reflexivity in *Handsworth Songs*." *Der Essayfilm: Ästhetik und Aktualität*. Eds. Sven Kramer and Thomas Tode. Konstanz: UVK, 2011. 241–256.
Evans, David, ed. *Appropriation*. Cambridge, MA: MIT Press, 2009.
Ezli, Özkan, ed. *Kultur als Ereignis: Fatih Akins Film 'Auf der anderen Seite' als transkulturelle Narration*. Bielefeld: Transcript, 2010.
Ezra, Elisabeth, and Terry Rowden. *Transnational Cinema. The Film Reader*. London and New York: Routledge, 2006.

Fanon, Frantz. *Black Skin, White Masks* [1952]. London: Pluto Press, 1986.
Farocki, Harun, and Antje Ehrmann. *Kino wie noch nie.* Wien: Generali Foundation/Köln: Verlag der Buchhandlung Walter König, 2006.
Fauteux, Brian. "Television, Live Transmission. 'Control' and the Televised Performance Scene" *Cinephile* 5.32 (2009): 24–29.
Fenner, Angelica. "Roots and Routes of the Diasporic Documentarian: A Psychogeography of Fatih Akin's *Wir haben vergessen zurückzukehren.*" *Turkish-German Cinema in the New Millenium: Sites, Sounds, and Screens.* Eds. Sabine Hake and Barbara Mennell. New York: Berghahn Press, 2012: 59–71.
Ferro, Marc. "Film as Agent, Product and Source of History." *Journal of Contemporary History* 18.3 (1983): 357–364.
Finzsch, Norbert. "'Gay Punk, White Lesbian, Black Bitch'. Zur Konstruktion des schwarzen männlichen Revolutionärs durch die Black Panther Party, 1966 bis 1982." *Lebendige Sozialgeschichte. Gedenkschrift für Peter Borowsky.* Eds. Rainer Hering and Rainer Nicolaysen. Wiesbaden, Hamburg University Press, 2003. 206–220.
Fisher, Jean. "In Living Memory … Archive and Testimony in the Films of the Black Audio Film Collective." *The Ghosts of Songs: The Film Art of the Black Audio Film Collective 1982–1998.* Eds. Kodwo Eshun and Anjalika Sagar. Liverpool: Liverpool University Press and FACT, 2007. 16–30.
Fisher, Tony. "Isaac Julien: Looking for Langston. Montage of a Dream Deferred." *Third Text* 12 (1990): 59–70.
Florida, Richard. *The Rise of the Creative Class.* New York: Basic Books, 2002.
Flückiger, Barbara. "Material Properties of Historical Film in the Digital Age". In: *Necsus*, 1.2 (2012).
Fossati, Giovanna. *From Grain to Pixel: The Archival Life of Film in Transition.* Amsterdam: Amsterdam University Press, 2009.
Foster, Hal. "An Archival Impulse." *October* 110 (2004): 3–22.
Foucault, Michel. *The Archaeology of Knowledge.* London and New York: Routledge, 1972.
Foucault, Michel. "Film and Popular Memory: An Interview with Michel Foucault." *Radical Philosophy* 11 (1975): 24–29.
Foucault, Michel. *Language, Counter-Memory, Practice: Selected Essays and Interviews.* Ithaca: Cornell University Press, 1977.
François, Etienne, and Hagen Schulze. *Deutsche Erinnerungsorte,* Band 1–3, München: Beck 2001.
Frei, Norbert, and Martin Sabrow, eds. *Die Geburt des Zeitzeugen nach 1945.* Göttingen: Wallstein, 2012.
Frey, Indra Sengupta, ed. *Memory, History, and Colonialism: Engaging with Pierre Nora in Colonial and Postcolonial Contexts.* London: German Historical Institute, 2009.
Frick, Caroline. *Saving Cinema: The Politics of Preservation.* Oxford/New York: Oxford University Press, 2011.
Friedman, Lester, ed. *British Cinema and Thatcherism: Fires We Started.* Second edition London: Wallflower Press, 2006.
Friedrich, Markus. *Die Geburt des Archivs: Eine Wissensgeschichte.* München: Oldenbourg, 2013.
From Two Worlds. [Exhibition catalogue] London: Whitechapel Gallery. 1986

Fusco, Coco. *Young British and Black: A Monograph on the Work of the Sankofa Film/Video Collective and Black Audio Collective*. Buffalo, New York: Hallwalls/Contemporary Arts Center, 1988.

Fusco, Coco. "Black Filmmaking in Britain's Workshop Section." [1988] *Cinemas of the Black Diaspora: Diversity, Dependence and Oppositionality*. Ed. Michael T. Martin. Detroit: Wayne State University Press, 1995.

Fuss, Diana. *Essentially Speaking: Feminism, Nature, and Difference*. New York: Routledge, 1989.

Gaar, Gillian G. *She's a Rebel: the History of Women in Rock & Roll*. Seattle: Seal Press, 1992.

Gabriel, Teshome H. "Third Cinema as a Guardian of Popular Memory: Towards a Third Aesthetics." *Questions of Third Cinema*. Eds. Jim Pines and Paul Willemen. London: BFI Publishing, 1989. 53–64.

Gagnon, Paulette. *Isaac Julien*. Montréal: Musée d'art contemporain de Montréal, 2005.

Garde-Hansen, Joanne, and Andrew Hoskins, and Anna Reading, eds. *Save As... Digital Memories*. Basingstoke: Palgrave Macmillan, 2009.

Garde-Hansen, Joanne. *Media and Memory*. Edinburgh: Edinburgh University Press, 2011.

Garnkarcz, Joseph. "Hollywood in Germany: The Role of American Films in Germany". *Hollywood in Europe: Experiences of a Cultural Hegemony*. Eds. D.W. Ellwood and R. Kroes. Amsterdam: Amsterdam University Press, 1994. 94–135.

Gatenby, Phill. *The Essential Smiths Tour*. Manchester: Empire Publications, 2009.

Gates Jr, Henry Louis. "The Black Man's Burden". *Black Popular Culture*. Eds. Michele Wallace and Gina Dent. Dia Center for the Arts, Discussions in Contemporary Culture, Number 8. Seattle: Bay Press, 1992. 75–84.

Gates, Jr Henry Louis. "Looking for Modernism." *Black American Cinema: AFI Film Readers*. Ed. Manthia Diawara. New York and London: Routledge, 1993.

Gates Jr, Henry Louis. "A Reporter at Large: Black London." *Black British Culture and Society: A Text Reader*. Ed. Kwesi Owusu. London and New York: Routledge, 2000. 169–180.

Geimer, Peter 2002: "Einleitung." *Ordnungen der Sichtbarkeit. Fotografie in Wissenschaft, Kunst und Technologie*. Ed. Peter Geimer. Frankfurt/M.: Suhrkamp, 2002. 7–28.

Geissler, Rainer, and Horst Pöttker. *Massenmedien und die Integration ethnischer Minderheiten in Deutschland*. Bielefeld: Transcript, 2005.

Genette, Gérard. *Palimpseste: Die Literatur auf zweiter Stufe*. Frankfurt/M.: Suhrkamp, 1993.

Gever, Martha, and John Greyson, and Pratibha Parmar, eds. *Queer Looks: Perspectives on Lesbian and Gay Film and Video*. New York/London: Routledge, 1993.

Gfeller, Johannes, and Agathe Jarczyk, and Joanna Phillips, eds. *Kompendium der Bildstörungen beim analogen Video*. Zürich: Scheidegger & Spiess, 2013.

Gilroy, Paul. *The Black Atlantic: Modernity and Double Consciousness*. London: Verso, 1993a.

Gilroy, Paul. *Small Acts: Thoughts on the Politics of Black Cultures*. London: Serpent's Tail, 1993b.

Gilroy, Paul. "Diaspora and the Detours of Identity". *Identity and Difference*. Ed. Kathryn Woodward. London, Thousand Oaks and New Delhi: Sage, 1997. 299–343.

Gilroy, Paul. *There Ain't No Black in the Union Jack. The Cultural Politics of Race and Nation*. [1987] London and New York: Routledge, 2002.

Gilroy, Paul. *After Empire*. London and New York: Routledge, 2004.

Gilroy, Paul. *Black Britain: A Photographic History*. Preface by Stuart Hall. London: Saqibooks, 2007.

Givanni, June. "In Circulation: Black Films in Britain." In: *ICA documents 7, Black Film, British Cinema*. London: ICA 1988, 39–41.
Givanni, June. "Black and independent." *Ecrans d'Afrique* 3, first quarter (1993): 90–92.
Givanni, June, ed. *Remote Control: Dilemmas of Black Intervention in British Film and TV*. London: BFI Publishing, 1995.
Givanni, June. "A Curator's Conundrum: Programming ‚Black Film' in 1980s–1990s Britain." *The Moving Image* 4.1 (2004): 60–75.
Göktürk, Deniz. "Verstöße gegen das Reinheitsgebot: Migrantenkino zwischen wehleidiger Pflichtübung und wechselseitigem Grenzverkehr." *Globalkolorit: Multikulturalismus und Populärkultur*. Eds. Ruth Mayer and Mark Terkessidis. St. Andrä/Wördern: Hannibal, 1998. 99–114.
Göktürk, Deniz. "Beyond Paternalism: Turkish German Traffic in Cinema." *The German Cinema Book*. Eds. Tim Bergfelder, and Erica Carter, and Deniz Göktürk. London: British Film Institute, 2002. 248–256.
Göktürk, Deniz, and David Gramling, and Anton Kaes, eds. *Germany in Transit: Nation and Migration 1955–2005*. Berkeley: University of California Press, 2007.
Gopal, Priyamvada 2004: "Reading subaltern history." *The Cambridge Companion to Postcolonial Literary Studies*. Ed. Neil Lazarus. Cambridge: Cambridge University Press, 2004. 139–161.
Gopaul, Lina. "Which Way Forward." [1985] *The Ghosts of Songs: The Film Art of the Black Audio Film Collective 1982–1998*. Eds. Kodwo Eshun and Anjalika Sagar. Liverpool: Liverpool University Press and FACT, 2007. 146–147.
Gopinath, Gayatri. *Impossible Desires: Queer Diasporas and South Asian Public Cultures*. Durham, NC/London: Duke University Press, 2005.
Gotto, Lisa. *Traum und Trauma in Schwarz-Weiß: Ethnische Grenzgänge im amerikanischen Film*. Konstanz: UVK, 2006.
Gould, Gaylene. "By Any Means Necessary." *Black Film Bulletin* 1.1 (1993): 11.
Grainge, Paul. *Monochrome Memories: Nostalgia and Style in Retro America*. Westport, CT: Praeger, 2002.
Grainge, Paul, ed. *Memory and Popular Film*. Manchester: Manchester University Press, 2003.
Graves, Matthew, and Elizabeth Rechniewski. "From Collective Memory to Transcultural Remembrance." *Portal. Journal of Multidisciplinary International Studies* 7.1 (2010): 1–15.
Green, David. "Veins of Resemblance: Photography and Eugenics." *The Oxford Art Journal* 7.2 (1985): 3–16.
Grever, Maria. "The Pantheon of Feminist Culture: Women's Movements and the Organization of Memory." *Gender & History* 9.2 (1997): 364–374.
Grever, Maria, and Kees Ribbens. "The Dynamics of Memories and the Process of Canonization." *The Gender of Memory: Cultures of Remembrance in Nineteenth and Twentieth Century Europe*. Eds. S. Paletschek and S. Schraut. Frankfurt/M.: Campus, 2008, 253–266.
Grierson, John. *Grierson on Documentary*. London: faber and faber, 1966.
Griffiths, Robin, ed. *British Queer Cinema*. London and New York: Routledge, 2006.
Gring, Diana, and Karin Theilen. "Fragmente der Erinnerung." *AugenZeugen. Fotos, Filme und Zeitzeugenberichte in der neuen Dauerausstellung in der Gedenkstätte Bergen-Belsen*. Eds. Rainer Schulze and Wilfried Wiedemann. Celle: Stiftung niedersächsische Gedenkstätten, 2007. 153–219.

Gripsrud, Jostein. *The Dynasty Years*. New York and London: Routledge, 1995.
Grønstad, Asbjørn. "Isaac Julien's *Looking For Langston* and the Limits of the Visible World." *Readings of the Particular. The Postcolonial in the Postnational*. Eds. Anne Holden Rønning and Lene Johannessen. Amsterdam/New York, NY: Rodopi, 2007. 119–131.
Groo, Katherine. "Cut, Paste, Glitch, and Stutter: Remixing Film History." *Frames Cinema Journal* 1.1 (2012) http://framescinemajournal.com/article/cut-paste-glitch-and-stutter/ (25 July 2014).
Groys, Boris. "Art Workers: Between Utopia and the Archive." *e-flux journals* 45, May (2013): 1–11.
Grusin, Richard 2004. "Premediation". *Criticism* 46.1 (2004): 17–39.
Grusin, Richard. "YouTube at the End of New Media". *The YouTube Reader*. Eds. Pelle Snickars and Patrick Vonderau. Stockholm: National Library of Sweden, 2009. 60–67.
Gunning, Tom. "Towards a *Minor Cinema:* Fonoroff, Herwitz, Ahwesh, Klahr, Lapore and Solomon." *Motion Picture* 3.1–2 (1989–1990): 2–5.
Gupta, Akhil, and James Ferguson. "Beyond 'Culture': Space, Identity, and the Politics of Difference." *Cultural Anthropology* 7.1 (1992): 6–23.
Gutiérrez Rodriguez, Encarnación. "Widerstand in der différance. Repräsentation, Vereinnahmung und Gegenstrategien von MigrantInnen und Schwarzen Deutschen." In: *iz3w, blätter des informationszentrums 3. welt, 253* (2001): 22–23.
Guynn, William. *Writing History in Film*. New York/London: Routledge, 2006.
Habermas, Jürgen. *The Structural Transformation of the Public Sphere: An Inquiry into a Category of Bourgeois Society*. Cambridge, Mass: MIT Press, 1989.
Habib, Imtiaz H. *Black Lives in the English Archives, 1500–1677: Imprints of the Invisible*. Aldershot: Ashgate, 2008.
Hackenberg, Dietrich. "Migration im Bild. Fotografie und Internet als Formen visueller Präsentation zur Migrationsgeschichte." *Geschichte und Gedächtnis in der Einwanderungsgesellschaft: Migration zwischen historischer Rekonstruktion und Erinnerungspolitik*. Eds. Jan Motte and Rainer Ohliger. Essen: Klartext, 2004. 181–188.
Hagener, Malte. *Moving Forward, Looking Back: The European Avant-Garde and the Invention of Film Culture, 1919–1939*. Amsterdam: Amsterdam University Press, 2007.
Halbwachs, Maurice. *The Collective Memory*. New York: Harper & Row, 1980.
Halbwachs, Maurice. *Das Gedächtnis und seine sozialen Bedingungen*. Frankfurt/M.: Suhrkamp, 1985.
Halbwachs, Maurice. *On Collective Memory*. Chicago: University of Chicago Press, 1992.
Hall, Catherine. *White Male, and Middle Class: Explorations in Feminism and History*. London and New York: Routledge, 1992.
Hall, Stuart, et al. *Policing the Crisis: Mugging, the State and Law and Order*. Basingstoke: Palgrave Macmillan, 1978.
Hall, Stuart, ed. *Culture, Media, Language: Working Papers in Cultural Studies, 1972–79*. London: Hutchinson in association with the Centre for Contemporary Cultural Studies, University of Birmingham, 1980.
Hall, Stuart. "Cultural Identity and Diaspora." *Identity: Community, Culture, Difference*. Ed. Jonathan Rutherford. London: Lawrence & Wishart 1990. 222–237.
Hall, Stuart. "The Whites of their Eyes: Racist Ideologies and the Media." [1981] *The Media Reader*. Eds. Manuel Alvarado and John O. Thompson. London: BFI, 1990. 7–23.
Hall, Stuart. "Reconstruction Work: Images of Post-War Black Settlement." *Family Snaps*. Eds. Jo Spence and Patricia Holland. London: Virago, 1991. 152–164.

Hall, Stuart. "What is This 'Black' in Black Popular Culture?" *Black Popular Culture*. Eds. Michele Wallace and Gina Dent. Dia Center for the Arts, Discussions in Contemporary Culture, Number 8. Seattle: Bay Press, 1992. 21–33.

Hall, Stuart. "Vanley Burke and the 'Desire for Blackness'." *Vanley Burke: A Retrospective*. Ed. Mark Sealy. London: Lawrence & Wishart, 1993. 12–15.

Hall, Stuart. "New Ethnicities" [1987]. *Black British Cultural Studies: A Reader*. Eds. Houston A. Baker, Jr., Manthia Diawara and Ruth H. Lindeborg. Chicago and London: University of Chicago Press, 1996a. 163–172.

Hall, Stuart. "Cultural Identity and Cinematic Representation" [1989]. *Black British Cultural Studies: A Reader*. Eds. Houston A. Baker, Jr., Manthia Diawara and Ruth H. Lindeborg. Chicago and London: University of Chicago Press, 1996b. 210–222.

Hall, Stuart. "Minimal Selves" [1987]. *Black British Cultural Studies: A Reader*. Eds. Houston A. Baker, Jr., Manthia Diawara and Ruth H. Lindeborg. Chicago and London: University of Chicago Press. 114–119.

Hall, Stuart. *Representation: Cultural Representations and Signifying Practices*. London, Thousand Oaks and Delhi: Sage, 1997.

Hall, Stuart. "Encoding, Decoding." *The Cultural Studies Reader*. Ed. Simon During. London and New York: Routledge, 1999. 90–103.

Hall, Stuart. "Constituting an Archive." *Third Text* (2001): 89–92.

Hall, Stuart "Whose Heritage? Un-settling 'The Heritage', Re-imagining the Post-Nation." [1999] *The Third Text Reader on Art, Culture and Theory*. Eds. Rasheed Araaen, Sean Cubitt and Ziauddin Sardar. London and New York: Continuum, 2002. 72–84.

Hall, Stuart, and Mark Seally. *Different*. London: Phaidon, 2001.

Hallas, Roger. *Reframing Bodies: AIDS, Bearing Witness, and the Queer Moving Image*. Durham, NC and London: Duke University Press, 2009.

Hammer, Barbara. "The Politics of Abstraction." *Queer Looks: Perspectives on Lesbian and Gay Film and Video*. Eds. Martha Gever, John Greyson, and Pratibha Parmar. London and New York: Routledge, 1993. 70–75.

Harvey, Sylvia. "Deregulation, Innovation, and Channel 4." *Screen* 30.1–2 (1989): 60–79.

Hasebrink, Uwe. "Die Beziehung zwischen Programm und Publikum als Emanzipationsprozess." *Programm und Programmatik: Kultur- und medienwissenschaftliche Analysen*. Ed. Ludwig Fischer. Konstanz: UVK, 2005. 386–399.

Haslam, Dave. *Manchester England: The Story of the Pop Cult City*. London: Fourth Estate, 2000.

Haug, Frigga. *Vorlesungen zur Einführung in die Erinnerungsarbeit: The Duke Lectures*. Berlin and Hamburg: Argument, 1999.

Haug, Frigga. "Memory Work: the Key to Women's Anxiety." *Memory and Methodology*. Ed. Susannah Radstone. Oxford and New York: Berg, 2000. 155–179.

Hauthal, Janine, and Julijana Nadj, and Ansgar Nünning and Henning Peters. *Metaisierung in Literatur und anderen Medien. Theoretische Grundlagen – Historische Perspektiven – Metagattungen – Funktionen*. Berlin and New York: de Gruyter, 2007.

Hebel, Udo J., ed. *Transnational American Memories*. Berlin and New York: de Gruyter, 2009.

Hebdidge, Dick. *Subculture: The Meaning of Style*, London and New York: Routledge, 1996.

Hediger, Vinzenz. "The Original Is Always Lost: Film History, Copyright Industries and the Problem of Reconstruction." *Cinephilia: Movies, Love and Memory*. Eds. Marijke de Valck and Malte Hagener. Amsterdam: Amsterdam University Press, 2005. 135–150.

Hediger, Vinzenz. "Original Work Performance: Film Theory as Archive Theory". *Quel che brucia (non)ritorna – What Burns (never) returns: Lost and Found Films*. Eds. Simone Venturini and Giulio Buris. Pasian diPrato: Campanotto Editore, 2011. (no pagination)

Heidenreich, Nanna, and Vojin Saša Vukadinović. "In Your Face: Activism, Agit-Prop, and the Autonomy of Migration; The Case of Kanak Attak." *After the Avant-Garde: Contemporary German and Austrian Experimental film*. Eds. Randall Halle and Reinhild Steingröver. Rochester, NY: Camden House, 2008. 131–156.

Heller, Franziska. "*Warum Filmgeschichte? Wie die Digitalisierung unser Bild der Vergangenheit verändert.*" Memento Movie. Materialien zum audiovisuellen Erbe. 2013. Online: http://www.memento-movie.de/2013/02/warum-filmgeschichte/ (10 September 2014).

Hemphill, Essex, ed. *Brother to Brother: New Writings by Black Gay Men*. Boston: Alyson Publications, 1991a.

Hemphill, Essex. "Looking for Langston: An Interview with Isaac Julien." *Brother to Brother: New Writings by Black Gay Men*. Ed. Essex Hemphill. Boston: Alyson Publications, 1991b. 174–180.

Hemphill, Essex. "Undressing Icons." *Brother to Brother: New Writings by Black Gay Men*. Ed. Essex Hemphill. Boston: Alyson Publications, 1991c. 181–183.

Hepp, Andreas. *Cultures of Mediatization*. Cambridge: Polity, 2012.

Herridge, Peter. "Television, the 'Riots' and Research." *Screen* 24.1 (1983): 86–91.

Hesse, Barnor. "Diasporicity: Black Britain's Post-Colonial Formations." *Un/settled Multiculturalisms: Diasporas, Entanglements, 'Transruptions'*. Ed. Barnor Hesse. London: Zed, 2000. 96–120.

Hickethier, Knut. *Einführung in die Medienwissenschaft*. Stuttgart: Metzler, 2010.

Higson, Andrew. "The Concept of National Cinema." *Screen* 30.4 (1989): 36–46.

Higson, Andrew. *Waving the Flag: Constructing a National Cinema in Britain*. Oxford: Clarendon Press, 1995.

Higson, Andrew. "The Instability of the National." *British Cinema, Past and Present*. Eds. Justine Ashby and Andrew Higson. London and New York: Routledge, 2000a. 35–47.

Higson, Andrew. "The Limiting Imagination of National Cinema." *Cinema and Nation*. Eds. Mette Hjort and Scott MacKenzie. London and New York: Routledge: 2000b. 63–73.

Higson, Andrew. "Re-presenting the National Past: Nostalgia and Pastiche in the Heritage Film." [1993] *Fires We Started: British Cinema and Thatcherism*. Second Edition. Ed. Lester Friedman. London: Wallflower 2006. 91–109.

Hill, John. *British Cinema in the 1980s*. Oxford: Clarendon Press, 1999.

Hirsch, Marianne. *Family Frames: Photography, Narrative and Postmemory*. Cambridge: Harvard University Press, 1997.

Hirsch, Marianne. "The Generation of Postmemory." *Poetics Today* 29.1 (2008): 103–128.

Hirsch, Marianne, and Valeri Smith. "Feminism and Cultural Memory: An Introduction." *Signs: Journal of Women in Culture and Society* 28.1 (2002): 1–19.

Hjort, Mette, and Scott Mackenzie, eds. *Cinema and Nation*. London and New York: Routledge, 2000.

Hjort, Mette, and Duncan Petrie. *The Cinema of Small Nations*. Edinburgh: University of Edinburgh Press, 2007.

Ho Tai, Hue-Tam. "Remembered Realms: Pierre Nora and French National Memory", *American Historical Review* 106.3 (2001): 906–921.

Hobsbawm, Eric, and Terence Ranger, eds. *The Invention of Tradition*. Cambridge: Cambridge University Press, 1992.

Hodgkin, Katharine, and Susannah Radstone, eds. *Contested Past: The Politics of Memory*. London and New York: Routledge, 2003.

Hohenberger, Eva, ed. *Bilder des Wirklichen: Texte zur Theorie des Dokumentarfilms*. Berlin: Vorwerk8, 1998.

Hohenberger, Eva, and Judith Keilbach. *Die Gegenwart der Vergangenheit: Dokumentarfilm, Fernsehen und Geschichte*. Berlin: Vorwerk8, 2003.

Holdsworth, Amy. *Television, Memory and Nostalgia*. Basingstoke: Palgrave Macmillan, 2011.

Holmberg, Jan. *Slutet på filmen: o. s. v. Göteborg:* Daidalos, 2011.

Hook, Peter. *The Hacienda: How Not to Run a Club*. London: Simon & Schuster, 2009.

hooks, bell and Isaac Julien. "State of Desire." *Transition* 53 (1991): 168–184.

hooks, bell. *Reel to Reel: Race, Sex and Class at the Movies*. New York/London: Routledge, 1996.

hooks, bell. "The Oppositional Gaze: Black Female Spectators." *Film Theory: critical concepts in media and cultural studies* 3 (2004): 233–248.

Hoskins, Andrew. "New Memory: Mediating History." *Historical Journal of Film, Radio and Television* 21.4 (2001): 333–346.

Hoskins, Andrew. *Televising War: From Vietnam to Iraq*. London: Continuum, 2004.

Hoskins, Andrew, and Ben O'Loughlin. *War and Media: The Emergence of Diffused War*. Cambridge: Polity Press, 2010.

Hoskins, Andrew. "Media, Memory, Metaphor: Remembering and the Connective Turn." *Parallax* 17.4 (2011): 19–31.

Houston, Penelope. *Keepers of the Frame – The Film Archives*. London: BFI Publishing, 1994.

Hutcheon, Linda. *The Politics of Postmodernism*. London and New York: Routledge, 1989.

Huyssen, Andreas. *Twilight Memories: Marking Time in a Culture of Amnesia*. London: Routledge, 1995.

Huyssen, Andreas. *Present Pasts: Urban Palimpsests and the Politics of Memory*. Palo, Alto, CA: Stanford University Press, 2003.

Iordanova, Dina. *Cinema of the Other Europe: The Industry and Artistry of East Central European Film*. London: Wallflower, 2003.

Irwin-Zarecka, Iwona. *Frames of Remembrance: The Dynamics of Collective Memory*. New Brunswick [N.J.]: Transaction Publishers, 1994.

James, D. E. *The Most Typical Avant-Garde: History and Geography of Minor Cinemas in Los Angeles*, Berkeley: University of California Press, 2005.

Jamin, Mathilde. "Migrationsgeschichte im Museum: Erinnerungsorte von Arbeitsmigranten – kein Ort der Erinnerung?" *Geschichte und Gedächtnis in der Einwanderungsgesellschaft: Migration zwischen historischer Rekonstruktion und Erinnerungspolitik*. Eds. Jan Motte and Rainer Ohliger. Essen: Klartext, 2004. 145–158.

Jarausch, Konrad H., and Martin Sabrow. "'Meistererzählung' – Zur Karriere eines Begriffs." *Die historische Meistererzählung: Deutungslinien der deutschen Nationalgeschichte nach 1945*. Eds. Konrad H. Jarausch and Martin Sabrow. Göttingen: Vandenhoeck & Ruprecht, 2002. 9–32.

Jenkins Henry. "Reception Theory and Audience Research: The Mystery of the Vampire's Kiss." *Reinventing Film Studies*. Eds. Christine Gledhill and Linda Williams. London: Arnold, 2000. 165–183.

Jenkins, Henry. *Convergence Culture: Where Old and New Media Collide.* [New ed.] New York: New York University Press, 2008.
Johnston, Claire. "Women's Cinema as Counter-Cinema." [1973] *Feminist Film Theory: A Reader.* Ed. Sue Thornham. New York: New York University Press, 1999. 31–40.
Johnston, Sheila, and John Ellis. "The Radical Film Funding of ZDF." *Screen* 23.1 (1982): 60–73.
Julien, Isaac. *Looking for Langston.* London: BFI, 1989.
Julien, Isaac. "'Black Is, Black Ain't': Notes on De-Essentializing Black Identities." *Black Popular Culture.* Ed. Gina Dent. (Dia Center for the Arts, Discussions in Popular Culture, Number 8). Seattle: Bay Press, 1992. 255–263.
Julien, Isaac. "Confessions of a Snow Queen: Notes on the Making of The Attendant." *The Critical Quarterly* 36.1 (1994): 120–126.
Julien, Isaac. "Burning Rubber's Perfume." *Remote Control: Dilemmas of Black Intervention in British Film and TV.* Ed. June Givanni. London: BFI Publishing, 1995. 55–62.
Julien, Isaac. "Confessions of a Snow Queen: Notes on the Making of The Attendant." *The Film Art of Isaac Julien.* Eds. Isaac Julien, David Deitcher and David Frankel. Annandale-on-Hudson, NY: Center for Curatorial Studies, 2000. 79–82.
Julien, Isaac. "Revealing Desires." *Looking at Class.* Eds. Sheila Rowbotham and H. Beynon. London: Oram Press, 2001. 173–183.
Julien, Isaac, and Kobena Mercer. "De Margin and De Centre." *Screen* 29.4 (1988): 2–10.
Julien, Isaac, and Colin MacCabe. *Diary of a Young Soul Rebel.* London: BFI Publishing, 1991.
Julien, Isaac, and Paulette Gagnon. *Isaac Julien.* Montreal: Musée d'art contemporain de Montréal, 2004.
Julien, Isaac, and Christine van Assche, eds. *Isaac Julien.* Paris: Centre Georges Pompidou, 2005.
Julien, Isaac, David Deitcher, and David Frankel, eds. *The Film Art of Isaac Julien.* Annandale-on-Hudson, NY: Center for Curatorial Studies, 2000.
Julien, Isaac, and Mark Nash. "Dialogues with Stuart Hall." *Stuart Hall: Critical Dialogues in Cultural Studies.* Eds. David Morley and Kuan-Hsing Chen. London and New York: Routledge, 1996. 476–483.
Julier, Guy. "Urban Designscapes and the Production of Aesthetic Consent". *Urban Studies* 42.5–6 (2005): 869–887.
Jureit, Ulrike. *Erinnerungsmuster. Zur Methodik lebensgeschichtlicher Interviews mit Überlebenden der Konzentrations- und Vernichtungslager.* Hamburg: Ergebnisse Verlag, 1999.
Kaes, Anton. *From ‚Hitler' to ‚Heimat': The Return of History as Film.* Cambridge, Mass.: Harvard University Press, 1992a.
Kaes, Anton. "History and Film: Public Memory in the Age of Electronic Dissemination." *Framing the Past: The Historiography of German Cinema and Television.* Eds. Bruce Arthur Murray and Chris Wickham. Southern Illinois University Press, 1992b. 308–323.
Kansteiner, Wulf. "Finding Meaning in Memory: A Methodological Critique of Collective Memory Studies." *History and Theory* 41.2 (2002): 179–197.
Kansteiner, Wulf. "Film und Fernsehen."*Erinnerung und Gedächtnis: Ein interdisziplinäres Handbuch.* Eds. Christian Gudehus, Anna Eichenberg and Harald Welzer. Stuttgart: Metzler, 2010. 217–226.
Kansteiner, Wulf. "Macht, Authentizität und die Tyrannei der Normalität: Aufstieg und Abschied der NS-Zeitzeugen in den Geschichtsdokumentationen des ZDF." *Die Geburt*

des Zeitzeugen nach 1945. Eds. Norbert Frei and Martin Sabrow. Göttingen: Wallstein, 2012. 320–353.

Kaplan, E. Ann. *Looking for the Other: Feminism, Film and the Imperial Gaze*. London and New York: Routledge, 1997.

Karpf, Ernst, and Doron Kiesel, and Karsten Visarius, eds. *Once upon a time... Film und Gedächtnis*. Marburg: Schüren (Arnoldshainer Filmgespräche, Bd. 15), 1998.

Kassabian, Anahid. *Hearing Film*. London and New York: Routledge, 2001.

Katz, Joel. "From Archive to Archiveology." *Cinematograph* 4 (1991): 93–103.

Keilbach, Judith 2008: *Geschichtsbilder und Zeitzeugen: Zur Darstellung des Nationalsozialismus im bundesdeutschen Fernsehen*. Münster: LIT.

Keilbach, Judith 2012: "Mikrofon, Videotape, Datenbank: Entwurf einer Mediengeschichte der Zeitzeugen." *Die Geburt des Zeitzeugen nach 1945*. Eds. Norbert Frei and Martin Sabrow. Göttingen: Wallstein Verlag. 281–299.

Keitz, Ursula von, and Thomas Weber, eds. *Mediale Transformationen des Holocaust*. Berlin: Avinus, 2012.

Kelley, Shannon, ed. *L.A. Rebellion: Creating a New Black Cinema. Catalog*. Los Angeles: UCLA. 2011.

Kilbourn, Russell J.A. *Cinema, Memory, Modernity: The Representation of Memory from the Art Film to Transnational Cinema*. New York and London: Routledge, 2010.

Kinter, Jürgen. "Gegenöffentlichkeit und Selbsttätigkeit – Ende einer medienpolitischen Utopie? Zur Geschichte und Theorie alternativer Öffentlichkeit." *Handbuch der Medienpädagogik*. Eds. Susanne Hiegemann and Wolfgang H. Swoboda. Opladen: Leske und Budrich, 1994. 205–222.

Kirstein, Arine. "Decentering the Subject: The Current Documentary Critique of Realism." *Realism and ‚Reality' in Film and Media*. Ed. Anne Jerslev. Copenhagen: Museum Tusculanum, 2002. 211–225.

Klippel, Heike. *Gedächtnis und Kino*. Basel/Frankfurt am Main: Stroemfeld, 1997.

Klippel, Heike, ed. *The Art of Programming: Film, Programm und Kontext*. Münster: LIT, 2008.

Kmec, Sonja, and Viviane Thill, eds. *Private Eyes and the Public Gaze: The Manipulation and Valorisation of Amateur Images*, Trier: Kliomedia Verlag, 2009.

Knight, Julia, ed. *Diverse Practices: A Critical Reader on British Video Art*. Luton: University of Luton Press, 1996.

Knight, Julia. "Agency vs Archive: London Film-Makers' Co-op and LVA vs Film and Video Umbrella". *Screen* 47.7 (2006): 469–475.

Koebner, Thomas, and Thomas Meder, eds. *Bildtheorie und Film*. München: edition text und kritik, 2006.

Koivunen, Anu. "Yes We Can? The Promises of Affect for Queer Scholarship." *Lambda Nordica* 15.3–4 (2010): 40–64.

Korte, Barbara, and Ulrike Eva Pirker. *Black History – White History: Britain's Historical Programme between Windrush and Wilberforce*. Bielefeld: Transcript, 2011.

Korte, Barbara, and Claudia Sternberg. *Bidding for the Mainstream? British and Asian Film since the 1990s*. Amsterdam and New York: Rodopi, 2004.

Kracauer, Siegfried. *Von Caligari zu Hitler: Eine psychologische Geschichte des deutschen Films*, Frankfurt/M.: Suhrkamp, 1984.

Kracauer, Siegfried. *Der verbotene Blick*. Leipzig: Reclam, 1992.

Kracauer, Siegfried. *Theorie des Films: Die Errettung der äußeren Wirklichkeit*. [1960] Frankfurt/M.: Suhrkamp, 1985.

Kramer, Sven, and Thomas Tode, eds. *Der Essayfilm: Ästhetik und Aktualität.* Konstanz: UVK, 2011.
Kristeva, Julia. *Desire in Language: A Semiotic Approach to Literature and Art.* New York: Columbia University Press, 1980.
Kuhn, Annette. *Family Secrets: Acts of Memory and Imagination.* [1995] New Edition. London and New York: Verso, 2002a.
Kuhn, Annette. *An Everyday Magic: Cinema and Cultural Memory.* London and New York: Tauris, 2002b.
Kuhn, Annette, and K Emiko McAllister, eds. *Locating Memory: Photographic Acts.* New York and Oxford: Berghahn Books, 2006.
Kuhn, Annette. "Photography and Cultural Memory Work." *Visual Studies* 22.3 (2007): 283–292.
Kuhn, Annette. "Memory Texts and Memory Work: Performances of Memory in and with Visual Media." *Memory Studies* 3.4 (2010): 298–313.
Lachmann, Renate. "Mnemonic and Intertextual Aspects of Literature." *Cultural Memory Studies: An International and Interdisciplinary Handbook.* Eds. Astrid Erll and Ansgar Nünning. Berlin: de Gruyter, 2008. 301–310.
Lagerkvist, Amanda. *Media and Memory in New Shanghai: Western Performances of Futures Past,* Basingstoke: Palgrave Macmillan, 2013.
Landsberg, Alison. "Prosthetic Memory: The Ethics and Politics of Memory in an Age of Mass Culture." *Memory and Popular Film.* Ed. Paul Grainge. Manchester: Manchester University Press, 2003. 144–161.
Landsberg, Alison. *Prosthetic Memory: The Transformation of American Remembrance in the Age of Mass Culture.* New York, NY: Columbia University Press, 2004.
Landy, Marcia, ed. *The Historical Film. History and Memory in Media,* New Brunswick: Rutgers University Press, 2001.
Lane, Jim. *The Autobiographical Documentary in America.* Madison: University of Wisconsin Press, 2002.
Lanyon, Josephine. "Foreword." *Ghosting: The Role of the Archive within Contemporary Artists' Film and Video.* Eds. Jane Connarty and Josephine Lanyon. Bristol: Picture This, 2006. 3–11.
Lawson, Alan. *It Happened in Manchester: The True Story of Manchester's Music.* Bury: Multimedia, 1998.
Leavy, Patricia. *Iconic Events: Media, Politics, and Power in Retelling History.* Lanham, MD: Lexington Books, 2007.
Lebow, Alisa, ed. *The Cinema of Me: The Self and Subjectivity in First Person Documentary.* London: Wallflower Press, 2012.
Leggewie, Claus, and Anne Lang, eds. *Der Kampf um die europäische Erinnerung: Ein Schlachtfeld wird besichtigt.* München: Beck, 2011.
Lessig, Lawrence. *Remix: Making Art and Commerce Thrive in the Hybrid Economy.* New York: Penguin Press, 2008.
Levy, Daniel, and Natan Sznaider. *Erinnerung im globalen Zeitalter: Der Holocaust.* Frankfurt/M.: Suhrkamp, 2001.
Levy, Daniel, and Natan Sznaider. "Memory Unbound: The Holocaust and the Formation of Cosmopolitan Memory." *European Journal of Social Theory* 5.1 (2002): 87–106.
Leyda, Jay. *Films Beget Film: Compilation Films from Propaganda to Drama.* London: Allen & Unwin, 1964.

Limoges, Jean-Marc. "The Gradable Effects of Self-Reflexivity on Aesthetic Illusion in Cinema." *Metareference Across Media: Theory and Case Studies.* Eds. Werner Wolf, Katharina Bantleon, and Jeff Thoss. Amsterdam: Rodopi, 2009. 391–408.

Lipsitz, George. *Time Passages: Collective Memory and American Popular Culture.* Minneapolis: University of Minnesota Press, 1990.

Littler, Jo, and Roshi Naidoo, eds. *The Politics of Heritage: The Legacies of 'Race'.* London and New York: Routledge, 2005.

Livingstone, Sonia. "On the Mediation of Everything": ICA presidential address 2008. *Journal of Communication* 59.1 (2009a): 1–18.

Livingstone, Sonia. "Foreword: Coming to Terms with 'Mediatization'." *Mediatization: Concept, Changes, Consequences.* Ed. Knut Lundby. Oxford: Peter Lang, 2009b. ix-xxi.

Löbbermann, Dorothea. *Memories of Harlem: Literarische (Re)Konstruktionen eines Mythos der Zwanziger Jahre.* Frankfurt/M.: Campus, 2002.

Loh, Hannes, and Murat Güngör. *Fear of a Kanak Planet: Hiphop zwischen Weltkultur und Nazi-Rap.* Höfen: Hannibal, 2002.

Lorde, Audre. *Sister Outsider: Essays and Speeches.* Freedom, CA: Crossing Press, 1994.

Loshitzky, Yosefa, ed. *Spielberg's Holocaust: Critical Perspectives on Schindler's List.* Bloomington: Indiana University Press, 1997.

Lovink, Geert. *Hör zu – oder stirb! Fragmente einer Theorie der souveränen Medien.* Berlin – Amsterdam: Edition ID-Archiv, 1992.

Lundemo, Trond. "In the Kingdom of Shadows: Cinematic Movement and its Digital Ghost." *The YouTube Reader.* Eds. Pelle Snickars and Patrick Vonderau. Stockholm: The National Library of Sweden, 2009. 314–329.

Lundemo, Trond: "Conversion, convergence, conflation: archival networks in the digital turn", *L'archivio: FilmForum 2011; XVIII Convegno Internazionale di Studi sul Cinema* 2012. 177–182.

Lundby, Knut, ed. *Mediatization: Concept, Changes, Consequences.* Oxford: Peter Lang, 2009.

Lupton, Catherine. "Speaking Parts: Heteroglossic Voice-Overin the Essay-Film." *Der Essayfilm: Ästhetik und Aktualität.* Eds. Sven Kramer and Thomas Tode. Konstanz: UVK, 2011. 159–174.

Lyotard, Jean-François. *La Condition postmoderne: Rapport sur le savoir.* Paris: Éd. de minuit, 1979.

Malik, Sarita. "Beyond the 'Cinema of Duty'? The Pleasures of Hybridity: Black British Film of the 1980s and 1990s." *Dissolving Views: Key Writings on British Cinema.* Ed. Andrew Higson. London: Cassell, 1996. 202–215.

Malik, Sarita. *Representing Black Britain: A History of Black and Asian Images on British Television.* London and Thousand Oaks and Delhi: Sage, 2002.

Malik, Sarita. "'Keeping it Real': The Politics of Channel 4's Multiculturalism, Mainstreaming and Mandates." *Screen* 49.3 (2008): 343–353.

Malraux, André. "Sur l'héritage culturel." *Commune. Revue littéraire francaise pour la défense de la culture.* 27 September (1936):1–9.

Manoff, Marlene. "Theories of the Archive from Across the Disciplines." *portal: Libraries and the Academy,* 4.1 (2004): 9–25.

Manovich, Lev. *The Language of New Media.* Cambridge, Mass.: MIT Press, 2001.

Margalit, Avishai. *The Ethics of Memory.* Cambridge, MA: Harvard University Press, 2002.

Marks, Laura U. *The Skin of the Film: Intercultural Cinema, Embodiment, and the Senses.* Durham, NC/London: Duke University Press, 2000.

Marriott, David. *Haunted Life: Visual Culture and Black Modernity.* New Brunswick: Rutgers University Press, 2007.

Marshall, Stuart. "Video: Technology and Practice." *Screen* 20.1 (1979): 109–119.

Marshall, Stuart. "Video: From Art to Independence." *Screen* 26.2 (1985): 66–72.

Martin, Michael T., ed. *Cinemas of the Black Diaspora: Diversity, Dependence and Oppositionality.* Detroit: Wayne State University Press, 1995.

Martin, S. I. "Inheriting Diversity: Archiving the Past." *The Politics of Heritage: The Legacies of 'Race'.* Eds. Jo Littler and Roshi Naidoo. London: Routledge, 2005. 196–201.

Maty Bâ, Saër. "Problematizing (Black) Documentary Aesthetics. John Akomfrah's Use of Intertextuality in *Seven Songs for Malcolm X* (1993)." *Studies in Documentary Film* 1.3 (2007): 221–244.

Mayer, Ruth, and Mark Terkessidis, eds. *Globalkolorit: Multikulturalismus und Populärkultur.* St. Andrä/Wördern: Hannibal, 1998.

Mayer, Ruth. *Diaspora: Eine kritische Begriffsbestimmung.* Bielefeld: Transcript, 2005.

Mazière, Michael, and Nina Danino, eds. *The Undercut Reader: Critical Writings on Artists' Film and Video.* London: Wallflower, 2003.

Mazierska, Ewa, and Laura Rascaroli. *Crossing New Europe: Postmodern Travel and the European Road Movie.* London: Wallflower, 2006.

McLuhan, Marshall. *Understanding Media: The Extensions of Man.* London: Routledge, and K. Paul, 1964.

McNeil, Legs, and Gillian McCain, eds. *Please Kill Me: The Uncensored Oral History of Punk.* London: Abacus, 1997.

Mead, Matthew. "Empire Windrush: Cultural memory and archival disturbance." *Moveable Type* 3 (2007): 112–128.

Mead, Matthew. "Empire Windrush: The Cultural Memory of an Imaginary Arrival." *The Journal of Postcolonial Writing* 45.2 (2009): 137–149.

Medienzentren und Videogruppen in der BRD, eds. "das andere Video". *Zehn Jahre politische Medienarbeit. Ein gemeinsamer Verleihkatalog von Medienzentren und Videogruppen,* Freiburg/Frankfurt/M: Medienwerkstatt Freiburg/EDN video, 1984.

Mercer, Kobena, ed. *Black Film, British Cinema.* London: ICA Documents 7. London: ICA/BFI, 1988a.

Mercer, Kobena. "Diasporic Culture and Dialogic Imagination". *Blackframes: Critical Perspectives on Black Independent Cinema.* Eds. Mbye Cham and Claire Andrade-Watkins. Cambridge, MA: MIT Press, 1988b. 50–62.

Mercer, Kobena. "True Confessions: A Discourse on Images of Black Male Sexuality." [1986] *Brother to Brother: New Writings by Black Gay Men.* Ed. Essex Hemphill. Boston: Alyson Publications, 1991. 167–173.

Mercer, Kobena. "Dark and Lovely Too: Black Gay Men in Independent Film." *Queer Looks: Perspectives on Lesbian and Gay Film and Video.* Eds. Martha Gever, Pratibha Parmar, and John Greyson. London and New York: Routledge, 238–256.

Mercer, Kobena. "Black Atlantic." *Black Film Bulletin* 2.1 (1993b): 24

Mercer, Kobena. *Welcome to the Jungle.* London and New York: Routledge, 1994.

Mercer, Kobena. "The Question of Difference" [1988]. *Rogue Reels: Oppositional Film in Britain, 1945–1990.* Ed. Margaret Dickinson. London: BFI Publishing, 1999. 197–201.

Mercer, Kobena, and Chris Darke. *Isaac Julien.* London: Ellipsis Minigraph, 2001.

Mercer, Kobena. "avid iconographies." *Isaac Julien.* Eds. Kobena Mercer and Chris Darke. London: Ellipsis Minigraph, 2001. 17–21.

Mercer, Kobena. *James VanDerZee*. London and New York: Phaidon Press, 2003.
Mercer, Kobena. "Post-colonial Trauerspiel". *The Ghosts of Songs: The Film Art of the Black Audio Film Collective 1982–1998*. Eds. Kodwo Eshun and Anjalika Sagar. Liverpool: Liverpool University Press and FACT, 2007. 43–73.
Merewether, Charles, ed. *The Archive*. London: Whitechapel Art Gallery, 2006.
Meyer, F. T. *Filme über sich selbst: Strategien der Selbstreflexion im dokumentarischen Film*. Bielefeld: Transcript, 2005.
Middles, Mick. *From Joy Division to New Order: The True Story of Anthony H. Wilson and Factory Records*. London: Virgin Books, 2002.
Middles, Mick. *Factory: The Story of the Record Label*. London: Virgin Books, 2009.
Minton, Anna. *Ground Control: Fear and Happiness in the Twenty-First-Century-City*. London: Penguin, 2009.
Mirzoeff, Nicholas. *An Introduction to Visual Culture*. London and New York: Routledge, 1999.
Misztal, Barbara A. *Theories of Social Remembering*. Maidenhead: Open University Press, 2003.
Mitchell W. J. T. *Picture Theory*. Chicago: The University of Chicago Press, 1994.
Monk, Claire. "Heritage Film Audiences 2.0: Period Film Audiences and Online Fan Cultures." *Participations. Journal of Audience and Reception Studies* 8.2 (2011): 431–477.
Monk, Claire, and Amy Sargeant, eds. *British Historical Cinema: The History, Heritage and Costume Film*. London and New York: Routledge, 2002.
Morley, David, and Kevin Robins. *British Cultural Studies*. Oxford University Press 2001.
Morrison, Toni. *Beloved*. New York: New American Library, 1987.
Morrow, Bruce. "An Interview with Isaac Julien." *Callaloo* 18.2 (1995): 406–415.
Morrow, Fiona. "Going back to the bottle." *The Guardian*, 5 June 2000.
Motte, Jan, and Rainer Ohliger, eds. *Geschichte und Gedächtnis in der Einwanderungsgesellschaft: Migration zwischen historischer Rekonstruktion und Erinnerungspolitik*. Essen: Klartext, 2004.
mpz. mpz Materialien 1. Zur Theorie und Praxis politisch-pädagogischer Medienarbeit. Hamburg: Medienpädagogikzentrum, 1976.
Mulvey, Laura. *Visual and Other Pleasures*. Houndmills: Macmillan, 1989.
Muñoz, José Esteban. *Disidentifications: Queers of Color and the Performance of Politics*. Minneapolis and London: University of Minnesota Press, 1999.
Murphy, Robert, ed. *British Cinema in the 90s*. London: BFI Publishing, 2000.
Murphy, Robert, ed. *The British Cinema Book*. Second edition. London: BFI Publishing, 2001.
Naficy, Hamid. "Phobic Spaces and Liminal Panics: Independent Transnational Film Genre." *Global/Local: Cultural Productions and the Transnational Imaginary*. Eds. Rob Wilson and Wimal Dissanayake. Durham, NC and London: Duke University Press, 1996. 119–144.
Naficy, Hamid. *An Accented Cinema: Exilic and Diasporic Filmmaking*. Princeton, NJ. Princeton University Press, 2001.
Nagib, Lucia, Christopher Perriam, and Rajinder Dudrah, eds. *Theorising World Cinema*. London: IB Tauris, 2012.
Nagl, Tobias. *Die unheimliche Maschine: Rasse und Repräsentation im Weimarer Kino*. München: edition text und kritik, 2009.
Negt, Oskar, and Alexander Kluge. *Öffentlichkeit und Erfahrung*. Frankfurt/M.: Suhrkamp, 1972.

Negt, Oskar, and Alexander Kluge. *Public Sphere and Experience: Toward an Analysis of the Bourgeois and Proletarian Public Sphere*. Minneapolis, MN: University of Minnesota Press, 1993.

Neiger, Motti, Oren Meyers, and Eya Zandberg, eds. *On Media Memory*. Basingstoke: Palgrave Macmillan, 2011.

Nero, Charles I. "Towards a Black Gay Aesthetic: Signifying in Contemporary Gay Literature." *Brother to Brother: New Writings by Black Gay Men*. Ed. Essex Hemphill. Boston: Alyson Publications, 1991. 229–252.

Nice, James. *Shadowplayers: The Rise and Fall of Factory Records*. London: Aurum Press, 2010.

Nichols, Bill. *Representing Reality*. Bloomington/Indianapolis: Indiana University Press, 1991.

Nichols, Bill. *Blurred Boundaries: Questions of Meaning in Contemporary Culture*. Bloomington: Indiana University Press, 1994.

Nichols, Bill. *Introduction to Documentary*. Bloomington: Indiana University Press, 2001.

Noordegraaf, Julia. "Remembering the Past in the *Dynarchive:* The State of Knowing in Digital Archives." Paper submitted for the conference *Media in Transition 7, Unstable Platforms: The Promise and Peril of Transition*, Boston, MIT, May 13–15, 2011.

Nora, Pierre, ed. *Les lieux de mémoire*, 3 vols. Paris: Gallimard, 1984–1992.

Nora, Pierre. "Between Memory and History: Les Lieux de Mémoire." *Representations* 26 (1989): 7–24.

Nora, Pierre. *Realms of Memory. Vol. I: Conflicts and Divisions: Rethinking the French Past*. Ed. Lawrence D. Kritzman. New York: Columbia University Press, 1996.

O'Connor, Justin, and Derek Wynne, eds. *From the Margins to the Centre: Cultural Production and Consumption in the Post-Industrial City*. Aldershot: Arena, 1996.

O'Pray, Michael. *The British Avant-Garde Film: 1926–1995: An Anthology of Writing*. Luton: University of Luton Press and Arts Council of England, 1997.

Olick, Jeffrey K. *The Politics of Regret: On Collective Memory and Historical Responsibility*. New York: Routledge, 2007. 85–118.

Olick, Jeffrey. "Collective Memory: A Memoir and Prospect." *Memory Studies* 1.1 (2008): 23–29.

Olick, Jeffrey, and Vered Vinitzky-Seroussi, and Daniel Levy, eds. *The Collective Memory Reader*. Oxford: Oxford University Press, 2011.

Orgeron, Devin. "Re-Membering History in Isaac Julien's The Attendant." *Film Quarterly* 53.4 (2000): 32–40.

Ortiz, Fernando. *Cuban Counterpoint: Tobacco and Sugar (Contrapunteo cubano del tabaco y el azúcar)* [1940]. Durham, NC/London: Duke University Press, 1995.

Owusu, Kwesi. *Black British Culture and Society: A Text Reader*. London and New York: Routledge, 2000.

Ozil, Seyda, and Michael Hofmann, and Yasemin Dayioglu-Yücel, eds. *50 Jahre türkische Arbeitsmigration in Deutschland*. Göttingen: V&R Unipress, 2011.

Paech, Joachim. *Passion oder die EinBILDdungen des Jean-Luc Godard*. Frankfurt/M.: Deutsches Filmmuseum, 1989.

Paletschek, Sylvia, and Syliva Schraut, eds. *The Gender of Memory: Cultures of Remembrance in Nineteenth and Twentieth Century Europe*. Frankfurt: Campus, 2008.

Pantenburg, Volker. *Film als Theorie: Bildforschung bei Harun Farocki und Jean-Luc Godard*. Bielefeld: Transcript, 2006.

Parikka, Jussi. *What Is Media Archaeology?* Cambridge: Polity Press, 2012.

Parmar, Pratibha. "Hateful Contraries: Media Images of Asian Women." *Ten8* 16 (1984): 71–78.
Parmar, Pratibha. "That Moment of Emergence." *Queer Looks: Perspectives on Lesbian and Gay Film and Video.* Eds. Martha Gever; John Greyson and Pratibha Parmar. London and New York: Routledge, 1993. 3–11.
Paul, Gerhard, ed. *Visual History: Ein Studienbuch.* Göttingen: Vandenhoeck & Ruprecht, 2006.
Peck, Jamie, and Kevin Ward. *Restructuring Manchester.* Manchester University Press, 2002.
Peeren, Esther. *Intersubjectivities and Popular Culture: Bakhtin and Beyond.* Stanford: Stanford University Press, 2007.
Peitz, Christiane. "Rettung der Schätze der Leinwand." *Der Tagesspiegel* 19.08.2014.
Perinelli, Massimo. *Fluchtlinien des Neorealismus: Der organlose Körper der italienischen Nachkriegszeit, 1943–1949.* Bielefeld: Transcript, 2009.
Pethö, Agnes. "Cinema and Intermediality: A Historiography of Methodologies." In: *Acta Universitatis Sapientiae*, Film and Media Studies 2 (2010a): 39–72.
Pethö, Agnes. "Media in the Cinematic Imagination: Ekphrasis and the Poetics of the In-Between in Jean-Luc Godard's Cinema." *Media Borders, Multimodality and Intermediality.* Ed. Lars Elleström. Basingstoke: Palgrave Macmillan, 2010b. 211–225.
Pethö, Agnes. "Introduction: The Post Media Life of Film." *Film in the Post-Media Age.* Ed. Agnes Pethö. Newcastle: Cambridge Scholars, 2012. 1–14.
Petty, Sheila. *Contact Zones: Memory, Origin, and Discourses in Black Diasporic Cinema.* Detroit: Wayne State University Press, 2008.
Phillipps, Kendall R., and Mitchell G. Reyes, eds. *Global Memoryscapes: Contesting Remembrance in a Transnational Age.* Alabama: The University of Alabama Press, 2011.
Phillips, Mike, and Trevor Phillips. *Windrush: The Irresistible Rise of Multi-Racial Britain.* London: Harper Collins, 1998.
Phoenix, Ann. "Interrogating Intersectionality: Productive Ways of Theorising Multiple Positioning." *Kvinder, Køn & Forskning* 2–3 (2006): 21–29.
Pines, Jim. "Introduction to the Black Workshops." London: BFI Publishing, 1989.
Pines, Jim, and Paul Willemen, eds. *Questions of Third Cinema.* London: BFI Publishing, 1989.
Pines, Jim. "The Cultural Context of Black British Cinema [1988]." *Black British Cultural Studies: A Reader.* Eds. Houston A. Baker, Jr., Manthia Diawara, and Ruth H. Lindeborg. Chicago and London: University of Chicago Press, 1996. 183–193.
Pines, Jim. "Black Films in White Britain" [1971]. *Rogue Reels: Oppositional Film in Britain, 1945–1990.* Ed. Margaret Dickinson. London: BFI Publishing, 1999. 116–118.
Polan, Dana B. "Brecht and the Politics of Self-Reflexive Cinema". *Jump-Cut* 17 (1978): 29–32
Polan, Dana B. "A Brechtian Cinema? Towards a Politics of Self-Reflexive Film". In: Nichols, Bill: *Movies and Methods: An Anthology. Volume II.* Berkeley, Los Angeles, London: University of California Press, 1985. 661–672.
Pollock, Griselda. *Differentiating the Canon.* London and New York: Routledge, 1996.
Portelli, Allessandro. "The Peculiarities of Oral History." *History Workshop* 12.1 (1981): 96–107.
Pratt, Mary Louise. *Imperial Eyes: Travel Writing and Transculturation.* London: Routledge, 1992.
Procter, James. *Dwelling Places: Postwar Black British Writing.* Manchester/New York: Manchester University Press, 2003.
Radstone, Susannah, ed. *Memory and Methodology.* Oxford/New York: Berg, 2000a.

Radstone, Susannah. "Reconceiving Binaries: The Limits of Memory." *History Workshop Journal* 59 (2005): 134–150.

Radstone, Susannah. *The Sexual Politics of Time: Confession, Nostalgia, Memory.* New York and London: Routledge, 2007.

Radstone, Susannah. "Nostalgia: Homecomings and Departures." *Memory Studies* 3.3 (2010): 187–191.

Radstone, Susannah. "What Place Is This? Transcultural Memory and the Locations of Memory Studies." *Parallax* 17.4 (2011): 109–123.

Radstone, Susannah, and Katherine Hodgkin, eds. *Regimes of Memory.* London and New York: Routledge, 2003.

Radstone, Susannah, and Bill Schwarz, eds. *Memory: Histories, Theories, Debates.* New York: Fordham University Press, 2010.

Rajewsky, Irina O. "Intermediality, Intertextuality, and Remediation: A Literary Perspective on Intermediality." *Intermédialités* 6 (2005): 43–64.

Rajwesky, Irina O. "Border Talks: The Problematic Status of Media Borders in the Current Debate about Intermediality." *Media Borders, Multimodality and Intermediality.* Ed. Lars Elleström. Basingstoke: Palgrave Macmillan, 2010. 51–68.

Rancière, Jacques. *Film Fables.* Oxford and New York: Berg, 2006.

Rascaroli, Laura. *The Personal Camera: Subjective Cinema and the Essay Film.* London: Wallflower, 2009.

Reade, Lindsay. *Mr Manchester and the Factory Girl: The Story of Tony and Lindsay Wilson.* London: Plexus Publishing, 2010.

Reading, Anna. "Gender, Memory and Culture: The Social Inheritance of the Holocaust." *Theories of Memory: A Reader.* Eds. Michael Rossington and Anne Whitehead. Edinburgh: Edinburgh University Press, 2007. 219–222.

Reading, Anna. "Memobilia: Mobile Phones Making New Memory Forms." In: Joanne Garde-Hansen, Andrew Hoskins, and Anna Reading, eds. *Save As...Digital Memories.* Basingstoke: Palgrave Macmillan, 2009. 81–95.

Reading, Anna. "Globalisation and Digital Memory: Globital Memory's Six Dynamics." *On Media Memory.* Eds. Motti Neiger, Oren Meyers, and Eya Zandberg. Basingstoke: Palgrave Macmillan, 2011. 241–252.

Redfern, Nick. "'We Do Things Differently Here': Manchester as a Cultural Region in *24 Hour Party People*." *EnterText* 5.2 (2005): 286–306.

Reekie, Duncan. *Subversion: The Definitive History of Underground Cinema.* London: Wallflower, 2007.

Rees, A. L. *A History of Experimental Film and Video.* London: BFI Publishing, 1999.

Renan, Ernest. "What is a Nation?" *Becoming National: A Reader.* Eds. Geoff Eley and Ronald Grigor Suny. New York: Oxford University Press, 1996. 41–55.

Renov, Michael. *Theorizing Documentary.* London and New York: AFI Film Readers, Routledge, 1993.

Renov, Michael. "New Subjectivities: Documentary and Self-Representation in the Post-Verité Age." *Feminism and Documentary.* Eds. Diane Waldman and Janet Walker. Minneapolis: University of Minnesota Press, 1999. 84–94.

Renov, Michael. *The Subject of Documentary.* Minneapolis and London: University of Minnesota Press, 2004.

Renov, Michael. "First-person Films: Some theses on self-inscription." *Rethinking Documentary: New Perspectives, New Practices*. Eds. Thomas Austin and Wilma de Jong. Maidenhead: Open University Press, 2008. 39–49.

Renov, Michael, and Erika Suderburg, eds. *Resolutions: Contemporary Video Practices*. Minneapolis: University of Minnesota Press, 1996.

Reynolds, Simon, and Joy Press. *The Sex Revolts: Gender, Rebellion and Rock'n'Roll*. London: Serpent's Tail, 1995.

Reynolds, Simon. *Rip It Up and Start Again: Postpunk 1978–1984*. London: faber and faber, 2005.

Reynolds, Simon. *Retromania: Pop Culture's Addiction to Its Own Past*. London: faber and faber, 2011.

Richards, Thomas. *The Imperial Archive: Knowledge and the Fantasy of Empire*. London: Verso, 1993.

Rigney, Ann. "Plenitude, Scarcity, and the Production of Cultural Memory". *Journal of European Studies* 35. 1–2 (2005): 209–226.

Rigney, Ann. "The Dynamics of Remembrance: Texts Between Monumentality and Morphing." *Cultural Memory Studies: An International and Interdisciplinary Handbook*. Eds. Astrid Erll and Ansgar Nünning. Berlin/New York: de Gruyter, 2008. 345–353.

Rigney, Ann. "Divided Pasts: A Premature Memorial and the Dynamics of Collective Remembrance." Memory Studies 1.1 (2008b): 89–97.

Rigney, Ann. *The Afterlives of Walter Scott: Memory on the Move*. Oxford: Oxford University Press, 2012.

Rigney, Ann, and Astrid Erll. "Introduction: Cultural Memory and Its Dynamics." *Mediation, Remediation, and the Dynamics of Cultural Memory*. Ed. Astrid Erll and Ann Rigney. Berlin: de Gruyter, 2009. 1–11.

Robb, John. *Punk Rock: An Oral History*. London: Ebury Press, 2006.

Robb, John. *The North Will Rise Again: Manchester Music City 1976–1996*. London: Aurum Press, 2010.

Roberts, Les. *Film, Mobility and Urban Space: A Cinematic Geography of Liverpool*. Liverpool: University of Liverpool Press, 2012a.

Roberts, Les, eds. *Mapping Cultures: Place, Practice, Performance. Basingstoke:* Palgrave Macmillan, 2012b.

Rodowick, David N. *The Virtual Life of Film*. Cambridge, Mass.: Harvard University Press, 2007.

Røssaak, Eivind. "Analysing Archives in Motion." *Journal of Scandinavian Cinema* 1.1 (2010): 79–81.

Røssaak, Eivind, ed. *The Archive in Motion: New Conceptions of the Archive in Contemporary Thought and New Media Practices*. Oslo: Studies from the National Library of Norway, 2011a.

Røssaak, Eivind. "The Archive in Motion: An Introduction." *The Archive in Motion: New Conceptions of the Archive in Contemporary Thought and New Media Practices*. Ed. Eivind Røssaak. Oslo: Studies from the National Library of Norway, 2011b.

Rosen, Philip. *Change Mummified: Cinema, Historicity, Theory*. Minneapolis: University of Minnesota Press, 2001.

Rosenstone, Robert A. *Visions of the Past: The Challenge of Film to Our Idea of History*, Cambridge/Mass: Harvard University Press, 1995.

Rosenthal, Alan, ed. *New Challenges for Documentary*. Berkeley, LA, London: University of California Press, 1988.

Rosenthal, Alan, and John Corner, eds. *New Challenges for Documentary*. Manchester and New York: Manchester University Press, 2005.

Ross, Karen. *Black and White Media: Black Images in Popular Film and Television*. Cambridge, MA: Polity Press, 1996.

Rothberg, Michael. *Multidirectional Memory: Remembering the Holocaust in the Age of Decolonization*. Stanford: Stanford University Press, 2009.

Rothberg, Michael, and Yasemin Yildiz. "Memory Citizenships: Migrant Archives of Holocaust Remembrance in Contemporary Germany." *Parallax* 17.4 (2011): 32–48.

Ruby, Jay "The Image Mirrored: Reflexivity and the Documentary Film." *New Challenges for Documentary*. Ed. Alan Rosenthal. Berkeley, Los Angeles and London: University of California Press, 1988. 64–77.

Ruby, Jay. "The Image Mirrored. Reflexivity and the Documentary Film." *New Challenges for Documentary*. Ed. Alan Rosenthal and John Corner. Manchester and New York: Manchester University Press, 2005. 34–47.

Runnymede Trust. *The Future of Multi-Ethnic Britain: The Parekh Report*. London: Profile Books, 2000.

Rushdie, Salman. "Songs doesn't know the Score" [*Guardian*, January 12, 1987]. *Black Film, British Cinema.ICA Documents 7*. Ed. Kobena Mercer. London: ICA/BFI, 1988. 16–17.

Russell, Catherine. *Experimental Ethnography – The Work of Film in the Age of Video*. Durham, NC and London: Duke University Press, 1999.

Ryan, James. *Picturing the Empire: Photography and the Visualization of the British Empire*. London: Reaction Books, 1997.

Sabrow, Martin, ed. *Erinnerungsorte der DDR*. München: Beck, 2009.

Samuel, Raphael. *Theatres of Memory*. Revised edition. London: Verso, 2012.

Sanders, Julie. *Adaptation and Appropriation*. London: Routledge, 2006.

Sandhu, Sukhdev. *London Calling: How Black and Asian Writers Imagined a City*. London: Harper Perennial, 2004.

Sandhu, Sukhdev. "Vagrancy and Drift: The Rise of the Roaming Essay Film." *The Guardian* 3 August, 2013.

Savage, Jon. *England's Dreaming: Anarchy, Sex Pistols, Punk Rock, and Beyond*. London: faber and faber, 2005.

Saxton, Libby. *Haunted Images: Film, Ethics, Testimony and the Holocaust*. London: Wallflower, 2008.

Schaffer, Johanna. *Ambivalenzen der Sichtbarkeit: Über die visuellen Strukturen der Anerkennung*. Bielefeld: Transcript, 2008.

Scheiding, Oliver. "Intertextualität." *Gedächtniskonzepte in der Literaturwissenschaft*. Eds. Astrid Erll and Ansgar Nünning. Berlin: de Gruyter, 2005. 53–72.

Scherer, Christina. "Zwischen Filmtheorie und Filmpraxis: Selbstreflexivität und Selbstreferentialität im Experimentalfilm." *Augen-Blick. Marburger Hefte zur Medienwissenschaft* 31 (2000). 20–35.

Scherer, Christina. *Ivens, Marker, Godard, Jarman: Erinnerung im Essayfilm*. München: Fink, 2001.

Schneider, Alexandra. *Die Stars sind wir: Heimkino als filmische Praxis*. Marburg: Schüren, 2004.

Schneider, Alexandra, and Vinzenz Hediger. "Vom Kanon zum Netzwerk." *Orte filmischen Wissens: Filmkultur und Filmvermittlung im Zeitalter digitaler Netzwerke.* Eds. Oliver Fahle, Vinzenz Hediger and Gudrun Sommer. Marburg: Schüren, 2011. 141–158.

Schulze-Engler, Frank. "Introduction". *Cross/Cultures – Readings in the Post/Colonial Literatures in English.* (Volume 102: Transcultural English Studies). Eds. Frank Schulze-Engler, and Sissy Helff. Amsterdam: Rodopi, 2008.

Schulze-Engler, Frank, and Sissy Helff, eds. *Cross/Cultures – Readings in the Post/Colonial Literatures in English* .(Volume 102: Transcultural English Studies). Amsterdam: Rodopi, 2008.

Schwarz, Bill. "The Legacy of Slavery and Emancipation: Jamaica in the Atlantic World." *Proceedings of the Ninth Annual Gilder Lehrman Center International Conference at Yale University* 2007. Online: http://www.yale.edu/glc/belisario/Schwarz.pdf (10 October 2013).

Scott, David. "Introduction: On the Archaeologies of Black Memory". *Small Axe* 26 (2008). v-xvi.

Scott, Joan Wallach. *Gender and the Politics of History.* New York: Columbia University Press, 1988.

Scott, Joan Wallach, ed. *Feminism and History.* Oxford: Oxford University Press, 1996.

Sealy, Mark, ed. *Vanley Burke: A Retrospective.* London: Lawrence & Wishart, 1993.

Sedgwick, Eve Kosofsky. *Between Men: English Literature and Male Homosocial Desire.* New York: Columbia University Press, 1985.

Sekula, Allen. "The Body and the Archive." *October* 39 (1986): 3–64.

Sekula, Allen. "Reading an Archive: Photography Between Labour and Capital." *The Photography Reader.* Ed. Liz Wells. London and New York: Routledge, 2003. 443–452.

Shandler, Jeffrey. *While America Watches: Televising the Holocaust.* New York: Oxford University Press, 1999.

Shin, Chi-Yun. "Engaging Theory and Making Film: Radical Black Cinema in Britain." *Postcolonial Media Culture in Britain.* Eds. Rosalind Brunt and Rinella Cere. Basingstoke: Palgrave Macmillan, 2011. 99–114.

Shohat, Ella, and Robert Stam. *Unthinking Eurocentrism: Multiculturalism and the Media.* London and New York: Routledge, 1994.

Shohat, Ella, and Robert Stam. *Multiculturalism, Postcoloniality, and Transnational Media.* New Brunswick, et al.: Rutgers University Press, 2003.

Siewert, Senta. "Soundtracks of Double Occupancy: Sampling Sounds and Cultures in Fatih Akin's 'Head On'." *Mind the Screen: Media Concepts According to Thomas* Elsaesser. Eds. Jaap Kooijman, Patricia Pisters and Wanda Strauven. Amsterdam: Amsterdam University Press, 2008. 198–208.

Silverman, Kaja 1988: *The Acoustic Mirror: The Female Voice in Psychoanlysis and Cinema.* Bloomington and Indianapolis: Indiana University Press, 1988.

Silverman, Kaja. *The Threshold of the Visible World.* New York: Routledge, 1996.

Sinha, Amresh, and Terence McSweeney, eds. *Millennial Cinema: Memory in Global Film.* New York: Columbia University Press and Wallflower, 2012.

Sitney, P. Adams. *Visionary Film: The American Avant-garde, 1943–1978*, 2nd edition. New York: Oxford University Press, 1979.

Sjöberg, Patrik. *The World in Pieces: a Study of Compilation Film.* [Dissertation] Stockholm: Stockholm University, 2001.

Smalls, James. *The Homoerotic Photography of Carl Van Vechten: Public Face, Private Thoughts*. Philadelphia: Temple University Press, 2006.

Smith, Evan. "History and the Notion of Authenticity in Control and 24 Hour Party People." *Contemporary British History* 27.4 (2013): 466–489.

Smith, Ian Robert. "The Exorcist in Istanbul: Transnational Processes of Intercultural Dialogue within Turkish Popular Cinema." *Portal: Journal of Multidisciplinary International Studies* 5.1 (2008a).

Smith, Ian Robert. "Beam me up, Ömer: Transnational Media Flow and the Cultural Politics of the Turkish Star Trek Remake." *Velvet Light Trap* 61 (2008b): 3–13.

Smith, Ian Robert. "Introduction." In: Cultural Borrowings: Appropriation, Reworking, Transformation. Special edition of *Scope: An Online Journal of Film Studies* 15 (2009).

Smith, Shawn Michelle. *American Archives: Gender, Race, and Class in Visual Culture*. Princeton: Princeton University Press, 1999.

Smith, Valerie, ed. *Representing Blackness: Issues in Film and Video*. London: Athlone Press, 1997.

Snead, James A. "'Black Independent Film': Britain and America". *ICA documents 7: Black Film, Black Cinema*. Ed. Kobena Mercer. London: ICA/BFI, 1988. 47–50.

Snickars, Pelle, and Patrick Vonderau, eds. *The YouTube Reader*. London: Wallflower Press, 2009.

Sobchack, Vivian, ed. *The Persistence of History: Cinema, Television and the Modern Event*. New York and London: Routledge, 1996.

Solomos, John, and Les Back. *Race, Politics and Social Change*. London and New York: Routledge, 1995.

Sontag, Susan. *On Photography*. New York: Farrar, Straus and Giroux, 1977.

Spence, Louise, and Vinicius Navarro. *Crafting Truth: Documentary Form and Meaning*. New Brunswick: Rutgers University Press, 2011.

Spence, Louise and Aslı Kotaman Avcı."The Talking Witness Documentary: Remembrance and the Politics of Truth." *Rethinking History: The Journal of Theory and Practice* 17.3 (2013): 295–311.

Spielmann, Yvonne. *Video: The Reflexive Medium*. Cambridge, Mass.: The MIT Press 2008.

Spivak, Gayatri. "Three Women's Texts and a Critique of Imperialism." *Critical Inquiry* 12.1 (1985): 243–261.

Spivak, Gayatri. "Can the Subaltern Speak?" *Marxism and the Interpretation of Culture*. Ed. Cary Nelson and Lawrence Grossberg. Urbana: University of Illinois Press, 1988. 271–313.

Spivak, Gayatri Chakravorty. *In Other Words: Essays in Cultural Politics*. London: Routledge, 2006.

Staiger, Janet. "The Politics of Film Canons." *Cinema Journal* 24.3 (1985): 4–23.

Stam, Robert and Louise Spence 1983: "Colonialism, Racism, and Representation: An Introduction." *Screen* 24 (2), 2–20.

Stam, Robert. "Bakhtin, Polyphony, and Ethnic/Racial Representation." *Unspeakable Images: Ethnicity and the American Cinema*. Ed. Lester Friedman. Urbana and Chicago: University of Illinois Press 1991. 251–276.

Stam, Robert. *Reflexivity in Film and Literature: From Don Quixote to Jean-Luc Godard*. [1985] New York: Columbia University Press 1992a.

Stam, Robert. *Subversive Pleasures: Bakhtin, Cultural Criticism, and Film*. Baltimore, Md.: Johns Hopkins Univ. Press, 1992b.

Stam, Robert. "Cultural Studies and Race." *A Companion to Cultural Studies.* Ed. Toby Miller. Oxford: Blackwell, 2001. 471–487.
Stam, Robert. "Beyond Third Cinema: The Aesthetics of Hybridity." *Rethinking Third Cinema.* Ed. Anthony A. Guneratne and Wimal Dissanayake. London and New York: Routledge, 2003. 31–48.
Stam, Robert. "Introduction: The Theory and Practice of Adaptation." *A Companion to Literature and Film: A Guide to the Theory and Practice of Film Adaptation.* Ed. Robert Stam and Alessandra Raengo. Malden: Blackwell, 2005. 1–52.
Stam, Robert, and Robert Burgoyne, and Sandy Flitterman-Lewis. *New Vocabularies in Film Semiotics: structuralism, post-structuralism and beyond.* London: Routledge, 1992.
Steedman, Carolyn. *Dust.* Manchester: Manchester University Press, 2001.
Stein, Mark. *Black British Literature: Novels of Transformation.* Columbus: The Ohio State University Press, 2004.
Stein, Mark. "The Location of Transculture." *Cross/Cultures – Readings in the Post/Colonial Literatures in English.* Eds. Frank Schulze-Engler and Sissy Helff. (Volume 102: Transcultural English Studies). Amsterdam: Rodopi, 2008. 251–266.
Steinle, Matthias. "Das Archivbild: Archivbilder als Palimpseste zwischen Monument und Dokument im audiovisuellen Gemischtwarenladen." *Medienwissenschaft* 3 (2005): 295–309.
Steorn, Patrik. "Mode och skam: Om Sighsten Herrgård, AIDS, garderober och arkiv", *lambda nordica,* no. 3/4, 2009, ss. 78–103.
Steorn, Patrik. "Queer in the museum. Methodological reflections on doing *queer* in *museum* collections", *lambda nordica* no 3/4, 2010, ss. 119–141.
Sterne, Jonathan. *The Audible Past: Cultural Origins of Sound Reproduction.* Durham, NC and London: Duke University Press, 2003.
Steyerl, Hito. *Die Farbe der Wahrheit: Dokumentarismen im Kunstfeld.* Wien: Turia und Kant, 2008.
Steyerl, Hito. *The Wretched of the Screen.* Berlin: Sternberg Press/e-flux journal, 2012.
Stickel, Wolfgang. "Medienwerkstatt Freiburg: Versuch einer Selbstdarstellung". *Medien praktisch* 4 (1990): 13–16.
Stiegler, Bernhard. "The Carnival of the New Screen: From Hegemony to Isonomy." In: Pelle Snickars and Patrick Vonderau (eds): *The YouTube Reader.* Stockholm: National Library of Sweden, 2009. 40–59.
Stoler, Ann Laura. *Along the Archival Grain: Epistemic Anxieties and Colonial Common Sense.* Princeton: Princeton University Press, 2009.
Street, Sarah. *British National Cinema.* Second edition. London and New York: Routledge, 2009.
Sturken, Marita. "Paradox in the Evolution of an Art Form: Great Expectations and the Making of a History." *Illuminating Video: An Essential Guide to Video Art.* Eds. Doug Hall and Sally Jo Fifer New York: Aperture/Bravc., 1990. 101–121.
Sturken, Marita. "The Politics of Video Memory: Electronic Erasures and Inscriptions from Resolutions: Contemporary Video Practices." *Resolutions: Contemporary Video Practices.* Eds. Michael Renov and Erika Suderburg. Minneapolis: University of Minnesota Press, 1996. 1–12.
Sturken, Marita. *Tangled Memories: The Vietnam War, the AIDS epidemic, and the Politics of Remembering.* Berkeley: University of California Press, 1997.

Sundholm, John. "Visions of Transnational Memory." *Journal of Aesthetics & Culture* 3 (2011). [no pagination].
Tai, Hue-Tam Ho. "Remembered Realms: Pierre Nora and French National Memory." *The American Historical Review* 106.3 (2001): 906–922.
Taylor, Diane. *The Archive and the Repertoire: Performing Cultural Memory in the Americas.* Durham, NC and London: Duke University Press, 2003.
Terkessidis, Mark. *Die Banalität des Rassismus: Migranten zweiter Generation entwickeln eine neue Perspektive.* Bielefeld: Transcript, 2004.
Terkessidis, Mark. *Interkultur.* Berlin: Suhrkamp, 2010.
thede, eds. *die thede 1980–1990.* Hamburg: Schwarze Kunst, 1996.
Thornton, Sarah. "The Social Logic of Subcultural Capital." *The Subcultures Reader.* Eds. Ken Gelder and Sarah Thornton. London and New York: Routledge, 1997. 200–209.
Tischleder, Bärbel. *Body Trouble: Entkörperlichung, Whiteness und das amerikanische Gegenwartskino.* Frankfurt: Stroemfeld/Nexus, 2001.
Tölölyan, Khachig. "The Nation-State and Its Others." In: *Diaspora* 1.1 (1991): 3–8.
Töteberg, Michael. *Filmstadt Hamburg.* Hamburg: VSA, 1997.
Tode, Thomas. "Demontage des definitiven Blicks." *Schreiben Bilder Sprechen: Texte zum essayistischen Film.* Eds. Christa Blümlinger and Constantin Wulff. Wien: Sonderzahl, 1992. 157–169.
TRANSIT MIGRATION Forschungsgruppe, ed. *Turbulente Ränder. Neue Perspektiven auf Migration an den Grenzen Europas.* Bielefeld: Transcript, 2007.
Trinh T. Minh-ha. "Documentary Is/Not a Name." *October* 52 (1990): 76–98.
Trinh T. Minh-ha. *When the Moon Waxes Red: Representation, Gender and Cultural Politics.* London and New York: Routledge, 1991.
Tucker, Jennifer, and Tina Campt. "Entwined Practices: Engagements with Photography in Historical Inquiry." *History and Theory* 48 (2009): 1–8.
Van Assche, Christine, ed. *Isaac Julien.* Paris: Espace Trois-Cent-Quinze, Centre Pompidou, 2005.
Van der Knaap, Ewout, ed. *Uncovering the Holocaust: The International Reception of Night and Fog.* London: Wallflower, 2006.
Van Dijck, José. *Mediated Memories in the Digital Age.* Stanford: Stanford University Press, 2007.
Van Dijck, José, and Karin Bijsterveld. *Sound Souvenirs: Audio Technologies, Memory, and Cultural Practice.* Amsterdam: Amsterdam University Press, 2009.
Vidal, Belén, and David Martin-Jones, and Dina Iordanova, eds. *Cinema at the Periphery.* Wayne State University Press, 2010.
Wallace, Michele and Gina Dent. *Black Popular Culture.* Dia Center for the Arts, Discussions in Contemporary Culture, Number 8. Seattle: Bay Press, 1992.
Wallenberg, Louise. *Upsetting the Male: Feminist Interventions in the Queer New Wave.* [Dissertation] Stockholm: Stockholm University, 2002.
Wallenberg, Louise. "New Black Queer Cinema." *New Queer Cinema. A Critical Reader.* Ed. Michele Aaron. Edinburgh University Press, 2004. 128–143.
Warburg, Aby. *Gesammelte Schriften: Studienausgabe.* Ed. by Horst Bredenkamp, et al. Berlin: Akademie Verlag, 1988–2009.
Warburg, Aby. *Der Bilderatlas Mnemosyne.* Ed. Martin Warnke and Claudia Brink. Berlin: Akademie Verlag, 2000.

Waugh, Patricia. *Metafiction: The Theory and Practice of Self-conscious Fiction*. London: Methuen, 1984.
Welsch, Wolfgang. "Transculturality – the Puzzling Form of Cultures Today." In: *Spaces of Culture: City, Nation, World*. eds. Michael Featherstone and Scott Lash. London: Sage, 1999. 194–213.
Welsch, Wolfgang. "On the Acquisition and Possession of Commonalities." *Cross/Cultures – Readings in the Post/Colonial Literatures in English*. Eds. Frank Schulze-Engler and Sissy Helff. (Volume 102: Transcultural English Studies: Theories, Fictions, Realities). Amsterdam: Rodopi 2008. 3–37.
Welzer, Harald, ed. *Das soziale Gedächtnis: Geschichte, Erinnerung, Tradierung*. Hamburg: Hamburger Edition (HIS), 2001.
Welzer, Harald. *Das kommunikative Gedächtnis: Eine Theorie der Erinnerung*. München: C. H. Beck, 2002.
Welzer, Harald, ed. *Der Krieg der Erinnerung: Holocaust, Kollaboration und Widerstand im europäischen Gedächtnis*. Frankfurt/M.: Fischer Taschenbuch Verlag, 2007.
Welzer, Harald, Sabine Moller and Karoline Tschugnall. *'Opa war kein Nazi': Nationalsozialismus und Holocaust im Familiengedächtnis*. Frankfurt/M.: Fischer Taschenbuch Verlag, 2002.
Welzer, Harald and Lenz, Claudia. "Opa in Europa: Erste Befunde einer vergleichenden Tradierungsforschung." *Der Krieg der Erinnerung: Holocaust, Kollaboration und Widerstand im europäischen Gedächtnis*. Ed. Harald Welzer. Frankfurt/M.: Fischer Taschenbuch Verlag, 2007. 7–40.
Welzer, Harald. "Re-narrations: How Pasts Change in Conversational Remembering". *Memory Studies* 3.1 (2010): 5–17.
White, Hayden. *Metahistory: The Historical Imagination in Nineteenth Century Europe*. Baltimore: Johns Hopkins University Press, 1973.
White, Hayden. *The Content of the Form: Narrative Discourse and Historical Representation*. Baltimore: Johns Hopkins University Press, 1987.
White, Hayden. "Historiography and Historiophoty". *The American Historical Review* 93.5 (1988): 1193–1199.
White, Patricia. *Uninvited: Classical Hollywood Cinema and Lesbian Respresentability*. Bloomington: Indiana University Press, 1999.
Williams, Raymond. *Television: Technology and Cultural Form*. London: Fontana/Collins, 1974.
Williams, Raymond. *Keywords*. Oxford: Oxford University Press, 1985.
Willis, Holly. *New Digital Cinema*. London: Wallflower Press, 2005.
Wilson, Rob/Dissanayake, Wimal. *Global/Local: Cultural Production and the Transnational Imaginary*. Durham, NC/London: Duke University Press, 1996.
Winker, Gabriele/Degele, Nina. *Intersektionalität: Zur Analyse gesellschaftlicher Ungleichheiten*. Bielefeld: Transcript, 2009.
Winston, Brian. *Claiming the Real: The Documentary Film Revisited*. London: BFI Publishing, 1995.
Winter, Jay. *Sites of Memory, Sites of Mourning: The Great War in European Cultural History*. Cambridge: Cambridge University Press, 1995
Winter, Jay. "Die Generation der Erinnerung: Reflexionen über den ‚Memory-Boom' in der zeithistorischen Forschung." *WerkstattGeschichte* 30. Hamburg: Ergebnisse Verlag, 2001. 5–16.

Winter, Jay. *Remembering War: The Great War between Memory and History in the Twentieth Century.* New Haven and London: Yale University Press, 2006.
Winter, Jay. "The Performance of the Past: Memory, History, Identity." *Performing the Past.* Eds. Karin Tilmans, Frank van Vree and Jay Winter. Amsterdam: Amsterdam University Press, 2010. 11–34.
Winter, Jay, and Emmanuel Sivan, eds. *War and Remembrance in the Twentieth Century.* Cambridge: Cambridge University Press, 1999.
Wolf, Herta, ed. *Diskurse der Fotografie: Fotokritik am Ende des fotografischen Zeitalters.* Band II. Frankfurt/M.: Suhrkamp, 2003.
Wolf, Werner, in collaboration with Katharina Bantleon and Jeff Thoss, eds. *The Metareferential Turn in Contemporary Arts and Media: Forms, Functions, Attempts at Explanation. Studies in Intermediality 5.* Amsterdam and New York: Rodopi, 2011.
Wollen, Peter. *Signs and Meanings in the Cinema.* London: Secker & Warburg und BFI, 1969.
Wollen, Peter. "The Two Avant-Gardes[1975]." In: Peter Wollen: *Readings and Writings: Semiotic Counter-Strategies.* London: Verso 1982. 92–104.
Wollen, Peter. "Godard and counter-cinema. Vent d'Est!" *The European Cinema Reader.* Ed. Catherine Fowler. London and New York: Routledge, 2002. 74–82.
Yelin, Louise. "Callin' out Around the World: Isaac Julien's New Ethnicities." *Atlantic Studies* 6.2 (2009): 239–253.
Young, James Edward. *Writing and Rewriting the Holocaust: Narrative and the Consequences of Interpretation.* Bloomington: Indiana University Press, 1988.
Young, Lola. *Fear of the Dark: 'Race', Gender and Sexuality in the Cinema.* London and New York: Routledge, 1996.
Yuval-Davis, Nira. *Gender and Nation.* London: Sage, 1997.
Yuval-Davis, Nira. "Intersectionality and Feminist Politics." *European Journal of Women's Studies* 13.3 (2006): 193–209.
Zelizer, Barbie. *Remembering to Forget: Holocaust Memory Through the Camera's Eye.* Chicago: University of Chicago Press, 1998.
Zelizer, Barbie, ed. *Visual Culture and the Holocaust.* New Brunswick, NJ: Rutgers University Press, 2001.
Zemon Davis, Natalie, and Randolph Starn. "Introduction." *Representations* 26 (1989): 1–6.
Zimmermann, Patricia. "'Introduction: The Home Movie Movement: Excavations, Artifacts, Minings." *Mining the Home Movie: Excavations in History and Memory.* Ed. K.L. Ishizuka and P. R. Zimmermann. Berkeley: University of California Press, 2008. 1–28.
Zimmermann, Patricia. "Speculations on Home Movies: Thirty Axioms for Navigating Historiography and Psychic Vectors." *Private Eyes and the Public Gaze: The Manipulation and Valorisation of Amateur Images.* Ed. Sonja Kmec and Viviane Thill. Trier: Kliomedia, 2009. 13–23.
Zryd, Michael. "Found Footage Film as Discursive Metahistory: Craig Baldwin's Tribulation 99." *The Moving Image* 3.2 (2003): 40–61.

Filmography (case studies)
Handsworth Songs. Dir. John Akomfrah. Black Audio Film Collective, 1986.
Looking for Langston. Dir. Isaac Julien. Sankofa Film and Video Collective, 1989.
The Alcohol Years. Dir. Carol Morley, Cannon and Morley Productions, 2000.
We Forgot to Go Back (*Wir haben vergessen zurückzukehren,* Dir. Fatih Akin, Megaherz, 2001.

Index of Names

Abramović, Marina 85
Achinger, Christine 53
Ajamu 172
Akerman, Chantal 103
Akin, Fatih 18, 26, 28, 32f., 50, 53–55, 57–60, 62–71, 196
Akomfrah, John 1, 5f., 39, 100, 126, 132f., 137, 141f., 146, 148, 178, 183, 185, 192
Alexander, Karen 31, 40, 125, 132, 138
Ali, Muhammed 186
Alter, Nora 66, 140
Amber 109
Anderson, Benedict 10, 12, 24, 91, 131, 141, 144, 195
Anderson, Lindsay 142
Andersson, Lars Gustaf 106, 115
Anger, Kenneth 175
Appiah, Kwame Anthony 178
Appudarai, Arjun 24
Arroyo, José 173, 176
Arsenal – Institute for Film and Video Art in Berlin 38
Arteabaro, Ainoah 55
Assmann, Aleida 4, 15, 34–37, 39, 58, 100, 106f., 197
Astruc, Alexandre 102
Attille, Martina 146
Auguiste, Reece 90, 126, 129f., 134, 139, 145, 154
Austen, Jane 52
Ayten, Hatice 55

Bad Religion 142
Bakari, Imruh 138
Baker, Houston A. jr 178
Bakhtin, Michail 75, 83, 140, 178
Baldwin, James 170, 175, 179–181, 183–185, 190
Barthes, Roland 6, 13, 178, 183
Basquiat, Jean-Michel 186
Bau, Christian 105, 116f.
Bauer, Petra 103
Bazin, André 102
Beam, Joseph 181, 190

Beck, Ulrich 32
Benjamin, Walter 175, 177, 185
Bergfelder, Tim 17, 26, 28–32, 71
Bergman, Ingmar 31, 40
Bergman, Ingrid 152–154
Berkhofer, Robert 9, 106
Bertillon, Alphonse 135
Berwick Street Collective 109, 139
Bhabha, Homi 12, 22, 24, 68, 136, 178, 188
Biard, François-Auguste 191
Bigelow, Kathryn 44
bildwechsel 104, 107–109, 112, 114–116, 118–125, 197
Bishton, Derek 143f.
Bitomsky, Hartmut 101
Bjerg, Helle 9, 56f., 60, 76
Black Audio Film Collective 1, 12f., 90, 100f., 103, 126f., 129, 131–134, 136–139, 144f., 147, 152, 154, 156, 167f., 173
Blackberri 172, 180
Blackwood, Maureen 146, 168
Blake, William 141
Bleibtreu, Moritz 66
Bloom, Harold 36
Blümlinger, Christa 100–102
Bodnar, John 10
Bolter, Jay 14, 41–43, 45–48, 51, 80, 84, 128, 198f.
Bottà, Giacomo 92
Bourdieu, Pierre 92
Bousdoukos, Adam 66
Boyce, Sonia 12
Boyle, Danny 141, 152, 157
Boym, Svetlana 78
Brabazon, Tara 80f., 92
Bradshaw, Peter 79
Bragg, Billy 142
Brakhage, Stan 110
Brecht, Bertolt 112
Briggs, Marlon 172
Brillowska, Mariola 121
Bronski Beat 177
Brown, Ford Madox 157
Bruhn, Jörgen 171f., 174, 193

Bruzzi, Stella 14, 86, 89
Bryan, Milton 138
Brynntrup, Michael 64
Buñuel, Luis 175
Burke, Vanley 142–144, 185
Butler, Judith 13f., 143

Cameron, David 94
Camus, Marcel 176
Caouette, Jonathan 85
Capa, Robert 48
Carter, Erica 53
Cavalcanti, Alberto 144
Ceddo Film and Video Workshop 138
Chadha, Gurinder 28, 31
Chambers, Eddie 139f.
Chtcheglov, Ivan 75
Cinema Action 109, 116, 139
Cinenova 120
Clarke, Dylan, 74
Cocteau, Jean 175–177
Confino, Alon 3
Cooder, Ry 64
Cook, Pam 14, 128, 133, 135, 173
Corbijn, Anton 79f., 83f.
Corrigan, Tim 101f., 127
Crofts, Stephen 28
Crusz, Robert 146
Cullen, Countee 170, 179, 183
Cummins, Kevin 80, 94f.
Curtis, Deborah 79, 82
Curtis, Ian 60, 79, 82
Curtis, Robin 53, 55, 59, 60, 62
Cvetkovich, Ann 37, 120, 182, 202

Darke, Chris 171, 189f.
Dash, Julie 169
Davies, Terence 90, 98
Delaney, Samuel 172
Deleuze, Gilles 16, 69, 71, 108, 180
Derin, Seyhan 55
Derrida, Jacques 10, 17, 37, 40
Devoto, Howard 80
Diawara, Manthia 126, 131, 138
Dickel, Simon 170, 190f.
Dieckhoff, Artur 117
Disney, Walt 43

Distelmeyer, Jan 29, 192
Dixon, Melvin 172
Documenta 126, 133
Donellan, Philip 141
DuBois, W.E.B. 183
Dulac, Germaine 175
Dunye, Cheryl 169
durbahn 109, 112, 114, 121
Dyer, Richard 8, 136f.

Eastwood, Clint 46
Egoyan, Atom 46
Einstürzende Neubauten 64
Eisenstein, Sergej 101
El-Tayeb, Fatima 8, 56
Elleström, Lars 47, 167, 184
Ellison, Ralph 172
Elsaesser, Thomas 28f., 58, 68, 71, 91f., 142
Emerson, Lake & Palmer 142
Emin, Tracey 55, 85f.
Enwezor, Okwui 126f., 137
Erll, Astrid 1–5, 12, 15, 17, 19, 21f., 25–27, 33, 38, 45–48, 52f., 58, 71f., 79, 84, 96, 128, 149, 156f., 196, 198
Ernst, Max 37, 58, 117
Eshun, Kodwo 12, 90, 126f., 131f., 136, 141f., 145, 147
Export, Valie 85
Ezli, Özkan 71

Factory Records 77, 80, 93f., 98
Faithfull, Marianne 177
Fani-Kayode, Rotimi 12, 172
Fanon, Frantz 188
Farocki, Harun 5f., 101–103, 127
Fassbinder, Rainer Werner 26, 33, 63, 190
Fellini, Federico 31
Feminale 125
Flaherty, Robert 64
Florida, Richard 93, 97, 99
Fossati, Giovanna 15, 35, 40, 103f., 106, 122
Foster, Hal 146
Foucault, Michel 8–11, 13, 37, 40, 66, 175, 178
Fox-Genovese, Elizabeth 14
Frears, Stephen 132, 171

Index of Names

Friedrich, Markus 38, 197
Fusco, Coco 133 f.
Fuss, Diane 13

Galton, Francis 135
Garde-Hansen, Joanne 2 f., 6
Garncarz, Joseph 32
Gaskell, Elizabeth 96
Gates, Henry jr 175, 178, 182
Gee, Grant 80
Gemünden, Gerd 70 f.
Genet, Jean 175
Getino, Octavio 139
Gill, Craig 93, 177
Gilroy, Paul 7, 12 f., 24, 26, 33, 59, 67, 127, 142, 151, 168, 174, 178, 181 f.
Godard, Jean-Luc 5, 47, 101, 103, 127, 139
Göktürk, Deniz 30, 60, 65
Gopaul, Lina 126, 132, 178
Gopinath, Gayatri 175 f., 193
Grafe, Frieda 102
Gramatke, Alexandra 117 f.
Grant, Duncan 190
Greenblatt, Stephen 36
Grierson, John 144
Gring, Diana 20
Grundy, Stella 84
Grupo Cine Liberación 139
Grusin, Richard 14, 41–48, 51, 80, 84, 128, 198 f.
Guattari, Félix 16, 71, 108
Güngör, Murat 55, 58
Gunning, Tom 16, 43, 108
Gupta, Sunil 176

H.D. [Hilda Doolittle] 190
Habermas, Jürgen 137
Haçienda (club) 74–76, 80 f., 83, 86, 92 f., 97
Hacke, Alexander 64
Hagener, Malte 110
Halbwachs, Maurice 4, 7, 35, 60
Hall, Stuart 6 f., 9, 12, 14 f., 24, 26, 33, 49 f., 52, 59, 64, 67, 76, 129, 131, 135 f., 141, 143, 145, 147, 150, 153, 156, 168, 171 f., 175, 178, 187–190
Hallas, Roger 87 f.

Hamburger Filmmacher-Cooperative 110
Haneke, Michael 32
Hannah, George 180
Hannerz, Ulf 29
Hart, Douglas 84
Hasebrink, Uwe 51
Haslam, Dave 73 f., 79, 84, 91, 93, 95, 98
Haworth, Gwen 85
Hebdige, Dick 73, 91
Hediger, Vinzenz 17
Heidenreich, Nanna 55, 60 f.
Heine, Heinrich 63
Helff, Sissy 17, 21–23
Hemmleb, Maria 116 f.
Hemphill, Essex 172 f., 175, 178–181, 187, 190
Herder, Johann Gottfried 23
Hesse, Barnor 151, 155
Hill, John 126, 131 f., 168, 175, 181
Hitchcock, Alfred 43, 153 f., 181
Hobsbawm, Eric 12, 24
Homer, Brian 143, 144
Homer 27, 47
Hook, Peter 75, 80
hooks, bell 170, 175, 178, 191
Hopper, Dennis 71
Howe, Darcus 145
Hubert, Antje 118 f., 141
Huckeriede, Jens 117, 119
Hughes, Langston 170, 173–175, 178–181, 183–185
Hurd, Douglas 141

Idle, Eric 81
Imperial War Museum 200
Inspiral Carpets 74, 93

Jacobs, Jane 91, 111
James, David E. 16, 78, 80
Jarman, Derek 157, 177
Jenkins, Henry 14
Jennings, Humphrey 127, 144 f.
Jobs, Steve 39
Johnson, Avril 126
Johnston, Claire 11
Joseph, Clare 30, 126
Joy Division 77, 79, 80, 84, 93, 94

Julien, Isaac 5, 13, 19, 76, 127, 137f., 143, 146, 149, 167–170, 172–181, 183, 185, 187f., 190–193, 199
Julier, Guy 93
Jureit, Ulrike 56f.

Kassabian, Anahid 68
Keilbach, Judith 65, 87f., 200
Keiller, Patrick 90
Keitz, Ursula von 4
Khan, Pervais 140
Kiefer, Anselm 46
Kinter, Jürgen 108f.
Klippel, Heike 40, 50f.
Kluge, Alexander 101, 104, 112, 127, 137, 139, 147
Knoop, Carsten 64
Knopp, Guido 66
Kramer, Sven 101f., 127, 140
Kristeva, Julia 83, 177
Kuhn, Annette 57–59, 67, 82, 157
Kureishi, Hanif 26, 171
Kurosawa, Akira 201

Lampalzer, Gerda 117
Landsberg, Alison 2, 6, 57, 74, 79
Lang, Maria 3, 121
Larsen, Nella 184
Lawson, David 87, 126, 178
Lebow, Alissa 85
Leggewie, Claus 3
Leigh, Mike 132
Lenz, Claudia 9, 56f., 60, 76
Levy, Andrea 152
Levy, Daniel 2, 3, 7
Leyda, Jay 100
Lipsitz, George 10, 72
Livingstone, Ken 132
Locke, Alain
Löbbermann, Dorothea 179, 183f.
Loh, Hannes 55, 58
London Filmmakers' Co-op 110
Lord Kitchener
Lovink, Geert 137
Lumière brothers 43
Lupton, Catherine 87, 140

Lynes, George Platt 183, 189–191
Lyotard, Jean-François 147

MacPherson, Kenneth 190
Maccarone, Angelina 70
Malcolm X 132, 145, 183
Malik, Sarita 10, 30f., 131, 158
Mapplethorpe, Robert 171, 176, 182f., 186–188, 191
Marais, Jean 177
Mark Stewart and the Maffia 141f.
Marker, Chris 6, 101–103, 127, 130, 139, 147, 170
Markopoulos, Gregory 110
Marks, Laura U. 64, 127
Marsh-Edwards, Nadine 146
Marshall, Stuart 110f.
Massive Attack 90
Mathison, Trevor 126, 136, 141
McCain, Gillian 78, 80
McKay, Claude 179
McLuhan, Marshall 4, 41
McNeil, Legs 78, 80
Meatball (Den Haag) 111
Medienladen 108, 113f., 120, 125
Medienpädagogikzentrum (mpz) 104, 107f.
Medienwerkstatt Freiburg 104
Medvedkin, Aleksandr 170
Mekas, Jonas 110
Melitopoulos, Angela 56, 103
memoriav 125
Mercer, Kobena 12f., 16, 126, 130, 135, 137–139, 145, 148, 168, 170–172, 178f., 185–190, 193
Metzlaff, Barbara 117f.
Meyers, Oren 7
Micheaux, Oscar 170
Middles, Mick 79f., 87
Middleton, Kate 141
Mikesch, Elfi 121
Minton, Anna 93
Mitchell, W. J. T. 5, 46
Moore, Michael 65, 87, 128
Morley, Carol 5, 18, 53, 73, 76, 79, 82–87, 89f., 98
Morley, Paul 79
Morris, Errol 89

Morrison, Paul 152
Morrison, Toni 175, 180f., 185f.
Morrow, Fiona 83f., 89
Müller, Matthias 101
Mulvey, Laura 39, 85, 136
Muñoz, José Esteban 168, 170–173, 176, 180–183, 187

Naipaul, V.S. 26
Negt, Oskar 104, 112, 137, 147
Neiger, Motti 4, 7
Nero, Charles 172
New Order 75, 77, 84, 93
Nichols, Bill 14, 87, 89, 140
Nietzsche, Friedrich 26, 35
Nolan, Christopher 46
Noordegraaf, Julia 38
Nora, Pierre 2–4, 34f., 75, 99, 195
Nugent, Bruce 175, 179, 190

Oasis 94
Obama, Barack 52
O'Connor, Justin 92
Odyssey (band) 68
Oppermann, Manfred 105, 116
Ortiz, Fernando 22
Ottinger, Ulrike 121

Pantenburg, Volker 5, 127, 140, 195
Paradjanov, Sergei 183
Parikka, Jussi 34, 37, 40
Parmar, Pratibha 86, 138, 183
Parry, Hubert 141
Pasolini, Pier Paolo 101
Pathé 1, 152f., 156, 160–163
Peel, John 83
pelze multimedia 120
Pet Shop Boys 177
Peters, Jan 64
Pethö, Agnes 47
Phillips, Mike 151, 155f.
Phillips, Trevor 151, 155f.
Pierre et Gilles 177
Pines, Jim 139
Piper, Keith 12
Polat, Ayşe 71
Ponger, Lisl 101

Porter, Edwin S. 100
Portishead 90
Potter, Sally 177
Powell, Enoch 131, 155
Pratt, Mary Louise 22
Prelinger, Rick 159
Press, Joy 82
Prince William 141

Rainer, Yvonne 103
Rajewsky, Irina 47f., 167, 184, 189
Rancière, Jacques 146, 170
Ranke, Leopold von 5, 84, 135
Rascaroli, Laura 59, 71, 85, 101f., 127f.
Reade, Lindsay 80, 82
Reardon, John 143f.
Redfern, Nick 75, 80f., 91f., 95–97
Reilly, Vini 81, 84
Reiner, Rob 81
Renov, Michael 63, 85, 87
Resnais, Alain 101, 147
Reynolds, Simon 77f., 82, 91
Richardson, Tony 142
Richarz, Claudia 121
Richter, Hans 101
Rigney, Ann 2f., 15, 19, 26, 33, 38, 45–47, 58, 198
Rippel, Nina 116f.
Rist, Pipilotti 121
Rivington Place 152
Robb, John 80
Robeson, Paul 190
Rodney, Donald 12
Rosler, Martha 121
Røssaak, Eivind 35
Rothberg, Michael 2f., 52f., 58, 74, 196
Rushdie, Salman 26, 145
Russell, Catherine 85, 126, 162

Sagar, Anjalika 12, 126, 131f., 136, 142, 145, 147
Salford Lad's Club 94
Sanders-Brahms, Hilma 48
Sandhu, Sukhdev 127
Sankofa Film and Video Collective 19
Savage, Jon 78, 82, 98
Saville, Peter 77, 93

Schiller, Greta 169, 176, 178
Schneemann, Carolee 85
Schneider, Alexandra 17, 57
Schulze-Engler, Frank 17, 21–23
Schwarz, Bill 70, 154
Schygulla, Hanna 63
Scorsese, Martin 64f., 68
Scott, Walter 19, 33
Sebald, W.G. 46
Sedgwick, Eve Kosofsky 80f.
Sekula, Alan 6, 135
Shabazz, Menelik 138
Shelley, Pete 83f.
Sherman, Cindy 85
Shohat, Ella 12–14
Shub, Esfir 101
Siewert, Senta 64, 68
Sillitoe, Alan 142
Silverman, Kaja 170, 185
Sitney, P. Adams 110
Sjöberg, Patrik 100
Sklovskij, Viktor 48
Sly and The Family Stone 68
Smalls, James 183f.
Smith, Bessie 170, 179
Smith, Harry 110
Smith, Mark E. 80
Smiths, The 74, 94, 99, 177
Snickars, Pelle 159
Solanas, Fernando 139
Somerville, Jimmy 177
Sontag, Susan 6, 135
Spivak, Gayatri 13, 103, 178
Stam, Robert 12–14, 129
Starn, Randolph 11
Steel Pulse 133
Stein, Gertrude 22, 184
Steyerl, Hito 6, 88, 103
Stiftung Kinemathek (Berlin) 118
Sturken, Marita 4, 11, 82, 106, 109
Sundholm, John 10, 32, 106
Syal, Meera 140f.
Sznaider, Natan 2f., 7

Tagg, John 5
Tai, Hue-Tam Ho 3
Tarkovskij, Andrei 180

Tate Britain 27, 126
Teno, Jean-Marie 87
Terkessidis, Mark 62
Test Department 141
Thatcher, Margaret 131f., 155
The Beatles 81, 92
The Durutti Column 80f., 84
The Fall 80, 84
The Film-Makers' Cooperative 110
The Happy Mondays 74
The Jesus and Mary Chain 84
The Otolith Group 103
The Stone Roses 74, 94
thede, die 104f., 107f., 114, 116–119, 124
Theilen, Karin 20
Thornton, Sarah 78, 82
Throbbing Gristle 177
Thurman, Wallace 179, 184
Tode, Thomas 101f., 127, 140
Tretyakov, Sergej 104, 112
Treut, Monika 114, 121
Tricky 90
Trinh T. Minh-ha 88, 103, 176
Trotta, Margarethe von 121
Turner, Debby 84

Van Der Zee, James 143, 181–183, 185f.
Van Vechten, Carl 183f., 187
Van Dick, José 3, 37
Van Sant, Gus 48
Varda, Agnès 6, 101, 147
Vertov, Dziga 101, 139, 145
Vidéo-femmes (Quebec) 114
Video-Inn (Vancouver) 111
Videoladen Zurich 104
Vonderau, Patrick 159
Vukadinović, Vojin Saša 55, 60f.

Warburg, Aby 4, 7
Warhol, Andy 110
Watts, Harry 88
Weber, Thomas 4
Weekes, Yvonne 140
Welsch, Wolfgang 17, 21–26
Welzer, Harald 10f.
Wenders, Wim 64, 70f.
West, Cornel 178

Wilson, Tony 75, 79–82, 84, 93
Windrush, SS Empire 1, 19, 50, 149, 151–165, 168f., 198f.
Winter, Jay 77
Winterbottom, Michael 18, 75, 79f., 83
Wise, Alan 84
Wollen, Peter 11, 39, 43, 110, 129
Woolf, Virginia 177
Wright, Basil 145
Wright, Stephen 94
Wynne, Derek 92

Yavuz, Yüksel 55
Yildiz, Yasemin 52f.
Young, James E. 4, 63, 89
Yuval-Davis, Nira 24, 77

Zaimoglu, Feridun 26
Zalcock, Bev 121
Zandberg, Eva 7
Zemon Davis, Natalie 11
Zimmermann, Patricia 9, 106
Zukin, Sharon 91

Index of Titles

Ab nach Rio. Die Akte Guggenheim 119
A Diary for Timothy 127
Aladdin 43
Alice in the Cities 71
All You Need is Cash 81
Another Philosophy of History for the Education of Mankind 23
Ararat 46
Aus Lust am Schauen 105

Beauty and the Beast 43
Before Stonewall 169, 176, 178
Bend It Like Beckham 28
Black Book 183, 186 f.
Black Orpheus 176
Bob and Rose 97
Borderline 190
Brother to Brother 181, 190
Buena Vista Social Club 64

Camera Lucida 41, 183
Chariots of Fire 142
Circus Notebook 110
Coal Face 144
Control 8, 17 f., 37, 54, 68, 79 f., 83 f., 88, 112, 121, 144
Coronation Street 96
Crossing the Bridge 64, 67 f.

Das Ding am Deich 118 f.
Daughters of the Dust 169
Derek 177
Der Vorführ-Effekt 64
Deutschland, bleiche Mutter 48, 53, 55, 58, 63, 65
Die kritische Masse 117–119
Die vergessene Generation 55
Downfall (Der Untergang) 5, 52
Dreams of a Life 83

Easy Rider 71
England's Dreaming 78
Expeditions One: Signs of Empire 126
Expeditions Two: Images of Nationality 126

Factory. The Story of the Record Label 79
Flags of our Fathers 46
Foyles War 152
From Joy Division to New Order 79

Gegen-Musik (Contre-Chant) 102
20 Geigen auf St. Pauli 118

Halfmoon Files 103
Handsworth Songs 1, 5, 19, 39, 100 f., 103, 126–149, 152, 154, 156, 167, 173, 178, 184, 194, 198
Harlot 110
Harry Potter 52
Head On (Gegen die Wand) 63, 67 f., 71
High Hopes 132
Home Stories 101
24 Hour Party People 18, 75, 79–82, 95 f.
Housing Problems 88

If 142
In July (Im Juli) 63, 66 f., 71, 125, 132
In the Life 100, 181
Invisible Man 172
Italianamerican 64 f., 68

Joy Division (documentary) 80
Joy Division. Piece by Piece 79
Jurassic Park 43

Khush 86, 183
Kings of the Road (Im Lauf der Zeit) 71

Last Angel of History 132
Letter from Siberia 102
Letter to Breshnev 132
Listen to Britain 127, 145
London 90
Looking for Langston 5, 19, 39, 75 f., 103, 127, 143, 149 f., 166–187, 189–194, 199 f.

Index of Titles

Macbeth 201
Manchester 9f., 18, 24, 33, 71, 73–80, 82–84, 87, 89–99, 177, 195f.
Manchester England 79, 98
Mein Vater, der Gastarbeiter 55
Memento 46
Memory Room 451 132
Milk 48f.
Minority Report 44
Monty Python's Flying Circus 135
Mr Manchester and the Factory Girl 80, 82
My Beautiful Laundrette 132, 168, 171, 176, 193

Nanook of the North 64
Night and Fog
Nigger Heaven 183
North and South 96
November 103

Odyssey 19, 27, 47
Of Time and the City 90, 98
Orfeo Negro 176
Orlando 177
Orphée 176f.
Otolith I–III 103
Outlines of a Philosophy of the History of Man 23

Passagen 101
Passing Drama 56
Please Kill Me 78, 80
Punk Rock 80

Queer as Folk 97

Respite (Aufschub) 103
Return of the Tüdelband 117–119
Rip It Off and Start Again 78
Robinson in Space 90

Sammy and Rosie Get Laid 168, 171
Sans Soleil 139
Saving Private Ryan 46, 48f.
Schindler's List 5
Seven Songs for Malcolm X 132, 183

Shadowplayers: The Rise and Fall of Factory Records 80
She's a Boy I Knew 85
Short Sharp Shock 63, 67
Small Island 152
Solino 55, 66
Song of Ceylon 145
Soul Kitchen 66f., 71
Sounds in the Silence 119
Spellbound 43
Spinal Tap 81
Strange Days 44
Surname Viet, Given Name Nam 88

Tarnation 85
Terminator 2 43
Territories 103, 168, 171, 173
The Alcohol Years 5, 18, 53, 73, 76, 79, 82–90, 97f., 194
The Archaeology of Knowledge 37
The Arrival of a Train at the La Ciotat Station 43
The Art of Vision 110
The Attendant 183, 190f.
The Color of Pomegranates 183
The Edge of Heaven (Auf der anderen Seite) 63, 67
The Fall of the Romanov Dynasty 101
The Haçienda. How Not to Run a Club 75, 80
The Harlem Book of the Dead 181, 186
The Last Bolshevik 130, 170
The Life of an American Fireman 100
The Loneliness of the Long Distance Runner 142
The Lost World 43
The Man With a Movie Camera 101
The Mirror 181
The Nine Muses 39, 148
The North Will Rise Again: Manchester Music City 80
The Patriot (Die Patriotin) 140
The People's Account 138
The Rise of the Creative Class 93, 97
The Stuart Hall Project 40, 148
The Thin Blue Line 89
Three Songs of Lenin 145
Tongues Untied 172

Torn Apart. The Life of Ian Curtis 79
Touching from a Distance 79, 82
Tour Abroad (Auslandstournee) 71
Toy Story 43
Twilight City 90, 103

Unknown Pleasures: Inside Joy Division 80

Vertigo 43
Viaggio in Italia 71

Watermelon Woman 169
We Forgot to Go Back (Wir haben vergessen zurückzukehren) 18, 50, 53–55, 57–60, 62–64, 67, 69–71, 196
Wondrous Oblivion 152

Young Soul Rebels 177, 190

Index of Terms

adaptation   26, 31f., 41f., 46, 51, 99, 142, 167f., 172, 177, 191f., 199, 201f.
affect   33, 50, 78, 182, 202
agit-prop   104f., 111f., 124, 138
Angry Young Men   96, 142
appropriation   19, 51, 76, 78, 99, 134, 159, 167, 172, 174f., 177, 183, 185f., 191f., 199, 201
archive   1f., 6–8, 12, 14–19, 21, 34–41, 45, 49f., 52–56, 58, 66, 70, 76, 79, 83, 86, 89f., 98, 100f., 104–109, 114, 118–125, 127–135, 140–142, 144–149, 151, 153, 156–160, 164–166, 168–170, 174–177, 182, 190f., 193f., 197–202
archive fever   37
archivology   21, 37, 41, 108
authenticity   45f., 48f., 59, 71, 80, 84, 86, 88, 117, 128, 135, 137f., 162, 179
autobiographical filmmaking   53, 63f., 85, 87, 197

Black British Cultural Studies   7, 12, 24, 33, 59, 147, 188
Bollywood   86, 202

Centre for Cultural Studies   200
Channel 4   31, 97, 132, 138, 156–158, 160, 168
Chronotope   66, 75, 94f., 99, 178, 180, 182, 193
Cinema Novo   139
cinéma vérité   104, 112
city branding   77, 90–93, 96–99
convergence culture   14, 42, 201
cultural capital   92
cultural memory   1–5, 7–10, 12, 14–21, 26f., 32–36, 41f., 45f., 49f., 52, 54–58, 60, 69f., 73f., 76–84, 89–92, 94, 96–100, 103, 105–107, 109, 119–122, 125f., 128–130, 133, 140, 142, 148–153, 158f., 162f., 165f., 169f., 174, 182, 184, 190, 192–198, 200–202
cultural studies   14, 16, 26, 29, 38, 127, 170
curating   121f.

digital memories   3, 90, 94
digitization   37, 39f., 103f., 106f., 118, 121, 123f.
Direct Cinema   104, 112, 117, 141, 163

entangled memories   52, 193

Facebook   2, 4, 6, 33
forgetting   15, 34–38, 56, 119, 130
functional memory   15, 34–36, 39f., 51, 107, 122–124, 127, 197, 199, 201

gentrification   67, 77, 90, 93, 119
Geschichtsfernsehen   88

Harlem Renaissance   168, 170f., 177–181, 184, 190, 193
Heimatfilm   67, 71
heritage   3, 9, 12, 15, 52, 76, 78, 90–92, 95f., 98f., 103, 106, 157, 170, 186, 188, 197f.
Holocaust memory   74
home movies   2, 16, 57, 115

Indymedia   104f.
Instagram   2, 6, 90
intermediality   19f., 41, 46f., 49, 51, 75, 134, 149f., 166f., 171, 174–176, 183, 193, 199, 201
intertextuality   20, 46, 74, 83, 167, 171

Kanak Attak   54f.

LGBT memories   97–99
lieux de mémoire   2–4, 45, 54, 75, 99, 195
longue durée   96

media memory studies   1, 14, 18, 20, 33f., 38, 194, 197, 201
mediatisation   45f., 193
memory films   5, 52, 79
memory work   57–59, 67, 69, 80–82, 107, 109, 169, 195
Merseybeat   92

Index of Terms

Middle Passage 25, 179
minor cinema 16 f., 25, 33 f., 39, 43, 51 f., 73, 103, 108, 194, 196
mnemotope 75, 96
multidirectional memories 2, 18, 98

New British Cinema 132, 142
New Film History 109, 202
New Labour 156 f., 199
New Romantics 175
newsreel 1 f., 4, 15 f., 19, 43, 46, 48, 128, 130, 134, 140, 152–154, 156, 159–163
nostalgia 25, 67, 74, 78, 90–92, 94, 96, 99

oral history 6, 20, 56–58, 80, 86, 156, 159, 163

palimpsest 96
Playstation 39
pop historiography 78, 81
post-punk memory 79, 83, 97
prosthetic memory 2

queer memories 97, 99, 168 f., 176, 180, 184, 193, 200

reappropriation 19, 51, 142, 149, 151, 183, 191–193, 198, 201
remediation 2 f., 5, 14–17, 19–21, 34, 38–52, 73–76, 78, 80, 84, 90, 94–96, 122 f., 125, 128, 141–143, 147, 149–153, 155–160, 163, 165 f., 168 f., 171, 174, 176, 185, 192–194, 198–202
remix culture 14
repurposing 42, 48, 98
retro culture 2, 18, 53, 79, 89, 91 f., 98 f.
reworking 5, 8, 16, 18 f., 40, 76, 83, 90, 100, 121, 126, 128, 133, 141 f., 146, 151, 155, 158, 160, 166, 168–170, 182, 185, 187, 190–193, 197–201

Screen (journal) 39 f., 42, 44, 85, 111, 114, 116, 121, 123, 136 f., 143 f., 188 f.
self-reflexivity 42, 74, 105, 127–129, 131, 134, 140, 143, 147, 167, 171, 194, 198
sticky-tape syndrome 105
storage memory 15, 34 f., 39, 51, 107, 122, 124, 127
subculture 18, 25, 72–78, 90 f., 95

tableaux vivants 86, 134, 167, 171, 183, 185, 189
Ten8 (journal) 187
testimonial witness 6, 45, 65 f., 82, 87 f., 159, 165, 194
transcultural memory 6, 18 f., 25 f., 32 f., 52 f., 71–73, 77, 92, 98 f., 149, 151, 202
translation 5, 26, 32, 49, 51, 53, 62–64, 99, 116, 159, 185, 193, 196, 199
transnational film studies 27 f., 32 f., 201
transnational memory 18, 21, 27, 32, 53, 95, 99
travelling memory 2, 72, 193
Tumblr 6, 15
Twitter 4, 6, 33, 94

VHS 121, 127, 159 f.
video 5, 11, 18, 20, 33, 36, 38, 40, 42, 52, 55, 85–87, 94, 100, 103–125, 127, 132, 138, 152, 159 f., 163 f., 168, 171, 173, 177, 194, 197 f., 202

Windrush generation 50, 145, 151, 156 f., 159, 161 f., 164 f., 169
witness testimonies 20, 65, 88, 163
working memory 35

YouTube 1, 4–6, 15, 19, 33, 36 f., 52, 77, 80, 90, 104 f., 118, 121, 149, 151–153, 158–161, 163–165, 198

www.ingramcontent.com/pod-product-compliance
Lightning Source LLC
Chambersburg PA
CBHW031805220426

43662CB00007B/539